politics@media

David D. Perlmutter, Series Editor

HOW A REDNECK HELPED
INVENT POLITICAL CONSULTING

FALLING UP

RAYMOND D. STROTHER

Published in cooperation with the Kevin P. Reilly Center for Media & Public Affairs

Louisiana State University Press   Baton Rouge

5|03

Copyright © 2003 by Louisiana State University Press
All rights reserved
Manufactured in the United States of America
First printing
12   11   10   09   08   07   06   05   04   03
5   4   3   2   1

Designer: Laura Roubique Gleason
Typeface: Minion text with Gill Sans Bold Condensed display
Typesetter: Coghill Composition Co. Inc.
Printer and binder: Thomson-Shore, Inc.

Library of Congress Cataloging-in-Publication Data:

Strother, Raymond.
   Falling up : how a redneck helped invent political consulting /
Raymond D. Strother.
         p.   cm.—(politics@media)
"Published in cooperation with the Kevin P. Reilly Center for Media & Public Affairs."
Includes index.
   ISBN 0-8071-2856-2 (cloth : alk. paper)
   1. Strother, Raymond.   2. Political consultants—United States—Biography.   3. United
States—Politics and government—1981–1989.   4. United States—Politics and
government—1989–1993.   5. United States—Politics and government—1993–2001.
I. Title.   II. Series.
   E840.8 .S69   2002
   324.7′092—dc21   2002151296

This book is dedicated to my father,
Albert Dolph Strother,
and others who give a damn
and are willing to fight
and to my grandchildren,
Dylan, Emma, and Nicholas,
who represent the future—
and of course to my wife, Sandy,
whose strength and comradeship
made my adventure possible.

I'm a sucker for crips. . . . And any son of a bitch who has been hit solidly, as every man will be if he stays, then I love him.

—Ernest Hemingway, *Across the River and into the Trees*

CONTENTS

Foreword, by David D. Perlmutter   xi

Acknowledgments   xvii

Prologue   1

Growing Up in Texas   14

"Get the Hell Out of Here. You Have a Future"   40

The Louisiana Years   45

A Short Sheriff and a Long Pistol   51

The First Lessons   55

Light Bulbs and Bookmarks   66

Sunshine Rains on Me   70

James Carville and Iceberg Lettuce   85

The Awakening   94

Season of Discontent   102

The Kingfish Lends a Hand   117

What Is It You Do, Sir?   130

I Know Lloyd Bentsen, and He Is a Friend of Mine   141

A Pretty Woman with a Smudge on Her Cheek   155

The Clock Ticks   165

The Wise Ones Stumble Again   172

Bill, Hillary, Al, and the Gang   206

Buddy Roemer and the Silver Bullet   222

Where Dreams Go When They Die   234

Marriage on the Rocks, Up with a Twist   246

Kicking Ass and Taking Names   263

Buying Friends and Influencing People   268

Blue Chips, Dwarfs, and Survival   274

The Sea Creatures Crawl to the Shore   282

The Chill Winds of September   288

Index   297

DAVID D. PERLMUTTER

Power politics and communication media have been intertwined throughout the history of hierarchical civilizations. Ancient monarchs, for example, propagandized by means of huge statues and reliefs of themselves praying to approving gods, hunting dangerous beasts, and smiting enemies. One Assyrian king, Esarhaddon (c. 670 B.C.E.), summed up the content of these mass(ive) messages of the pre-printing and electronic world when he proclaimed, "I am powerful, I am omnipotent, I am a hero, I am gigantic, I am colossal." The success or failure of such hyperbole and hypertrophy helped determine the rise and fall of dynasties and peoples.

But today's global mass media, where scenes of distant wars and Senate hearings are delivered to our television and computer screens instantly, inundate us with a greater volume of and more complex information about the world than ever before. According to a 1998 United Nations report, for example, a greater number of people have access to a television set than to a flush toilet. An American can travel to a remote yurt in Mongolia and find the occupants curious and opinionated about Michael Jordan and Monica Lewinsky. Moreover, through a Web connection, we can virtually visit any spot on earth, read any text, and be informed (or misled) about any issue. Furthermore, whatever is being aimed at us in a million different sales pitches, spin cycles, and propaganda broadsides—a presidential candidate, toothpaste, new offshore drilling legislation—relies on mass media to "get out the message," "target the audience," and "engineer public opinion." Hence there is a need for all parties involved, from the salesperson to the public, to manage what is put out and what is taken in.

The politics@media book series is an effort to help clarify this disjointed, overwhelming, and amazing modern world of politicized mass media and mass-mediated politics. It is predicated on the assumption that for the democratic experiment to survive, we must understand how it interplays with today's converged electrodigital communication environment. Accordingly, this project—a joint effort by a public affairs, policy, and research foundation and a university press—also endeavors to innovate. Specifically, we will feature books that are distinctly contemporary, that concentrate on today's political problems. The concepts that these books put forth will eventually become part of the world of media and politics that they study. Naturally, we will favor titles that promote turning ideas into action: applied lessons and practical advocacy.

The books will be aimed at both the trade public affairs market and the college classroom. We will produce works that teachers will employ to outline modern issues in political communication and that journalists and political workers might use as sourcebooks and guidebooks for their writing and research. Since these books are meant to attract the literate public affairs reader (and student), they will not be bulky, thousand-footnoted tomes. As recently explained to a political consultant, "We want this to be a book series whose titles you can use in your job and professors can use in their classes with equal enthusiasm."

A critical decision, therefore, was choosing our debut text. Should it be a book that dealt with such issues as money and mass-mediated politics, or a case study in mediated public policy or mass-mediated foreign affairs, or ethics and morality, or media credibility and faith in public institution, or mass media and governance, or mass media's impact on the popular culture of politics, or online politics? Moreover, should it be a book written with learning and critical insight by a political or media professional or a hands-on, applied study by an accomplished academic? All such texts would have been and will be welcome.

Raymond Strother's *Falling Up*, we decided, was a good example of the hybrid we seek to solicit and produce. It is, of course, primarily a political memoir. Yet it is also a book with richness and lore for many audiences, from students of politics and media to experienced pros in the field to academics with mostly research-level familiarity with modern campaigns and elections. It is neither a dry-as-dust textbook nor a breezy but empty kiss-and-tell pathography; however, it manages to both teach and entertain. It offers us a glimpse of a netherworld of back rooms and commercial sets that is both unalloyed and unromanticized but also fascinating and revealing. Finally, it highlights problems and offers solutions; Strother wants to make things better, to prescribe what works and proscribe what is harmful.

Strother is uniquely qualified to write this book. He was, indeed, present at the early days of modern political consulting in the 1960s and came of age professionally when political consulting exploded in size, wealth, and power in the 1970s and 1980s. Such experience allows him to tell us stories and make observations that give us an insider's perspective without an insider's myopia. In addition, Strother was and is not just a man of affairs or an adviser to power. He is an artist, a man who feels more at home splicing celluloid and appraising the light of the "magic hour" than smoking a cigar in the poker hall. His combined pragmatism, idealism, and aesthetic sensitivity allow him to make insights that a one-dimensional businessman would ignore.

In general, I think he makes four main points of use to ordinary voters, journalists, researchers, and political workers. First, there were no "good old days"; rather, in Strother's lifetime, the political/mass-media complex has been a source of abuse of power. This is a point well worth repeating for all of American history: each era had its problems. George Washington may have dreamed that the new republic's politics would sustain itself without factions and tomfoolery, but when he first ran for a legislature he lubricated voters with hard cider. And Thomas Jefferson would probably not have won the presidency without a tremendous get-out-the-vote and "image" campaign by his ace political consultant John Beckley. Modern readers of *Moby-Dick* (set in the 1840s) will be wryly amused to note that the novel's headlines of the day were a contested presidential election and a war in Afghanistan. And, of course, today's campaign reforms are after all only revisions of previous reforms.

Each generation, Strother reminds us, creates it own vices and virtues, and often they are mixed in the same person or movement. For example, one of the heroes in these chapters is the late Mississippi senator John Stennis—a great and good man, but a near-lifelong segregationist, too. That does not mean these are the best of times—far from it. Modern politics, as Strother reveals, is driven by an almost unprecedented obsession with and need for mass media exposure and mass mediated public approval. Worse, political leadership is a product of intensive polling to answer the question, "Will this look and sound good on TV?" The result is worse than an empire of spin: the very nature of who runs for office has been changed. Once upon a time we had senators, like Stennis, who, whether you agreed with them or not, sincerely believed in what they advocated and didn't confer with a team of "consultants" before they made decisions. They asked men like Strother to help them win elections, not, as do the pols nowadays, to actually govern. The men and women of that generation may not have been more honest than candidates and legislators today, but at least they were leaders in the now archaic sense of the word.

Third, money, while not actually power, is increasingly the arbiter of who has power. Modern mass media politics is expensive. Strother shows us how and why that money is spent and, often, wasted. He provides us a portrait of men and women who generally have good intentions but whose consciences are ground down by the relentless need to raise bigger and bigger war chests. (Most of that money, of course, goes to pay for television ads.) The result is frightening: only people who have devoted their lives to getting rich or getting rich friends can run for higher office. The perpetual candidate is also a bottomless money pit. While it's not impossible to remain concerned with the common good and stay honest in such a system, it's very difficult.

Strother's final point is more subtle. Certainly much is wrong in his world of media and politics. Modern mass media have created a dystopia where private life is as fair game for the klieg lights as public speech, where increasingly journalists are fascinated with the horse race, not with the issues, where principles take a second place to polling numbers, where money is the holy grail, and where winning is the only test of virtue. But if this were just a back-room-at-Babylon scandal revelation or a sky-is-falling jeremiad, *Falling Up* would not be useful for our series or our intended readers. Strother does not believe that the situation is hopeless; he consistently makes the point that good people can make a difference, that the public are not dupes who will buy any inane idea or vote for any worthless fop. His cynicism is moderated by a deep patriotism, the belief that America still works if we want to fix it and make it better. He underlines that if we wait for a mighty pharaoh to solve our problems for us, hope wanes. *Falling Up* is a call for the American people themselves to correct the deficiencies of media and politics.

For the reader, there is also a fascinating personal struggle. Strother is a real-life Horatio Alger, one who candidly assesses how he thinks he has lived up to his father's ideal of always looking out for the working man.

Indeed, *Falling Up* is much more than a "getting even" score-settler or a "present at the creation" political testament. In fact, it might be categorized in literary genre as an old-fashioned two-fisted tale of the sea. This a rousing adventure, but one that speaks to clear and present dangers that affect our lives.

That is why *Falling Up* will become a classic political memoir and a staple of every political library and classroom, not just because it provides us insider views of famous politicians, but also because—and here the scholar and student of political communication will be particularly rewarded by the reading of this book—we learn how the process of becoming a candidate, winning an election, and staying in power actually works.

I always wanted to leave a trail, some sign that I had been there, a fluorescent painted tag on a wall of human experience. And I wanted to do it alone without committees forcing compromise. As with James Fenimore Cooper's vision of the strong American, individuality was more important than soup.

But, alas, it is impossible.

There are people around you who force an altered course in your journey. And the wisdom of years is proving that these can be shortcuts rather than obstacles. Often new courses become the shining path. This book could never have been completed without three people who didn't stand in my path but took to my side: my wife, Sandy, and two friends, Carl Cannon and David Perlmutter.

Sandy told me to be true in the book and not spare feelings or shade truth, even if it caused her personal pain. And it did. David read a few pages of the manuscript, saw that I had lagged and grown sensitive to dealing with the ghosts that were bouncing around in my head, and encouraged me to start again. Carl scrutinized every word, edited, called bullshit when it was necessary, and forced me to expand my vision of what I was doing. His name should be on the cover with mine.

And there are others. The first time my mind was clear enough for the vision of the book was during my fellowship at Harvard. How can I ever thank the former director of the Kennedy School's Institute of Politics, Senator Alan Simpson, my colleague Dan Lungren, or staff members Catherine McLaughlin, Jennifer Phillips, and Bill White? Or the incredible students I was allowed to mentor? Harvard will always be a special place to me.

And what about the people who were ignored while my mind wrestled with which parts of the story to tell—like my daughter, Kristan Trugman, and my son, Dane? Could I have spent more time at the zoo with my grandchildren, Dylan, Nicholas, and Emma, if I had not attempted this book? Could I have helped sell more campaigns for Jim Duffy and Dane?

In this book I mention the country-and-western song "Mama Tried." Well, my mama tried and should not be ignored. Thanks.

And there are others in my life who mattered—many others—some who will have hurt feelings for being left out. I know you were important. And to those scores of people, I apologize. I only have about three hundred pages.

FALLING UP

In political consulting winning is everything. There is no good second place. No runner-up award. As a result, no cost is too great. Survival depends on it. A win, even a fluke victory over a scandal-ridden opponent, throws the spotlight on the consultant and allows him to prosper. A noble and principled campaign that did not use negative ads and talked about issues of substance turns into ashes if it loses by even one vote. Even winning four races in a season and losing six puts the consultant in the same position as a wounded gazelle being tracked by lions. Thus, political consulting becomes a Darwinist, ferocious business in which the law of the jungle rules and the weak are massacred by bigger and stronger predators.

This almost epic struggle is waged in a climate of near hysteria in which the perception of a consultant is more important than reality. The result is a constant battle for recognition. Consultants cozy up to the press so they will be mentioned or interviewed on politics. Television producers are courted for an occasional appearance on fourth- or fifth-rate cable shows. And as hard as a consultant works to spin his brilliance, there are people trying just as hard to damage his or her reputation.

Anonymous letters are sent to candidates in an attempt to poison a consultant who appears to have an advantage or is close to being hired. Records of a firm's defeats are carefully researched and collected. Backward spin begins after an election, and great efforts are made to diminish the impact of a victory and to amplify the pain of defeat. Blame is assigned, victories are dampened. A newspaper article, even an obviously planted one in some small weekly newspaper, blaming the defeat of a candidate on bad professional advice or bad media is clipped, copied, and disseminated. Spin, spin, spin.

Starry-eyed young staff members and low-level party bureaucrats on Capitol Hill with more ambition than talent or experience become clubs to beat down consultants at the top and to promote those at the bottom who may hold promise of a future job. Elected officials make promotional calls on behalf of their consultants as a form of continued payment to a people they believe helped them win. Even if they are not sure why they won, few successful candidates want to take chances that their 52 percent victory could turn into a 49 percent loss next time.

Senator Edward Kennedy, for example, has been the winning lottery ticket for one firm in Washington. I doubt Kennedy is insecure; he is perhaps only helping his former press secretary Bob Shrum, who obviously served him well. But a call to a naive first-time Democratic candidate somewhere in middle America from this huge celebrity, this keeper of the Kennedy flame, usually makes the difference when insecure candidates decide on a consultant to hire. Because of this kind of namepower, many consultants stud their demonstration television reels with testimonials from well-known winners. Never losers.

There is great insecurity in all candidates. Ted Kennedy's brother John F. Kennedy once remarked that wanting to be president is not a normal ambition. And since Capitol Hill and the fifty statehouses are full of men and women who think they have the right stuff to someday sit in the Oval Office, consultants are by definition dealing with some of the bigger egos in America. But ambition is not the same thing as expertise. Strange as it may seem, politicians themselves seldom know a good media campaign from a bad one. Media campaigns are a necessary form of black magic. Even the most successful incumbents have been involved in only a handful of campaigns, though their egos seldom allow them to admit that they do not understand how they got elected. So they turn to people who have been in hundreds of campaigns for advice.

From the time they throw their hats into the ring, candidates are besieged by calls from hungry consultants looking for bucks or an opportunity to enhance their reputations. Friends and relatives of the candidate are recruited as allies of one hopeful consultant or other. Party hacks with control over badly needed campaign dollars dial in to recommend people they think will later help them in their own scramble for recognition and riches. Mail pours in. FedEx packages of demonstration television reels proliferate. Poison telephone calls begin. Newspaper clips arrive.

Influence is also brought to bear within the consulting industry itself.

Pollsters try to promote media people who allow them control over message. Consultants who know how to produce quality television ads align themselves with direct mail companies, campaign managers cozy up to party bureaucrats for recommendations, researchers go to their Rolodexes and try to ally themselves with all of the logical contenders for a campaign. Pollsters are usually hired first in a campaign, and media producers call them for favorable treatment in the merry-go-round that constitutes the campaign selection process. Consultants often make unspoken agreements with the pollsters to acquiesce and produce literal, numbers-driven, nothing-but-the-facts, emotionless television—the type pollsters like, but which the best consultants also realize is turning off the American audience. And most important, large contributors who are familiar to the party's worker bees because of past donations are called for their input. These big donors usually want to do more than just write a check. They want to give advice. And their advice carries weight. California Assembly Speaker Jesse Unruh used to say that "money is the mother's milk of politics," and even though reformers like Senators John McCain and Russ Feingold passed legislation in what may be a futile attempt to change all that, you'd have to repeal the laws of nature before a call from a rich businessman or special interest carries no influence with a candidate. Candidates may not understand much about the inner workings of professional politics—but they all know that money is essential to a campaign.

Insecurity about money then begins to drive the selection process. The most successful firms in the business compete with upstarts who will promise to perform magic beyond their capabilities for almost nothing. Fees are cut or eliminated, commissions from media are negotiated down to less than a profitable margin. To become a successful consultant one must be perceived as a successful consultant. That requires a couple of notable victories or help from people who carry the mantle of influence. In the mid-1980s, when the consultant industry began to bloom, two now-prominent firms worked almost free for long-shot candidates and won the gold ring.

In the 1985–1986 election cycle, the Democrats got their first chance to run against the 1980 class of Senate conservatives who'd come to Washington on the coattails of the "Reagan revolution." The night Reagan defeated President Jimmy Carter, the Republicans captured twelve Senate seats that had been held by Democrats. A few of those Republicans, including Charles Grassley of Iowa, Warren Rudman of New Hampshire, and Frank Murkowski of Alaska, went on to distinguished Senate careers. A fourth, Don Nickles of Oklahoma, is now the second-ranking Republican in the Senate; a fifth, Dan Quayle, made it as far as the vice presidency. Some of the others were of decidedly lesser cloth and would never have been heard of outside their native states if not for Reagan. The outcome left the Democratic Party—and consultants like me—with a score to settle. Quayle beat one of our stars, Birch Bayh. And we lost other Democratic icons in the Reagan landslide: Frank Church of Idaho; Warren G. Magnuson of Washington state; George McGovern, our 1972 presidential nominee, in South Dakota; Gaylord Nelson of Wisconsin, one of the most respected men in the Senate; and a Georgian, Herman E. Talmadge, who distinguished himself as a member of the Senate Select Committee on Watergate. All of them were beaten by upstart conservatives we either didn't like, didn't respect, or had never heard of.

Six years later it was payback time, and our guys got back the Senate. There may have been an inevitability to this swing, but our business is about winners and losers. Suddenly the perceived long-shot candidates' consultants found themselves where they longed to be—in the hot glare of the spotlight. They had overnight recognition, new best friends in high places, and the key to the bank vault. They would become rich in the next four years. Were they talented? A couple were. Perhaps sooner or later these two would have emerged anyway, but the quirks of 1986 gave them a head start.

I had similar luck. I was adopted by the powerful chairman of Finance, Russell Long, and later his successor on Finance, Senator Lloyd Bentsen. Though I had been in business for about fourteen years and had done well financially, their endorsement propelled me into the top of Washington's political elite. I was invited to the black-tie dinners, assemblies of the White House Correspondents, television personalities, publishers, and show-business types. There was almost no competition. On the entire East Coast there were only three prominent Democratic media firms, and mine soon became one of them. I picked and chose clients. For one cycle I even haughtily made a rule that I would not represent clients farther away than the 900-mile range of my airplane, a Mooney 231, because it was a great bother to land and refuel. I ate with presidential candidates and was invited to dinners with American legends on Martha's Vineyard.

I was forced to hire an assistant to handle my personal finances, which had swelled to such a point that I became careless. In fact, I became like the rest of Washington: money was no longer important. My drugs of choice were recognition and power. But money can never be ignored in Washington. The establishment itself is a giant machine that must raise hundreds of millions of dollars to finance communications. Political parties now exist almost solely as money-raising vehicles. Consultants must be paid because without them one has little chance of being elected. Television and radio must be bought. Researchers must be hired. Polls must be taken.

Power equates to money. Though he is from a state with fewer than 900,000 people, Max Baucus raised millions for his 2002 reelection bid. The chairman of Finance can get people of money and influence and captains of industry on the telephone. Senator Baucus is known as a principled man, but he had no choice but to lean on the people who need him. The Republicans on the other side had the same needs and were trying to raise money from the same people with vague hints of future access or favorable tax philosophies. A tiny squiggle in the tax code can mean millions of dollars to a single individual or large corporation. That squiggle becomes more important than a party label, and big money dances with both parties.

As consultants grow prominent, they are dragged to fundraising events to mix with people looking for influence with their candidates. The aim is to spin a hopeful picture of the candidates' chances for victory. Often we show commercials and give short talks to insiders munching on boiled shrimp, little squares of cheese, and roast tidbits, and drinking glasses of white, not red, wine. (Even rednecks learn that spilled white wine is not as visible on a tie.)

So the tom-toms beat, the jungle animals prowl, the machines belch, the spotlights are focused, coins jingle, testosterone surges, sharp elbows poke, and the clumsy but effective campaign industry surges forward. How the hell did a redneck from Port Arthur, Texas, and then the swamps of Louisiana ever end up here with a little tiny piece of cheese in one hand, a microphone in the other, and a trail of Chardonnay down the front of his pants?

I never really thought being called a redneck was derogatory. The people I grew up and lived with in the first forty years of my life wore the title like a badge of brotherhood. We laughed among ourselves when a country singer released a song called "Red Necks, White Socks, and Blue Ribbon Beer." Most of us wanted a pickup truck with a gun rack in the back as a symbol of cultural identity—even after we grew up and parked a Mercedes or Porsche in the garage.

In Baton Rouge, I knew one redneck wannabe who didn't actually own any firearms but who had a full gun rack with shotguns and deer rifles painted on the rear window of his Ford truck. As a redneck society we had our own language and set of rules. We even spawned a whole industry of redneck bumper stickers and jokes. This didn't mean we all agreed on everything. We simply enjoyed drinking long-neck beers in kicker bars with Hank Williams or Merle Haggard playing on the jukebox. I still enjoy the symphony of clicking pool balls, country music, too-loud laughter, and the dull thud of beer bottles hitting the bar in unrhythmic patterns. The joy of being a redneck didn't prohibit you from putting on your dinner jacket and attending the opera or from reading T. S. Eliot, but redneck culture is fun and it is always politically incorrect. My friend Howell Raines, who hails from Alabama and occupies the lofty position of editor of the world's most powerful newspaper, the *New York Times,* touches on the culture in his fine book *Fly Fishing through the Midlife Crisis.* Howell reminisces fondly about pulling crappie out of a lake in prodigious numbers without regard for sportsmanship or conservation, then frying them up redneck-style. Roy Barnes, the brilliant governor of Georgia and an accomplished redneck storyteller, says rednecks will eat anything from green tomatoes and grits to sections of fence posts, so long as it's deep-fried. The pillars of redneck culture are storytelling, football, hunting, fishing, beer drinking, and food. The sacred redneck temple is a dilapidated hunting camp perched on stilts in a swamp, marsh, or piney woods. There we congregate to play cards, lie about sexual exploits, watch college football, talk trash—and, of course, cook our kind of kick-ass food.

"Come taste this, Billy Bob. It's so good it'll make you slap your grandma," somebody will say. Or someone else: "Come take a suck out of this pot. It'll knock your dick in the dirt." To be a successful redneck one must have a middle name that rolls right out of the first name. If you don't have one, the boys at the hunting camp give you one by tacking on a Bob or Joe to your first name so you aren't embarrassed to be different. Rednecks aren't always bad boys. They just like to have fun. And their way of life is a cultural quilt they can pull up to their chins when they feel the cold draft of change closing in.

So you might say that I was already attuned to how the outside world views southerners when I went to Wisconsin to bid on the job of trying to get some Democratic officeholder elected governor. As I cooled my heels in a waiting room, I could hear through the thin walls one of my competitors, a Yankee from Illinois, applying the word redneck to me as a way of trying to undermine the pitch I hadn't yet made. In our business, you don't let them see you sweat, so I may even have smiled as I heard the characterization.

But it was a thin smile.

And as I waited to make my presentation to the prospective candidate, I heard more descriptions of myself through those thin walls. "Good ole boy" was one phrase I picked up. He strung that one together with expressions like *washed up, too old, too rich, out-of-touch, too southern*. That's when I remembered Governor Michael Dukakis of Massachusetts.

In 1982 I was called to make a presentation in Boston because Mike Dukakis, after sitting out for four years, was searching for a consultant to work for his reelection to the statehouse in a comeback he and his aides hoped would lead all the way to the White House. Dukakis and his top aide, John Sasso, made a great first impression when I sat with them. They were courteous, thoughtful, and receptive as I explained how my television ads would emphasize his good character.

Their confidence in me and my style were confirmed when, a few weeks later, I was called for a second visit and asked to present my television concepts to a group of necktied, starched-shirted men seated around a long conference table in a stylish Boston law firm. They had narrowed their search to two firms. These were serious men, humorless really, and there was no light conversation as I set up my video reel. I tried to respect their somber mood and stick to the business at hand instead of my usual digression into political stories and light banter in the style of rednecks. I admit I was a little put off by the stone countenances of the group and didn't do my best job, but as I finished and reclaimed my tape from the machine, Dukakis asked to see me privately. We went into a secretary's office.

"You aren't going to be hired," Dukakis told me bluntly. "I just wanted to tell you personally."

"I just finished, governor. They didn't vote. Did I do something wrong?"

"No," he said, "I could read their faces. It's just your accent. People up here equate the southern accent with people who aren't as smart as they are. Those are mostly Harvard graduates, and they will never have confidence in you."

"Governor, we shoot our commercials with a camera made in France by a company named Aaton, but the commercials don't have a French accent."

He understood the point and explained that he himself didn't agree with his aides' prejudices, but that when it came time to make hard decisions in the toughest days of the campaign ahead I would never have the confidence of the group assembled at that boardroom table. I knew he was right. It was a battle I had fought repeatedly since moving from Louisiana to Washington, D.C. Besides, it was hard to get angry with a person as decent as Dukakis, even if he was telling me that his friends considered me a stupid redneck.

A few months later, Dukakis fired the firm he'd hired over mine and asked me to come to Massachusetts and finish the campaign. My redneck pride and my workload made me refuse, but I was touched that he asked— and I remained friends with both Dukakis and Sasso for years.

In 1988, however, after he became the Democratic nominee, Dukakis surrounded himself with those same smug people he had around him when I made my presentation. This time, they cost him his election—cost him the presidency—and helped take the Democratic Party into near-ruin. Mike Dukakis carried not one southern state. Obviously his problems went beyond not understanding rednecks. But that turned out to be an apt symbol. He and his group just never had an ear for the American voice.

When Dukakis chose courtly Texas senator Lloyd Bentsen as his running mate, a lot of political professionals took one look at the ticket and thought it was upside-down. Bentsen was not only tougher, older, richer, and more experienced than Dukakis, he even *looked* more like a president. Bentsen was also a longtime client of mine. (Raised on a ranch along the Mexican border, he had no problem with a southern accent.) In fact, he and I were already working that year on his reelection campaign to the Senate, which, by a quirk in Texas law, he could continue while simultaneously appearing on the ballot as Mike Dukakis's vice presidential running mate.

I don't know for sure if Lloyd Bentsen would have made a good president—I like to think he would have made a *great* president—or even if he would have beaten George Bush if he had been the Democratic nominee in 1988. But it's an established fact that Bentsen was a stronger candidate in Texas than Dukakis: while the Dukakis/Bentsen ticket lost the state in a landslide—56 percent to 43 percent—Lloyd Bentsen was winning his Senate race by a million votes. Of course, that's because Bentsen, and not those smart boys from Boston, was in charge. Bentsen tried to help the Dukakis ticket in Texas—I know this because he was always telling me to do things that would have helped. But those Boston boys were always thwarting him. In the process, they sabotaged their own campaign.

Bentsen instructed me to create a series of television spots for the ticket about gun control, with the idea that they would be shown only in Texas. It turns out that in that race the only candidate to have ever favored gun control was George Bush. After the commercials were finished and Bentsen approved them, he had me send them to Boston for approval. Almost daily, he would ask if I had heard from the message managers in the Boston campaign headquarters. I always answered "No," and he always shook his head in disbelief. Finally one day he called and said I was to call Boston and ask for a man named David D'Allesandro, an insurance advertising executive, exactly at 11 A.M. Texas time.

I was on the streets in Dallas shooting commercials for his Senate reelection campaign and stopped all production about ten minutes before the hour. I asked Gay Erwin, Bentsen's executive assistant, to drive me to a pay phone at the edge of a park. That seems quaint now, but 1988 was still the pre-cell-phone era. At exactly 11, I dialed the number in Boston and was told by a receptionist that Mr. D'Allesandro was too busy to talk to me. I explained with some urgency that this call was made at the direction of their own candidate for vice president and that I would not be ignored. I hung onto the phone in the Texas heat for several minutes while cars roared around me. A young man finally answered. He was obviously screening calls for Mr. D'Allesandro. I explained my dilemma. He asked again who I was. I replied that I was the media person for Senator Bentsen's Senate campaign. In the middle of my explanation he cut me off. "Look, sport," he said. "I don't know you, I don't know what you're talking about, and you're wasting my time. So go fuck yourself."

He hung up on me. I returned to the car in a blind rage and related the conversation to Gay. She went to the phone and called Senator Bentsen, who was on the campaign plane. Bentsen had me recount the conversation word for word. There was a long pause and then, in his calm and dignified voice, he said, "Raymond, you did all you could do. Just forget it. This campaign is over."

So I was tempted on that cold midwestern night, as I listened to my character and my firm being assassinated, to rush into the room and whip my competitor's Yankee ass in front of the entire selection committee. That was the instinctive redneck reaction that was in my blood. How dare this unproved pretender challenge the skills and knowledge I had acquired through decades of high-profile campaigns for people like Gary Hart, Bill Clinton, Lloyd Bentsen, Al Gore, Paul Simon, John Stennis, Russell Long, and a parade of candidates I thought should all have statues in their honor. How dare this fool who had only a lay-down mayor's race to his credit think he was qualified to dismiss the years of painstaking work learning our craft, the thousands of hours spent in the air, the hangovers, family problems, insults, and sublime exhilaration that I had attached to me like the bent nose on a honky-tonk brawler?

There is an ever-expanding group of campaign consultants, but a stable pool of candidates requiring their services. As a result, competition among consultants for new business is not only fierce, but often dishonest, deceitful, slanderous, and petty. I knew this about the new consultants, so my agitation at my young rival soon gave way to anger at the candidate I had not yet even met. How could this guy be so stupid that he would listen to the unschooled rookie paint a picture of a "low-budget, guerrilla campaign fought door-to-door"? It was bad enough that this unprincipled pretender of a consultant was pandering desperately to get a fee and a few commissions by telling the candidate he could win without raising much money, weaving a spell of magic solutions that would reduce the need for broadcast communications. But it was worse that the candidate bit like a largemouth bass trying to savage a lazy frog on a shady afternoon bayou.

My anger grew as the thin walls allowed me to hear the group agree because the huckster had told them exactly what they wanted to hear. Stupid leading the stupid. By the time it was my turn, I was no longer interested in being hired and was already regretting the money I had spent on airfare and lodging. I had even fallen in the snow and ice trying to find the low-rent building. My trousers had a wet knee and their crease was long gone. I knew my situation was hopeless. I couldn't honestly duplicate the promises my competitor made. It would have required more than just stretching the truth. It would take what my mother called "telling a story," her southern way of saying "lie." Maybe the inexperienced consultant had not yet learned his limits and his pitch was truth as he saw it. I knew the campaign for governor was doomed if they followed his advice. I seethed at having to humble myself before a committee of amateurs who thought they were going to "think outside the box" and find a consultant with New Ideas. I resented talking to a group that even *used* the phrase "think outside the box." So by the time I arrived in my rumpled suit and sat in the eye of the half circle, I was belligerent and defensive. They would have to hire me on my terms.

"I don't think I'm going to show commercials," I told them and put the tape back into my shoulder bag. "That's no way to hire a consultant. No person is capable of looking at a commercial and declaring it good or bad without knowing something about its campaign purpose and the poll numbers it reflects. I offer you the following: I have never lost a race for an incumbent U.S. representative or senator. I have helped elect eleven governors and been involved in three presidential campaigns. I make the best television commercials and am perhaps the best speechwriter of all the consultants. Only one or two other consultants surpass my experience, and I will personally work in your campaign without sending in college interns or second-string employees. My fee is $50,000 and we retain the 15 percent commissions allowed by media on all the money you spend on advertising. Any questions?"

The committee members just looked at each other. They had had their asses kissed for a solid week by consultants who had multimedia presentations, little inside stories studded with illustrious names, and glib jokes. They had been entertained and flattered. And now they had been insulted. They were not going to hire me, but they couldn't resist asking a question anyway.

"How much money will it cost to win this campaign?"

I answered that it would take almost two million dollars. They visibly blanched.

"Well, our budget is $500,000. How would you run a campaign with that kind of money?"

This was the point in the process, I guess, where the other consultant began talking about "guerrilla" campaigns.

"If that is all you raise," I replied, "my advice would be to drop out now before you waste half a million dollars and have a loss on your record."

I wasn't there much longer. The committee members all suddenly remembered meetings they had to attend. The candidate shook my hand and asked if I knew anyone who could raise money for him. I did, but didn't offer free advice. I left there figuring they were doomed. My instincts turned out to be right. The candidate came in dead last in a crowded field. But the "guerrilla" consultant took his show on the road and is still hoodwinking candidates with the same routine to this day.

After the Dukakis experience, I became even more aware of my accent and began to spend time reading my audience. With most southern candidates it was an advantage, but there were exceptions. When Dick Morris first took me to meet one of his clients, the governor of Arkansas, I realized that I had better keep the lid on the box of grits. Bill Clinton and his wife, Hillary, I quickly learned, did not think highly of the southern intellect. I cleaned up my act and was hired, but my relationship with Clinton would have been much closer if I had a diploma from Harvard or Yale hanging around my neck. Later, when Mrs. Clinton took over the campaign for president and brought in most of her own people, the team included few southerners until James Carville was hired.

Political consulting is a rough business. It requires no license, no college degree, no experience. All one needs to open a practice are a business card and some contacts in one of the political party offices who know even less than you. They will put your name on lists of acceptable consultants and throw you into the pool of salesmen roaming the country with a bag of tricks and sharp tongues. Not to say they are all hacks. Some of the brightest and most principled people I know are consultants, and I am proud to be in their number. Initially, they came into the business in an attempt to involve themselves nobly in the process of democracy. Some of us looked up one day and found our bank accounts overflowing and were amazed. We were also too pleased to spend much time wondering what compromises we had made along the way—or what we had done to American politics.

In 1999, a poll of political consultants showed a clear line of demarcation. Most consultants who had been in the business more than ten years had gotten in almost by accident while trying to advance some candidate or cause. The generation of consultants who came later were attracted by the figurative dollar signs that hang like constellations over the dome of all state capitols. Candidates themselves can't seem to tell the difference between the two types. Even old incumbents who have been in office for twenty-five years have been involved in only five or six campaigns. Most of them don't really understand why they were elected. All tend to see their victories as evidence of some special genius on their own part. They are not much better at distinguishing good from bad consultants than the obscure mayor or state legislator who dreams of someday being president, which most of them do.

I have stayed around long enough that rednecks are coming back into style. James Carville, a former employee of mine, has taken his accent and quirky down-home persona and stuck them in the eye of the effete establishment. Now rednecks rule. At my invitation James joined me for a forum at Harvard, where in 1999 I had been awarded a fellowship in the John F. Kennedy School of Government, Institute of Politics. I was amused to watch students fight for his autograph and occasionally try to wrap their tongues around a mellow redneck pronunciation. The next day I looked around Harvard Square to see if anyone was painting gun racks in the rear windows of their cars. They weren't, but I loved my stay at Harvard. If they would hire me again I could offer an advanced degree in Redneckism and be one of their most popular instructors. I'd ask the students to call me Ray Bob.

In my childhood home we were fierce Democrats on the picket line against the abuse of working people. We knew that if one dropped his guard for only a minute the Republicans would have him by the throat like a jungle predator feeding on the weak. Republicans individually were limp, sexless, selfish cowards and we, collectively, were strong. Workers with sweat on their backs and dirt under their fingernails could defeat the rich capitalists who devoured our young for breakfast and built roads for their Cadillacs and Packards from the crushed bones of working people. Workers had to stand together, shoulder to shoulder, with clubs in our hands and righteousness in our hearts.

In the fall of my fifth grade I was sent to school on an urgent assignment from my father. I was to correct the teacher's misinterpretation of history and explain to her that Franklin Roosevelt, and not George Washington, was the father of our country.

"Washington was just another aristocrat who rose to power on the backs of dead soldiers and working people. He could afford to throw dollars across the Potomac and chop down his family's fruit trees because they had more money and more trees. But working people don't. We have to squeeze our dollars and hang on because the world is filled with people who want to cheat us out of it."

My teacher looked at me with wonder but I wasn't rebuked, because she taught in a union town. My attitudes were spawned at Local 23 of the Oil, Chemical and Atomic Workers. Preachers and teachers knew to cower when Port Arthur was in the middle of a strike and blood had been spilled at the plant gates. My father, Albert Dolph Strother, was a smoldering, 230-pound, six-foot-two-inch, khaki-clad, Lucky Strike–smoking, hard-muscled malcontent who sometimes lashed out in his sleep at intruders trying to take away something he had earned through sweat. I shadowboxed behind him, learning to call strikebreakers "scabs" with the corners of my mouth turned down and occasionally spitting in the grass. I carried candy Lucky Strikes in my shirt pocket. What my father hated, I hated. What he believed, I embraced as universal truth. So of course Franklin Roosevelt was the father of our country. I learned to read from the CIO newspaper and from picket signs:

See Dick.

See Dick strike.

Strike, Dick, strike.

See Jane.

See Jane picket.

Picket, Jane, picket.

See Dick and Jane.

Dick and Jane are union.

According to our code, to budge off of a truth in the face of an argument or to compromise merely showed a lack of character. To forgive one's enemies was for the pale-faced preachers in my mother's church who pleaded for larger collections in the Sunday sermons my father occasionally attended as the price of peace at home. We listened vigilantly to those tearstained sermons, especially closely when the union was on strike, to make sure the preacher didn't ask God for anything that would give aid and comfort to a scab or a union-busting company. Strikes made collection plates awfully light in Port Arthur, and preachers were known to ask for heavenly intervention when they couldn't make the payment on the church's new Ford.

The city of my birth needed Jesus to help cushion its workers against its climate of violence and its fear of unemployment. Port Arthur was an acid-smelling, soot-covered union town of people who earned their living at one of the local oil refineries or chemical plants. The city was a festering sore that infected the Gulf, the marshes, and the bayous. Even the air smelled of something singed and sour. Bosses, Republicans, and professional people moved to Beaumont, eighteen miles away. In Port Arthur our houses looked the same, we all dressed the same, we even thought the same because the center of our collective universe was the Oil, Chemical and Atomic Workers Labor Hall of Local 23. When Pete Seeger sang about "ticky-tacky" little houses that "all look the same," he could have been talking about the houses and the society of Port Arthur. All of our fathers made, within a few cents, the same salary. Women didn't work. Our beaches were covered with globs of oil and the earth around the banks of the Intracoastal Canal had the consistency of asphalt as the result of dumped oily ship bilge. Democrats always received 95 percent of the vote. In 1951, when I was eleven, two friends, Robert Jones and Earl Harbert, pedaled their bikes at breakneck speed to my house. "We know where a Republican lives. You want to go see?"

I jumped on my Western Flyer bike and rode three or four blocks to a nondescript frame house not unlike where most of us lived. We sat across the street in the shade of a chinaberry tree waiting. Finally a man, a woman, and two children emerged. We were astonished. They looked like us. I don't know what we expected, but they didn't resemble monsters who would suck the blood from working people and leave their families to starve. In fact, the youngest girl was a classmate of ours. Later, true to my father's predictions, the Republican became a scab when he breached the picket line and entered Gulf Oil's gates to work during a strike. Of course we stopped talking to his daughter at school, and some of the boys from high school broke her father's windows and slashed his tires. It was to be expected. What was unexpected, however, was my father's lecture to me when I explained that we had shut the daughter out of class activities. "You can't do that," he said. "You go to school and be nice to that little girl. She can't help it if her daddy's a damned scab and a snake. She didn't ask to be born to such a miserable son of a bitch. You set a good example in school by playing with that little girl. You hear me?" I did what my father said but was ridiculed by a few of my friends.

My father was a brooding man who would enter blue periods and sit for hours under a cottonwood tree staring at things in the bottom of an empty coffee cup like a reader of tea leaves. His fury was almost as visible as the worm-eaten leaves scattered around his bent metal chair. I would sit close by and carve wooden sticks for fishing corks and repair broken fishing reels. Occasionally I would feel his presence as his big fingers reached out and tightened a screw I had forgotten or tied a knot in a line about to unravel. Once in a great while he would pat me on the head or ruffle my hair. Men like my father didn't hug. It just wasn't part of the code. These little acts of love and kindness were done without comment. Silence was part of our communication. It seemed more important to listen to the dry rattle of the cottonwood leaves than to pollute the quiet with meaningless words. But for some reason, when we were in the Gulf of Mexico out of sight of land in our tiny, fourteen-foot pea shell of a boat, he would share his secrets of life, both of us looking at the horizon while gulls threw themselves out of the sky to prey on the shrimp jumping across the surface to escape schools of speckled trout beneath them. I remember the smell of the fish breaking salt water and the thousands of frantic shrimp doing tailstands on the mirror surface.

"Not much difference in those shrimp and working people," my father said. "If they go down the fish eat them, if they jump out of the water they get eaten by the gulls." I just nodded. Occasionally as we sat watching our hand-carved popping corks bob on the water, he would say, "Raymond, go to school and get an education. We need some lawyers who can help working people."

In the depths of the Damned Republican Depression, before I was born, my father was infrequently employed as a deckhand on a Texas Oil Company tanker taking heating oil to New York. For some reason the company always fired all of the deckhands once they were in port and hired new ones. My father's theory was they didn't want men together long enough to organize. After being released my father would hop freight cars back south. As the unemployed deckhands and assorted displaced rail riders watched America slide by their boxcar, they sang Jimmy Rodgers hobo songs and talked about a new order where working people had job security and the bosses would be put in their place—wherever that was. They rolled their own cigarettes and talked freely about the experiment in Russia and how maybe it wasn't such a bad idea.

"We'd all be Communists now if it weren't for Franklin Roosevelt," my father once told me. "We were about ready to pick up guns when he came along. Damned Herbert Hoover almost destroyed this country."

My teachers, though, again seemed to have a warped sense of history. They talked about a world depression and global economic factors. One of them actually had the gall to say Hoover wasn't responsible for the depression. She didn't even know that his first name was "Damned." Her lack of understanding of a basic truth about Damned Hoover shook my confidence in the infallibility of teachers. I had already learned that preachers could not be trusted.

The only curse word allowed in our house was "damned" but only as a prefix before Nazi, Jap, or Republican. You could also use "damned" before the given name of any Republican, such as "Damned Herbert Hoover." Even my mother understood that some things were so awful they demanded an awful word. I didn't learn to say Japanese instead of Damned Japs until I was in high school. They bombed Pearl Harbor.

"You can't forget about what they did just because time passes," my father said. To forgive one's enemies exhibited a weakness of character.

The worst thing in the world would have been to mix my father's hatred of the Japanese with his skepticism of the Baptist Church. And it happened just that way one memorable day.

Fundamentalist Baptist churches love religious freak shows. Converted Catholics, dried-up drunks, and Jews reclaimed by Jesus were great favorites. A flashy traveling preacher named Angel Martinez, who wore white coats and pink shirts and drove a 1956 Ford T-Bird, made an annual stop at North End Baptist. Angel had it all. He was a Mexican, a former drinker, a former Catholic, and with his Elvis swept-back hair with one curl over his forehead, he looked like something that would bop down at the local honky-tonk. The old women loved him and the young girls in the congregation swooned. A few of the boys, me included, were concerned that he would deflower our virgins before we got to them. My dad only laughed at the flashy Mexican and shook his head in wonder when dollars were heaped onto the collection plate. But a Japanese revivalist was another matter.

The day he arrived, we filed glumly into a pew three rows from the back of the church. The night was heavy with the sound of crickets, and all of the windows were open to let the sparse wet breeze drift through. Even today I remember the smell of freshly cut St. Augustine grass, Texas dust, refinery poison, and the singed starch in our shirts. My father, brother, sister, and I all looked as though we were being led to an execution. But my mother was bubbling. She had stayed in the choir until she was sure we were actually entering the church and rushed to meet us. On those rare times when my father consented to attend church, she would leave her place in the choir behind the preacher and sit close to her unsaved, un-born-again man. There was always a chance that Jesus would sweep out of the sky and whisper in his ear, and she wanted to be close enough to help in such an important event.

I looked to the front and realized that this night was going to be different, but hardly the way my mother would have fantasized. Seated on the elevated stage to the side of the pulpit was our preacher in his usual place. Next to him sat a diminutive Asian in a suit.

The preacher introduced him as "the man who led the attack on Pearl Harbor but has found Jesus." I was only ten, but I could have predicted what happened next. My father held the Japanese responsible for the death of his younger brother, Claud, a mate on an oil tanker that was sunk by a submarine in the Caribbean in 1942. The truth was that it was a German sub that sunk the ship, but my father always held "the Japs" equally responsible with the Nazis. Many years later my younger brother, also named Claud, was killed in Vietnam and my father blamed Robert McNamara and Lyndon Johnson with the same fervor he had the Japanese. In his bitterness and grief he actually talked more than once of wanting to dig up the corpse of Johnson, a fellow Texan, and hang him from a public tree as a warning against all warmongers.

The night of the revival my father tried to behave himself, I'm sure of it, if only to please my mother. But something took hold of him, and before the poor man could even get started on his guest sermon, my father stood up, jammed on his hat, and said loudly enough that even the preacher in front could hear, "Let's go. We're not going to listen to a damned murdering Jap." We marched out of the church and through the swinging doors. My mother was weeping and was soon joined by my sister, Clara. I held my shoulders back a little straighter. My dad, my small and bewildered brother Claud, and I had just won World War II again, and I felt like John Wayne. Real men didn't listen to born-again Japs. Jesus had missed another chance at my father, and the Japanese had lost another war. And it was the only time I ever saw my father wear a hat indoors. His code was rigid.

We didn't have the same feeling about the "Nigras." In fact, we had no feeling about African Americans. They lived across the tracks in the West Side, and we never came into contact with them. It might seem strange today, but they were simply not mentioned in my house. We had tolerance created by distance. The schools weren't integrated, and I can't recall as a youth seeing blacks except when they borrowed the track at our school, Thomas Jefferson High, to train. The coach, as ordered by the school board, announced that anybody who had strong beliefs didn't have to train with the black visitors, but he made it clear that he felt it was right to make our track available once a week because they didn't have one over at Lincoln High under the separate but unequal rules that existed then in the South.

As captain of the track team and a local sensation in the mile, I was willing to train with the shiny black boys because I felt—though it was unspoken— that the coach wanted me to set an example. Most of the first-string runners joined me and trained with the black kids. The boys on our track team who were lazy or lacked talent—or who had no heart—availed themselves of this easy excuse to get out of practice. "I don't run with niggers, coach," one of them said as they drifted toward the corner drive-in. I could see Coach's face redden in anger as he looked the other way in disgust. Thus, without speaking a word, did my track coach send the clear signal that in his eyes, those boys were losers. But in those days, even with my coach's tacit support, our interaction with the black athletes was little more than nods and greetings. I couldn't invite them to Frostop Root Beer if I wanted to because segregation shut them out of most business places. This was before American heroes like John Lewis, a future client of mine and current member of Congress, were beaten bloody at lunch-counter sit-ins.

So we competed in time trials and that was all. But after four or five weeks, I began to benefit from that interaction directly. A black runner who always put his medal of the Virgin in his mouth when he ran began pushing me in practice harder than I'd been pushed before, making me go all-out to earn practice victories that before I had won easily. As a result, I shaved five seconds off my time. After practice one day Coach Cornelius gripped my shoulder in an iron grasp that I interpreted as affection—or at least approval.

"Real men don't judge a man by his color, do they, Strother?" He wanted badly to tell me about justice, but the school system would not have allowed it. But most of all he wanted to show comradeship and affection. Texans didn't touch. This is as close as a coach could come to a hug.

But my experience with the coach and the black runners did make me reconsider the local prejudices against Mexicans. I began inviting a Mexican half-miler home with me after school. Though they, unlike the blacks, went to school with us, there was a tremendous bias in Texas against Mexicans. An Anglo girl in our high school would become an outcast if she dated or even walked down the halls with a dark-skinned classmate. To my surprise, my father treated the thin, nervous boy with respect. Mexicans, to him, were just working people trying to survive.

It was always assumed I would work. When I was eleven I talked a distributor into giving me a delivery route for the *Port Arthur News,* my first adventure in newspapering. I delivered afternoon papers daily and the Sunday paper before daylight on a bicycle until I was thirteen. After I saved $85, I bought a broken-down old Harley Davidson motorcycle that could more easily accommodate the seventy-five pounds of newspapers on Sunday morning. My younger brother and I would wake at 3 A.M., push the Harley for half a block to start it because we couldn't afford a new battery, and then roar down the streets to meet the distributor. One time it fired prematurely and left us standing on the street watching it pile into a frame house. They were understanding neighbors and just waved at the crazy Strothers standing bewildered under a streetlight watching their still-puttering bike. One important piece of equipment was an old stopwatch we used in our constant attempts to set new records each week putting a newspaper in the door handle of each of the 140 houses on our route. We always doubled back to make sure we had forgotten no door. To have a complaint in a time when a hundred boys wanted a route could be grounds for losing the franchise.

We kept that route in the family for more than ten years. When he was a little older, my brother took over the afternoon deliveries so I could run track and bought himself a small fleet of ancient, worn-out motor scooters that he learned to expertly repair and resell. We must have been a Sunday-morning nightmare to the shift workers trying to sleep as our mufflerless machines split open the cricket calm of dew-wet mornings. They didn't seem to hold it against the Strother brothers. When the salute was fired across my brother's casket after his body was shipped home from Vietnam, I saw several of our old customers standing weeping in the rain. Their paperboy had gone off to save democracy by flying helicopters in Vietnam. While I cursed the god that created LBJ and Robert McNamara, they celebrated my brother's valor. I don't blame them. It was their connection to the war, and we had served them well as news delivery boys. But they must not have read carefully enough those papers we put in their doors—or they, too, would have wept at the injustice instead of the glory. They didn't understand that ignorant working people like them and the Strothers were only cannon fodder for the bastards.

In our family, work was a virtue and I was constantly looking to prove my manhood by finding another job. In junior high, while still delivering papers, I got a job in the school cafeteria scraping plates and stacking them onto a conveyer belt that went through the dishwasher. There was no pay, but you got a hot breakfast if you arrived at the school early, and all the lunch you wanted. I was proud not to need the twenty-five cents a day for lunch that always came out of my daddy's deep khaki pockets. There was always a strike on the horizon, and I thought working for free meals meant that our family strike fund would grow large enough there would be no fear when the big one hit. I lost my cafeteria job when the cafeteria manager discovered my father had a job at the refinery. She tried to reserve the lunchroom jobs for poor children who had to work or skip lunch.

By the time I was fourteen, I supplemented my paper route with a weekend job in a discount gas station. By now I needed that extra money to pay for gas for my dad's old Chevrolet he kept to drive to the acid-spewing plant. I had discovered girls. The manager of the station was a disabled man with a speech problem. For some reason he was sure all of his teenaged employees were "getting laid two or three times a day at school," and with each paycheck he gave us packages of Trojan rubbers from the vending machine hidden in the back room. We carried them in our wallets and flashed them to friends. Once when I was collecting for my paper route, a handful of foil packages fell out of my pocket at the feet of a woman customer as I fumbled for change.

Junior, the manager, showed me where he hid the long-barreled revolver under the cash register and gave me permission to shoot any bastard who tried to take his money. When working after midnight I would often stick the pistol in the front of my jeans with the pearl handle showing when a rough bunch of drunks wheeled in and asked for a dollar's worth of gas. A buck bought four gallons in 1954.

All-night service stations became a specialty for me. I enjoyed the people who came in late to buy the least expensive gas in town. In those dark hours I learned to hot-wire cars, change oil, replace spark plugs, fix flats with either hot or cold patches, and handle drunks who were lost or down on their luck. Almost every weekend an illiterate traveler would drive an old truck under the lights and ask me to write a letter to a wife, mother, or lover. The stories were always about some sort of misery like a lost job or being in jail. "Write a bunch of stuff in there about how much I love her and when I get on my feet I'll be back," was a typical instruction. That was perhaps the start of my "creative" writing, as I would weave their hard luck stories into some sort of poetic tome, taking liberties and inserting Hemingway expressions like, "You make my earth move." Even with my ninth-grade education it was easy to write words they didn't understand, so I learned to be careful with my vocabulary, which in truth wasn't really that great. Later I traded up and began working in a Mobil station at the intersection of the highways to Beaumont, Orange, and Galveston. About two in the mornings I began to get unwashed frog hunters with their croaker sacks filled with hopping frogs. They would sit around the office drinking Cokes from our vending machine and telling tales. Most of them would sell their sacks of frogs to a restaurant and drink cheap wine until they ran out of money and were forced back into the marshes.

Filling station work was not terribly lower than my expectations. When I was born in Port Arthur it seemed I was predetermined to be one of those people who work with their hands for hourly wage. The dream of most people in my position was to graduate from Thomas Jefferson High School and win a job at one of the refineries that surrounded the city. I cheated fate in part because of a turn-of-the-century philanthropist, a man I simply knew as Gates because his name was etched in marble over the door of Gates Memorial Library. John Warne Gates, I learned later, was indeed a memorable person. As a young man during the mid-1870s, he was working in a small hardware store in his hometown in Illinois when a businessman who'd invented a new kind of fence—barbed wire—happened in. Soon Gates, who had a natural talent for verbal expression, was selling barbed wire in Texas, where he helped alter the very landscape with his silver-tongued descriptions on the wonders of the product, a vision he espoused in Grange halls from San Antonio to Amarillo. Until then, western ranchers had no economical way of fencing their cattle. Gates ended up with his own barbed-wire company, and from there he branched into oil, banking, and railroads. Eastern bankers considered him not only an ill-mannered lout, but a pirate. Hard to imagine, then, what the few blue-nose types in Port Arthur thought of Gates. He drank whiskey, smoked, and gambled constantly. In fact, it is said that he made at least one bet every single day of his life. These tended not to be small wagers: his biography, which gathers dust in the library that bears his name, is titled *Bet-a-Million Gates*. When he died, his widow donated the land and the money for the building of a library. And it was the discovery of the library and the free books inside it that changed my life. Gates Memorial was the light that illuminated knowledge and art. A good teacher had given my class an assignment in the "big" library, and I pedaled my bike there on a spring afternoon. The marble facade, the orderliness of the shelves, and the reigning silence both attracted and intimidated me.

When my bare feet squeaked across the waxed wood floors, I was overcome by the powerful scents of books, mildew, dust, and furniture oil. It was a spiritual place that became my tabernacle. The librarian explained the card system and astonished me by saying I could read all of the books free— and even borrow them and take them home. So I set out to conquer the shelves. I would sit on the floor at the end of the stacks and read entire works of Stevenson, Dos Passos, Sinclair Lewis, Hemingway, and occasionally Faulkner, though I had trouble understanding "a tale told by an idiot, full of sound and fury." Because my parents didn't monitor my activities and didn't seem to care what I did with my time, I would ride my bike and later my motorcycle to the columned building and spend three or four hours a day. And I took books home, always careful to return them before the two-cent fine kicked in. I buried myself in books. One Saturday morning my mother jerked a book from my hands and ordered me to "go outside and play like a normal boy." I could hear the neighborhood kids playing baseball in a vacant lot. After she determined I wasn't normal because I spent too much time reading, I smuggled the books out of the house and sat out of sight behind the huge cottonwood, absorbing ideas and feeling an adrenaline rush when a passage was so beautiful that even a twelve-year-old boy understood there was a world that reached far beyond a drab, oil-soaked town hunkered down under smoke-filled skies. Years later my mother told me that she had been afraid my reading would ruin my eyes, but the truth was that it wasn't manly to read so much.

After I had gained the librarian's respect, she introduced me to one of the two listening rooms and the library of music on huge records. The first recording she put on was Beethoven's Fifth Symphony. I was hypnotized by the heroic recurring theme and listened to that record for weeks. Then she let me sample Brahms Piano Concerto no. 2 in B-flat Minor. I was now hooked on classical music. It must have been a funny picture, a tiny barefooted boy lying on the floor between two giant speakers with his eyes closed and his mind leaping through stars. When I was a senior at Thomas Jefferson, a junior member of the track team, Jim Langdon, stuck his head into what had become accepted by most regulars in the library as my room and asked me to listen to jazz. He played the trombone in the high school dance band. I was immediately attracted to the intricate patterns and creative energy in jazz, and began to join Jim and his friends occasionally. They were as devoted to jazz as I was to classical. Years later, when he was a fellow newspaper reporter, Jim would remind me that one of the members of his listening-room group was a girl who later turned out to be a tragic, exploding roman candle in the music world. Her name was Janis Joplin. I barely remembered her. She seemed mousy and distant, and had little to say. I guess she, too, had dreams larger than Port Arthur.

When I look at the scope of my life, the ups and downs, that librarian becomes one of my most important and influential figures. My father read union newspapers and Mickey Spillane novels, and my mother didn't touch any printed material but the Bible. Because the librarian introduced me to books, I developed intellectual curiosity. And when she opened the listening room to me, I learned that Hank Williams wasn't the most important composer of our time. The shame is that I don't even know her name. But because of her kindness I did not leave high school for the refineries. In those books she let me see beyond the smog and the board-and-batten, weatherbeaten culture of violence and fundamentalist preachers.

In my party, the Democratic Party, we believe that all of us are assigned places in life by our environment and economic condition. In some ways, the great philosophical debate we've had with the Republicans for the last seventy years in this country has revolved around this one principle. The Republicans say they emphasize the power and wonder of every individual. They believe that Democrats have discounted the factor of personal determination and, thus, personal accountability.

I'm a lifelong Democrat, but my own history is a testament to the fact that Republicans are sometimes right—that people of modest origins can work their way up the ladder and fully realize the American Dream. But I remain a Democrat. We Democrats don't want to leave barefoot little boys to the vicissitudes of chance—or leave in place a playing field that rewards only the most tenacious of the poor. We believe that despite the wealth of this country, it still often requires a government program—or a progressive labor union—to break the cycle of poverty and ignorance that holds people back.

Sometimes, of course, what is needed is something else entirely. Sometimes we all just need a lucky break. That luck can come in many forms. In my case it came, fittingly, in the form of a building named after a gambler who honored the written word. Gates's library was my luck.

The only mistake the librarian made was inviting me to participate in a quiz bowl on literature with my junior high classmates. It was one of the Friday afternoon assemblies with hundreds of bored students sitting in a hot auditorium.

I didn't relish the idea of going on stage in front of three hundred kids, but my obligation to her overcame my self-doubt. I sat starched and shined with seven other students on stage while the principal asked questions about literature. It was terrible. I had never heard of any of the books. *Rebecca of Sunnybrook Farm* and the Hardy Boys adventures had never been part of my reading list. Where were Zola, Hemingway, Steinbeck, and Hugo? I knew about Robert Jordan, Quasimodo, and the whore Nana, but not about anybody named Tess or Rebecca. I knew I was disappointing the librarian, and the audience was beginning to notice I had not answered a single question. Toward the end I finally scored a point when they got to *Huckleberry Finn* and I was able to identify the Ohio as the river Huck had planned to go up in order to help Jim escape from slavery. I had read all of Twain. But the assembly program ended in shame as I came in last. I was never asked to participate in another school program.

We all have books that helped us focus or expanded our vision. Mine came at the end of the stack of Twain after I had finished all of the known works like *Connecticut Yankee, Tom Sawyer,* and *Huckleberry Finn.* The critics were never kind to the book, but my discovery of the irreverent *Mysterious Stranger* with its wacky logic and cynicism helped me understand my continued problems with fundamentalism, a discovery that put me on a collision course with my mother—who, in league with the Baptist Church, had tried to convince me that God would strike you down if you questioned anything in the Bible or made jokes about its inconsistencies. Mark Twain helped me question a version of religion that required that one shut down one's mind and believe narrow interpretation without question. I remember the preacher saying, "The Bible says it, I believe it, and that settles it." Then he would interpret Scripture to make it mean something other than the words on the gold-edged paper. According to him, the Bible said that kids at North End Baptist Church couldn't dance, go to movies on Sunday, or swim with girls. They called it mixed bathing and said it was specified in the Bible. I don't know if it is or not, but years later I learned that mixed bathing could really be a lot of fun. I am convinced that freed fundamentalists have a lot more fun with sex. My theory applies to both Bill Clinton and Jimmy Swaggart—and me.

My father kept my life from being a religious boot camp. He worked out an arrangement that required me to go only to Sunday school and worship services on Sunday mornings and Training Union and church on Sunday night. This took at least four hours of my Sunday, but I didn't have to attend revivals, Bible study, or youth activities like the Royal Ambassadors that would have captured several hours every week. When I was about eleven I was talked into attending a Royal Ambassadors week-long retreat in the piney woods of East Texas. Some of the more affluent kids in town had gone to summer camps, so I bought into this as the same sort of thing, with Jesus paying the tuition. This camp consisted of six to eight hours of various mind-numbing religious services a day broken only by lunch, two swimming sessions, and dinner. On the third gruesome night I was stopped by one of the preachers, who led me between two cabins, put his hand on my shoulder, and asked if I had hair around my pecker. When I said I did, he said, "Let me see." When I refused, he reached for my zipper. I broke away and ran to the safety of the next Bible study. That night I walked three miles to the highway and hitched a ride back to Port Arthur. My mother cried when I showed up at home. I had insulted Jesus and the good people who had sacrificed for me to attend camp. I didn't tell her then—or ever— why I had fled. I shudder to think what my father would have done if I had told him.

My father was passive on church rules. He always had his guard up when the preacher's lips were moving. What he was not passive about, though, was law enforcement against strikers. In my father's world the Texas Rangers belonged in a level of hell with scabs and bankers. He considered Rangers to be little more than thugs sent in by the rich oil men to beat and murder people trying to organize a union or exercise their rights on a picket line. My father loved me and my brother but would have rather seen us dead than wearing a Texas star. When television came along later and glorified the Rangers' exploits as Indian fighters and kindly peace officers, my father would scream at the black-and-white images on the Admiral set, and my mother would dance around to protect the precious picture tube.

There were certain unwritten rules about being a man in my father's house. In the third grade, Bobby Clayton, the class bully, sent me home from school in tears with a torn shirt. Then he stood in our front yard yelling that I was a coward and should come out and fight. In my eight-year-old eyes he looked the size of a Ford coupe. Because he had failed the third grade, he was not only bigger, but older. My father looked at me and shook his head.

"You got to go out there and fight."

And so I did. Soon I was bleeding from the nose and one ear and retreated inside the house again—only to be sent back into the yard. My mother was weeping and my father was glum.

"It's what he has to do, Mildred. If he runs now he'll spend the rest of his life running."

Albert Dolph Strother was a man of few words, but the ones he used had the force of a recoil from the old 12-gauge shotgun we kept in the closet. The day after the mauling he took me out under the cottonwood tree, where we had our serious talks. He sat in the old metal lawn chair and I stood before him. We didn't touch.

"I know you hurt, but you did what you had to do. A man can't run. But he's a big boy and you got to even the odds. He outweighed you about twenty pounds, so you needed to pick up something that made up for the difference. Maybe a baseball bat or a wrench."

I nodded, even though I was only beginning to understand this tough Texan who was my father.

"And another thing you got to remember," he said, "Never cry. Never let 'em see you sweat. Wade in, don't blink, and don't wear your feelings on your face. Don't whimper. Life is a poker game. Keep 'em guessing about what you could do next. You never have to worry about a talker. Don't ever let the bastards see you sweat."

This advice has served me well in the business of political consulting. When things fall apart and the candidate looks in your direction, he needs to see someone who appears to be in control. A panicked consultant would not be trusted. In fact, the slogan "Never let the bastards see you sweat" hangs on my office wall to this day.

But if my father's lessons about standing and fighting were helpful when I became a political consultant, they could be damaging in personal relationships. It took me many years to learn the need for compromise and to make an effort to see other viewpoints. And many times, I found myself relitigating with my own wife my parents' epic struggle over the rage that is in men's souls. My mother's church taught her to turn the other cheek; the violence of the real world taught my father that any fool who does that is likely to be cold-cocked with a tire iron on the other side of his face. *Don't turn your back on the bastards and don't let them see you sweat.* It took me the better part of a lifetime to see that they were both about half right.

My family took miserable Sunday drives with my brother, Claud, my sister, Clara Sue, and me in the backseat squabbling and my mother pressed into the passenger door, slightly more than arm's length from my father. I don't know why she did that, because my father never touched her in anger. That would have violated his rigid code of being a man.

It was on such a miserable Sunday in the country when our old polished black Hudson was more than halfway across a single-lane bridge and another car started across, stopping ten feet from our bumper. Three men were in the car. The driver leaned out his window, a cigarette hanging from his lips, and yelled, "Back up, I want to get across this bridge." He turned and looked at the other men in the car. They laughed.

My mother inched down in her seat.

"Honey, back up. Those fellows want to start trouble."

My little sister began crying and Claud hid on the floorboard. I knew that no matter what my mother said, the issue was settled. A man didn't run. I wasn't worried. My father was Jack Dempsey, John Wayne, and Babe Ruth rolled into one huge, contained missile of passion and strength. He slowly climbed got out of the car, and so did the front-seat passenger of the other car. My mother began to cry. My father slowly took off his Dobbs snap-brim hat and gently laid it back in the car, precisely folded his suit coat and tie over the window, and rolled up his sleeves a single roll at a time. Every motion was cool and deliberate. He leaned over the bridge rail to look at the rushing water as though he was making sure a fall into the muddy, swollen, stump-tumbling currents would be fatal, and then looked at the man in cowboy boots leaning against the door of the Ford with a snarl-like smile on his face.

Suddenly it dawned on Mr. Cowboy Boots that he had to make a quick choice between backing up or being thrown over the bridge by a big redneck in a cold fury. He considered the odds. There were three of them and only one giant with ice-blue eyes who was walking slowly toward him. But the truth was evident. It was a mismatch. There were not enough men in that car to stop the deadly rage coming their way. Their sedan scraped the bridge twice as it burned rubber in reverse trying to outpace my father, who continued walking toward them on the chance they might stall. One long piece of chrome rattled on the asphalt. When he returned to the car and put on his coat and tie there was no conversation. Because men didn't talk, they acted. And my mother didn't want to start an argument that would continue the rest of the miserable Sunday. If life is a woven cloth of experiences, then ours was corduroy with each of the ribs representing anger.

Though my father wasn't the only person or institution that taught me violence, it was part of my education. Port Arthur, like most seaport and mining towns, rotated around a core of violence. I had to fight or bluff almost every day. And to be able to bluff, one had to occasionally fight. It was part of being a man in a town founded on union violence and drunk merchant sailors on binges. In high school, I once accidentally brushed shoulders with Wayne Johnson, a local tough, making him drop his cigarettes. The school grapevine soon announced that he had called me out for a fight in the vacant lot across the street during lunch. There was never a thought that I would not show. A gang had already gathered in the grassy lot next to the Bloody Bucket, a hamburger joint frequented by the rough crowd. They parted to let me through.

Johnson and I took off our shirts and the fight began. He was a huge and eager brawler and he knocked me down five or six times with blows to the head. But I kept getting up and tearing into him. I was not physically imposing like my father, but I was Dolph Strother's kid. Also, my body was hard from years of training, both on the track and in tough manual labor. As big as he was, he was a beer-drinking, Camel-smoking slacker.

Soon his breath was coming in gasps.

"You had enough?" he gasped.

Now I was angry and could see an advantage. I answered by wading back into him with my fists, finally able to use the boxing moves I learned on Wednesday and Saturdays at the VFW gym after track practice. I moved and darted. He panted. Soon he dropped his hands down by his sides in fatigue and I bloodied his nose and ears. Then I continued to punish him as he held his arms over his face and tried to turn his back. I punched him in the kidneys. Fury consumed me. He vomited down his chest. The boys who were calling for my blood were now yelling encouragement. They wanted more violence and more blood.

Over the shouts of excited, bloodthirsty punks we heard a loud whistle. I kept pounding Johnson with unrestrained fury until somebody said,

"Run, that's Coach Jones." The coach was leaning out of the second-story library window directly across the street, blowing the whistle that always hung around his neck. Coach Jones was known as a head-thumper and tough disciplinarian. He was the assistant to most sports and was my home-room teacher.

"I want to see you in the track office, Strother," he yelled.

Worried, I walked to the track office and sat in an old straight chair. I couldn't afford to be kicked off the track team. My main chance at going to college in a strike year was to win an athletic scholarship. The coach arrived. He sat behind his desk and put his boots up and laced his fingers behind his head.

"Strother, you're not afraid of anything, are you?"

I didn't respond. I noticed that my shirt was bloody and my nose was bleeding. The coach handed me a tissue, which I stuffed up my nose.

"That big boy could have killed you."

I still said nothing.

"Well, you gave him a good ass-kicking and he deserved it. But I need to talk to you officially now. I'm your counselor." (I didn't know I had one. Texans would have never gone to a counselor or even admitted one existed.)

"Miss Crisp, your English teacher, says you are a hell of a writer. So we think you ought to consider going to college in journalism and becoming a sportswriter. That's my advice. Your math grades are shit. I don't think you'll be an engineer."

It was the first kind word I had ever heard said about my academic ability. And he was right about my math grades.

"So, are you planning to go to college?"

"If I can get a scholarship, Coach."

"Well, I don't know about that. The milers at the big-time colleges now all run right around four minutes. You never will. You're all guts, but you'll never get much better than you are now. Not enough talent. But I'll call around little schools and junior colleges. You got any idea what part of the country where you want to go?

"Just away."

"Like where?

"As far as I can get from Port Arthur."

"I'll call around and see what I can do. Small colleges can use a slow miler in small meets and relays and stuff. You're good in cross-country. Maybe they'll go for your endurance. I like your guts. I'll even lie for you. Now you go out there and tell everybody I reamed out your ass for fighting with Johnson."

That was the beginning and the end of my high school counseling.

The Wayne Johnson fight allowed me to bluff and not exchange blows until just before graduation, when a kid about my size insulted my girl-friend, Sandy, who would later become my wife. I called him out, as was expected, and the seconds who took over arranged for us to fight in the baseball stadium at lunch. Before going to the stadium I went home and put on an old shirt and took off my shoes so I would have mobility in the Texas dust. The kid showed up along with more than a hundred spectators who ganged around. A big lineman, Mickey Walker, made some rules. We couldn't kick or wrestle. When one of us hit the ground, the other fighter had to back away and let him up.

I gave the kid a chance to back down. I didn't want to fight and I could tell he didn't. But the crowd had skipped lunch for a fight and Mickey would have no compromise, no apology. Soon we were standing toe-to-toe and slugging. Most schoolyard fights are two or three blows, some cursing, and some shoving—mainly posturing. But this was a bare-knuckle fight that went on for fifteen minutes. Finally, when we were both cut and cov-ered with blood, the kid held up his hands and apologized. I looked at him and wanted to cry. I had pounded a decent boy into hamburger. I damaged his face so badly he never regained vision in one eye.

Two days later he sought me out in school. He had a patch. "I'm sorry," he said, and extended his hand. "I was being a smartass."

"I didn't mean to hurt you," I said, and swore to myself to never fight again if I could just get the hell out of Port Arthur. I had never been any-where else, but I knew that every place had to be better than there.

Coach Jones made good on his promise to help me find a scholarship, and one day I received a handwritten letter from the track coach at North-western State College in Natchitoches, Louisiana. He offered to pay all of my costs of college and give me a make-work job changing light bulbs in girls' dormitories for spending money. It was about 175 miles from Port Arthur but my only opportunity to leave town. Lamar Tech in Beaumont had offered me a similar deal, but it was only sixteen miles away.

I had never talked to my parents about college. My father may have harbored dreams I could go, but I knew they couldn't afford to send me. My mother didn't seem to care. I didn't want to hurt their feelings, so I didn't discuss my ambitions with them. My father was sure that because of the union he could get me on at Gulf Oil, and that was my heritage.

The day after receiving the letter I packed some jeans, my only suit, and some shirts in a duffle bag and found my father sitting in a metal lawn chair under that huge cottonwood tree in the backyard, drinking coffee from a chipped cup. The grass in front of his chair had been worn to dirt like the carpet at the bottom step in an old public building. I explained that I was going to college and that I would hitchhike there so I could start early training for the cross-country season. He looked at me with almost no expression. "I'm glad. I always wanted you to go to college. But being on strike and all, I don't know how we can pay."

"I have a track scholarship."

"So where are you going?"

"Northwestern Louisiana State."

"Where's that?"

"Natchitoches, Louisiana."

"I know where that is. I once worked for a logging company that cut around Natchitoches. What are you going to study?"

"Journalism. I'm going to be a writer."

"Not a labor lawyer?"

"No."

"Well, maybe you can tell the union side. Nobody ever does that. You got any money?"

"Yes, sir. I've been saving this summer." I had worked on a highway crew.

He reached into his thin brown wallet that was shaped like the contours of his hip and turned out a leather flap that covered what he called his strike fund. He unfolded a $100 bill and handed it to me. It smelled like a damp newspaper. It was the last money he ever gave me.

He took a swallow of coffee and looked off into the blue, over the tops of the scrub trees, where he could see the gulls endlessly circling over Sabine Lake. He always looked south as though pain ended where the earth met the water's edge. Often I tried to look at the same spot to see if I could see the same things he did. I could not. At least not yet. He offered to drive me to the highway, but I walked and hitched until, ten hours later, the last of a long series of cars left me at the front gates of a college I had never heard of before seeing it on the stationery of the letter that said I had been accepted as a student there.

After my first year in college I returned to Port Arthur for the summer, tried unsuccessfully to sell encyclopedias door to door, and when I found that I was too shy to be a salesman, took a job that nobody else wanted, working with the paint crew on the Rainbow Bridge over the Neches River. At that time it was the highest bridge in the South—when it was built in the 1930s, it was specifically designed so that the navy's tallest ship, a dirigible tender with a dirigible moored to the mast, could safely sail under it on the way to Beaumont and Houston. The low bidder to paint the bridge was a scab outfit that hired misfits off the streets to do dirty work like clean inside the huge legs that extended from the top of the bridge deep into the marsh. I qualified as a leg cleaner. I was small, rock-hard from college training, and a misfit because of my education. The highest education level other than mine on the bridge crew was third grade. Only four or five could read. There is a great folk wisdom among the unschooled that educated people don't have common sense and therefore can't do manual labor. It is a defense they use to protect their self-esteem. My presence on the crew challenged those assumptions, and because of this attitude I became a punching bag for all of their doubts.

Loaded with a gallon of red lead paint, a scraper, a chipping hammer, a paintbrush, and a heavy wire brush, but not burdened by any safety gear, my job was to crawl through the openings of the legs, put my back against one wall, my feet against the other, and brush my way hundreds of feet from the top to the bottom. I would chip out rust, wire-brush the spot, and paint it with red lead. This was to prepare the leg for the spray painters who dangled from long cables and for amusement tried to drop five-gallon cans of paint down the smokestacks of passing ships. There was great delight one day when one of the cans broke open on the deck and splattered four or five foreign sailors. When that same ship came back through several days later headed for the Gulf, a man stood on deck with a pistol and fired a full magazine at the dangling painters, who responded with buckets of paint and raised center fingers. After that, Legs, the crew pusher—a kind of foreman whose entire job was to walk around yelling that we weren't working fast enough—kept a long-barreled pistol tucked into his belt. Sometimes I would hear gunfire as he shot at rabbits and small marsh animals far below us. He never hit anything as far as I know—he was usually drunk and the distances were too great for a pistol. But it did help break up the monotony of the day.

Every ten feet there was a platform in the leg. When I had finished a section of the leg and brushed off the platform through drain holes, I would worm out into the sunshine through one of the portholes and loop back into another below the platform. It took about three days to complete an entire leg. On my third day when I dropped the final two feet to the platform in a low section, it sounded as though I had fallen on fragile seashells. When I began to sweep out the dark platform, though, I discovered it was six inches deep in skeletons of marsh rats. It was disgusting, but later, when I dropped to the floor of the final chamber, I encountered worse. Huge rats swarmed all over me. The three-foot-square leg was home to dozens of the animals, and they were trying to get away through the drain holes around the bottom of the chamber. In panic they crawled over me looking for escape. It was thirty seconds of terror until the last rat had found its way out. I was not even scratched. When I brushed the next leg, I warned the rats by pounding the steel with my hammer at least two chambers away. Then I leaned out the porthole and watched as they jumped into the brackish water below. My father called that summer of 1959 the "Eisenhower Depression" and didn't approve of my working for a nonunion outfit, but I needed the money to go back to college. I was also soon to be married. And so I tolerated the rats for twelve dollars a day.

What I never learned to deal with was the ignorance of the crew or the callousness of the bosses. The company discouraged use of safety equipment because they said it slowed us down. So after the cavernous legs were finally cleaned and I was reassigned to the daylight, I walked boldly on ten-inch steel beams hundreds of feet above the water and the lacework of structural steel.

Because my education made me the oddest of the crew, there was always hope I would fall and earn them a holiday. Only one crew member died while I worked there. We were given the day off with pay to attend his funeral. But the crew didn't attend the funeral. They didn't even know the victim. Instead, they went to the B. O. Sparkle honky-tonk, listened to Hank Williams records, and drank beer all afternoon. "Why can't you die, College Boy, and give us a day off?" the pusher Legs would ask me every day when we broke for water.

Usually, I was assigned far away from the water cooler, and by the time I got there for the afternoon water break at about two o'clock, it was empty. The crew's hangovers drained the iced water all day while the temporary people like me worked far down the bridge. Then they sucked the ice. Port Arthur is one of the hottest, most humid places in America. I tried wearing a military canteen, but it caught on the steel and threw me off balance. Relief finally came when a black man showed up to clean legs. The white-trash crew would not drink from the same cup as a black man. He had his own cooler of wonderful ice and water

"Can I share your water?" I asked him on the first day.

"Might turn you black." His smile told me he knew volumes about prejudice and I had only peered through a crack in the door.

"I'll take that chance."

He handed me his bean can with the top cut out. Legs saw me sharing the tin cup with the black man.

"College Boy's drinking out of the same cup as the nigger," he yelled across the spans of the bridge. I heard laughter from the men dangling from cables. The black man smiled at me in conspiracy. A brotherhood of misfits. But he needed the $1.50 an hour worse than I did. He had children.

Another outcast soon joined our water-bucket team, a Mexican who had been in the country only a few days. The crew immediately named him Wetback and told him he had to drink with Nigger and College Boy. At lunch I would trade the thick ham sandwiches my mother packed for the Mexican's exotic soft tortillas filled with goat or chicken or beef and peppers. He spoke no English and I spoke no Spanish, but his smile was enough communication. One afternoon while driving home in my two-door-hardtop, lowered-rear-end, slicked-trunk, bought-real-used '53 Chevrolet, I passed him walking toward town on the long marsh highway, slapping at swarms of mosquitoes. I backed up. When I opened the door he smiled and quickly climbed in the car while madly swatting the clouds of insects. "Gracias, señor, gracias, señor," he repeated dozens of times. I nodded and smiled. I drove him to Houston Avenue, the dividing line between whites and the "others"—a cultural no-man's-land so lightly regarded the city fathers even allowed ten whorehouses to line its sidewalks.

Wetback never asked me for a ride. Every day he would start the five-mile walk home, and every day I would pick him up and take him to the same corner on Houston Avenue. Soon Wetback Two joined the crew and my car pool. It was hard for the company to find workers so desperate for a job that they would risk their lives for $1.50 an hour. On Friday the Mexicans would pull gently at my arm and plead with me in Spanish and sign language to do something that I couldn't understand. Finally one day I surrendered to the pleas and followed them about two blocks to a shack held together with beer signs. It was a Mexican bar. I was introduced in Spanish and every patron in the bar applauded. I don't know what they said, but soon I had a free Lone Star beer in my hand and no ability to explain to them that I didn't drink. I was an athlete. My body was my temple. My scholarship. My future. But soon my thirsty temple had sucked down about seven of their gift Lone Stars. It was my first drink. I liked it. I don't remember driving home, but my father was sitting on the back steps cleaning his nails with a penknife, in one of his blue moods. I must have tried conversation, but he kindly told me to go to bed.

"What's wrong with Raymond?" my mother asked.

"Oh, he's just tired. He works for a scab outfit that don't treat their workers right. He's just tired. Let him sleep. "

When I woke later that night, my father whispered to me, "Go take a bath and brush your teeth and try to stay downwind from your mother."

Although my father kept a couple of flat bottles of bourbon in his old tool chest in the back of the garage, drinking was a sin akin to bank robbery and would have been the cause of much crying and prayer—and, if my father was working the night shift at the refinery, maybe even a visit from the preacher (my mother would not invite him over when my dad was at home).

Many years later, when I finally had achieved success in Washington and sat with other consultants in posh watering holes over ten-dollar martinis, I listened when they recounted their adventures as counselors at summer camp and figured my experience gave me a leg up in helping candidates connect in their campaigns with working people. Later still, when competitors began saying I didn't understand working people because I was too rich or not tough enough—and when potential candidates agreed—I tried to laugh it off. But it cut deeply. Couldn't they see the scars on my soul?

Because of my work experiences, I never consider myself superior to Wetback or the black man who shared his water—or even the pusher Legs, or the drunk job boss Meachie. Nor any of the members of the illiterate bridge crew, refinery workers, or even the tramplike frog hunters who hung out in the predawn hours at the Mobil station When I watched lower-income people on the other side of a focus-group mirror, I truly understood their prejudices—while a prep school researcher just shook his head in wonder.

I had a great shock when I was asked in 1996 to make a presentation to the AFL-CIO. They wanted to hire a consultant to produce media for a national campaign to help Democrats. I made my pitch sounding a lot like those Lucky Strike–smoking picketers of my youth, and I could soon see I was not communicating. None of the bureaucrats on that selection committee had ever had dirty fingernails or walked a picket line or stood at a plant gate fighting for a few cents more an hour. None of them had been hungry. The union men I knew had blood on their hands and fire in their hearts. My father's generation had been replaced by people he would have considered the enemy—Chablis-drinking committee attendees. Of course they didn't hire my firm, and I don't blame them. I didn't speak the same language as these union bureaucrats whose pasty faces were an open deck. The heroes of my youth were gone.

I thought I was finally finished fighting when I arrived in college. It all seemed so peaceful and academic. But there are bullies everywhere, and violence is part of the human condition. In my first year at Northwestern State, I was minding my own business, quietly working on a term paper I had neglected because of out-of-town track meets. The dormitory was deserted and quiet as usual on Saturday night. At eleven o'clock, however, a 250-pound former football player, in college only by the grace of a disability scholarship because of a history of mental problems, began his customary weekend drunken rampage up and down the hall. He cursed and kicked beer cans down the concrete floor. Then he began to kick doors.

"Hey, is anybody around here?" he bellowed. "I want to kick some ass!"

Suddenly my door swung open and he stood there taunting me from the hall.

"Come on out here, bookworm. I'm gonna kick your ass for practice."

"Look, I'm just trying to study. Please be quiet and leave me alone."

"Come out here you dried up cocksucker, queer-faggot-motherfucker, or I'm coming in."

I saw Bobby Clayton standing in my front yard. I saw Wayne Johnson waiting without his shirt in the lot across from school. I saw the kid taunting Sandy, the Texas Rangers clubbing strikers, and all of the misshaped lessons of being a man I had learned from my father. I was conditioned to do what I did. It was beyond my redneck control. I began unbuttoning my shirt and walked to my closet just out of his sight. I made my father's calculation. He outweighed me by a hundred pounds, so I picked up a heavy wrench I kept to work on my bicycle and hid it bootleg fashion.

Of course I didn't talk. I walked slowly until I was less than an arm's length from him and smashed the heavy wrench across his head before he had braced himself to swing his balled fists. He was still talking about my sexual orientation when the lights went out. He sank to his knees and I raised the wrench again in case a second blow was necessary. Blood was pouring down his face onto his chest. He looked up at me.

"I'll fight anybody, but I'll never fight a little dried-up faggot with a wrench again."

The following week while I was in the library, he went back to my room in a drunken rage with sixteen stitches in his head and a pistol in his hand. The campus cops talked him out of the gun and took him away for good.

But he didn't see me sweat.

There was a reason I understood his calling me a faggot. I guess it was my father's fault. I had let my smart mouth overload me in a class labeled "Health and Fitness," which all scholarship athletes were required to take to help them keep up their average. It was a cinch "A" for an athlete.

The teacher was a coach who would ramble on for an hour for those of us who attended because our sports were out of season or we didn't have anything better to do that day. He gave slide shows of various venereal diseases and told us to "keep our wicks out of bad girls." He was assistant track and football coach and would march us all down to the infirmary the day before meets for huge injections of vitamin B. During the meet he was the one with the bottle of "pep" pills that we swallowed a few minutes before our event. In the late 1950s amphetamines were not considered a health threat, and most college students used them to stay awake for finals. All athletes I knew used them before their events.

While most of the lectures were about bad girls, the evils of drinking, and the benefits of red meat, his favorite subject was perversity.

"I want to talk to you fellows today about queers," he began one lecture. "You don't have to take notes, but these guys sometimes look like normal people. But what they really want to do is get you in a dark corner and suck your dick. You look around schoolyards and you can see these people watching little children and playing pocket pool in their pants. It don't matter how bad you want sex, never let one of them at you, because they'll turn you queer."

His conclusion was for us to be vigilant in the showers and locker rooms and "bust 'em good in the mouth if they reach for you."

I don't know why I did it. I guess it was like arguing with the teacher about the real father of our country. But unfortunately I raised my hand.

"What you want, Strother?"

"Coach, what if they can't help what they are? What if there's some kind of third sex and they're just born that way? It doesn't seem right to hit people simply because they don't think like us."

I was getting warmed up and I could see my roommate, Robert Brooks, sitting next to me in the class, hold up his hands in surrender. But I was forced to add one more thought. "Coach, what if they're right and we're wrong?"

There was some nervous laughter among the jocks. A seething Coach stared at me. "Fellows, I don't think any of you should get in the showers with Strother anymore. Watch him. He sure sounds like one of them." He was serious.

"Why did you do it?" Brooks pleaded with me as we walked across campus. "I'm your roommate. They're going to think I'm queer. I understand that he made you mad with his ignorance. But he's just a football coach. He can't help being what he is. But son, you let your mouth overload you."

Brooks had courage and didn't move out of our room, but my fame spread throughout campus. It didn't abate until I showed up the following year with a beautiful red-haired wife.

My stay at Northwestern, however, didn't improve when I married. And again, it was my fault—or my father's.

The school had refused to allow a labor leader—thus a "man with known Communist leanings"—to talk about racial equality on campus. But two weeks later the administration invited Robert Welch, founder of the John Birch Society, to address the students. I was a budding journalism student who knew enough to understand how outrageous this was. I picketed the meeting, along with one other student. The next day the president of the college called me into his office and suggested that I might be happier in "one of those liberal schools," like the University of Texas or Louisiana State.

I walked over to the small Department of Journalism and told my adviser, Dr. John Merrill, about the administration's suggestion to move on.

"I've been invited to leave, too," he told me. "Get the hell out of here. You have a future."

He headed to the University of Missouri. My new wife and I packed all of our possessions into a small trailer clamped to the back of my old '53 Chevrolet and drove south toward Baton Rouge, the state capital of Louisiana and home of LSU. We had about $100 in a savings account from my working in service stations and a cotton compress and Sandy's job as a secretary on something called the Sibley Lake Project. It wasn't much, and we were apprehensive. But as we drove south, my life was about to finally assume some direction. It was 1960.

In Baton Rouge we found two rooms and a kitchen in a converted motel on the wrong side of town. I registered in the LSU School of Journalism. Sandy almost immediately landed a job working for a restaurant supply company. She held the job a few months, typing with one hand and fending off the boss with the other. Finally she came home in tears and said she could not go back to work. She offered no other explanation. It was years before I learned that the sexual harassment had almost become rape. She didn't tell me, I guess, because we had been children together and she knew how I had been trained to handle situations that dealt with honor. I might have killed the man. We had no cushion in life like family money to fall back on. A week without work would have meant the street. Sandy endured the endless sexual assault that tens of thousands of desperate women did in the '60s. After she fled the restaurant supply company, she took a civil service test. Her scores were so high that she was hired almost immediately at the LSU Department of Education. There, her boss was a gentleman, Dr. Lemos Fulmer, who treated her like a daughter.

While Sandy was fending off the roving hands of her boss at the restaurant supply company, the Journalism School secretary, Patty French, arranged for me to work as the darkroom assistant for a professor, R. H. Wiggins, who became almost as important in my life as the Port Arthur librarian. He taught me photography and allowed me to run my own business out of the university darkroom. I was a natural. I mastered the enlarger and chemicals, learned tricks from other pros, and again spent hours in the library, reading about composition and studying the masters like Steichen. Soon I was experimenting with various films in the huge Graflex cameras that shot on a big 4-by-5-inch negative. Photography was an opportunity to express myself and make visual statements. Little did I know then that this would be the most valuable training to become a political media consultant. Later Professor Wiggins arranged for me to begin shooting pictures for the Associated Press, and that turned into a job as the night reporter in the Capitol Bureau. My experience in photography gave me the feeling for composition that carried over into my television production. R. H. Wiggins became another one of those strangers who took my hand and led me. He arranged for me to take football pictures at the Tiger games. I was an assistant to a great AP photographer named Jim Boutier, who taught me how to shoot rapid-fire multiple images with a motorized camera and then at halftime sprint to the darkroom to develop and put a picture on the wire for the early editions. We used warm developer to speed up the process. When the negatives were done, we held them up to a light and picked possible usable shots. With a hole punch we clipped the edge of our selections. In the dark we ran our hands down the 35-millimeter film to find the notches. Then we slammed them into the enlarger and reexamined them. Within twenty minutes we had a wet print wrapped around a spinning drum that sent primitive wire photos to newspapers around the country.

Soon I was taking pictures of student rodeos, weddings, and nudes in a studio I rigged up in the J-School attic. In the early sixties in Baton Rouge it was fashionable for women to give their husbands "bedroom" pictures. My photography along with being an advertising salesman and later an editor of the student newspaper, the *Daily Reveille,* brought in badly needed money for Sandy and me.

Today it seems selfish that I went to school while Sandy worked. Yet, we had come from so far down on the ladder that we had an agreement that both of us working could produce one degree. We were hacking our way into life, and we both paid a high price. But by working together we finally saw opportunity begin to peek over the horizon, and we moved toward it like moths flying toward a red, consuming fire. Our internship for life was over and we were ready to move toward our ultimate goals. After a short stint with the Louisiana Press Association, and the Associated Press and a failed business trying to sell advertising for weekly newspapers, I met a young advertising agency man who dabbled in political campaigns, Gus Weill, who hired me to be his assistant. So, in 1967, I officially became a political consultant. I had a sign on the door. In reality I was a driver, bartender for politicians, and companion.

My father died on his seventy-fifth birthday, December 29, 1982. Cancer had invaded his bones and brain. He didn't know me when I stood next to his bed. He was reaching up and tightening imaginary bolts with an imaginary wrench, perhaps fixing the car of some boss, or a machine in the refinery. The latter part of his life had not been pleasant. The system had beaten him. He was forced to retire by the company rules, and no union leader came to his rescue. He spent his last years staring into the old cotton-wood tree in the backyard. At night he would watch television, the window to a world he did not understand that disappointed him terribly.

His youngest son had been killed flying helicopters in a war he opposed. His eldest son was a tool of politicians and associated with the same business people and bosses he had spent all of his life fighting. I was flown to Port Arthur for the funeral in a private jet lent to a politician I was representing who wanted to make sure my time was efficiently spent, and I got back to the campaign as soon as possible. After the funeral I walked into the backyard of the old house to the worn spot under the cottonwood tree. On a still afternoon the worm-eaten, sun-parched winter leaves rattled together into a moan of mourning and reproach. I stood under the old rotting tree and wept.

Ancient warriors often point to a time on a small island or a bloody battlefield where they fought as twenty-year-olds as the most important moment of their lives. Never again would they feel the fear, the comradeship, or the desperation. Never again would their entire existence be determined by actions completely out of their control. Survival of such circumstances seemed to give them an advantage over those who stayed on safe shores—an understanding that many shared but even the best novelists could not describe.

Louisiana was my foxhole, and I wear the scars on my soul. I can make a lot of excuses like the culture and desperation for some of my youthful high jinks. At that point in my life I was having trouble seeing my own compass, and even now I must occasionally shut my eyes tightly to try to seal out what I perceive as disregard or flagrant tolerance for behavior that sometimes began to fit me like a tailored coat. But temptation was all around me, and I was hungry for everything. The old governor of Louisiana, Huey Long's brother Earl, once observed to a young reporter as they drove down a desolate road lined with shotgun shacks with junked cars in the front yard, bent basketball goals nailed to pine trees, and decorated with leaking sofas on the front porch, "Son, you see the people who live in these houses? They're good people, honest people. You know why?" He paused and looked out the window of the black Cadillac and then lamented, "They never been tempted."

Louisiana political life was studded with temptations and yet it was—and is—a hothouse for political consultants. While the rest of the nation's candidates were still raising money with twenty-five-dollar pig pickings and lobster roasts, oil money swamped campaigns in Louisiana. Candidates spent more per voter there than anywhere else in the nation. There was ample money to pay people with specialized knowledge. As a result, a few professionals found they could earn a living just by doing campaigns. This was in the 1960s. Though their methods were primitive by today's standards, campaign techniques and technicians there began to mature. That has continued.

James Carville, a former staff member in the firm of Weill/Strother, has become world famous. William Morgan, a former employee and perhaps the best political consultant I have ever known, is dead but distinguished himself in consulting. When I left Louisiana in 1981, he folded his law firm to follow me. He had worked in Washington for Congressman Gillis Long as an attorney for the Rules Committee and had been involved in numerous Baton Rouge campaigns. He was my best friend and was willing to take the wild ride with me with no promises and only pipe dreams for the future. Officially he died of cancer of the throat. But I believe that what really killed him was Louisiana hedonism.

Besides Morgan and Carville, others have also done well. James Farwell, a Republican consultant from New Orleans, a highly cultured man who changed from Democrat to Republican, has begun to attract attention across America.

Roy Fletcher, another of my former employees, is the top gun now in Louisiana and is looking out at distant horizons. He helped elect Republican governor Mike Foster in an upset in 1995 and was courted by both Pat Buchanan and John McCain.

Ray Teddlie, a quirky but creative man who came to work for me in 1978, has become successful in Louisiana races. Deno Seder moved from Shreveport to Washington in the '80s and made an impact with his creativity. And there are others fighting to make the break from provincial to national standing and reputation.

Fate took me to Louisiana, but strength of will and desperation took me out of there in 1981. It was so easy to be seduced. It would be overly dramatic, but only a slight exaggeration, to say my career in political consulting started in a whorehouse and ended on the steps leading to the White House.

In only my second campaign, my candidate routinely frequented a whorehouse owned by a Louisiana sheriff, and in the 1980s I did eight years helping Governor Bill Clinton get ready for his presidential campaign. After years of faithful service, and I think good work, Clinton brought in another political consultant for his 1992 presidential race. I learned about it from the newspapers. He then brought in another and then another. Clinton was known as a "star fucker" and moved to the hot consultant of the week. I had several years with him before there were bolder headlines with other names.

I created media and consulted with Al Gore, Gary Hart, Lloyd Bentsen, Russell Long, and dozens of others along the way, but my career began in Louisiana, where corruption flavors the politics like Tabasco seasons the food.

In an irreverent variation of Bismarck's dictum that politics is the art of the possible, wizened political pros in Baton Rouge used to describe Louisiana politics as "the art of the deal." But in Louisiana there was no art to it. Subtlety isn't a common commodity. Louisiana was wide open and proud of its title of acting like a third world nation. Fifty-dollar-a-day legislators drove Cadillacs and kept flashy mistresses. Few state insurance contracts were signed without kickbacks to agents who also served the people as legislators. Candidates sold jobs and land that mysteriously became exit ramps for new highways. Ramps to nowhere. One candidate had a beautiful woman released from prison in his care. And care for her he did. She lived in a beautiful apartment and drove new cars.

"She murdered her husband and the son of a bitch deserved killing," is the justification that particular "public servant" gave me. "And will you look at that ass? How could you let that go to waste in jail?" The girl did two model turns so I could survey her charms while listening to the crude praise being heaped on her. I guess it sounded better to her than the slamming of the cell door.

At that time I was not morally offended. I was young, brash, hungry, and thought of myself as an expatriate living in a lost generation of adventures that would be the stuff of novels when I had ripened, matured, and paid all of the car notes. (In fact, I wrote such a novel. It was titled *Cottonwood* and E. P. Dutton published it in 1991 to fair sales and surprisingly positive reviews. Friends would ask if half the stuff in the book really happened. The answer is that a lot of it did. In fact, I left out a great deal in the cause of preserving harmony at home. Still, my wife left me just as it was published. She came home after a year and maintains *Cottonwood* had nothing to do with her sabbatical. I now agree that her leaving was a result of a distracted husband who had trouble maintaining personal relationships while a political consultant.)

As my career in politics began, I fancied myself the bemused outsider dispassionately watching the political landscape as though it were flickering on a wide screen in a movie theater. Later in life, like a Woody Allen character, I was sucked into the screen and began having trouble discerning the obscene from the ideal. I began to feel a festering in my soul; principles and ethics long buried began to fight to the surface . . . but that took a while.

The truth is I was utterly charmed the first time I met Daly Joseph "Cat" Doucet, sheriff of St. Landry Parish. He handed me a nickel-plated pistol to guard the virtue of a woman candidate, Mary Evelyn Parker. The second time I met the good sheriff was in a whorehouse called The Gate, in Opelousas, Louisiana. I was working with a candidate for school board in Lafayette who decided after a campaign speech to make a twenty-mile side trip to Opelousas for female companionship. "Let's go get us a little poontang," was actually how he expressed it when he whipped the steering wheel to the left and we entered the dark swamp road to Opelousas. The Gate was surrounded by tall hedges and a corrugated metal fence. For convenience, it was only a few hundred yards from a small rural airport. Customers drove into the enclosure and entered the house through a door guarded by a uniformed man seated at a small desk who checked ID and confiscated drivers' licenses and pistols. I didn't have a pistol but my client did. I turned over my documents and nervously followed my candidate into the perfume-smelling, dark air.

The girls paraded around us in a sort of erotic cafeteria line, each trying to showcase her most attractive assets, each attempting to look the most enticing. There were redheads, brunettes, and blondes, wearing exotic garter belts and spike-heeled shoes, their bodies covered with the suggestion of fabric that offered more color than cover. Most were in their early twenties, about my age. I can't say that any of them looked like the girl next door— and I came from a downscale neighborhood. They did, however, look like the girls I knew from high school who after school parked a huge black Mercury behind the Frostop drive-in restaurant, smoked cigarettes, and passed around a bottle of vodka. When I saw them on the drag on Port Arthur's Procter Street, where kids made endless circuits in their cars or leaned against their customized chrome monuments in selected locations on Saturday nights, these girls' heads were always melted into the shoulders of older guys with tattoos driving slicked-down Fords with rumbling dual exhausts and lowered rear ends.

After surveying the real estate, my candidate took a redhead by the hand and started toward the hall. Over his shoulder he said, "You pick, College Boy, I'm buying."

Although it sounded like a great adventure, I passed on his $50 offer and instead drank two-dollar Coca-Cola out of 6-ounce bottles in the living room with the unoccupied girls, taking some pleasure in their careless posture and slipped straps while my client attended to other business upstairs. Suddenly I recognized one of the girls. She was from Port Arthur. She had gone to Thomas Jefferson High School at the same time I did. She had obviously decided to turn her backseat training into an occupation after dropping out of school. We had both traveled about two hundred miles. I had become a consort of politicians and she had become a prostitute.

We ignored each other. I guess she looked down on a freeloader who sat in the living room of a whorehouse drinking two-dollar Cokes instead of five-dollar beers. I stuck with the Cokes because I already had a rule that I would never drink while working for a client. I didn't know any rules for political consultants and had no role models, so I had to write my own. The no-drinking policy seemed like a fine standard and a good start for my self-imposed Bible of discipline. Because of my Baptist upbringing I understood that any truly good rule had to hurt a little. I was also aware that there had to be a lot more to political consulting than what I had learned in two campaigns. I was confident that, in the end, just one rule would never suffice. But I had to start somewhere. Thus far in my life, my motto had always been to blunder ahead and make up rules as I came upon necessity. However, as I sat and drank Cokes with the prostitutes, I was a little puzzled about the ethics of waiting downstairs in a whorehouse. Was this what other consultants did? I even entertained the notion that perhaps candidates in other states didn't frequent whorehouses, but I had no way of knowing. In my frame of reference it seemed improbable. Nevertheless, I decided to enter the whorehouse restriction as Rule II.

There is, of course, a larger point to this story, even if it eluded me at the time. Only a year removed from my newsman days, I still thought of myself as working for the common good. Yes, I was a hard-living young man, and my candidates were not exactly proving to be plaster saints. But at least they were all Democrats, weren't they? I was working for Democrats, for the party of my father, the party of working people. And the presence of what we euphemistically called "a working girl" from my hometown didn't prompt much self-doubt. True, if this scene was in those books I'd devoured in the Gates library, I would have gotten the symbolism. But I was young and on the rise and it didn't hit me until much later that the girl from my high school and I were more alike than I care to think about.

We were both in the process of selling a part of ourselves—a part that is not always easy to get back.

Years ago, a well-meaning and talented writer named Mary Alice Fontenot, author of the "Clovis Crawfish" series of children's books, wrote a biography of "Cat" Doucet. In it, she claimed the good sheriff did not own the brothels he frequented. But I rather doubt that the nice woman had the benefit of my firsthand experience.

The night I was in The Gate with my client, Cat strode into the room as though he owned the place. When I saw the sheriff, I immediately visualized my wife reading in the newspapers about my being caught in a whorehouse raid, and I contemplated jumping out a window. But I quickly came to understand that the good sheriff had a proprietary interest in the brothel and wasn't there to arrest customers. He was slightly drunk and boiling over with good cheer as he flipped through drivers' licenses collected by his deputy at the front desk. Framed medical certificates attesting to the girls' good health hung in a neat row behind the bar. As Cat said, this was a "class joint." That was my second meeting with Cat. The first was when he gave me a pistol and a shooting lesson.

The day of my shooting lesson I had driven down an oak-shaded lane to a plantation house decorated with political signs, crepe paper, and banners. Each of the oak trees lining the long lane through the cotton field displayed pictures of my smiling candidate for state treasurer, Mary Evelyn Parker, giving the arriving participants the festive feeling that would help spawn large contributions to her campaign. Ladies stood on the long verandah drinking sherry, awaiting Miz Parker. (For some reason, older southern women often claim not to partake, but will do serious damage to a bottle of sherry: "No, dear, I don't drink, but I will have a little sherry.") I went around the car and opened the door for her in the style to which southern ladies were accustomed and watched her climb the high steps to her waiting admirers and political contributors. After parking the big white Buick under the shade of a huge moss-draped oak tree, I rolled down the windows and lit a cigar. It was midafternoon and the Louisiana sun was set on high bake. The metal in the Buick groaned when the shade began to cool it, and a breeze that smelled of dust stirred up by the cotton-picking machines brought some relief and kept my smoke headed in the right direction. My white suit stuck to my body. On the porch I could see women in hats and gloves exchanging hugs and occasional laughs.

I was slumped down in the seat in that nether land between hangover sleep and daydreaming when a weathered hand squeezed my shoulder. The hand was connected to a small man in boots, a large Stetson, and a uniform with a gunbelt that held two pistols. A badge identified the wearer as a lawman, specifically, the sheriff of St. Landry Parish. I could smell bourbon on his breath. A few yards behind the Buick in the same shade, a deputy picking his teeth leaned against a squad car.

"You driving Miz Mary Evelyn around?"

We in the South were years ahead of the politically correct speech dictated by the women's movement that required that all women be addressed as Ms. We always combined Miss and Mrs. and made a Miz sound that sort of slipped off the tongue and was pleasing to married women, widows, young girls—or even whores.

I was almost compelled to explain to the sheriff that I was a political consultant, but my better judgment won out. It is never good to correct a man wearing two pistols. The truth was that I was sitting behind the wheel of a campaign car waiting outside a party like a chauffeur. Of course I saw myself in a more glamorous light as a strategist, creative genius, and political expert. Yes, I told myself, I did drive her around and open car doors, but I also created her speeches, produced her media, and wrote press releases on an old Smith Corona portable in the backseat. The sheriff didn't know all that—and wouldn't have cared if he did. This was the legendary Cat Doucet, and you might say he was preoccupied with more earthly concerns.

Once, years later, a *New Orleans Times-Picayune* reporter learned that Cat owned the whorehouses that dotted the landscape in St. Landry Parish and gleefully phoned Cat's farm for a statement.

"I'll give you a statement if you will print what I say exactly like I say it," Cat told him.

"Certainly, Sheriff. Just give me your statement. It will be printed verbatim."

"OK. Here's my statement, and you can say I said it. 'The way I look at it, a little pussy on the side never hurt nobody.'"

Reportedly the newspaper man hung up the phone without comment. The news story said that Cat had said something unprintable. Another story widely reported in Louisiana was that Cat gave the same statement on camera to a television station. There is also a story about Cat being told the cost of love was too expensive in his brothels. "That's a shame," he said. "Those young fellows and them college boys, they don't have that kind of money. They ought to fix it like at the restaurants; you know, like a child's plate."

Cat was never even indicted. In fact, he is today in the Louisiana Political Hall of Fame. Most of his constituents in this Cajun community thought the good that Cat did far overshadowed the few indiscretions they knew about. He dropped out of school in the sixth grade, but as the local district attorney, Morgan Goudeau III, put it years later, "Cat probably should have had a doctoral degree in psychology. . . . He had an uncanny ability to understand people and size them up." And that's what he was doing on this day in 1967 as I sat in the big old Buick.

"Yes, sir, I drive her around." It seemed the only appropriate answer, even if my ego did get slightly bruised.

"You got a gun?"

"No, sir." I was a southerner. My parents had taught me to "sir" or "ma'am" every adult. It always endeared me to old women and amused the young ones. I continued the practice through most of my life, partially as an irritant to Washingtonians, who can seldom be accused of gentility. In the case at hand, I was also showing respect to a legendary sheriff who, despite his short stature, instilled some fear.

"How you gonna protect that fine lady if you get in trouble?"

"I never thought about it, Sheriff."

"Tee Boy," the sheriff shouted to his deputy, "bring me that .38 Police Special out the backseat."

The deputy handed Cat a nickel-plated pistol, and he checked the cylinder. It was fully loaded except for the chamber under the hammer. "Go get a box of shells out of the trunk," the sheriff told Tee Boy. Then he turned to me.

"Got this pistol off a woman who murdered her husband. Good-looking woman. She's up at the jail now. I'm gonna give you her pistol to protect Miz Mary Evelyn."

He had me get out of the car and pointed to a spot about ten yards from the car.

"You see that stump over there?"

I nodded.

"Let me see you shoot it."

Like all Texans of my age, I knew guns. I even have the malady of many southerners—a loss of hearing in my right ear from exposure to shotgun blasts. As a youth I illegally killed rabbits while poaching on the Country Club golf course at night with spotlights, and later nutria rats along the bayous for the bounty. So, though the pistol barrel was short, I hit the stump three out of the first five shots. Cat watched as I reloaded and nodded approvingly when I left the hammer chamber empty. Ladies, sherry glasses in hand, began filing back on the porch to watch the shooting. They lined up against the rail and applauded every time I hit the stump as I emptied the box of shells. I liked the approval. The sheriff patted me on the back and handed me a fresh box of shells.

"Now put that under the seat so you can get to it."

He watched as I slid the shells and pistol under the seat. Then he sauntered up to the porch to greet the ladies with practiced gentility and affability.

Political Consultant. It was what the sign said on my office door, but I was not sure what it meant. Maybe carrying a pistol was part of the job description. Driving the lady around certainly seemed to feel right. I had exhausted all of the LSU library books on politics and still didn't know how to conduct myself because there were no role models. My partner, Gus Weill, who always wanted to be a playwright, had not done the reading and knew even less than I did, but he was the world's greatest salesman. Only my longtime buddy Dick Morris, the consultant from New York who had to resign from the Clinton campaign because he was exposed cavorting with a call girl whom he allowed to listen in on conversations with the president, rivaled my partner at painting images and making a candidate's pulse race with the possibilities.

Because Weill had worked for Louisiana governor John Mc-Keithen and because Miz Parker was the handpicked candidate of the powerful chief executive, we were able to peddle our services to other Democratic candidates. But before the campaign season began, Weill abruptly flew to New York to produce an off-Broadway play he had written. I was left with a box of his cigars, a tiny office, and my first candidate.

In 1968 candidates had a great fear of political television. They were convinced that John F. Kennedy had beaten Richard Nixon because of his ability to use the medium, and they wanted experts to help them. My partner persuaded the candidate and many candidates thereafter that I was the budding genius who could solve their problems. He did this partly because he had an ill wife who required a lot of attention and partly because he was uninterested in the developing new science of political communication. He was, like many, convinced that our business was an art instead of a blend of art and science, and that most good political communication came from the gut. Though not an unintelligent man, he did not see the changes that would soon transform politics and government.

I was able to bluff my way through the production of signs, newspaper ads, and bumper stickers because I knew artists in New Orleans, like the famous Harry Mayronne, who produced wonderful work. And because of all of my graduate school reading in propaganda, I was able to dazzle candidates with long discussions of the subconscious impressions of color and texture. I glibly explained that red quickens the pulse and causes the eye to dilate, green suggests nature, blue is calming. I could discuss the gender of various fabrics and make a convincing argument about design because of my study of Plato and his theory of the Golden Mean. But I only knew enough about television to turn on the black-and-white set. The library was not much help. But all things are possible to a creative young man on the hustle.

I drove to New Orleans and made an appointment with Paul Yacich, the dean of Louisiana television production. He was a director at WDSU, located on Royal Street in the French Quarter, and had helped turn on the station to broadcast its first signal. The Yacich family was part of a group that two generations before had come in from Croatia to form a fishing village south of New Orleans. I gave him a $100 bill and he walked me through video machines, editing, lighting, and sound. Then he gave me back the hundred. The only portable video equipment at the time was a huge sixteen-wheel truck loaded with tape machines and cameras that took two or three people to lift. The hourly rental cost was in the hundreds. The only other alternative was to shoot costly and hard-to-process film that had to be developed in New York or Dallas, or to take the candidate into the studio at the television station. Yacich was a likable man with a quick smile and an obvious tolerance for ignorance.

"Look, tomorrow I'm bringing my candidate into the studio to produce a commercial, and she thinks I know something about television," I said. "You have to keep me from being embarrassed." Yacich smiled and promised he would make me look like a hero.

Miz Parker arrived early to rehearse a few times with the Teleprompter. I had only learned about Teleprompters the day before. We were producing a live half-hour program. In the late 1960s and early 1970s, the thirty-minute, issue-oriented program was still a respected and watched medium. She and I had rehearsed for days. Miz Parker was a great speaker, with great intellect and a quick tongue—a natural who had found her way into politics because of speeches she gave as a young woman for a candidate for governor, Bill Dodd. When John J. McKeithen ran for governor in 1967, she was his designated television attack dog, for which she earned the nickname "Hatchet Mary." The governor thought a woman could get away with more-scurrilous charges than a man. In those days, at least, he was right. And she was a master of the thirty-minute speaking format, hardly looking at notes and always conscious of the time-left signs held just off camera.

Still, television is a tricky medium, and before her half-hour show was over, I established another of my rules. Never, never, go live on television. I didn't know enough about dress and the disasters that awaited to advise her not to wear a heavy charm bracelet that was a gift from her deceased husband. She was a demonstrative speaker, using her hands to make points. But every movement sounded like a locomotive collision, and when her hand hit the desk it sent knives of pain through the sound man's head. I looked over and saw him holding his headset a foot from his ear. After about ten minutes I made a sign and held it close to the camera. Miz Parker read the sign and shook her head in a negative signal.

She continued to drive daggers through the sound man, and I shrugged my shoulders. It was another rule in my evolving book:

1. No drinking with clients.
2. No going to whorehouses with clients.
3. No live television.
4. Carefully inspect every garment and item worn by a candidate before the camera is turned on.

In time, there would be others.

With Paul Yacich's help, however, this program and the other television I produced for Parker was good enough to attract the attention of other political professionals and hacks in Louisiana. Suddenly I was known. My phone began to ring. Even after splitting the money with Weill, I had earned $35,000 in about five months—more money than I had ever dreamed I would make in two years. I replaced my worn blue blazer with attire fitting a successful political consultant. I bought my wife a new Buick. Although it made me gag at first, I switched from bourbon to scotch because I read that scotch was what the Kennedys drank. I was rolling. And from that campaign until today I have never had to look back. The $35,000 bonanza exploded into multiples. Eventually our tiny rented house on Rhododendron

Street in Baton Rouge became a historic house on Capitol Hill in Washington. My small getaway in north Louisiana became a log home on forty acres perched over the Big Hole River in Montana. The Buicks became Mercedes. I no longer had to look in the folds of the sofa for pennies to buy milk for my children. I owned an airplane and a real estate development of airplane hangars in Virginia. It was a fast ride from driving Miz Parker in the white Buick and following a minor league candidate into a whorehouse to sitting in strategy meetings with candidates for president of the United States.

With my partner Gus painting dreams and me exploring and continuing to try to understand political consulting, the Louisiana years were heady. Youth helped. At twenty-eight one can drink whiskey most of the night and stand behind a camera the next day. In fact, it was part of the romantic image I had fabricated. I was creating a political consultant from whole cloth. The only problem with my new lifestyle and fame was the electoral calendar. Louisiana still had elections only every four years for statewide offices and every two years for U.S. Congress. That meant we had to represent nonpolitical clients. Our list included a four-state distributor for Volkswagen in its glory days, a chain of bakeries, a bank, a racetrack, and various political plums like the Louisiana Superdome in New Orleans. Except for the Superdome Commission, which put me back into the company of political hacks, I hated the advertising business. Looking back, that wasn't a great sign. Politicians like Cat Doucet and John McKeithen had spoiled me. I found the world of business too tame. A good year with a bank resulted in a small dinner with the bank president to celebrate an infinitesimal growth curve. A wild night was three scotches instead of two and an off-color joke told behind a napkin. In contrast, a political campaign was an orgy of noise, money, fistfights, bad-weather flying, midnight telephone calls, quick romances, intrigues, storytelling, scheming, dreaming, lying, and hyperactivity that resulted in an orgasm of frayed and overstimulated emotions on election night.

A bank president might say, "Well, our depositor growth was 3.4 percent and our EPS $3.03. That is up from $2.95 last year."

In contrast, on election night a campaign manager would take a swig from a bottle of bourbon and declare at the top of his lungs, "We kicked their asses." Or, if you lost, he would take a hit from his bottle and declare, "The damned television you produced was for shit." But it was always black and white. Win or lose. The beat was louder. Opinions became absolutes.

Enemies were clearly defined. And, best of all, it was over. In one television moment when the check mark went up next to a candidate's name declaring him the winner, it was over. The morning after the dinner with the bank president, one would trudge to work and start writing the next catchy jingle or storyboarding the next television ad. The day after an election, one would take a handful of aspirin, pack up the car, and go on a long vacation. I spent my downtime trout fishing in Scotland.

But my children got older and their needs greater. The notes from the public-school teachers came home with six and seven misspelled words, and one entire year my daughter was not taught math because her teacher couldn't add, so I turned to private schools. Louisiana's public schools are still one of its obstacles to progress. Our new house on Broussard, blocks from the little house on Rhododendron, had a larger mortgage and many rooms that needed furnishing and repainting. The Buick had to be replaced and I wanted a Porsche to keep up with my new high-octane image. So I buttoned down my collar, bought a few new suits, and became an advertising account executive. Few candidates in other states had begun to use political consultants, and I had the southern insecurity that people in "them northern towns" were smarter than me. A decade later I found out that a lot of them truly thought they were smarter than anyone with southern manners or accents, but that turned into a great advantage. My client Gillis Long, who was Democratic majority whip of the U.S. House of Representatives and well on track to be Speaker of the House before his ambition was stopped by death, once told me that while he sat out a couple of terms in defeat and became an investment banker, he would go to New York, turn on a heavy southern accent, and "take all of their money instead of just a few dollars. I always let them know how much smarter they were than me. It worked every time."

As a southerner, it still galls me when people equate my accent with a lack of intellect. My experience with Dukakis is an example of the prejudice I found when I got to Washington. But the East Coast bias continues today. Chris Matthews, the former flack for Speaker Thomas J. "Tip" O'Neill Jr., as well as author of the book *Hardball* and moderator of a cable television show of the same name, had my son Dane on his show in 1998. Dane, who is one of my two partners in the firm that bears our names, is an accomplished political consultant in his own right. But that didn't matter to Matthews. After the show he actually asked Dane why he didn't get rid of the southern accent.

A shortage of ego, however, was never my problem in the Louisiana years. I was confident I could meet any challenge. We needed off-season work, and my partner with the golden tongue, Gus Weill, sold our firm's services to Willard Robertson, who owned the Volkswagen distributorship for Louisiana, Alabama, Arkansas, and Tennessee. Robertson had been a major contributor and player in the McKeithen campaign for governor. As a young GI, he had ordered a couple of the goofy-looking bugs as a curiosity for his used car lot. The Germans followed the cars to his door and talked him into becoming a distributor for a good hunk of the country—a decision they later regretted when there was a bug in every other driveway and Robertson was one of the only bent cogs in their well-oiled distribution machine. He was strong enough to divert millions of advertising dollars to his control, which in turn resulted in hundreds of thousands of dollars in commissions in our pockets.

Despite the size of the account and the huge revenues, I couldn't seem to get out of the whorehouse. Robertson hired a new director of advertising who had come out of sales in a sleazy, down-market radio station. He was a walking deal. He traded and wheeled. He picked out a lavish apartment in New Orleans for himself to live in and made me rent it in my name, ostensibly so I could be close to the account, but really so he could live for free. He was ignoring all the rules of orderly media buying and forcing us to place radio and television time on low-rated stations that supplied him with cases of whiskey, off-brand cameras, fun-filled trips to Disney World, be-the-fifth-caller-and-win television sets, and airplane tickets to exotic Mexico. It was hard to walk through the apartment because of the cases of booty. Instead of New York crews that produced national-quality work, I was forced to use near-amateur production people from a local television station who had made some sort of deal with the advertising director. Finally I worked up enough courage to confront Robertson's CEO about the declining situation, but retreated when I found cases of scotch and several television sets lining his office walls as well. He was getting a share of the plunder. Payola has always been a problem in television and radio. I don't know if it was illegal to accept "gifts" in exchange for media buys, but it trampled ethical standards. In this case, it also made my production less effective and hurt the quality of the product.

When I complained to my partner about the poor quality of the work we were producing and the problems I was having in what was turning into *Let's Make a Deal*, he said, "You like the money? You like those $500 suits? You like those sports cars?" I got the point. Like the girl in the whorehouse, I was obviously for sale.

Another client was the Boustany family, who owned Evangeline Maid Bread in Lafayette and Bunny Bread in New Orleans. The elder Boustany, Frem, was a Lebanese immigrant who had gambled on the American dream and, through hard work, won. Judge Edmund Reggie, the son-in-law of the old patriarch, was a sophisticated, handsome, bright, attorney who was and is a major player in Louisiana and national Democratic politics—for example, his daughter, Vicki, is married to Ted Kennedy. My children went to private schools and I prospered in the early days solely because of the faith Reggie placed in Weill and me. (By this time I had become an equal partner in the Weill/Strother political and advertising business.) Reggie and his family were our first nonpolitical client and sheltered us through the rough times of establishing a business. These people were straight shooters. They were also damned good businessmen.

The family had bought a bakery in New Orleans and changed the name of the bread to Bunny. It floundered at the bottom of the market despite the incredible quality controls these people brought to the business. They were not content with their market share, and we began planning a product change. In their wisdom the Boustanys decided to lengthen their loaf and make it about five slices longer than their competitors'. These shrewd business people knew their chief competitor, Sunbeam Bread, the company that dominated the market, would not be able to follow because their ovens were too narrow. That gave the Boustanys the advantage they sought. I was assigned to introduce the product.

Bread commercials are all music and smiling children. In testing we found that people don't really care about bread and tend to buy the loaf that is familiar or is at eye level on the grocery shelf. Bread to the consumer is only to hold together the salami and lettuce. I was looking for a difference that would give us an edge. The difference was the size of the loaf. It was natural that I resorted to political techniques. I viewed the bread companies as candidates for office, and it was obvious we had to compare them for the voters. I had an art studio compose a full-page, color newspaper ad that had Bunny and the two competitors standing on end. It was obvious that our loaf was larger. The copy across the page read simply, "Big Bunny vs. The Little Guys." My television commercials showed bread racks with our large loaf hanging off the edge of the shelf while our competitors sat there, shorter and a smaller value.

The business community of New Orleans went crazy. These foreigners were coming in and taking away something from one of their insiders. To this day, the reason New Orleans is not a top-tier city economically is because of the myopic view of its business community. One's position in a Mardi Gras krewe was always more important than the balance sheet. Outsiders threatened them. As a result, Atlanta, Dallas, and Houston became major commercial hubs while New Orleans basked in the glory of its mildew, pedigreed families, and rusty iron railings. Somehow, the working people of New Orleans sensed this even when they chose what loaf of bread to buy, for the more the establishment bakeries complained, the more Bunny sales climbed. We loved it. We gave salesmen large buttons reading, "I've Got the Longest." The competition's salesmen didn't see the humor in having their manhood challenged (on top of their livelihoods) and fights broke out in the grocery aisles. The clever Boustanys and Judge Reggie smiled at the all-too-typical New Orleans response. These smart business people were playing with spoiled children. Soon they controlled more than half of all bread sales in New Orleans, and one of the "little guys" had gone out of business.

My only rough spot with the Boustany family came at one of their company family gatherings in Lafayette, where they brought in all of the salesmen and their wives to introduce the new advertising program, conduct some training, and feed them mountains of Cajun food with beer. They treated their employees as honored guests. I was in charge of making remarks about the new campaign and showing the new commercials to the sales people. Though the Boustanys were the nicest people I had ever met, they demanded perfection. They didn't want to hear excuses, nor would they accept second-class work. A presentation to their "bread family" was a terribly important event to them, and thus it was important to me.

I had a videotape made without color registration bars at the beginning because the Boustanys disliked having to wait two minutes for the commercials to start. I reduced the time between commercials to five seconds for the same reason. I put the tape on the machine in my office and played it dozens of times to be sure it was perfect. I even cued it so the first commercial started a second after pushing the button. Then I carefully wound the power cord around the machine and went home to sleep.

The next morning, before daylight, my partner and I carefully picked up the machine and put in the trunk of my car. At that time, before VHS machines, the 3/4-inch versions weighed about sixty pounds and were about three feet long. It usually took two people to lift them.

In Lafayette, while the hundreds of sales people took their seats, I hooked up the machine to the television sets and turned them on to warm up. Monitors were wired all over the large hall so that no person was more than about five feet from the images. Men with long sideburns and tattoos sat next to wives with big hair and polyester pant suits. They didn't want to be there any more than I did, but they loved the Boustanys and they liked their jobs and paychecks enough to show up for an annual command performance. I was introduced with a flourish as the man who had originated the Big Bunny campaign and was applauded. I gave some brief remarks and asked for the lights to be dimmed. I signaled for the button to be pushed. I had turned to speak to Weill when I heard shouts and applause. I looked up to see at least two Boustanys and Judge Reggie rushing toward the machine. On every screen in the hall Linda Lovelace was performing her famous act on a well-endowed man in ecstasy.

Just as he exploded in the obvious reaction to the manipulations by Lovelace, someone found the button, but it was the pause button, stopping the action on a most unfortunate picture. Two or three seconds later I managed to pull the plug on the machine to a chorus of boos from the audience. I was stunned. This could not have happened. Was it a dirty trick from a rival? I mentally reviewed my steps. I had been too careful. Where did the tape come from?

Later, after retreating to Baton Rouge, I learned that my art director, who often smoked an illegal cigarette, had taken a young lady into my office for some late-night romance on my couch. He was careful to put everything back in perfect order, even winding the power cord as I had left it, but he took the bread tape home instead of his copy of *Deep Throat*. I guess the men of the Boustany family had no choice. I was never privy to their conversations about our firm's future, but the very Catholic family made a show of firing us.

A few weeks later, after we had been properly shamed, they let us back into their family.

These smooth but tough-minded people were one of the pleasures of nonpolitical advertising. I gave them full measure of my ability and loyalty, and they treated me like a family member. I lost the contract when they sold to Flowers Industries, a large chain from Georgia who only knew about jingles and smiling faces. Flowers even ran an ad in New Orleans showing a man fly fishing in a mountain trout stream. It was as though they wanted to separate themselves from their customers. They didn't have the Boustanys' feelings for employees. When the Flowers people were introduced to their sales force, they said they intended to run their business with Christian values. I guess they decided to fire me when I spoke up and asked if they thought that maybe Jews liked bread, too. I have always had a smart mouth.

But our agency was growing larger as we took on more nonpolitical business. With my shined shoes and French-cuffed shirts, I began to look and feel like a flashy radio time salesman on the make. People even invited me to join the Jaycees and the Lions. But I wasn't happy. It was a bank client that finally pushed me over the edge to politics and nothing but politics.

Bank vice-presidents in charge of advertising were usually people who were miscast as bankers. At least that was my opinion. I was called into the vice-president's office one morning and shown a brilliant promotion premium on which he had spent tens of thousands of the bank's advertising budget. Turquoise jewelry. This fake Indian silver jewelry was to be awarded to depositors who made significant additions to their bank accounts: a bracelet for $1,000, a gaudy necklace for $10,000. His office was filled with boxes left by the huckster who had finally found a pigeon who would empty the trunk of his dirty Plymouth. And I was in charge of selling it.

I did my best. I still thought then, as do all young men, that I was a genius and there was no communications task I could not handle. I made high-style, art-directed television commercials and produced slick mail pieces that made the junk look valuable. We had a style show for women's groups. I exhausted every creative idea I could find. And no deposits came into the bank. Louisiana isn't turquoise jewelry. It's gold Rolex watches with diamond faces. It's the flash of diamonds and necklaces of 18-karat gold spelling out one's name. Turquoise jewelry is New Mexico. Louisiana is gaudy Mardi Gras beads, mink coats in a tropical climate, and shiny workout suits. And what woman who could afford to deposit $10,000 wanted to show up for her garden club meeting wearing jewelry that had been advertised on TV as a premium for deposits? But I made an effort and the VP kept telling me things were going well.

One summer morning I was summoned to the bank president's office for a meeting. He greeted me coolly. The vice-president in charge of advertising sat in the corner. He only nodded in my direction.

"I think you have done some good work in the past," the stern president said, "but I am disgusted at your completely senseless turquoise jewelry campaign. It has embarrassed us and cost $100,000 for absolutely no return."

I looked over at the VP. He was making a careful examination of his shoelaces. The president continued to explain my failings and how much I had cost the bank. I took it, occasionally glancing across the room at the man trying to reinvent shoes. The president, Embree Easterly, was a warm, good man of great dignity, and I liked him. I liked him enough to keep my mouth shut.

An hour later I stormed into Weill's office, where he was lying on the couch watching a soap opera on television and smoking a Churchill cigar.

"I'm through with advertising. I will never again in my life kiss the ass of another bank vice-president. You take my stock in the advertising agency. I am going to open a political office across the hall and you will be a partner, but I will never again . . ."

I ranted for about ten minutes and Weill listened without comment. He was a longtime master at handling my outbursts. Finally he simply said, "O.K." That was the only acceptable answer. And so in 1976 I became a full-time political consultant and began looking beyond Louisiana's borders.

By the time I shucked the agency business, Weill and I had dominated the political scene in Louisiana for several years. No Democrat ran for any major office without first offering us the campaign. Our nonpolitical clients always got short shrift when the political carnival rolled into town. In those years candidates in Louisiana spent more per capita on campaigns than any in America. They still come close. Because oil was abundant, there was a lot of new money floating around—and for reasons I have never quite understood, a lot of it was always in cash. Some people have suggested that the oil industry had a subeconomy that dealt in cash. My fees were often paid in $100 bills. My wife grew so accustomed to my wallet being filled with hundreds she began to call them "bookmarks." She picked up the expression during a campaign. I had been to the Pentecostal Camp Ground at Tioga, Louisiana, with a candidate who was addressing a gathering of fundamentalist preachers. I stayed in the back of the large tent listening to people talk in tongues and scream at the Holy Ghost. It was a sweaty, helmet-haired, white-suit-clad bunch. After an hour of testimony from various members of the clergy who had strayed but were seeking redemption, my candidate gave an emotional address about sin. The preachers endorsed his candidacy and he gave me an exit signal. As I turned to walk through the parched grass stubble and dust to our car and driver, a preacher with an open Bible stopped me.

"Brother Strother," he said, "ain't you gonna leave me a little bookmark?"

I was looking at him blankly when my candidate stepped in and put a newly minted hundred-dollar bill between the pages. Bookmark? Of course! Once, my wife bought a table that she said cost her only eleven bookmarks. It became a good way in our house of sanitizing dirty talk about what might have been dirty money.

Early one Sunday morning I got a call from an oilman who was a prominent political contributor, asking me to meet him immediately at my office. He was calling from the Governor's Mansion and had just been given blessings by Edwin Edwards to run for office.

Tommy Powell was a rumpled, bald man with a thick Cajun accent. He opened the conversation by saying, "I want to run for the Public Service Commission. How much will it cost?"

I wasn't surprised that Tommy wanted to run for a seat on the Public Service Commission. It was the elected body that regulated public utilities and common carriers in the state. It had been the stepping stone to higher office for several governors, including Huey Long. But it was one of those offices with a six-year term that didn't attract much attention. In fact, I couldn't answer Tommy's question about costs because I didn't even know the size of the district. I knew it covered several media markets in smaller cities but had no idea of advertising rates. Tommy, though, was insistent and would not allow me time to do even basic research in the books on the shelves behind me.

"How much? I want to get this business done."

"I don't know exactly," I told him.

"Well, about how much?"

"I guess about $250,000."

I threw out the figure without any foundation at all. Some people might even call it a wild-assed guess. The prospective candidate accepted my word the way a Protestant fundamentalist accepts anything out of the King James Version of the New Testament.

Tommy opened his briefcase and piled neat packages of hundred-dollar bills on my desk until they totaled $250,000.

This piqued Weill's interest. His eyes narrowed as he observed Tommy count out the money. Gus leaned over my shoulder, his cigar only inches from my ear. "Plus our fee, Tommy," he added—and watched as Tommy counted out another $50,000.

Weill, always cautious and terrified of breaking the law added, "You know we must declare this money on our taxes."

Powell looked a little hurt.

"Declare anything you want. That's good money."

I didn't know what "good" money meant, but I assumed it was money with all the taxes paid.

Tommy closed his briefcase and looked menacingly into my eyes. "Don't let me lose."

I didn't, but in his victory we created a story that is still told in Louisiana and gave him a name he proudly wore for the next twenty-five years: "Lightbulb Powell."

Here is how it came about: Tommy had entered the race for Public Service Commission late. It was necessary for us to go on the air immediately, so I booked production time at a studio in New Orleans and began writing scripts. The resulting spots were to be simple. Tommy was going to talk about high utility rates to camera. But he couldn't do it. At first I thought it was because he had a couple of drinks to "calm his nerves." But maybe he just couldn't deliver to camera. After hours of failing to produce an even fair reading, I sent Tommy back to his hotel. I went to a hardware store not far from the French Quarter and bought a length of extension cord, a plug, a pull-switch socket with a long chain, and a low-wattage light bulb. I assembled the elements in the back of the studio and looped the wire over a light standard so that the bulb hung about seven feet off the floor. Then I told the lighting director to illuminate only a spot under the bulb, leaving the rest of the studio black. I hired a local announcer to read a rewritten script, and at the end, Tommy simply walked under the bulb and pulled the chain. When he pulled the chain we turned on another light to help the bulb appear to illuminate the area and Tommy's face.

Tommy liked his TV commercial. The voters liked his TV commercial. In fact, he liked his commercial so much he tripled his TV exposure so that the light bulb illuminated every quarter hour on every station until the election. The commercial ran thousands of times. Some people began to scream at their TV sets. But the unknown oilman rushed to the lead in a large pack of candidates. People began calling him Lightbulb Powell. He handed out pencils with a small light bulb where the eraser should be. His CB handle, when CB was an important medium in rural areas before cell phones were invented, was "Lightbulb." He swept from last to first place and won without even having a runoff contest. On victory night he said in his poetic fashion, "Strother, always remember, money talks and bullshit walks."

I never forgot it.

My most remarkable race in Louisiana, though, took me back in time.

After agreeing to work for a young congressman named Edwin Edwards, a man who would eventually dominate the Louisiana political scene for thirty years, our firm was asked to change sides by Judge Edmund Reggie, our friend and savior from the lean years. Reggie, it seems, had an argument with Edwards and withdrew his important support. Later he would go back to Edwards, but we were left holding the bag, working for the ancient and bewildering candidate Jimmie Davis. My debt to Reggie was so large, I never resented his interference.

Davis was a country music star known for his gospel singing and some solid classic country hits, such as "Columbus Stockade Blues" and "You Are My Sunshine." It was certain to be a losing campaign, but by now I had an expensive lifestyle to maintain. So the tension of that campaign for me (since Davis never figured to win) was to separate the candidate from some of his cash. To be sure, Davis had money—lots of money—but he spent most of his time trying not to spend it. He was the most parsimonious man I have ever met. When we took trips in his Cadillac, we could not run the air-conditioning in the sweltering Louisiana heat because it increased the gas consumption. He made passengers sit on towels so they would not wear out the leather.

The campaign itself was a haunting time warp that gave me one last look at the campaigns of yesterday and helped me understand the campaigns of the future.

In Louisiana they call Jimmie Davis "Sunshine" after his classic country song "You Are My Sunshine." He had been elected governor first in 1944 and reelected in 1961 as a reformer.

But by 1971 all that remained of his constituency was the hardscrabble, depression-scarred, red-dirt farmers and small-town religious fundamentalists who built white frame churches and drove pick-up trucks with "Jesus Saves" bumper stickers and gun racks in the rear windows. Many of these voters shared racism as their bond and worshiped Davis as their George Wallace, although during my exposure to Davis he never in any way expressed any racist sentiment of any kind. Later, a black friend of mine explained that his slogan, "He's one of us," was an old southern rallying cry used by racists as a code that conveyed a stamp of approval. Davis was a dinosaur that had escaped the tar pits. He would never tell us his age, but I estimated him to be seventy-two when he began his last campaign with me in 1971. Apparently, that guess wasn't far off. In 1999, Davis sang his famous song at his own 100th birthday in Baton Rouge. In 2000 he was still working. He died in his sleep after his 101st birthday, November 5, 2000.

By the time I went to work for Jimmie Davis, times had changed. The economy had changed. People had migrated to the cities. Television had illuminated the world. But Jimmie was still Jimmie. He insisted on running the same campaign he had run during WWII. He used the same speech and the same techniques. Our campaign was an antique museum of the political past, a 78-rpm recording with all of the scratches and warps of time. I felt like a cultural anthropologist studying the rituals, speech patterns, and political techniques of some vanished tribe.

Davis's stories fascinated me. He came from a town so isolated by mud and gravel roads, so deep in the fundamentalist piney woods, that his schoolteacher had been fired for teaching that the earth was round, in apparent contradiction of the Bible's description of its four corners. As a child, the only gathering of more than twenty-five people Davis ever saw was in church. Even into his early adulthood, he lived where there was no automobile within fifty miles. People traveled by horseback. When he was a young man, he and two of his friends borrowed bits and pieces of neighbors' wardrobes to wear on their first visit to a city, Shreveport. Davis claimed that they wore everything from spats to tailed coats when they dressed for their debut. They were a curious trio in the city and immediately attracted the attention of a uniformed policeman, the first they had ever seen. They were so frightened, Davis related, that they turned and ran in fear, and the policeman drew his pistol and killed one of the trio.

One lesson I learned during this strange campaign was that the isolation of rural southerners can still mark the children of their children with caution, paranoia, and rebellion. Rural people resist authority, perhaps because they have never lived in a complex, ordered society. As a result, resistance for the sake of resistance becomes a mark of pride. Standing in a honkytonk with one's back against the wall and taking on the whole house against all odds is how manhood is measured. The fight, the symbol, is more important than victory. George Wallace stood in the courthouse door. Confederate general Thomas Jackson stood like a stone wall and earned his famous nickname. Robert E. Lee bucked the odds to take on the industrial giant of the North. In his second term as governor, Davis rode his horse Sunshine up the steps of the Capitol and into the governor's office. The newspapers captured the historic scene. A decade later people would approach me and say, "Remember when Jimmie rode his horse into the office?" I would nod. "He showed 'em, didn't he?" I only had a vague notion of who the "them" was, and no concept of what Davis had proved, but this symbolic act of defiance resonated with his red-dirt voters.

Politicians and consultants who don't take this attitude of redneck defiance into account are really handicapped in southern races. I have learned after spending two decades out of the South that these attitudes are expressed by most men who feel they are shut out of the system. They are powerless and know it. These frustrated voters made a difference for Ronald Reagan and Bill Clinton. With his cigarette boats and Ivy League background, George Bush never really understood. And it was obvious Dukakis didn't.

* * *

I didn't know what to expect when I signed on to the Davis campaign but I was told by the money people that it would be necessary for me to stay on the road most of the time, so I bought a new suit, some wash-and-wear shirts, a new manual portable typewriter, and a bottle of Johnny Walker scotch to tuck in my suitcase. At that time large areas of Louisiana were still dry, and my religious candidate didn't drink. At least I was so informed. (Later I found that wasn't true. In fact, little the public knew about the old politician was true.) As with the Parker campaign, I was expected to serve as press secretary, traveling companion, and media consultant.

Our campaign team was a strange group. Because the real Jimmie Davis band had disbanded decades before, the old campaigner assembled a group of players and a singer and simply gave them the old band's name. We were beginning a march to yesterday. Music had always been the center of his campaign, so it would be the center this time too—the flame that attracted the moths to the edge of our stage. A young singer named Eddy Raven, who at the time was working in a music store in Lafayette, was hired because of his rendition of the Merle Haggard classic "Mama Tried." In the early 1980s Eddy was to become a famous country singer himself, but he signed on with the campaign for $500 a month just because he wanted to sing with the great Jimmie Davis. "Doc" Guidry, a locally famous Cajun fiddler, was added to a group of Louisiana and Texas musicians who played under the name of the Jimmie Davis Band. The leader was Leon Gibbs from Fort Worth. Guidry, a older, balding man, told me he cried when he was asked to join the band. "I would go to hell for that man," he told me. For his part, Gibbs had that great Texas smile and look. The last time I saw him was on the screen of *The Last Picture Show*. The director of that film hired Leon for that look and cast him as the leader of a country band in what turned into a classic movie about the death of innocence and the decline of a small town. I was amused that even the band was a fraud, as it posed as part of the Davis music family.

The final ingredient in a Davis campaign was a gospel group, so he hired the famous Speer Family from Nashville. They came complete with a deluxe touring bus and a beauty queen who kept the band circling the bus like wolves waiting to spring through any open window. But this religious Nazarene family immediately made the bus off limits and put a padlock on its door to protect the little darling as she slept in her secure bunk. Later Davis decided Eddy Raven had prurient designs on the recently married Mrs. Davis and put a padlock on the outside of his own bus so he could lock her away when he was in a meeting. Sometimes I could hear her weeping in her prison quarters in the rear of the bus. I was assigned to take the message to Eddy that he would be fired if he took a shot at the governor's new wife. Eddy was astonished.

"Me, try to have sex with one of the Carter family?" he said. "Me? Me? That would be like taking a shot at the Virgin Mary."

Anna Carter Davis was a beautiful, soft-spoken, kind, bewildered former member of the famous Chuck Wagon Gang gospel group who had been swept off her feet by the old governor. To Eddy, Anna was older than his mother and a member of untouchable country music royalty. His feelings were bruised, but I still advised him to stay more than thirty yards away from the bus.

While the Speer family bus was ultramodern, with the amenities of a hotel, the Davis bus was a tired old retread selected only because of the minimal cost. The driver was a religious man who abandoned us one night in some remote village because when he was hired the governor had told him he would be paid "five" per month, which he interpreted as thousands and found in his first paycheck that Davis had meant as hundreds. A compromise was reached, and he returned. Later I found vagueness was a Davis technique to set up bargaining that was advantageous to him. He usually covered his mouth with his hand when he spoke and mumbled in incomplete sentences, so one was never sure exactly what he had said. Often he would reprimand us by claiming he had not given the specific orders we thought he had. Along with mumbling, he used code words in all conversations, so that one was never completely sure what he meant.

A typical Jimmie Davis command would be, "Find that man who did that thing yesterday and tell him to go to the place we went yesterday and to bring his things."

That might have meant something as simple as, "Find the mechanic who fixed the bus yesterday and tell him we will leave the bus at the service station on Main Street and he should bring his tools."

But there was never a straight statement. Davis had apparently broken so many laws and committed so many near-crimes as governor that he had become not just careful, but paranoid. One of his chief lieutenants, George

Dupuis, told me that when the gamblers came to the governor's office to make their payoffs, he would turn and look out the window at Capitol Lake and talk about the beautiful weather until the door closed behind them. Then George would pick up the bags and drive the cash to a north Louisiana bank owned by Davis and his friends. Davis could then say with conviction, "With the Lord as my witness, I can honestly say I have never touched a dollar of gambling money." (He played with words in the manner that my former client Governor Bill Clinton would do years later when he answered questions about marijuana smoking by saying he had "never broken the laws of his country." Clinton had smoked dope in England.)

Jimmie Davis appeared to be terribly rich. And terribly suspicious. He lived in a house separated from the Governor's Mansion only by a chain-link fence. To indicate his future intentions, there was even a gate. A "friendly" contractor and large contributor to Davis, Wilson Abraham, had built the house at the same time he built the Governor's Mansion. Some people thought the accounting must have been difficult when workers with materials on their shoulders walked from one project to the other. Two vicious guard dogs trained by the state police protected the house. Only Davis and his most trusted friend, Chris Fazier, could open the gates and put the dogs away. Before one could enter the house, there were at least two infrared beams to cross that, when activated, set off alarms. Every drawer and cabinet in the place had a lock; only Davis had the keys, which he kept on a huge ring. I always imagined the house was stuffed with old hundred-dollar bills.

Davis once called me at home and asked me to pick up his green show suit and shirt from his closet. His housekeeper, Harriet, a huge and ancient black woman whom, it was rumored, Davis had taken out of prison as a trustee and who was never allowed to leave his employ, let me in. When I explained what I wanted, she stepped back. "You go to that room and get that suit. I don't go in there. I never been in there."

It was a small bedroom with the usual furniture. Careful not to touch anything, I walked around looking for the mystery that frightened Harriet. The only unusual thing in plain sight was a long-barreled pistol serving as a paperweight for a $1,000 bill on a bedside table. I had never seen a bill of that denomination and bent to examine it. The real shock came when I opened the closet door. It was lined with suits on one side. There could easily have been fifty. The rest of the closet was filled with new shirts still in their original wrappers. Each package had a new tie folded neatly under the cellophane as when the clerk had sold it to the old singer. My conservative estimate was 300 new shirts and ties. Like formerly starving people often hoard food, Davis hoarded clothing. When we had spare moments in the campaign, I would accompany him to a men's clothing store, where he would buy two or three shirts and matching ties. This candidate had more kinks than a box of macaroni.

So our campaign began its slow trek to yesterday with two buses with captive women in them, a young man trying to invent political consulting as he went, and an assorted group of shiny-suited pickers and singers, hangers-on, campaign groupies, Jesus freaks, music fans, petty thieves, white-collar criminals, arthritic, gray-haired political hacks, and a living legend who was in reality a master of deception. We were full-tilt boogie, determined to re-create 1944.

The stage for our road show was a marvelous invention. When pulled behind the station wagon driven by the convict son of one of our insiders, it looked like a traveling sandwich board on wheels. But it became a mechanical cocoon when the sides came down and were propped into level position. Inside was an upright piano, amplifiers, bass drums, a mike, and a carpeted area for the band and singers. All we needed was access to an electrical plug for our long extension cord and we were ready for a performance.

Davis had decided that his press secretary/political consultant/speechwriter/television ad producer (me) should manage the events in each of the small towns. It seemed to fit his conception of what I did. So on the morning of the first day we moved into Jonesboro, where he had started his other two campaigns. I positioned the stage in a large flat area to allow room for crowds, but close enough to the courthouse to tap into an electric power socket. Davis, still living in the 1940s, told me confidently his voters would "come out of the pine trees by the thousands."

To alert these redneck masses, the convict and a Cajun boy known only as Muscles (because he had dropped out of a comic book body-building course) drove through the countryside playing Davis music out of huge speakers affixed to the top of the vehicle, interspersed with information about our appearance the next day. At night the two reported to Davis about how many people waved and promised to attend. They lied.

The next day there was pre-performance tension in the band as they tried out the strange stage and tuned their instruments. Davis's bus and the Speer Family's bus pulled up about half an hour early and I could hear their auxiliary air-conditioning motors roaring to fight back the humid heat that was nearing 90 by 9:30. It would get much hotter that day, but my new suit was already sticking to my back and last night's drinks with the band were beginning to pour from my face and into my eyes. I paced around the stage checking things that didn't need checking, asking questions of the band about the amplifier volume, making official-looking notes on a small pad. And waiting for the people to pour out of the pine trees. But they didn't.

By show time, a few dozen people stood in the shade of some distant oak and pine trees, fanning themselves with newspapers and Davis hand-bills. They were a motley group of country people interspersed with a few public officials in wet white shirts and wilted ties. At the appointed hour the bus horn honked and the driver beckoned me into the cool but hostile core of the machine.

"Where are all the people?" Davis asked. "Did that convict and that drunk Cajun forget to canvass the area with the sound truck?" He was screaming.

"And who ever taught you to set up a stage on hot asphalt instead of near the shade?"

I don't remember my answers. They were really irrelevant. That after-noon I was relieved of my duties as show manager and replaced by one of the old-timers who had done it in previous campaigns.

"I don't know where you learned your politics," Davis said. "But you got a whole lot to learn." He was right. I had failed show promotion and production.

But we opened. Doc Guidry played "Under the Double Eagle." Eddy Raven sang "Mama Tried," the Speer Family sang something about Jesus, and Anna Davis of Chuck Wagon fame did a beautiful rendition of "Help Me Make It through the Night." Then Jimmie jumped onto the stage to speak. He always jumped up the steps to show his youth and vigor, as Ronald Reagan would do years later. Though Davis knew hundreds of country songs by heart, he could not remember the speech he had given most of his life. He read it haltingly from large note cards.

My friends, today I am back at the old home place where I started from. And if I never go a step further, I have come a long ways. . . .

I look beyond this election. I look beyond all elections. I look to the time when they're going to take me, just like they're going to take you, to that silent city on the hill and we're not coming back.

That's the last ride. A place where there will be no rich men and no poor men; no big shots and no little shots; where six feet of earth—the great equalizer—makes 'em all the same size.

The speech lasted about twelve minutes, loaded with platitudes and cliches, not a single word of which related to any concern a voter might have—or even to the second half of the twentieth century. When Davis finished speaking he would pick up his guitar, an instrument he had never learned to play, and hang it around his neck as a prelude to singing a couple of his standards. Davis was usually accused of being a better musician than a governor. Therefore, he was defensive about his campaign's being built around music instead of issues. He always preceded the music with a little introduction that was only as deep as a song lyric itself: "I never make any apologies for strumming a guitar and singing a little. My old guitar is kinda like an old friend. It fed me when I was hungry and clothed me when I was ragged, and I don't run out on a friend."

He held his crowd pleaser, "You Are My Sunshine," until one of our shills in the audience would scream, "Play 'Sunshine,' Jimmie." The audiences would genuinely go wild and demand encores, which he never gave. "Always leave 'em wanting a little more," he told me. "Besides, they're getting this for free."

The only thing he always wanted more of was money, crisp hundred-dollar bills. Our most successful fundraising was done in New Orleans at the Fairmont Hotel. Davis would rent a suite and call in all of the people who had profited from his previous administrations. The people who built the bridges to nowhere, constructed the redundant buildings, warehoused the voting machines, sold the cheap food to the schools, built highways that potholed months after completion, poked holes in the earth for oil, soiled the air with pollution, and poisoned the bayous—all these grifters came at regular intervals through the lobby of the elegant old hotel and up to the suite. They understood that although checks were acceptable, cash was the commodity that would win favor with the past and future governor. Davis called me into the room and whispered into his hand that I was to go into the lobby and position myself ahead of a prominent contractor who lurked near the potted plants in order to get to the contributors before we did.

"Ten thousand turns into five by the time it gets up here," is how he explained the suspected treachery of one of his best friends.

Late in the afternoon I barged unannounced into the bedroom of the suite, where Davis sat on the bed surrounded by piles of bills. He had the look of a drunk with a new bottle of wine. The bills were in neat stacks and he was smiling. I didn't see what became of the money, but when our private plane landed we were met by our campaign chairman, Rolfe McCollister. It was his duty to pay for the television commercials I was producing, and he was nervous about making the Friday payment. McCollister was a straight shooter who held Davis in some awe. I never understood his attraction, unless it was religion. Many fundamentalists liked the old governor because of his gospel singing. Rolfe had a tendency to follow helmet-haired fundamentalists like Jimmy Swaggart. I knew Rolfe as a good man with deep religious convictions but poor judgment when it came to people.

"How did the fundraising go?" he asked me.

"Great. Davis has a lot of money."

Rolfe turned and rushed to confront Davis near the tail of the airplane as the old performer tried to escape to the safety of his huge bus that was purring next to the hangar. I couldn't hear the conversation, but I saw Davis shrug his shoulders and pull both of his trouser pockets inside out to show they were empty. There was a brief conversation and Davis pulled out a paper clip holding a few meager bills and gave Rolfe two twenties and a hundred. The bill for television that week was about $25,000.

It was a grinding country-music road tour with Davis collecting greasy bills and running away from voters to the safety of his bus. Tires began to blow out. The air-conditioning was constantly belching hot air and rattling death gasps. Our convict sound-truck driver stole the sound car and its equipment and disappeared forever. It was the courthouse parking lot in Coushatta at 10 A.M. and Front Street in Natchitoches at noon. The Little League ballpark at Ruston was at 2:30 and Monroe at 5. Meals along the trail were at Tastee Freezes and Big Burgers. We had to buy our own food. (Davis kept a stash of drinks and junk snacks in a small refrigerator, but he wouldn't share with the other riders on the bus no matter how long we had gone between meals.)

We bounced along between parched cotton fields, leaving a cloud of smoke behind our gasping engine. Eddy sang, the Speer Family harmonized, Davis spoke, Anna cried, the band got drunk at night in seedy redneck honky-tonks. The drink of choice was Canadian Club and Coke. A gourmet meal was fried catfish and hush puppies. The band's traveling van smelled of tobacco, marijuana, rye whiskey, and sweat. Breakfast was aspirin and Twinkies. At most stops there were braless girls in tight jeans or miniskirts cooing over Eddy and eager to lead him to backseats for erotic gymnastics. For me it was a never-ending journey through hell. But I still had children in private schools, a mortgage, and a taste for a lifestyle that sucked up money like a wino sucks at a muscatel bottle.

I was learning history like Mark Twain's Connecticut Yankee dropped back in time. But I was both Merlin and the fool. I was known as press secretary, but I was not allowed to talk to the press. My former colleagues were the enemy. Sometimes I had to look out the window as they knocked on the door for an interview. But they didn't really bother us in the hell days of summer when our shirts were wet by nine. They stayed in their air-conditioned metropolitan newsrooms. Our caravan seldom saw a traffic jam or even a suburban neighborhood.

"There's people all out in those pine trees," Davis would admonish me when I tried to present research or demographic data, "and on election day every unwashed son of every Bible-fearing mama will find their way to the voting machine."

We were basically irrelevant in the campaign, so our first press crisis came late, when an old friend called with a warning that reporters were fed up with our strategy of avoidance and the sprints to the bus. He said they were going to surround the stage so that Davis would have no place to escape. I tried to reason with the candidate that night as the bus bumped down secondary roads toward the next performance.

"Governor, all you have to do is answer a few questions for ten minutes."

"That's easy for you to say. You've never been anything." Then he gave me the old line he used in every speech. Everything to Davis was a song lyric:

If you want to see yourself as you have never seen it before
Find out some things about yourself you didn't know,
Get a real picture of yourself, bird's-eye view, close-up shot, inside-outside shot, half shot and every other kind of shot,
You just announce for public office and let somebody think you might win it

And they'll open your eyes.

"Those bastards will want to talk about that bridge."

Again I didn't know what he was talking about. I assumed it was about a bridge to nowhere he had built during his last term. The bridge, across the Mississippi southeast of Baton Rouge, began in a canefield on the east bank and ended in a canefield on the west bank. It was named the Sunshine Bridge in honor of Davis. Actually, the bridge became of immense value as industry flocked to the banks of the Mississippi and workers crowded the small towns on both sides of the river. But this year the old governor didn't want to talk about the bridge. I argued for more than an hour as we rattled down moonlit roads, with the candidate increasingly agitated by my insistence that he was going to have to meet the press.

"Stop the damned bus!" Davis finally screamed at the driver. "Get out!" he said to me.

I gladly obeyed his order and jumped to the ground without using the steps. I watched the bus pull away until the taillights and black smoke disappeared over a hill. Only then did I take stock of my situation. I was on a tiny, blacktopped road that was only a gash in a great pine forest. A band of stars twinkled above me in a moonless sky. It was unearthly quiet except for small animal sounds in the undergrowth. I sat on the side of the road with my back against a pine tree that seemed to vibrate with life because of a hot breeze that bent its top and mosquitoes that took sips of my blood. I was in a state of serene peace for more than half an hour until I saw headlights bobbing up and down the distant hills. I stood in the road and waved my arms until a white Buick screeched to a stop.

"Shit, Strother, what you doing standing in the middle of the road?"

It was George Dupuis, the former confidant for Davis. He was only slightly drunk and had two cases of beer iced down in a chest covering most of the backseat. I discovered that without Davis's knowledge he trailed the bus in case of trouble. He was a heavily armed, self-appointed commando. On this night he had fallen far behind the bus when he had to search for beer because he was in a dry parish.

I turned the air-conditioner vent on my chest full blast, drank three of his cold Budweisers, and slept for more than an hour until we found the bus parked at a seedy motel.

The next day Davis acted as though nothing had happened. Around noon, the press rebellion took place. When he finished his last number and the shill was to scream for "Sunshine," the old governor leaped from the back of the stage and began running toward the bus with a gaggle of shouting reporters chasing him.

To all of their questions he answered, "Ask Raymond."

After Davis was safely inside and the bus door was locked, my former friends in the press turned on me. They didn't want to talk about issues. They wanted to know what the candidate had to hide and why he wouldn't talk to them. I had no answers but was saved from having to admit it by a giant redneck who suddenly broke through the ranks, grabbed the most persistent reporter—who was only inches from my face—and lifted him about four feet into the air.

"I'm gonna kill this son of a bitch!" the redneck screamed.

My response became part of the campaign lore in Louisiana for years.

"Please don't kill the reporter," I said. "I have enough trouble as it is."

The huge man looked up at me and said, "Mr. Raymond, can I just break one of his arms then?"

The editorial cartoon in the *Shreveport Times* the next morning showed a huge redneck holding a reporter by the neck and a depiction of me yelling, "Please don't kill the reporter."

I never went back to riding the bus. I became traveling companion to George and the huge chest of beer. The campaign was a professional embarrassment, but the genial Cajun and his bottomless cooler took off some of the rough edges. Our opponents, more in humor than concern, began distributing buttons reading, "Where's Raymond?" I was finally a complete fool. I fell into surrender. The dollars continued to pour in, so I made commercials and went limp.

One day Davis asked me into the bus. "You tell me you can get me in the newspapers. They don't cover my speeches."

"Well, governor, you don't say anything. You don't talk about any issues or say what you will do if you get elected. We give the same speech at every stop. If we had some new material, we might make news."

"Then we'll add something to the speech. What do you think is important now?"

"Drugs, governor. Parents are concerned about their kids and drugs."

"Well, then, we will put something in my speech about drugs. You work it up."

I spent the next two days in a library and talking to law enforcement agencies until I came up with a program to educate children about drugs and to increase the penalties for selling. I gave it to Davis, who told me he would study it and make some cards, meaning that he would add some new 4 x 5 index cards to his old speech. I notified the few reporters still on speaking terms with me about our new position and stood in back of the crowd when Davis began his old speech.

Abruptly, he stopped at the point where he was to inject the new drug material. The pause seemed to go on forever. He wasn't used to deviating from his set piece and was trying to process the added sentences. People in the audience began to cough.

Finally he looked up and literally screamed into the mike, "DOPE!"

He paused and screamed again. "DOPE!"

He looked around the crowd, which was obviously mystified. "Dope!" he continued. "Some people are for it—some people are against it. Myself, I don't know. Ask your mommas and daddies."

Then he went directly back to his old speech, full of outdated expressions from his agrarian past like, "I've been to the mill and had my corn ground." I'm not sure exactly what that means, but it perhaps is a metaphor of experience. The press laughed, and I went to the car and guzzled four beers. At dinner that night Davis came over to my table.

"How you think that went?"

"Brilliant, governor. You were just brilliant. I guess if the press doesn't cover that speech, it just proves they're against us."

He nodded in satisfaction. He never again asked for new material, and I never again asked him to talk to the press.

I tried once more to resurrect my declining self-worth when I confronted Davis with the fact that he would run third or fourth in a six-person field.

"Well," he said, taking small sips from a soda, "I guess we will just continue to do our best and leave the rest to the Lord."

With the Lord taking over, I was freed of conscience and purpose, and began traveling more with the band. I enjoyed their talk about performing and their dreams of the big time. They were like children meeting a new world every morning. None of them could have told me whether Davis was a Democrat or a Republican. In fact, few of them could have identified more than two or three states on a map. They lived in a land of steel guitars, drums, fiddles, big hats, boots, and honky-tonks. They viewed their lives as country song lyrics filled with drinking, fighting, lost loves, unbroken horses, and cheating hearts. And they had a kind of joyful, uninhibited fun.

One September night the band and I were all doing battle with huge platters of fried frog legs, fried catfish, fried crawfish, and shrimp etoufée in an Opelousas restaurant when Sheriff Cat Doucet stumbled in. I said stumbled because Cat was having trouble keeping his head higher than his feet, swaying slightly at some imagined shifting of the earth. He spotted me across the restaurant and wove his way to me. I stood to shake his hand and he hugged me.

"Raymond, I love you so much for what you're doing for Jimmie that my heart is about to break." Cat of course knew that, as governor, Davis would take the heat off of his whorehouses and gambling, as he had in his last administration. Cat went around the table, first hugging Eddy and then each member of the band.

"I love all of you boys so much I go to do something for you."

He unsnapped the pearl-covered fastener on his shirt pocket and took out a stack of business cards. He counted the band members and wrote something appropriate on the backs of the same number of cards and handed them to us.

The card was illustrated with a line drawing of a winking woman holding her breasts, with huge protruding nipples. Over her head it read, "Bet you didn't know we handled these?" Under the drawing was the name of the brothel, The Gate, in which Doucet had a proprietary interest. On the back of the card the good and generous sheriff had written, *"Give this boy anything he wants free. Cat."*

The card was a free pass to the whorehouse, and some of the band members understood immediately the value of such a gift. With hot frog legs still on the table, the boys were piling into the station wagon for the five-minute drive to The Gate. Life was never the same again. After every evening performance I watched most of the band run for their station wagon. I went back to George's white Buick that, despite the fact it was only six months old, had one door wired shut, a smashed rear fender, and missing chrome that had been scattered in bar parking lots. By this time I had kindly explained to George we were going to lose, so he joined me in hedonistic free fall. We smoked cigars, ate Cajun food, and watched a lot of sunsets. Our resignation gave us a free pass around emotional involvement. We no longer worked. We simply traveled with the candidate like beer-soaked pilot fish following the bus as though it was the host shark.

Many Louisiana highways were made by digging earth from both sides to form high ground on which to lay the pavement. The resulting ditches, sometimes called borrow pits or bar pits, usually held water and often alligators as well. George and I were headed south toward Crowley from an afternoon Davis performance when we found the sides of the highway studded with signs on stakes. The signs were for one of our opponents, Congressman Gillis Long. It was a taunt by some mischief-seeking campaign workers who knew that every car leaving the huge Davis rally would go down this particular road. George, fortified by liquor, accepted the challenge, straddled the shoulder of the road, and began mowing down the signs. About every twenty yards we hit a sign and it flew over the top of the battered Buick. George would laugh and take a swallow of beer as he aimed at the next sign. It was great fun until the road turned and we didn't. The white Buick made a tremendous splash and then settled into the muddy bottom with water about three inches deep in the floorboards. George and I waded out of the stranded whale of a car.

"Bring the beer box," George said.

We pulled the heavy box to the side of the road and sat at the edge of the water watching the sun go down. It was only two days until the election. The bus was heading home from its last trip.

"Well," George said, "I guess this is the last stump speech in ole Sunshine."

The sky grew dark and stars poked through. Frogs began looking for mates, and an occasional gator bellowed in the distance. It was Hindu peaceful. Later a wrecker pulled the Buick clear of the water. We paid the driver $20 to allow us to ride in the towed car with our beer box. Anything is possible in Louisiana if you have enough money.

Jimmie Davis lost, of course, but my bank account swelled and I was a walking history of yesterday's politics. The lessons were tough but profitable. When he died in November of 2000, Davis was almost canonized by the press. Once again they proved that they have become desensitized to corruption and are more interested in the legend than the reality. Without perhaps even realizing it, they were thereby helping to perpetuate the corruption.

The ability of a political consultant is usually misunderstood, or at least exaggerated. This is all the more true in our celebrity culture, but one secret of our business is that the natural abilities of the candidate probably matter more than who is hired to give that candidate advice. Another is that a lesser opponent with a huge bank account can overwhelm even a good candidate with a good consultant. Money usually trumps talent.

Winning with or without a well-funded candidate, though, gives a consultant the aura of being talented and creative. It almost becomes part of his or her title. RAY STROTHER WHO ELECTED MARY LANDRIEU or RAY STROTHER WHO ELECTED ROY BARNES will be my title until I have a showcase loss or another dramatic victory.

Nobody illustrates this better than James Carville, the hyperkinetic leatherneck from the Louisiana bayous whose unofficial title is THE MAN WHO ELECTED BILL CLINTON PRESIDENT. That is a lovely thing to wear around one's neck. However, at one time it could have been THE MAN WHO HAS NEVER WON A MAJOR CAMPAIGN. The distance between those two epithets is not as big it seems.

Carville's abysmal won-lost percentage as a consultant prior to hooking up with Bill Clinton is a matter of record. But this doesn't mean that he lacked talent in those years. Carville was as good in some of his losses as he was in the famous 1992 Clinton campaign. In fact, Carville is still the only consultant I have ever heard of who gained credit while losing. And he deserved it. Dick Davis, candidate for governor of Virginia, was one of a long string of losers managed by Carville, but even in defeat James's work won him respect in the Washington political community.

But that respect was a long time in coming. In fact, in the seventies I had trouble seeing Carville as anything but an amusing novelty who did everything in excess and could go into emotional frenzies over things as simple as iceberg lettuce or a missed field goal in a professional football game. To spend time with the young James was exhausting. He was quirky, good company, and a thousand laughs as he said and did things others would blush even to think privately. He was different. I can best describe him then as a wind-up toy that would race madly across the room into a wall, spin upright, and race toward another wall. And the spring never ran down. Despite some of his quirks and early troubles getting established, there was something about him that, while sometimes not particularly endearing, made him stick out in a crowd, a character trait that hinted he would be tough to keep down.

I don't remember exactly when I met James. I knew him casually—as did almost everyone in Baton Rouge who dropped by any of the saloons around the area. But he and I began to spend time together because of my friendship with his boss, Shelly Beychok, a fiery Russian Jew born in Brooklyn who was as volatile as James. Shelly and his law partners, Jerry McKernan, Mary Olive Pierson, and Whit Cooper, put James in a back room of their firm, and he spent most of his time running errands for them. They said he was a terrible lawyer. The person who agreed most with that assessment was James. But he was fiercely loyal and made them all laugh.

Beychok, a major political player in Baton Rouge, was one of the people who convinced Congressman Edwin Edwards to become Governor Edwin Edwards. And in Louisiana, being the best friend of the governor is a powerful position. Like others in the Edwards crowd, Shelly lived very large even by south Louisiana standards. He drove big cars, had a flashy mistress, wore expensive suits, refused to wear neckties or dinner jackets, and generally made his own rules. And he loved James Carville.

In fact, everyone loved James. He was the product of a rock-solid Catholic family from the little town of Carville, down the Mississippi River from Baton Rouge. He claims to have set some sort of record for longevity as a student at LSU and to have barely squeaked through law school. His self-deprecating humor made everyone feel good. That sort of humor, unfortunately, only occasionally peeks through now, as James has begun to take himself seriously. But maybe he should. I think he saved a president of the United States and exposed the personal agenda of Special Prosecutor Ken Starr.

Had I paid more attention, perhaps I would have been able to see the future for James. But I was too self-absorbed and laughing too hard. So, perhaps, was Beychok, his mentor, who also missed the qualities that would later make James stand out. Those were the days of laughter.

Finally, I think in exasperation, Shelly asked Weill and me to hire James. "Hell," Beychok said, "if you take him off my hands I'll even pay his salary." We hired James but didn't take Shelly up on his offer of reimbursement.

The green Carville was of little value. He was not yet a disciple of message and believed too strongly in gimmicks and organization. But he was fierce even in his misunderstandings. Often, as an exercise, we are asked to define a person or place with one word. My word to explain James would be "obsessive." Carville's first campaign with me was in Joe DiRosa's gleeful and doomed romp for mayor of New Orleans in 1978. DiRosa, an affable city councilman, was convinced the way to win votes was to visit bars and buy drinks. It was Carville's job to give the campaign structure, run the headquarters, and to help the organization raise money. He was the campaign manager, the slot he would fill in future campaigns that eventually brought him fame.

For the DiRosa campaign, Carville and I moved into the luxury townhouse of Beychok and his business associate in a soft drink company, Jim D'Spain, who kept it as a New Orleans retreat. Deep in the Garden District, it was resplendent with four marble bathrooms, four bedrooms, and a beautiful patio. Shelly was a gourmand who kept the kitchen stocked with delicacies from New York, Europe, and San Francisco. D'Spain was a prodigious drinker who always had a pantry overflowing with Scotch. The two business associates kept a plane and pilot and would occasionally get a hankering for barbeque from a stand in Marshall, Texas, and send the pilot for carry-out.

The Russians briefly used New Orleans as a port for one of their cruise ships, and Beychok made a deal with an officer on the ship to smuggle us kilos of the best Russian caviar for only one hundred hard-currency dollars per tin. We would often sit with a kilo of caviar, some toast, and a bottle of champagne and eat the silky, uncrushed black eggs directly from the tin with teaspoons. About every three months Dave Wilson, the manager of Brennan's restaurant on Royal Street, would prepare a special dinner for eight or ten, served in a private wine cellar. We called it "The Gluttony." We gorged on course after course of the finest of foods over several hours, and topped it off with Cuban cigars cut and lit by scantily clad girls who came in at the end of the meal from the local Playboy Club to serve the cognac. The good times never ceased to roll.

Carville's and my campaign day consisted of going down to the head-quarters on Poydras, where I would watch him yell at people. He only had two levels, mute and scream, and he was seldom mute. When I first heard him begin his crusade on television against Ken Starr in 1996, I agreed with his premise that Starr was a partisan Republican zealot, but I still almost felt sorry for Starr, knowing what he was facing.

Carville is a snapping turtle that won't let go until it thunders . . . and he is deaf to thunder. When he was my friend he would develop passions about strange subjects. He would rant for hours about the lack of taste in iceberg lettuce or Washington Delicious apples. He once went on a crusade against vitamins because the physician father of a woman he dated told him that vitamins were useless. One would have to hide vitamin C in the back of the medicine chest to avoid a harangue. And if a waiter had the gall to put a salad of iceberg lettuce on the table, I would retreat to the men's room until quiet was restored. We had long conversations about the merits of Granny Smith apples and the tastelessness of Washington Delicious. So when I first heard James's tirade on *Meet the Press* attacking Starr, I started laughing. All I could think about was iceberg lettuce. When I see James go off into space with one of his overreactions, I now call it the "iceberg lettuce treatment."

I think he saved a president of the United States, unmasked an overzea-lous special prosecutor, and exposed to scrutiny an independent counsel system that was undermining self-government in this country. If that sounds like a polite way to describe the nasty jihad between James and Ken-neth W. Starr, perhaps it is. But consider the facts. From the moment Starr was appointed, every instinct in Carville's body told him to go after the guy tooth and nail. He was talked out of it, at least for a while, by cooler heads such as top Clinton adviser George Stephanopoulos, White House commu-nications director Mark Gearan, and White House counsel Lloyd N. Cutler. But these cooler heads were not wiser heads. A lowly political consultant shooting from the hip won the day. And James had an interesting motiva-tion besides his dislike of Republicans and his bulldog loyalty to Bill Clin-ton. It seems that in October of 1993, James was waiting for his wife's plane in the USAir Club at National Airport, sipping on a cup of coffee, thumbing through the sports pages, checking to see how the LSU Tigers were doing, when a stranger he described as "an intense, bespectacled man" grinned at him and made a crack about Clinton. "Your boy is getting rolled," the man told James. "He doesn't stand for anything."

James had become famous, and such things happened to him all the time, so he gave it no more thought—until early August the following year when a new Whitewater special prosecutor was appointed by a panel of federal judges. Staring out at James from the television set was the face of the bespectacled man at National Airport. Or at least this is how James tells the story. Starr claimed it never happened. But those of us who've known James also have a feel for him, warts and all. We know that although he exaggerates, name-calls, and rants about iceberg lettuce, he does not lie.

The cooler heads in the White House who suppressed James for two years finally lost the battle in November of 1996 when he appeared on *Meet the Press*. He declared war and began the rant.

Carville criticized Starr for lecturing to the law students at Regent University, a Virginia college founded by Christian Right leader Pat Robertson. Carville criticized Starr for not taking a leave of absence from his law firm, Kirkland and Ellis. He criticized him for the firm's client list, which included Big Tobacco, an industry that hated Clinton. He criticized Starr for accepting, and then declining, a deanship at Pepperdine University in a chair funded by right-wing billionaire Richard Mellon Scaife, a full-time Clinton basher. Mostly, James characterized Starr as a right-wing zealot who had partisan motivations and was obsessed with sex and bringing down Bill Clinton. As James hammered away, this mantra became the Democratic Party's position and later the public's perception.

Ken Starr had gotten the iceberg lettuce treatment.

When we were working together on the DiRosa campaign, Carville and I ate lunch across the street from the campaign headquarters at Mother's restaurant, a unique spot even for New Orleans. It was a hangout for Marines and policemen. The owners would ring a bell behind the bar when a Marine or a cop came in to stand in line for the great portions of fried speckled trout or oyster po-boys, red beans and rice, gumbo, or giant Ferdi Specials, which were a combination of chunked roast beef with gravy, ham, cheese, and shredded cabbage on half a loaf of fresh French bread.

Of course Carville told the owners he had been in the Marines, because it resulted in larger portions of potato salad and more sausage in the gumbo. The bell would begin ringing as we opened the door, and the insults would fly.

"You bunch of dagos don't ring that damned bell, I got a hangover."

"If I was as ugly as you, I'd drink too."

"You got any food today you didn't spit in?"

"No, but we can handle that if you wait just a minute."

And so on. Most of the customers in Mother's in those days were locals and accustomed to flying insults, ringing bells, ethnic slurs, and loud laughter. It was the way New Orleans was before it was called the Big Easy. After lunch Carville and I would go back to the apartment to watch Andy Griffith reruns or tune into the monitor of the entranceway security camera for the apartment building attached to our garden apartment. Carville would make wild speculations about who was entering and why. He invented sexual affairs and crimes going on all around us. He also had memorized most of the Andy Griffith shows and kept up a running commentary just a few seconds ahead of the action on the screen. "Watch Floyd get after his ass," he would scream as Andy arrived at the barbershop. After Andy, we would nap in our chairs for half an hour, weighed down by the copious and greasy food from Mother's, and drift back to headquarters about three. At seven we would meet Beychok and D'Spain and drink scotch while engaging in lively arguments about which of the great New Orleans restaurants we would hit that night. It was hard on my marriage, my liver, and my waistline, but a good time filled with lifetime stories and laughs. On Sundays we watched pro football and drank bloody marys. D'Spain and Beychok bet heavily enough that the bookie, Mitch, made house calls to take our sheets and money. Carville and I were $50 or $100 bettors. Beychok and D'Spain bet thousands each week.

When I packed up to move to Washington, Carville took my wife and me to dinner in Baton Rouge to celebrate my new business venture and my separation from Weill. But we drifted apart as he met other media producers and formed new friendships in Washington. Carville fell into the same trap as most rednecks; people from other places were smarter than people from home. The last time we worked together was in 1986 after Congressman Gillis Long of the Eighth District of Louisiana died and his widow, Cathy, ran for his seat. It was a badly managed campaign, and I hired James to go to Baton Rouge and guide it. Carville's entire fee for the rather short campaign was $10,000 (about half of what he now charges for a single speech), and he was broke, without a car, and behind on his rent. He saved the campaign with his tenacity and attention to detail.

Though we have never worked together in another campaign, James has repaid me several times over. When I have asked him to participate in presentations to the American Association of Political Consultants, he has always shown up and given remarkable performances. When I was a resident Fellow at the Institute of Politics at Harvard, he donated a day of his now-expensive time to lecture my class and to appear in one of the famous Kennedy School forums. So even though we are casual friends or just casually friendly, I am able to examine him with some objectivity.

I guess I was still partially blind to the Carville phenomenon until he met me at Harvard in November of 1999. I walked over to the Charles Hotel to escort him to my classroom and maybe even to talk about old times. James and I had shared many laughs in another life. We crossed the street to get money from an ATM machine and to stand outside Dunkin' Donuts to drink a quick cup of coffee. Three of about ten students who walked past stopped for autographs. I was stunned then, but my amazement grew when we got to my classroom and found people bunched around the door unable to go in. Some of them were my regular students. Later, after helping Carville fend off reporters who wanted only a minute of his time while he used my office to make calls, I walked with him to the core of the Kennedy Center, where the ARCO Forum is held. I was to be the moderator between Carville and Dan Lungren, a former congressman, attorney general, and failed candidate for governor of California. The right against the left. When we entered the large forum room, six hundred students stood and cheered Carville. Now I was really stunned. This man had become a major celebrity of movie-star status. Some of it was luck, but he made most of his luck.

What his critics should understand is that James was willing to pay the price for success and winning was a long time coming. He told me a story once of being broke in Washington, walking through the rain, when his suitcase popped open and spilled his jeans and shirts into the gutter. He sat on the curb with the understanding that he was at that point no better off than the homeless people sleeping on the subway grates. He considered what to do with his life: quit and return home to Louisiana or to push ahead. His decision is obvious. He was willing to try once again to establish himself as a political consultant. And that is the secret of his success.

Carville was willing to live in a campaign headquarters, take out the trash, answer the telephones, be a punching bag for enraged candidates and a morale booster when times were bad, while deferring his own salary. He had no wife, no children, no car notes, and no pretense. He made Brooks Brothers blue blazers last until they were threadbare. Winning was his only goal and there were no distractions.

James forced some candidates to win through force of will. He never claimed to be creative or even to have exceptional intelligence. It is Carville who calls himself the world's worst lawyer. James has the focus of a prizefighter in the late rounds who keeps punching from behind swollen eyes.

Could Clinton have won without Carville? Who knows? The best consultant in that campaign was Bill Clinton. But I wonder occasionally if the team could have maintained its focus without Carville's disciplined insistence on returning to the central message every time the campaign faltered. It was a campaign low on money with less than average media and periodic scandals. All it had was a good message, a bad opponent, and bulldog determination by the Clintons, Carville, and some of the other professionals. Most of all, though, Carville contributed the iceberg lettuce treatment.

But Carville was noticed. How could he not be? Some people point to the IT'S THE ECONOMY, STUPID sign that hung over his desk as the gimmick that first attracted attention, but I think if the wall had been bare Carville would have had people peering into his cage. For one thing, he was different. Few people other than those who have lived on the bayous have ever witnessed such an outrageous personality, so unhampered by conventional norms of behavior. When other consultants were kissing the asses of politicians and reporters, Carville was screaming at them. He didn't fit the mold. He was quirky, different-looking, and explosive. Those characteristics make good newspaper copy when reporters get bored listening to the same speech day after day. When rumors began to surface about his relationship with Mary Matalin, the Republican operative working for President Bush—the woman who would later become Mrs. Carville—he grew even more prominent in the media spotlight. Even his romance was quirky. Their marriage turned into a high-priced political carnival act that they both use to keep up their speaking fees. Once Mary called James a "frothing, rabid dog" on television. When asked by a reporter how he responded, the ever-quick Carville said when he got home he bit her. Carville is good copy.

Then, to make up for all of the bad luck Carville had in his early years as a consultant, a documentary filmmaker who could not get enough time with an elusive Bill Clinton became fascinated with James's outrageous personality and focused a film on him, *The War Room*, that made him a superstar. I even saw him in the audience for the Oscar awards. The rest has been all dollar signs.

Soon after Clinton was elected, and after losing a high-profile mayor's race in Los Angeles, Carville gave up domestic campaigns. It was a smart move because if he had stayed he would have become just another consultant when more than half of his nonincumbents lost—as they tend to do. He quit while still champ, with the luster on his star untarnished. Doors have opened for movies, television commercials, foreign campaigns, and celebrity events that pay bucks. Now James is rich and, because of his understanding of the fragile state of celebrity, will stay an important personality in Washington for the rest of his life. He has learned to play the game.

But I don't think James is the best political consultant I ever worked with. I still give that title to the deceased Bill Morgan . . . or maybe Bob Squier, or Joe Napolitan. Hell, it might even be my son, Dane, or my other partner, Jim Duffy, or even me. It is impossible to judge. James is first-rate, however, and I am proud that he came out of my gang of Louisiana consultants who made good. Actually, I take great pride in James's success, even though he achieved it on his own, long after he had left our firm. But who knows? If Shelly hadn't persuaded us to take him on, maybe he would have made it as a lawyer down on the bayou. And maybe Bill Clinton would never have been elected. And Ken Starr would be on the Supreme Court. Only God knows.

By the mid-seventies I had become part of the folklore of Louisiana political culture. Every political steakhouse and bar had Strother stories. My picture from that era still hangs in the famous Antoine's restaurant in the French Quarter. I was becoming a caricature of myself. My office had grown, and I began to hire talented people to assist me: Ray Teddlie, Roy Fletcher, Charlie East, James Carville—all of whom would become fairly prominent political professionals. They all shared two characteristics: they were bright, and they were amusing. They made me laugh. They told great stories. They were fun to drink with and good traveling companions.

With only a few disappointments, I have helped spawn many careers of competent or even brilliant consultants. Teddlie, Carville, and Fletcher were unique because they were all from Louisiana during the incubation period of my professional march from Port Arthur to Washington. My relationship with the most brilliant of them all, Bill Morgan, actually started in Louisiana when he was my LSU classmate and later my attorney. Even though his main contribution to my political career took place in Washington, as described later in this book, Louisiana campaigns helped define us all.

The DiRosa campaign for mayor was my awakening. Usually there was a meeting in the afternoon with the candidate and his friends to discuss money and strategy. I walked in on one of these meetings to learn that Matt Reese, the legendary organizational consultant, had been hired. It would turn out to be one of the most important events in my professional life, but I only saw red that day. Matt sat at the end of the table, a huge 300-pound Gibraltar that dominated the entire room. My hackles went up.

It was obvious that Matt was there to raid my bayou territory, because his first recommendation was to bring in an out-of-state filmmaker to produce television, a new artist to design campaign literature, and a Washington pollster named Peter Hart. Later I learned that this was Matt's "take charge" act to convince the candidate he had wisely spent his money, but at the time I was threatened and angry. I still had children in private schools. Matt wanted to bring an infection of outsiders into my private political honey-hole. I didn't know him or his ability, and he was not aware that I was Louisiana's king consultant. I quietly but aggressively puffed my cigar and bided my time. In late afternoon I paid a visit to Matt at the plush French Quarter hotel, the Royal Orleans. I interrupted a meeting he was having with his assistant, Ralph Murphine.

"Mr. Reese," I asked him, "how much money are you making from this campaign?"

Matt stuttered a little and waved his hands around as though he were conducting a symphony—gestures and mannerisms for which I later discovered he was famous, "I guess about $200,000 give or take a few dollars."

"Well, I have a deal for you. You forget about bringing in another film producer and you can make your $200,000. You bring in the producer and you will be back on a plane to Washington with nothing in your jeans but your dick. I'm the best film producer you have ever met, and I own the territory."

Matt studied me for a minute and looked back at Murphine with amusement or alarm, I never knew which. He said he would get back to me by morning. The next day he called and said, "I don't know why we can't do business. I'm told you're awfully good." Matt and I never again had cross words. He was soon recommending me to campaigns around the country, and when I moved to Washington he invited me to his monthly poker games with the national reporters. When he was named to the American Association of Political Consultants Hall of Fame he asked that I produce the film clip about his life. I did the film as an act of love because Matt had become a true friend. I learned more about organization and politics from Matt, who died in November of 1998, than I had learned in all the campaigns I had been involved in and all of the books I had read.

Matt's recommendation of Peter Hart as a pollster was also serendipitous. Hart enhanced my political education by showing me the importance of in-depth research and how it could make a huge difference in a race when combined with good judgment and experience.

Even today polling is the most misunderstood part of politics. In the

1970s, however, it was considered a sort of black magic, and one had to blackmail or trick the candidates into using pollsters. Even when the candidates reluctantly consented, they were interested only in what we call the "horse race"—who is ahead and who is behind. That is the least important part of a poll. What is important is the voluminous information that explains intensity of feeling about issues and the mood of various groups. It is important to know the difference in attitudes between the old and young, black and white, North and South. Are people without children willing to raise taxes for schools? How strongly do they feel about it? Will this issue make a difference or is it simply part of many concerns?

In the seventies the most common argument was that you could not talk to five or six hundred people on the phone and understand the attitudes of hundreds of thousands of people.

"You can't tell me you can talk to six hundred people and predict how people are going to vote," was the line I heard constantly.

"Just a waste of money. Let me tell you how we did it in Big John's election."

"First you got to have the sheriffs and the clerks of court for you. Then go buy you a few Negro leaders and get old Vic Bussie over at the AFL-CIO to back you. That's all you need."

Louisiana, which has always prided itself on the quality of its campaigns and elections, was behind the curve even in 1977. They didn't know the difference between name recognition and substantive name recognition. (Name recognition is when one knows the name Burger King. Substantive name recognition is when one knows the name and the ingredients of a Whopper.) Politicians in Louisiana at that time still thought one could shake hands or ride in parades and win elections. The most important medium was the "yard sign"—a paper sign on a stick with the candidate's picture and name. It would have been impossible then to persuade any candidate that he could have 100 percent name recognition and still lose. Yard signs are still a major industry there though this illusion has been shattered several times now by candidates who didn't use them and still won.

I spent much time in the seventies explaining how people were selected for interviews and the difficulty of phrasing questions that were not misleading. We know beyond argument that random selection works, but it is frustrating to try to explain it. If a person is selected randomly, he or she can represent thousands. Dr. Wiggins at LSU, who taught me photography and gave me my first lecture on polling, explained random selection as being like a huge bingo game. Theoretically, if one put the name and phone number of every voter in the state on individual ping-pong balls and tossed them in a huge cage, the six hundred taken out would represent a cross section of all issues and demographic groups. Instead of ping-pong balls, a computer makes random selections from the population. This usually results in a representative number of men, women, old, young, black, white, rich, poor, and many other social groups. It may still sound like black magic, but it works. Polling—in the hands of an experienced pro like Hart—became highly reliable and a road map for a campaign.

For example, in the New Orleans mayor's race that Reese, Hart, Carville, and I worked on together, Hart found that potholes and street repair were at the top of the list of unaided mentions or problems. By "unaided" I mean that the respondents were not asked specifically about streets, but simply to name problems that immediately came to mind. All the other pollsters obviously found the same thing. However, Hart recommended that we not deal with streets in our campaign but focus instead on crime. He saw in his cross tabulations that fewer people mentioned crime but those who did felt passionately about it. Soon all the other candidates were on television in commercials standing on battered streets. Our candidate, DiRosa, talked only about crime. Hart taught me a lesson that encouraged me to learn more about polling and pollsters. I immediately saw that if I was going to be successful in politics outside Louisiana, I had to work with better information than I had in the past.

Peter Hart's advice and Matt's genius at organization allowed us to surge into a lead and win a spot in a runoff election against an African American candidate, Dutch Morial. Carville was learning the same lessons I was, and we would spend hours discussing the window that had been opened to our eyes. But Carville was still Carville. Reese assigned an assistant, Skip Webb, to the campaign on a day-to-day basis, and immediately he and Carville began to antagonize each other. Carville was constantly inviting Webb to "hit the sidewalk" and fight. I don't think they ever came to blows, because Skip was terrified by the mad Cajun. He had never seen a person like him.

It was during this New Orleans orgy that something began to stir deep in my chest—a craving for something decent that didn't become merely titillating gossip. This sort of craving could not be satiated with whiskey or rich food. I was becoming a cultural chameleon, blending into the rusted wrought-iron lifestyle of an out-of-control hedonism. I wasn't helping working people as my father had wanted. I had made a fortune helping perpetuate a corrupt political system. Of course that is a generalization. There are actually many hardworking and well-intentioned political figures in Louisiana. But they are handcuffed by the hijinks of yesterday and a tolerance for corruption that permeates even into the press corps.

My father never said anything when he visited my house and saw my friends drink more whiskey and eat more gourmet food than he could afford to buy with a month of his meager retirement pay from Gulf Oil. He seemed happy with my acquisitions and my notoriety, but when I paid $50 for a bottle of wine or ordered smoked salmon from New York or Scotland, I always knew that he was stung by my excess and lack of direction. I wasn't the hawk-faced young labor lawyer in a back room of the union hall helping injured workers win dignity. And I couldn't change the tainted feeling in my chest by buying him and my mother expensive gifts or sending them to Israel to see where Jesus walked. I was a slick, Porsche-driving, thrill-seeking bon vivant. But I began to feel the stirring that would later lead me to Washington and a fight for a sort of separate peace, a shot at redemption.

As the battle raged for my soul, the political beat went on at a faster and faster pace. While the pundits and insiders were shocked with DiRosa's success in what they considered almost a freak accident, I had already seen the future and knew the outcome of the election. Peter Hart told me a few days before the vote that we would be in a runoff with Morial. I placed a $10,000 bet on the outcome, getting 2 to 1 odds from a bookie who usually based his line on information from the hacks of ancient political organizations who hung around the bars in the Irish Channel. They had always been right before. More important than the money I won, though, was the new appreciation I developed for the methodical, scientific approach to politics.

I watched Carville soak up new techniques. We had gone to school together in the DiRosa campaign, and he shared my respect for Hart's methods. After the mayoral race, James assembled a campaign team for Bubba Henry, a good-government reformer who was running for governor. I liked Bubba but could not work for him because of an old grudge between him and my partner. Carville was finally on his own. He assembled the best team I had ever seen in a political campaign. He had Hart as his pollster, the late Charlie Guggenheim to produce his media, and the great Mark Shields as a general consultant. It was a team that could have handled a presidential campaign without apology. Bubba's failed campaign reminded me of what I had read about one of Adlai Stevenson's races for the presidency. A woman had told him, "Oh, Governor Stevenson, you can't lose. You have all the intelligent people with you." Stevenson is reported to have responded, "Yes, madam, but I need a majority." Bubba had most of the thinking people with him. His campaign taught me another lesson: Even the best campaign team can't overcome a lack of campaign funds. I was a disciple of Guggenheim's. My own work in television during those years was based solely on the work done by the fine filmmaker. I studied his techniques for years. Every edit in his film *John F. Kennedy, 1917–1963* was etched into my brain.

The DiRosa campaign was the first stirring of my awakening, both personally and professionally. We defeated the powerful machine politician Nat Kieffer and earned a runoff position against Ernest "Dutch" Morial. Dutch was a Creole and lighter-skinned than DiRosa. He was the first African American to graduate from the all-white LSU Law School. Many of his classmates did not know that he was black.

The demographics of New Orleans, like most cities, had changed as whites fled to the suburban areas of Metairie, New Orleans East, and across the lake to Slidell, Covington, Mandeville, and other white enclaves. At this time, though, it was still almost impossible to elect a black in New Orleans. The great sitting mayor, Moon Landrieu, had brought blacks into city government in huge numbers, so whites were accustomed to seeing black officials. But still, Morial could count on only about 10 percent of the white vote, from the portion that was liberal and well educated.

Powerful black leaders in New Orleans headed organizations called BOLD (Black Officials for Leadership Development), COUP (Congress of Urban Politics), and SOUL (Southern Organization for Unified Leadership). Sherman Copelin, head of SOUL, one of the most powerful leaders, agreed to support DiRosa, as did Copelin's partner, Don Hubbard. With the support of these two powerful men, DiRosa more than overcame the 10 percent of the liberal white vote he would lose. Carville was busy working on get-out-the-vote operations. Our offices began to fill up with preachers and minor leaguers and would-be leaders looking for a part of the election-day cash. Beating Kieffer had been the hard part . . . or so we thought. Because of the inside information we had about our black votes, we knew we were going into the election with a comfortable lead.

And then Joe got drunk.

I was in Baton Rouge spending the weekend with my wife and children when the phone rang. Joe was raging. He said that some reporter had written a story accusing him of using racist terms. He said he had run into the reporter outside the bar of the Fairmont Hotel the night before, but he had never said any of the things that were reported in the morning *Times-Picayune*. He wanted a retraction. The reporter was Walter Isaacson, who became editor of *Time* magazine and is now head of news for the CNN television network. I called him and politely inquired about the story. I knew that Walter had impeccable integrity and was known for his accuracy. There was a sinking "Oh shit" feeling in my chest when Walter played the recording of the conversation over the telephone.

DiRosa, when asked about his election, had told Isaacson, "I got jungle bunnies coming out of the woodwork to help Morial. It looks like Idi Amin has sent in troops."

The only sensation I can compare to that would come years later, in 1987, when a *Miami Herald* reporter woke me early on Sunday morning for a quote about my client Gary Hart being caught with a beauty named Donna Rice.

I thanked Walter and gently put down the phone. It was over. The black leaders could no longer deliver votes. Even they didn't have the power to overcome those racist statements. Our 25 percent of the black vote vaporized.

A few days before the final election, three men showed up unexpectedly at the apartment. One of them was Mitch, the bookie who had taken my bet on the primary. The two men with him were jovial, and we all had a drink, but Mitch was shaking and tapped his foot incessantly.

"What we come to see you about, Mr. Raymond, is how you gonna bet on the election next week."

I looked over the top of my scotch. I really did not intend to bet, because I would not bet against my own candidate, and that was the only sure money. I had a small sense of propriety that had not yet leaked out onto the French Quarter streets.

"We can't take as big a bet as we did last time, but we can go for maybe five dimes straight up," Mitch said.

"I'm not going to bet on the election."

They looked at one another. After a long pause the second man spoke: "If you're not going to bet, would you help us set the line?"

"I don't think so."

"Look, we'll give you five grand if you tell us who wins and by how much."

"I can't do that."

They talked about how much they respected me and how I had proven they didn't understand elections and all they wanted was an opportunity to do business with a minimum of risk, like setting the line on a football game. I continued to refuse.

"Look, we'll be straight," Mitch said. "I need to get well on this election. I got a guy willing to bet one hundred big ones on the nig—ah, ah, black guy, and we want to know if we should take the bet. I know Joe will win, but I just want you to confirm it because I want to take the bet. I got a kid about to go to college. I need the money."

I held my ground, but as they left I felt terrible. Mitch was truly a small-timer who did a little nickel-and-dime booking on the side, like hundreds of others in New Orleans. He was in trouble with the people who covered his bets—possibly the two guys with him that day. My $10,000 bet had cost them $20,000. To make himself look good he had invited them to meet with me. I realized he had elevated himself in their eyes by knowing me. His face spoke quiet desperation.

I walked to the door and waited until they were almost to their car, then called for Mitch to come back for a minute.

He walked up to the top step and stopped. I was standing in the door. "Don't take that bet, Mitch." I quickly closed the door.

Of course DiRosa lost that election. Later, his explanation for his defeat was that his television wasn't good.

There is always depression after losing an election. That is to be expected. You exert your creative energies and your will to win. You lose sleep and live on the edge of an emotional abyss for months. Then it is over. After a loss the only consolation prize is the money you made during the campaign. A loss contributes nothing to the growth of your business or to your future. But this time there was something deeper. I was morally depleted after the DiRosa campaign. A great sadness consumed me that could not be quenched by hedonism or travel. Maybe one reason for the sadness was that I suddenly realized I didn't truly know what I was doing. My efforts were all creative and derivative of other hacks in Louisiana who knew less than I did. I had written my own rules and formed my own philosophy of winning. Some of my attitudes were even correct, but most of my victories, I realized, were mainly luck. Of course I was famous in my small pond and had been a part of many winning campaigns, but suddenly I saw that I had contributed far less to the victories than I thought. People convinced me that my brilliant media had won countless races. In accepting their praise, I stopped growing. I learned in the DiRosa race never to trust the instincts of even experienced politicians because they, too, were only perpetuating the errors they had learned from other politicians.

Hart and Reese gave me a glimpse at the science of political communications. Reese had a wonderful presentation on targeting that explained why we need not worry about all voters. His theory was that if you found in statistical research that green-haired and purple-nosed people tended to like the description of your candidate, you directed your campaign communications toward those people. If blue-eared people would not vote for your candidate under any circumstance, you ignored that group and didn't waste money talking to them. It seems elementary now, but then it was like a light coming on. I remembered my classes at LSU in rural sociology. Certain demographic groups shared common characteristics. We tend to live in neighborhoods of people like ourselves economically, socially, educationally, racially, and by age. In all of our American individuality we were exactly like our next-door neighbor, or at least an average of the entire neighborhood. Therefore, if Peter Hart could give me a description of target voters, all I had to do was find their neighborhoods and concentrate our resources where we had the best chance of harvesting votes. This lesson sent me back to the library for a reeducation in political science. I even retained an LSU professor, Dr. Donald Cundy, to brief me on the latest research being published on targeting, polling, and political motivation. I worked my way out of my depression by opening my mind to new ideas.

Then I went to Europe.

Still infatuated with the Lost Generation of Hemingway, Fitzgerald, Stein, and Dos Passos, after the unsuccessful DiRosa campaign I tried to escape. I leased an ancient cottage in rural Scotland. Called Burns Cottage because the famous poet was supposed to have bedded down there occasionally on his trek between Selkirk and Dumfries, it was warmed only by a small coal fireplace. For lights it had an electric meter that required the insertion of fifty-pence coins. There was a fine old desk at a west window looking out on a stone wall where peacocks held court. Soon I was helping a Scottish farmer rebuild the wall on the Moffat Water and catching tiny trout from the streams. I cooked my own meals, hung out in the Black Bull pub (where Bobby Burns had scratched his name into the window behind his drinking stall with a diamond ring), and occasionally caught the train to London for a day. I began a novel that was published in 1991 as *Cottonwood*. After a few months I felt restored enough to return to the States and to business. However, while I was gone, my partner had signed us onto a new campaign, Paul Hardy's run for governor, even though we had agreed before I left that we would not represent him. I had misgivings about his ability to govern. But I had an obligation to live up to the contract negotiated by Gus Weill. Like me, he had a child to educate and doctor bills to pay. I can't really blame him.

Despite my misgivings, the carnival started again. As per our mutual agreement, my partner withdrew to his couch, spending hours staring at his cigar smoke and ministering to his sick wife, and I immersed myself in a campaign that I didn't want.

It was 1979. Things had already begun to change in the campaign business. I was besieged with calls from pollsters who wanted this off-year work. (Unlike all but four other states, Louisiana has its elections in odd-numbered years. New Jersey, Mississippi, Kentucky, and Virginia join Louisiana as off-year oases in the parched electoral dry seasons.) The most persistent caller was a New Yorker who spoke about two hundred words a minute named Dick Morris. After about fifteen calls he began to threaten that if I didn't hire him soon, he would go with another candidate and defeat us.

I wasn't impressed by that line, only amused, but one day Weill walked into my office.

"Why don't we give the Jewish kid a chance?"

I acquiesced. It wasn't because Morris was Jewish, I don't even think it had even occurred to me. It was because my senior partner asked me to and he seldom interfered in my campaign work. I think he simply got tired of the phone ringing

I now believe that Dick Morris has been one of the most significant figures in politics and a major influence on political campaigning in America. It's probably not too much to say that this one man's persuasive and unrelenting drive, fueled by necessity of feeding his hedonistic lifestyle, has helped endanger the very fabric of democracy. He symbolizes, in one five-foot-six-inch package of insecurities, everything that has gone wrong with American politics. It was Morris who broke down the rest of the wall between campaigns and governing.

Two days after I agreed on the phone to hire him, Dick stepped into my office in Baton Rouge. Soon I discovered he was just another hustler who wanted to make a fast buck from my clients. Dick was a slim, kinetic, frenetic, sweaty huckster overdressed in a cheap wool suit from Orchard Street—it looked like bad felt that had long since cast off its creases. His mouth moved almost as rapidly as his hands, which seemed constantly to be trying to pick individual words out of the air. Had he been raised a thousand miles south, he might have been a door-to-door Bible salesman. Because of his size, he could efficiently curl up in a coach seat of an airplane on cheap red-eye flights and hop from city to city hawking his political services. That made him a potent selling machine. His sales approach was the same as an LSU fraternity boy I knew who believed that if you asked enough girls for sex, you would score a predictable percentage of times. Dick scored. But I wasn't seduced. In only a few minutes I was amused, impressed, and insulted almost simultaneously. When he burst into my office I was listening to *Turandot,* a Puccini opera. I often did that in the late afternoon just before cocktail hour.

"You listen to opera?"

As he leafed through the dozen or so albums of opera next to the stereo. I explained that I didn't know a lot about opera but had spent the past five years developing a taste for the music. He was astonished.

"I mean you're a southerner. I didn't know southerners listened to opera."

Dick Morris had grown up in a rent-controlled luxury apartment overlooking Central Park, son of a prominent real estate attorney father and a mother in publishing. He had all of the intellectual snobbery of an only child who had been taught that Manhattan was the center of the universe and that southerners were ignorant backwoods bigots who could be played like a Steinway by a smart New Yorker. Rednecks are accustomed to such assumptions and look at those smart Yankees with practiced tolerance.

"Sure, Dick, I can even read whole books without moving my lips."

Morris is a quick study. It took him only seconds to realize he had insulted me. He began machine-gunning compliments about my reputation, which he said had spread far and wide. His voice would have been pure cane syrup except for its brittle New York precision. I still prefer the sound of hominy grits rolling out like honey, caressing and prolonging words. It is my redneck prejudice.

In the next few years I came to know Dick well. He made me laugh. He made me think. I even liked him. Hell, I still like him, although I should not. Dick has a roaring intellect, a quick wit, and the best memory I have ever seen. He would rattle off dozens of possible scripts for commercials. They sounded vaguely familiar, and I found later that Tony Schwartz, the legendary radio producer and creator of the infamous "Daisy" spot for President Lyndon Johnson, had written them all. (The ad, pulled after only one airing, showed a little girl picking daisies while an announcer counted down from ten to zero—and at zero a mushroom cloud filled the sky. LBJ's voice then intoned how "we must love each other, or we must die." The ad was vicious, brilliant, and effective. It never mentioned Republican presidential nominee Barry Goldwater by name—but it didn't have to. Goldwater had talked about the tactical use of nuclear weapons in Vietnam, and the spot was supposed to make Americans ponder whose finger they really wanted on the button.)

Dick Morris shared his mentor's instinct for the jugular. He surpassed Schwartz, and almost everyone else in politics, in energy and creative ability. Dick's only failing was he knew less about polling than I did. This was odd, because Dick passed himself off as a pollster. But he would make major campaign decisions based on interviews with only twenty or thirty people. The reliability of polls is based on the accuracy of random selection and probability. As the total number of people interviewed comes down, so does the reliability. Dick would write poll questionnaires that would test three or four message paragraphs to the exclusion of all other possibilities. In effect, what we were doing was testing which of Dick's shoot-from-the-hip messages or Tony Schwartz adaptations scored best. He would explain that if we used Paragraph A we would win 37 percent of the vote but Paragraph B would give us 42 percent. This is, of course, junk political science, and I am confident that Morris's "research" was responsible for the failure of at least two great politicians—Texas governor Mark White in 1986 and Bill Clinton in Arkansas when he was defeated after his first two-year term. Clinton made some Morris-inspired decisions that angered the Arkansas voters. The irony is that Clinton then hired another pollster, Peter Hart, to do his first reelection. When he lost he went back to Morris for most of his career. They were a great team.

During Clinton's first term as governor, Morris produced a poll proving that more than half of the voters approved of an increase in the auto license tag tax. Because Morris at that time seldom carefully examined the intricate cross tabs of demographic information in a poll, he failed to see that most of those who said they were against the tax belonged to the Clinton's base.* Therefore, when Clinton embraced the tax he lost many dependable Democratic voters and was defeated.

A few years later, in 1985, when the South was still hot on the issue of education, Morris convinced Governor Mark White to institute "no pass,

---

*Cross tabulations are the guts of a poll. They allow the reader to view the reactions of each demographic group to each question. Poll total numbers can be misleading. Though the auto tag tax appeared to win a majority, the cross tabs revealed that most of the support came from hard-core Republicans who would not vote for a Democrat. A close examination of the cross tabs would have shown that the issue was a losing one for a Democrat and a winning one for a Republican.

no play" legislation originally cooked up by a Ross Perot–led blue-ribbon commission on education. This simply meant that children with a failing grade could not participate in extracurricular activities like band or, more to the point in Texas, football. White, determined to distinguish his administration with improved education, like Clinton, embraced the poll without enough information. It is tempting to say that a nerdy New Yorker like Morris, who never spent any time with rednecks, didn't know Texas culture, and never played a down of high school football, was out of his element.

But the truth is that the mistake Morris made was, for a political pollster, even more basic than that: Democratic governors get stars in their eyes when a poll shows them improving their position with Republicans and this "no pass, no play" legislation was more popular with Republicans than Democrats. At least it was briefly. Soon all hell erupted in Texas when star football players found themselves locked outside the stadium. The hysterical Texas football fans of both parties took it out on a fine governor, White. He was defeated when he ran for reelection.

But Morris kept on. He is truly an amazing salesman. When we used a message he had prescribed and the numbers in the next poll didn't go up, he would shrug his shoulders and immediately come up with a new plan and new paragraphs, in a new poll, wowing the candidate, who seldom ever questioned what had happened in the failed attempt. Later, when I worked with Governor Clinton, he was so enamored of Morris that he would not allow even a word to be changed in a message paragraph and would not hear of independent interpretation of the cross tabs and core data. In fact, Morris seldom gave us cross tabs or data. Usually he came in with a memo explaining which message worked and guaranteeing results. Despite his weaknesses as a pollster, I am convinced that he helped create a presidency and was terribly important in Clinton's reelection. Though he seems to have faded in America, Dick is in great demand in foreign elections and is back on a winning track.

The 1979 Hardy campaign had all the potential for wackiness of the Jimmie Davis catastrophe. But I had changed. Corruption was no longer funny, and casual racism angered me. Hardy was no overt racist, but I was bored with the Louisiana politician's tired old retread stories from Huey and Earl Long. I thought I would slap the next person who tried to mimic a gravel-voiced Earl Long. Edwin Edwards with his shiny suits, widely admired libido, and taste for high-rolling gambling was godlike among political hacks.

Louisiana laughed when Edwin said on television that he would be reelected unless he got caught in bed with a dead girl or a live boy. But I thought it was sick. I was starting to see the cost of all these shenanigans to working-class Louisianians—to the people my father cared about. The corruption Louisiana found so cute kept business from expanding into the state. No CEO wanted to live or work in insecurity, knowing that on a whim, corrupt politicians could change the rules for doing business so as to benefit another company or their friends. No wife of a CEO wanted to move her children into a school system that had been systematically looted by corruption until it was the worst in the nation. Most of all, I was tired of laughing at misdeeds. In fact, many people were proud of their state's rakish reputation.

The tolerance for corruption had even permeated the press corps. They weren't individually corrupt. But they had been immersed in corruption for so long they no longer could distinguish it when it was in front of their faces. One reporter who exposed a scandal of illegal parking permits at the New Orleans airport had an illegal parking permit. He wasn't corrupt. He had just grown insensitive to it. The best journalism was done by reporters who had come from out-of-state or who were young enough that they had not become part of Louisiana's chuckle-at-corruption attitude.

When Congressman Gillis Long was asked if he was for good government, he replied with a wink, "I'm for pretty good government." Though Gillis was straight, he knew his public loved it. They laughed while the potholes grew in their highways and people got sick ingesting toxins from their drinking water and the schools became, unbelievably, even worse. Senator John Breaux denied selling votes for campaign contributions. He said he "just rented them." He was using acceptable Louisiana humor that the rest of the nation didn't understand. Senator Breaux is a great politician.

Our candidate for governor, Paul Hardy, thought it would be a macho stunt if he went into the black Desire Housing Project in New Orleans and spent the night with a family. The area was a festering sore of drugs, murder, and poverty. On the surface, sleeping in the projects and showing concern for those poor people seemed a good idea, and I was on hand with cameras the next day when he walked out of the development on a humid, warm morning wearing his macho leather jacket. The press gathered around him as he defined people in the projects in racist terms and didn't even understand he was doing it. "These people are just like us. They love their children and keep themselves clean." Racism—even unintended—

bothered me as much as the corruption. Racism was so deeply ingrained that Hardy was innocent because he simply didn't understand. I stood in the back of the crowd listening and knew at that moment I had to get the hell out of Louisiana. Finally, I had reached saturation.

But the show wasn't quite over. I couldn't just desert a campaign. We did research and found that many people did not think Hardy was smart enough to hold the lofty office of governor. He resented that characterization and said, "You think you are so smart. I'll tell you how smart I am. I went all the way through USL [University of Southwestern Louisiana] and I have never read a book all the way through." I tried not to react, but I countered the perception regarding his lack of intellect by shooting commercials with him talking to environmentalists, engineers, and scientists. I scripted short, poignant questions for him to ask. Then we spent hundreds of thousands of dollars running the commercials. He jumped to first place in the polls.

By this time I was determined to leave Louisiana. The only remaining question was when. My new company logo was already designed and sitting on my desk. However, I still felt some insecurity about my ability to make it in Washington. As usual, Weill and I had more campaigns than we could handle. Because I was buried in Louisiana work and needed help quickly, I reached out to a man I had once met with Shelly Beychok, a New York producer named David Sawyer. Not only would he relieve me of my production load, he would serve as a clinic for me to test my own ability. I wanted to watch each step of his process in getting a candidate ready to film. David was impressive. He was smooth and engaging, and his work had the highest production values I had seen outside of that done by Charles Guggenheim, the man who had made the marvelous John Kennedy memorial film for the Kennedy Library.

For Hardy, Sawyer wanted to do speech coaching and to dress the candidate. The candidate turned the speech coaching into a party and arrived in New York with a group of Cajuns looking to be entertained. Sawyer had wonderful resources; he secured reservations for the group at America's best restaurant at that time, Lutece, and managed to get orchestra tickets to the hottest Broadway show, *Ain't Misbehavin'*. I joined Tommy Mathieu, the "money man" for the campaign, and we ducked the group and had cocktails at the Polo Lounge in the Westbury Hotel and then went to "21" for dinner.

Tommy was a bold and brash north Louisiana oilman decked out in handmade maroon alligator-skin cowboy boots tagged with his initials. He sported a diamond-and-18-carat-gold tiepin in the shape of an oil derrick. He was a decent man in spite of all this. In his circles in Houston, Dallas, and Shreveport, Tommy looked like most of his oil friends. In New York, however, he stood out.

The next morning I went downstairs for breakfast and found the Cajun delegation sitting around a large table. When I inquired as to how they had enjoyed their evening, Hardy said, "I wish you wouldn't have asked." He went on to explain that the food at Lutece was terrible—the chef needed to go to Pat's in Henderson, Louisiana, to learn how to cook. (Pat's is known for its piles of fried catfish, shrimp, frog legs, crawfish, and gumbo—satisfying food, but it could never be defined as haute cuisine.) When I asked about the musical, a woman at the table said, "That was worse. It was nothing but a bunch of black people dancing. I can see that on Bourbon Street sidewalks any night."

I separated myself from the group and took Tommy, still in a daze over the reactions of the Louisianians to the evening, to the Russian Tea Room, where he gave the maitre d' $100 for the corner booth in the back. We drank wine and met the Cajuns later outside the Stage Deli, where they waited in their two limousines to escape to the airport. They did not like New York. They had bags of tee shirts with cute slogans and other souvenirs from a shop across the street. I tried to make conversation.

"I see you did some shopping."

One of the ladies snorted. "Well, if you call it that. Lucky we found that shop across the street. We couldn't find anyplace to shop in this city."

I was bewildered.

"You're on Seventh Avenue. Two blocks over is Fifth Avenue. Many people think that may be the best shopping in the world."

"Nobody told us. We went the other way. Besides, I don't want to be out on these streets without a gun."

I stumbled away from the car. I could see tears coming out of Tom Mathieu's eyes as he tried not to laugh.

The Sawyer contract was a complete success. Hiring David filled in another blank in my "invent as you go" education. I had been self-schooled in production, and David's crews were the first top-quality professionals I had encountered. His attention to detail and selection of talented people in every position on the crew impressed me as examples of the finer arts of film communication. I was interested in the amount of preproduction time David spent before he shot film. He sent a producer to Louisiana for several days to scout locations. Then, the day before we were to begin shooting, the film crew arrived. Until this time, I had used only Louisiana crews who were talented but had come out of television instead of film. I would soon discover that the techniques were entirely different.

Television is slam-bam shooting with little preparation and almost no additional lighting except for the bright primary lights placed close to the camera. Sawyer, however, brought in a "gaffer"—the film name for a lighting director—and a moving van filled with exotic lights and equipment. My first reaction was impatience and annoyance at the hours the crew spent lighting one location. He had a New York makeup artist, a sound man who noticed every slight noise that might distract the viewer, and a cameraman, Bob Fiore, who could put a camera on his shoulder and move as though on ball bearings, ducking and weaving through the people gathered around the candidate and always being in the right place when the candidate was on our message target. He not only shot film, he listened. Sawyer gave Bob a message briefing before we began. The entire professional crew worked like a team of ballet dancers, always moving the light, camera, and sound to best advantage. It was an intensive three-day class in film production. And I learned. I made an appointment to review the rough television spots and pay David ten days later in New York. It was to be one of the last times I would see my friend Tommy.

Tommy was originally from Monroe, Louisiana. He owned oil wells and oilfield equipment, drove Rolls Royces, flew a large twin-engine airplane, and overindulged a beautiful mistress in Houston. He bought her a business there and was delighted when she showed a profit. He seemed close to his wife and children, though I never remember meeting them until his funeral. The mistress, I can't even remember her name, was just another example of his thirst for life by the barrel. It was my job to show her New York.

For some reason Tommy and I left his plane behind and flew Delta to Kennedy. When we stepped outside the terminal, a black limousine filled with red roses and Dom Perignon champagne met us. We uncorked a bottle and drove to LaGuardia Airport to meet his girlfriend. I had never seen her, but she was immediately identifiable as she stepped through the doors. Not only was she uncommonly beautiful, she was a sparkling Milky Way of diamonds and gold. Her dress, even in an era of short dresses, was a little too short on one end and a little too low on the other. Impatient people rushing for cabs paused briefly to study her flawless lines, ripely bulging flesh, and fireworks sparkle. The driver almost slammed his finger in the car door peering down her dress.

We were the best of Big Louisiana and Big Texas combined. Being slightly champagne drunk made it amusing, and I was glad to be there as an observer and confidant. I guess had I been sober I would have felt a tad conspicuous. But even after two more bottles of champagne that had begun to taste slightly of roses, I was self-conscious when we pulled up in front of the Pierre Hotel. The girl I knew only as "Sweetie" did her best to get out of the limo without exposing acres of flesh but mostly lost the battle despite the southern female trick of smiling at your gentleman friend to divert his attention. The rest of the pack gathered around the limo were obviously not gentlemen.

I gave the couple the hour and a half they requested to "relax a little" before lunch, then met them at the bar. Our plans were to review the commercials, pay David, and go to "21" for lunch. When they arrived, though, the plans changed. She said she had always heard of the Stage Deli and wanted to eat there instead of at "21." And she wanted to do it before we paid David because she was "famished." I asked her if she minded leaving some of the diamonds in the hotel safe, and she complied, though Tommy thought she looked much better with them. Walking to the Stage, I asked Tommy if he had remembered to bring a check so we could go by David's office immediately after lunch. "No," he said. "I don't have a check, I brought cash."

"You brought $90,000 in cash?"

"No, I couldn't remember exactly how much it was, so I brought $110,000."

"Where is it?"

"Oh, I left it in the room in a briefcase on the bed."

I was stunned. "You left $110,000 on your bed? Let's go back and get it."

"No," Tommy answered, "I don't want to walk all the way back there, and besides, the briefcase is locked." He thought for a minute. "That's a big hotel. Why would a thief pick out my suite instead of hundreds of others?"

I guess Tommy had not noticed the impression we had made getting out of the limo.

Lunch was great fun and we attracted still more attention. When we got back to the hotel the briefcase was on the bed. Tommy unlocked it and proved to me that I was paranoid. The cash was in neat stacks of hundreds, sealed with paper bands. It was all there. David Sawyer, however, was perplexed. He didn't know what to do with the mound of money heaped on his desk. This had never happened before. He had never worked in Louisiana before.

"You know I'll have to declare this?" David asked.

"Sure, son, do anything you want to with it. Just give me a receipt."

The little caper with Tommy was my last such adventure of my Louisiana years. In 1981, I was doing business in Congressman Long's office on Capitol Hill in Washington when an aide told me Tommy had died of leukemia. I was immediately filled with guilt. He had been reaching out to me, and I had pushed him aside in my haste to leave Louisiana. I had brushed aside two or three invitations to fly to South America with him in his new airplane. He wanted to go dove hunting, he said, but as I look back, Tommy just wanted to be going somewhere exotic, doing something, anything. As I flew my small plane to Monroe for his funeral, I had a lot of time to think. Finally I understood that he knew he was dying and was trying to cram as much life as he could into his final days with newer and better toys, flashier women, and more exotic trips. But as I flew halfway across the country, I wondered if that's what everyone in our insular little world was doing.

More was always better.

Loud was preferred to quiet.

Anything bland was a sin.

Tommy looked down at his fists filled with money and asked, "What do we do now?" He squeezed life until it hurt, with the oilman's knowledge that good fortune was transitory. There were no cultural reference points with subtle meanings built into club ties, symbols, or generations of wisdom. He was living life one day at a time, learning as he went, experimenting and never afraid to fail. He wasn't evil, he was simply a product of a culture that lived by the same rules. Tommy was good. Tommy was Louisiana.

For that reason, my time with him was an appropriate ending to my Louisiana days. He was one of them and a part of what I liked, admired, disdained, and hated. His corruption was ingrained and innocently guileless. He was bighearted and generous and had a gift for friendship. His excesses were of the Louisiana oilman, new-money sort, filled with diamond Rolex watches and cars with personalized license plates.

When I left Louisiana in 1980, about a year after Hardy lost, I was close to falling off the edge. I learned political consulting as Tommy had learned oil drilling and big money, with some of the same disregard for rules and convention.

I needed a change, and change came. This time my luck came in the form of two totally different men, William Hamilton and Richard Morris.

When Paul Hardy lost in 1979, my partner and I were asked to take over media for the campaign of Louis Lambert, the winning Democrat who would now face a Republican, David Treen, in the general election. Morris was out of the picture after the Hardy loss. Lambert already had a famous pollster, and Morris was still only a hustler on the make. The retiring governor, Edwin Edwards, who was term-limited out of running again, ran the state's Democratic Party as though it were his own. He determined that the work of Democratic consultant Bob Squier lacked an understanding of Louisiana. I didn't necessarily agree, but Weill and I accepted the job happily when they fired Squier.

I had lost with Hardy—and I would subsequently lose with Lambert—but if I was falling, I was falling up. Morris and Hamilton changed my life. Bill was a southerner who had conquered Washington. He and I decided that it was time for me to do the same. Morris was a relentless salesman and needed a media producer.

Bill knew more about interpreting poll data in 1980 than almost all political pollsters and media consultants know to this day. He gladly spent hours with me in late-night bars discussing how the pieces of a campaign could fit together and work in harmony. His advice didn't stop with numbers. It included explaining how to put together constituencies of labor unions, blacks, teachers, and hard-core party activists. He knew how to stroke candidates' egos without compromising the integrity or meaning of his data. He was a straight arrow who could sit in a meeting and not be splashed by the corruption around him—and yet he was an insider.

In contrast, Morris operated out of his hip pocket, often showing up with nothing more than a few numbers written on a legal pad. Though I am critical of Morris's techniques and occasionally his ethics, I still appreciate his putting me into the campaigns of some of America's most successful politicians. Along with my campaign for Russell Long that I did with Bill in 1980, I produced television for a Morris client, Lieutenant Governor Zell Miller of Georgia, who was running for a Senate seat against the Democratic incumbent, Herman Talmadge.*

I made some badly needed money from this and other Morris contacts, but it was Hamilton and Matt Reese who discovered me, taught me, and allowed me to leave Louisiana. Although I was involved in the Lambert campaign for only a few weeks, Hamilton and I became friends, and beyond our friendship, I earned his respect. He recommended me to a Senate campaign in Florida for a Democrat named Bill Gunter, and I made every effort to live up to his billing. I used this campaign to open my new business. We defeated a seated senator, Richard Stone, in the Democratic primary but were upset in the general election by a Republican named Paula Hawkins (and her chameleon political consultant, Dick Morris) in the great Reagan wave of 1980. A day after winning the primary, the affable Gunter called me into his office and told me to take some time off. "We're running against a crazy, Mormon, Republican woman, and none of those things have ever been elected in Florida." We just didn't see the Reagan revolution coming out of the western mountains. But with Gunter, I had reached outside Louisiana and was never again going to be satisfied living next to the Mississippi River. It was the only time I would ever lose and feel that I had won. Even in defeat I had attracted the attention of Washington. I didn't know it then, but defeating an incumbent U.S. Senator in a primary election is almost impossible.

About the time I went to work in Florida in 1980, I received a call from Kris Kirkpatrick, the chief of staff for Senator Russell Long. I was hired to produce media for the Long reelection campaign. That campaign was high profile and was in part won with a documentary called *The Fight for Louisiana*, which I still measure with the best of my work. After Long was elected, suddenly I had a Washington following of my own.

*Miller and I had instant chemistry but didn't work together again until 2000, when he was appointed to fill the office of deceased Republican senator Paul Coverdell. Zell told Governor Roy Barnes he would accept the brief appointment if the governor could talk me into handling his election campaign three months later. With a powerful feeling of obligation to Zell for having lost in 1980 and to Governor Barnes out of friendship, I moved into an apartment in Atlanta. This was one I could not afford to lose. We won with 58 percent of the vote.

Weill and I, after many years of partnership, went our separate ways. He had given me my start and promoted me into stardom for various reasons before I was ready or capable of it. But I was ready now. In just six months, I had garnered recognition in Washington. The *Washington Post* even called me a "rising star."

In 1980, however, the field was small. In those days, not every out-of-work political hack in the country had started hanging out a shingle calling himself a campaign consultant. It's only a slight exaggeration to say that Bob Squier was my only major competitor and that we divided up the juiciest Senate races between us. We were friends as well as competitors, and we were on top.

Washington, D.C., is a city of power. In 1982, I was the Delta Airlines seatmate of the CEO of a major telecommunications company. We had a couple of cocktails and he was lamenting that his was one of the largest private employers in Washington—and he didn't even count. He was ignored by the *Post* and never invited to the A-list parties. My advice was simple: move to New York, where money counts. In Washington the currency is power. And power blew open the doors for me in the capital and allowed me to start a new consulting business without any downtime for start-up.

My ticket to ride was Russell Long.

United States Senator Russell Long was chairman of the powerful Finance Committee and respected by all. He was a "senator's senator." Long was a master of Capitol Hill, but because I came from outside the Washington Beltway, it took me a long time to understand the significance of having such a powerful and decent friend. For a while I thought my own wit and intellect had paved the way for my success.

Long was the son of the historic Louisiana populist Huey Long. Yet when Bill Hamilton took his first poll for Russell Long, he found that most people in the state did not know of this kinship, even in a time when Huey was a reconstructed hero because of the Pulitzer Prize–winning biography by T. Harry Williams, *Huey Long*. Like many senators of his generation in the South, Russell Long had seldom been challenged for reelection. As a result, he had lost contact with the people of Louisiana. They, in short, didn't know him. Hamilton suggested that we needed to put Russell Long in context by explaining the link with his father. Long, at least at first, was reluctant to bring Huey into the documentary. I never understood it, but I guess he had been forced to run on his own for so long without ever mentioning his father he was finding it difficult to change. In fact, he often seemed embarrassed when his father's name was mentioned.

Our opponent was a bright right-wing conservative named Woody Jenkins, who has made a career of being defeated by Louisiana icons. Two years previously he had run against the junior senator, J. Bennett Johnston, and didn't really threaten him but gave him a big scare. All candidates run scared, even if they are as secure as Johnston was then. Therefore, at the advice of Johnston, Long didn't just swat at Jenkins like he was an insect, he brought out heavy artillery. And my conduct in Long's war against Jenkins distinguished me enough to roll into Washington with banners flying.

Jenkins was an attractive media candidate who had played around the edges of communications by owning a small advertising agency and a weekly newspaper. His main media vehicle was the thirty-minute program that had once been so popular in American politics. Though the programs were poorly produced, they were effective enough that we could not allow them to go unchallenged. At a meeting in Long's Baton Rouge farmhouse, we decided to produce a thirty-minute piece of our own, so that when Jenkins went on the air we could immediately respond. Hamilton gave me a list of issue points to cover and admonished me to tie the senator closely to his father.

We found that Jenkins was scheduled to run his first program seventeen days after our meeting at the farm. I had a certain clarity, almost a vision, that those seventeen days would be the most important in my professional life. As Hamilton spoke and the Russell Long kitchen cabinet droned on about the tactics of the upcoming campaign, I made mental notes of things that had to be done immediately. I could truly hear distant drums. I decided then to produce our program on film in various locations to give it the most contrast with Jenkins's video project. Film is warmer and has a better feel of reality. And because I wanted this to be a showcase for my production skills, I wanted the best help money could buy.

After the meeting, Hamilton and I retired to a bar. While he ordered drinks I was on the phone contracting the entire crew that had worked for David Sawyer in the Hardy campaign. The peerless hand-held cameraman Bob Fiore would shoot; the now-prominent lighting director Michael Barrow would be the gaffer; Big Harry Lapham would fly in from New York to record sound. Bob hired a woman from Washington, Lillian Brown, to do makeup. Lillian would later work for me on a Bill Clinton campaign—and ended up in the White House to make up the president for all of his on-camera appearances. That was the kind of talent we assembled for Russell Long's movie. It was expensive, because these folks were pros and knew how good they were. But even this experienced crew had doubts that we could write, produce, shoot, edit, and complete a thirty-minute documentary in sixteen days. The clock was ticking.

The next day I flew with Long to Washington, and on the third day my crew met in his office, where I did a series of interviews while glancing at the Hamilton poll in my lap. I didn't have time for research about Long or even to write a script. That would evolve, I thought, out of the interviews. We shot one day in his office and the next day in his Watergate apartment. Long was good. The interviews were laced with wonderful stories and stood by themselves. His wife, Carolyn, was a lovely woman who helped in every way she could. After we finished a breakfast scene with her, I put the cameraman in the front seat of Russell Long's car and climbed in the back with a lighting man with a hand-held battery light, and we continued the interview as he drove by the familiar monuments. I hovered over the sound man and assistant cameraman, pushing them for extra seconds in my day even as they changed film and tape. I was in a race for my future and I knew it.

The ticking of the clock grew louder in my head. Occasionally Harry Lapham would ask, "Are you sure you can't get a two-week extension on this project?" No, Harry, I could not. This was my big chance, and I wasn't going to blow a deadline.

I needed to impress Louisiana with Long's power. When John F. Kennedy assumed the presidency and was asked about his plans for fiscal reform, he responded that he would have to ask Senator Long before he proposed any legislation. Long was truly king of the Hill, and in Louisiana he was being threatened by a man who wouldn't have qualified to serve on his staff. My film was about power, and I asked Kris Kirkpatrick and Senator Long to contact some well-known names in the Senate who might give testimonials. I wanted men recognized as powerful to talk about the greater power of Louisiana's Russell Long. I believed that people in Louisiana understood power and even had an exaggerated sense of the importance of government in their lives.

We all swung into action. Long picked up the telephone and Kris and I moved quickly to find a room for filming. Everything was double time. Tick-tock. Minutes later I had the crew of ten setting lights and a camera in a conference room down the hall. We didn't have to wait long. Soon there was a parade of political superstars waiting outside. Senators Daniel Patrick Moynihan of New York, Sam Nunn of Georgia, and the timeless John Stennis of Mississippi all agreed to be filmed. Others offered to help in any way they could. One of the great surprises came when Republican senator Bob Dole asked to be filmed to help his friend Russell. I had this inspiration of having Dole and Moynihan sit together on a sofa and argue about why Russell Long was the most powerful man in government after President Carter.

This type of collegial understanding and friendship is rare in Washington these days. Sure, Ted Kennedy and Orrin Hatch have a friendship—off the Senate floor when they're not beating each other's brains out on the issues. But such friendships rarely transcend partisanship in today's Congress, and are often a casualty of it. Moreover, just plain good manners seem in short supply in the halls where John Stennis once comported himself like such a gentleman.

There are many culprits. The Republicans like to blame Bill Clinton for the decline in simple civility; my side blames Newt Gingrich. Surely both those men have a lot to answer for: The Clintons decried the "politics of personal destruction" while practicing it. Gingrich went on a self-proclaimed crusade to bring down House Speaker Jim Wright—and succeeded. Then, in 1994, Gingrich's Republican Party won a single election cycle in the House, giving them a narrow majority in Congress, and he ridiculously declared himself the leader of a "revolution."

But despite the outsized egos of Washington's most colorful antagonists during the decade of the nineties, the true reasons for the systemic incivility run much deeper than Gingrich or Clinton. The reasons include: districts so gerrymandered that Democratic congressmen never need consider the wishes of Republican constituents—and vice versa; a 24-hour-a-day news cycle dominated by talking heads whose only currency is conflict and who have no institutional memories and no sense of discretion; single-interest groups who exert ferocious pressure on the two major parties, thus pulling the Democrats to the left and Republicans to the right and leaving the vast majority of Americans in the middle without adequate representation; and, finally, we consultants—we too have a role in the decline of comity. We run campaigns of such vitriol that neither the candidates nor the electorate can ever quite move on when it's over.

I certainly understand that Washington cannot return to the days when three of my fellow Texans, President Dwight D. Eisenhower, House Speaker Sam Rayburn, and Senate majority leader Lyndon Johnson got together in the Oval Office in the afternoons and ran the country over their bourbon and branch water. Nor am I saying that showing good manners is a substitute for showing backbone in matters of principle. Actually, I believe they go together. In 1954, John Stennis was among the Democratic senators tapped by Lyndon Johnson to investigate Senator Joseph McCarthy, the notorious Red-baiting Republican from Wisconsin. It was a shrewd choice. When it was over—and McCarthy was finally put in his place—Stennis's manners had won the day over McCarthy's brutishness.

As George Reedy, a Johnson aide, put it in Merle Miller's oral history of LBJ, "It had never occurred to me that anybody as gentle as John Stennis could actually get up in a cross-floor debate and not only hold his own, but mop up the floor with an Irish brawler like Joe McCarthy."

It's a lesson I wish more of today's senators knew.

As I interviewed senators, as I ate, as I paced behind the camera, the film began to take shape in my mind. As I absorbed the comments of the senators, I knew that if Washington was about power, filming in Louisiana would have to be about the human side of Long. Frantically we made Delta reservations and rushed to National Airport. Within hours my crew was on the ground in the piney woods of north Louisiana, shooting film with rural sheriffs and good ole boys sitting on the porch of a redneck hunting lodge drinking beer, chewing tobacco, and telling stories. I got there an hour before Senator Long and opened two cases of beer for the older men who sat in rocking chairs on the end of a long porch. Michael, the lighting man, pasted yellow boards to the roof of the porch so that when he bounced our powerful lights off of them it bathed the scene in a golden afternoon glow. I talked to the men and loosened them up by listening to their stories. An hour and four or five beers later, they were ready for Long when he rolled up. The tub of beer hidden just out of sight was the perfect lubricant for a session of storytelling that would have made a film by itself. The senator, who didn't drink, began telling stories about his father and about Huey's brother Earl, who had also been governor of Louisiana. (The colorful "Uncle Earl" was the subject of a 1989 Paul Newman movie called *Blaze*, the title being taken from the name of Earl's longtime paramour, New Orleans stripper Blaze Starr.) The only problem was that my hardworking camera-man's lens sometimes jiggled because he was laughing so hard.

"My Uncle Earl had a way of talking, you know. He had an opponent, and Earl never said anything really bad about his opponents. He said, 'My opponent is a fine man. Has fine children and fine parents. G-o-o-d people. He's a Ford dealer. If I wanted to buy a car, I'd buy it from him. But if I wanted to buy two cars, I'd go somewhere else because the deal would be too big.'"

Soon the old men on the porch were telling their own stories about the Longs, and the senator became better and better as he relaxed. I simply stood to the side and watched it unfold.

"Uncle Earl used to say this: 'You know how you can tell that fellow's lying? Just watch his lips. If they're moving, he's lying.'" The porch scene was as warm as the light created for us. It would connect Long with the working people of the state, reestablish his Louisiana roots, and make a fine contrast with the sprayed-down, helmet-haired newcomer Jenkins.

I soon realized in my dealing with Russell Long, as I would later with other senators of his generation, that the institution of the Senate was far more important to him than any political party. That's why Bob Dole volunteered to help a Democrat. Russell Long understood the importance of the traditions he had inherited and the impact his decisions in the Finance Committee could have on the country and the world. He did not take his responsibilities lightly. And he measured the ability of his fellow senators but refused to even bruise the character of the Senate by naming them.

"You know," he mused in one of our Washington scenes, "sooner or later you learn to know who you can count on up here, who to turn to when you need something done." He was peering beyond my camera into the past as though he had forgotten film was running.

In 1980 the charismatic ex-governor of California, Ronald Reagan, was enthusiastically embraced by America. He swept a Republican majority into the Senate, and Long lost his powerful chairmanship. (Chairmen are chosen by the party in power.) Loyal to my party and my client, I tried to console him and offered my condolences in a tone that might have suggested death.

Long only smiled at me and explained in an almost fatherly manner: "Oh, don't worry about that. Bob Dole will take over, and he's a good man. We can do business with him." Dole, Bentsen, Stennis, Nunn, Moynihan, and a host of others from both parties represented a dying generation of comradeship and decorum in the Senate. They have been replaced in large part by petty partisans who care more about their party than about the institutions of the Senate or even about their country. I always think of Long's gentlemanly explanation after losing to Dole and wonder how American voters allowed giants to be replaced by midgets.

Much of my interview with Long involved the place of the Senate in America and the responsibilities that go with the job. He seldom even mentioned political parties. Because the average American's vision is only about as far as his own city limit sign and sometimes his own wallet, I continually had to turn Long from national and global issues to local concerns for the purpose of my film.

"Tell me something that your power in the Senate has meant to Louisiana in jobs."

"Well," Long said as he sat back in his chair and smiled, "there was that time when President Kennedy called me over to the White House to discuss a trade bill that was stuck in the Senate. His administration was about to close Fort Polk."

This was a World War II base in red-dirt-poor northwest Louisiana that may have no longer been essential to America's national defense but did employ thousands of people.

"I tried to talk to him about that matter while I was there. So I only talked about Fort Polk, and he only talked about that trade bill. Finally President Kennedy said, 'Russell, I just don't understand. What has that trade bill got to do with Fort Polk?'

" 'Well, Mr. President, it's got just this much to do with it. About half the senators on the committee see the trade bill your way and about half don't. And then there's me. If I get my way about Fort Polk, I suspect you'll get your way about that trade bill.' "

The story made my "greatest hits" list. When I edited the film, I showed Long in his office talking to the camera about the trade bill. Then, when he said, "If I get my way about Fort Polk, I suspect you'll get your way about that trade bill," I cut to him standing in a jeep with a three-star general as they reviewed the troops at Fort Polk. It was not subtle, but it was one of the highlights of a film that won numerous awards, made my reputation nationally, and more to the point, helped Russell Long win reelection.

After six days of filming I finally had covered most of the issue and character ingredients suggested by Hamilton's polling. I had Long with Cajuns, with conservatives, with the rich and powerful—and, of course, with rednecks. Now all I needed was to tie him to a father who was still immensely popular in Louisiana, but whom Long rarely talked about in public.

Looking everywhere for something I could use as a link, I blindly purchased several minutes of Huey Long footage from a California film archive. Meanwhile Kris Kirkpatrick found a box in the attic of the Russell Senate Office Building filled with Huey Long material. Part of it was a thick set of 78-rpm records. It turned out to be a recording of what is thought to be the first paid political broadcast, a thirty-minute talk to the nation for Huey's presidential campaign. When one record crumbled in my hand, I took the others to the Smithsonian Institution for restoration. They kept the originals and gave me an audiotape. The recording opened with Huey singing his theme song, "Every Man a King." Finding this song was the first of what turned out to be several miracles.

As a reporter I had always understood the importance of silence, and in filming Senator Long my silences proved to be more important than the questions I asked him. After Long would finish answering my questions and the camera was still rolling, I would sit quietly. Before too many seconds passed, he felt an obligation to fill the empty spaces. The resulting dialogue far exceeded what he had given me in his answer to the question.

I found that the Long campaign was changing my attitude about political communication. Once more I was learning new lessons. Perhaps it was my great respect for him and his office, or perhaps I realized I was moving up a rung in my career, but I began to understand that all of my preconceived ideas about how to prepare candidates for filming were simply knee-jerk conventional wisdom. I didn't try to talk Long into hiring tailors for perfectly cut suits and I didn't rehearse lines with him. Russell Long was what he was, and it was my job to communicate the best parts of his character and not to try to change anything. He wore expensive but baggy suits, so I filmed him in baggy suits. He occasionally stuttered, and I recorded his stutters.

It was as though my mind opened up and I realized that I was not God behind a camera. It was not my job to remold. John Ruskin said, *"The greatest thing a human soul ever does in this world is to see something and tell what he saw in a plain way."* That is a lesson that I have never forgotten, and the quotation hangs on my office wall. When a consultant tries to change a candidate, the result is a cardboard figure. Of course I used makeup. But even that was minimal. Lillian Brown, who was close to Long's age, was cultured and respectful. It would have been disastrous if I had hired some youngster who wanted to impress the senator and chattered away his focus or self-confidence. Lillian was perfect.

I was beginning to understand that everything contributed to a successful camera shoot, from the personality of the makeup artist to the dress of the crew. I began to watch not only the candidate but the many people who swarmed around him. The crew was not allowed to engage in idle conversation with the candidate or among themselves. They were merely planets that orbited the sun.

Once, years later, on a Gary Hart presidential campaign shoot, a fill-in sound man from New York showed up in silky red gym shorts and no shirt or socks. I told him to go dress and he refused.

"You can't tell me how to dress," he said.

"No," I agreed, "I can't tell you how to dress, but I can tell you to get your ass back on an airplane for New York and never try to work with me again."

So in the middle of Red Rocks Park outside Denver, I had to kill a half day of shooting while we waited for a new sound man. Hart said the half-naked fill-in didn't bother him, but he bothered me and he questioned my authority. If I was going to sink or swim as a result of my work, I was going to control every aspect and nuance. I did. The director must be in charge of everything around him. Russell Long taught me that.

The Long film was possible because of an expensive but highly professional crew and discipline. When the assistant cameraman put the lid on the last can of film and Harry Lapham handed me his last reel of recording tape, I caught a plane to New York. I had only eight days until the film went on the air. There was no script on paper, and the old professionals on the crew offered their encouragement but little hope. Fiore did more than his part. He arranged for rush film processing at a friendly lab and found an editor, Sharon Sachs, who could handle the job. Sharon got us a small room and an editing machine at the Film Center on Ninth Avenue. I told her we only needed it for eight days, and she shrugged her shoulders in what I thought was resignation. (Later, when we finished, she said she thought the task impossible and the shrug was disbelief.) Sharon hired two assistants to organize and wind film behind her, and I put my chair at her right shoulder.

I had a vision of my film opening with the antique recording of "Every Man a King." One can't explain creative impulses, but that impulse, combined with pure luck, transformed the film. When we looked at the California footage, the first scene was of Huey standing by a piano singing. There was no sound, but the recording from the attic almost perfectly fit Huey's lip movement. That was another of the miracles. In 1978, I was president of the Baton Rouge Symphony and had connections with LSU and Baton Rouge musicians. Calling on old friendships, I used Delta Dash counter-to-counter service to send a copy of the "Every Man a King" recording to Rick Mackie, the executive director of the orchestra. Rick picked up its rhythm and feel in a one-finger piano rendition that I would lay down under the body of the film. I listened on the phone. Another miracle. He put the new music back on a Delta plane to New York. Sharon and I added scratches to the recording to make it better match the quality of the original material. It was perfect.

The interviews carried the film, and I wrote transitions to be delivered by an announcer between Long's on-camera segments. I selected the announcer, Ed Rose, from an agent's demonstration tape. I picked Ed because he had a rich, older voice that did not fight with Long's. We would build a minute of film and review it several times while I decided what would come next and how to write my way to it. Then I would send a runner down the street with the script for Rose to do what we called a "scratch track." This was just a rough recording, without theatrics or inflection, used only for timing and content. I knew we would have to record the announcer again as I made adjustments.

It turned into an endurance-testing marathon. Occasionally, for an hour, I lay down in the corner and napped with my coat under my head. From time to time the editors switched chairs. The only thing that distinguished night from day was the food the assistants brought in. I knew bagels were breakfast and sandwiches were lunch. Every twenty hours or so I walked to my hotel room at the Algonquin and showered. We could no longer afford to spend the time reviewing the entire film before inserting segments. I looked only at the last completed minute before writing copy or finding a film clip to connect it to the next. Then, suddenly, with two days left, we finished. It was short by about two minutes! I had no choice. I went back to the antique footage, interspliced it with the new, and returned to the original music. The film now ended as it had begun. A circle. It worked. Another miracle.

Computers have changed the way we edit film. But the methods we were using in 1980 were not much different from those used in the first talkies. Film editing was still a hand operation. Film is shot on a negative, and then a dirty "slop" print is made to work with. The negative is fragile and scratches easily, so it is kept in a tin and never touched. All of the cutting and splicing is done on the slop print. Even the color is not exact (that adjustment takes place when the final negative is transferred either to video-tape or to a finished film format). What one ends up with is a patched and taped series of edits. There are grease pencil marks to indicate dissolves and effects. In short, it is a mess that must be decoded by a highly paid profes-sional called a negative matcher or cutter. Sharon didn't even take time to rewind our original. She simply spun around in her chair and handed me the can of negative and our rough-edited documentary. In a sleepless trance I put the negative and print under my arm and carried it across town to a woman who had agreed to do a rush job for double pay. I gave the cab driver a twenty and didn't wait for change. As he sped away, I realized I had left the negative in the backseat. I was finished. Doomed. The film was lost and could not be re-created except by starting over and shooting new mate-rial. My finger had reached for the brass ring and I had been jerked from my horse. In terror I sprinted down the street and caught the taxi at a light. The film and my future were both saved. The driver had stopped for a fare and had missed the light. Another miracle.

(Two years later, the scene would almost repeat itself in an important project for Senator Lloyd Bentsen when I left the final commercials for his campaign in a phone booth in the Atlanta Airport because of fatigue. But that is another story. I guess that is why so many of my friends in the busi-ness have such short lives.)

Our film, *The Fight for Louisiana,* hit the airwaves a few hours before Jenkins's thirty-minute bio was broadcast. I had won the toughest race in my life with endurance and desperate determination. *Fight* was a hit with the public and the press. Soon my phone began ringing as senators and even the White House asked for copies. I was a star. I had fought my way out of Port Arthur and now I had fought my way out of the moral swamps of Louisiana.

So after slugging away, I finally made my permanent escape from Louisi-ana on the wings of Russell Long, Bill Gunter, and Zell Miller. But the get-away wasn't pretty. As with most things I had done in my life, I left casualties. In my ambitious sprint I had neglected my friends, my wife, and my children. The split with Weill was unnecessarily rancorous, and I neglected to tell my wife that the Louisiana chapter of our lives had been closed and I was writing a new edition. Today I regret my handling of Weill and how I dealt with Sandy.

My final day in Baton Rouge came as I walked into my office and a confrontation with Weill. I had just come from the opera in New Orleans and still wore my tux. My parting wasn't heroic. I had already made contact and was in the process of being hired by Senators Lloyd Bentsen, Dennis DeConcini of Arizona, and Paul Simon of Illinois. The terms of my split with Gus meant that I sent him half the profits from these campaigns in 1982. I was too anxious to leave Louisiana to make a good deal. Normally when partners split in an advertising agency, the person leaving takes his personal accounts. In this case, however, I determined that I owed Weill. He had given me my start and promoted me when I didn't deserve it. The accounts were mine, had been sold by me, but I shared the profits partially out of guilt.

I met Bill Morgan, my best friend and attorney, in a bar and asked him if he would like to move to Washington. I had already opened a one-room office and hired a woman to answer the phone and receive mail.

"When do you want to leave?" Morgan asked.

"Today or tomorrow."

"I'll meet you there," he replied and took a long swallow of scotch.

I arrived in Washington with a big reputation and big friends. With the Bentsen, DeConcini, and Simon campaigns I was assured of a good income for at least one year. I didn't know if it would last, but I had spent my whole life betting on the come. It really didn't matter.

After a few weeks in a rental house where Morgan and I holed up, my wife showed up in her Cadillac with her giant Labrador, Mulligan Stew, and a couple of suitcases. She rearranged the furniture, ran Morgan to a hotel, and filled the refrigerator with edibles. She had come for what she considered a visit because I had not shared the little secret that I was never going back to Louisiana. She thought I was only in another campaign that kept me away from home (I still returned to Baton Rouge on most weekends). She had her club memberships, house, and family in Louisiana. By following me she had moved into a dump that smelled of Morgan's cigarettes, spilled scotch, and dust. Even our retriever's tail drooped as though he were depressed.

After a few weeks, Sandy sold her huge boat of a car that never fit into a Capitol Hill parking place and went home and fetched my new but unused two-door Mercedes from the garage where it sat on a flat tire. One morning while she was driving me to Dulles Airport, I was expansive about the beauty and magic of Washington. I had been thoroughly seduced by the Capitol's pearl-white dome. She glanced over at me and said, "We're never going home, are we?"

"No," I said. "This is home now." She began silently weeping.

I was a captive of Washington and was cautiously learning its ways. People didn't laugh at sexual hijinks, and hookers didn't loiter in the corridors. People talked about what they could do rather then what they could get away with. Cocktail parties were used to raise money and sell ideas instead of to get drunk. It was a great change from Louisiana.

Let me make it clear, if I haven't already, that not all of my experiences with Louisiana public officials had been disappointing. Many fought the good fight and tried to make a difference. Moon Landrieu, the great mayor of New Orleans, saved the state millions when the Superdome was being built by slapping as many greedy hands as he could. While I represented the Superdome board with Weill, Landrieu became my political hero for doing the right things for the right reasons. But for reformers it was like trying to swim in cold cane syrup. John McKeithen was a good man and a reform governor (1967–1975) who made changes in how Louisiana did business. His problem was that he was shackled by a system that allowed only adjustments instead of major reform. Mary Evelyn Parker and Mary Landrieu were notable state treasurers. Generally, though, corruption lubricated the gears of government, and the system would have ground to a halt without the ability to cut deals with legislators.

I laugh when people find Washington sinister. Perhaps it is, but compared to the type of politics I knew, it looks simon-pure. In the first year, I began to change. I became more comfortable with myself and developed a growing respect for government and those who govern. The hope fostered by my father took root. The edges smoothed out. For the first time in my life, I relaxed. My suits became conservative Brooks Brothers, and I virtually stopped drinking. The year of 1981 gave me a chance to mellow before I tumbled into new wars that I had never imagined. Finally I was in the big arena in the headline fights.

Senator John Stennis was a gentleman of the old school. His gentility, however, was not simply a matter of standing for women or tipping one's hat. His was a style found today only in period movies and in the memory cupboards of ancient park-bench nappers.

But more than a gentle anachronism, he was a monument to a Senate of yesterday, a Senate closer to the House of Lords than to the casual gathering of sometimes mean-spirited breast-beaters and dwarves whose informality is accepted in Washington today.

I met Senator Stennis by accident one day during a friendly, nonbusiness lunch with Senator Russell Long in his Capitol hideaway just off the majestic dome. A white-coated waiter served us from a cart while we talked about our mutual interests and campaigns. The chance meeting with Stennis would fine-tune my appreciation of the Senate as an institution and wrench the old Mississippi senator out of a comfortable past.

He pushed through the door without knocking. "I'm so sorry for the intrusion, Senator Long. I didn't know you had company. I have a small, private matter of state to discuss with you, but it can wait until another time. Please pardon me, sir." He turned to leave.

"Come in, Senator." Long rose from the table. "Come meet my friend Ray Strother. If you run for reelection, you may need his help." Long winked at me. It was common knowledge that the courtly gentleman was not going to run again. He was a frail, small man with thin hair swept straight back. He wore suspenders—he called them braces—and a suit coat that was never removed in the presence of others. To appear without a coat, or even wearing a coat that did not match his trousers, would have been akin to appearing naked. His speech was from another era, closer to the nineteenth than the twentieth century. Born August

3, 1901, he retained the manners of those who raised him and those who taught him in a more formal time at the University of Virginia.

He shook my hand as I stood to greet him. "I've heard your name, sir, tell me what it is you do, sir, that might help me in my reelection, if I decide to run for reelection, of course." And then he winked at Long. There were a lot of signals flying around the room.

The old senator had reasons to retire and, as it turned out, reasons to stay. When he was seventy a thug had shot him in the stomach outside his D.C. home. A man of iron constitution, he recovered, but his health was never quite the same. He could have retired with grace. But the Senate was his entire existence. His wife had recently died, and he mourned her deeply. His was a solitary and lonely life that found meaning only in the corridors of the Capitol.

His colleagues didn't think he had the stamina for a modern campaign. In 1980 the Democrats had lost control of the Senate in a reaction to runaway inflation, an oil shortage, and American citizens being held hostage by a mob in Iran. Most working Americans thought the Democratic Party had let them down. Ronald Reagan, though he disagreed with labor unions and most Democratic Party beliefs and institutions, won convincingly and dragged into office such unlikely senators as Jeremiah Denton in Alabama, Paula Hawkins in Florida, and Matt Mattingly in Georgia. Because of their success at electing such unelectables, the 1982 Republican professional wolf pack was confident, well funded, and eager to pick off weakened Democrats like Stennis. If they could win with people like Denton and Hawkins, they were sure they could defeat the tiny man from Mississippi with a good candidate. They had an attractive prospect, Haley Barbour. Politics had become a bloody business, and the hardened veterans on the Hill didn't think Stennis was up to the race. Politics had changed, they told each other, and this eighty-year-old man lived in another day.

"What is it you do, sir?" Stennis asked as I sat with Senator Long at that lunch table. It seemed an easy question, but I was stunned. I had never been asked in exactly that context. Often candidates wanted to know if I used film or videotape, or if I specialized in one particular medium. What I do is make television commercials. No, what I do is communicate a campaign message. No, what I do is give a campaign direction and coordination. No, what I do is bring to bear years of experience in two hundred campaigns to help you win. What I do is meet with pollsters and drink with mail consultants. For God's sake, everyone knows what I do. How could I have so much trouble explaining it?

If a space alien landed and asked why we live as we do, it would take forever to fill in all of his blanks. Why do we drive on the right? Why do women wear skirts? Why do trees grow up? Why do leaves turn green? Why do some people live stacked on top of each other and other people live in patches of grass? If the alien asked, "What do you do?" you might respond, "I am a collection of cells that multiply, and I spend a lot of my life eating chicken-fried steak and green beans so that various chemicals move through those cells and generate waves in my brain that allow me to earn enough money to buy more chicken-fried steak."

"Ah," the extraterrestrial might say. "What is money?"

The size of the old senator's question stunned me, and I rambled and stumbled through an answer about film, opinion polls, phone banks, and the marriage of technologies. It was a foreign language, and I got the same response I get from Colombians when I attempt to speak my never-practiced college Spanish. They nod pleasantly without a clue to my meaning. Senator Stennis nodded pleasantly, but I had made little impression. He had worked in the Senate for thirty-seven years without campaign technology or experts. He had served his state well and had been returned again and again to office without heated opposition. In his previous campaign he had spent only about $5,000. He was truly one of the Senate's prized institutions. He was a legend. I met a Mississippi woman one night at a Washington cocktail party, and she expressed her state's feelings best. "How dare that Haley Barbour run against Senator Stennis? Has he ever thought what Mississippi would be like without the senator?" (Barbour was Stennis's last opponent and later became chairman of the National Republican Party. He is now a prominent lobbyist.)

The simple fact that Senator Stennis had to ask "What is it you do, sir?" was testimony to how truly old-school he was.

"So you take pictures?" he finally concluded after I had rambled on for several minutes trying to answer his question.

I was tempted to try again to explain, but I didn't. It was like when Sheriff Cat Doucet asked if I was Miz Parker's driver. I acquiesced.

"I guess I am a sort of photographer," I agreed.

"So you have me walk up and down in front of the Capitol and you take my picture?" I was stunned by the innocence of the question.

"Well, I guess so, Senator."

"Well, then what do you do with those pictures?"

"I put them on television, Senator."

"Well, I've never had much luck with that. I've sent those films home, but I'm not sure they ever ran them."

He was referring to the public-service tapes that senators make in an effort to communicate with their electorate. They are offered to television stations for discretionary use in public-service time, usually late at night or early on Sunday mornings.

"Senator, we pay them to run the pictures." I had fallen into his idiom.

"Well," he said, shaking his head with some enthusiasm. "You pay them. That changes things, doesn't it? We need to have a meeting, sir."

If campaign technology had come before the Senate, Stennis would have known the business inside out. But until this impetuous young Republican, Haley Barbour, announced against him, he had merely watched his friends leave every six years for election activities while he minded the Senate.

A few days after this meeting I received a telephone call from one of Stennis's staff members asking if I would be in my office to receive a call from the senator at 11 A.M. I confirmed I would wait for the call. She then asked if I would be available for a meeting with the senator in his office at 2 P.M. I said I would hold open that time.

At exactly eleven the phone rang.

"Mr. Strother, this is Senator John Stennis. You may remember me. I met you with Senator Russell Long a few days ago."

"I remember you well, Senator."

"I was wondering if we might not get together this afternoon about two o'clock."

I confirmed the time and we said good-bye. A minute or so later the phone rang again. It was the staffer confirming that Stennis had called and had set a meeting for 2 P.M. I confirmed to the staff member. However, about an hour later my phone rang again.

"Mr. Strother, this is Senator John Stennis. You may remember me. I met you with Senator Russell Long a few days ago."

"I remember you well, Senator." Needless to say, I was puzzled.

"I was wondering if we might not get together this afternoon about two o'clock."

I confirmed again and later walked across the Capitol grounds to the

Russell Office Building. I arrived about ten minutes early. An elderly secretary hurried to meet me.

"Are you Mr. Strother?"

"I am."

"I'm so sorry, the senator forgot. He went to his apartment to take a nap."

I soon forgot about it too. I had more work than Morgan and I could handle anyway. I was in West Texas with Senator Lloyd Bentsen shooting film when he asked me about Stennis's campaign. I said that I knew nothing about it.

Bentsen looked puzzled. "You're not doing his campaign?"

"No, sir. I only met him one time. We never even talked about it."

Bentsen shook his head, obviously confused. "What would it take for him to contract you?"

"Same as you, Senator, a handshake."

A few days later I received a call from Stennis asking me to come immediately to his office. He was sitting behind a large desk. He rose and extended his hand.

"A firm handshake, sir," he said with some enthusiasm. "Now how's my campaign coming?"

Thus we began. During long afternoons spent sitting at the large table in his office, I explained phone banks and he gave me insight into the Senate of yesterday. If Jimmie Davis had shown me yesterday's campaigning, Stennis gave me a feel for the dignity and tradition of a Senate that was quickly fading as blow-dried pretenders performed under the glare of television lights.

"Wood is nice," he told me one day as he rubbed his hand across his old table (which had once been Harry Truman's). "New wood is beautiful, but it is the old wood that gets luster through years of hand-rubbing that seems to give it surfaces under the surfaces."

One decision I made was to limit the number of technicians exposed to Senator Stennis. He was looking to me to do whatever vague things were necessary for victory and had difficulty understanding that there were some specialties I lacked. The Washington pollster Peter Hart and I became his campaign contacts. Peter used poll numbers to gently help the senator make campaign decisions. Until a confrontation near the end of the campaign,

Peter, a complete gentleman himself, behaved like a grandson talking to the parent of his parents.

Age was the only possibly volatile issue in the campaign, and Peter and I both encouraged the senator to avoid situations that might focus attention on his advanced years. Barbour was a youthful Republican who wanted his fresh face, vigor, and broad shoulders on the same stage with the legend. Peter and I were professionals determined not to provide such an opportunity to a man who was born the year Senator Stennis took office. Barbour screamed debate and we ignored him. Or we ignored him until the senator's gentlemanly pride was wounded by repeated suggestions that he was a coward.

I called Peter in desperation one afternoon and he met me in Stennis's office. The senator had forced a confrontation with us about debates.

"I'm going to debate that young man. I'm not afraid of him."

Peter carefully explained the numbers and public attitudes in Mississippi, and the dangers of making age a legitimate issue. Stennis countered again and again with arguments about his depth of experience and understanding of government. We were losing our battle until Peter, in a desperate last attempt, made the final argument.

"Senator, every morning when you get up and shave, you see the same man. Age comes slowly. It takes years to change a face, so we don't notice. But when you debate Haley Barbour, the people watching television will see an old man. They will see an eighty-one-year-old man they haven't seen in a long time except in carefully prepared television commercials, and they will vote against you because you are older than all of the voters in the state. If you debate, I think you might lose reelection."

It was painful for Peter. His voice was low, almost a whisper when he finished, and there was silence in the room. When we left, Senator Stennis was still sitting at the table looking at his weathered hands.

We won that battle but almost lost another when Senator Stennis showed up at the largest political event in Mississippi, the Neshoba County Fair. The fairgrounds were decorated with banners congratulating him on his eighty-first birthday, and the Republicans attempted to present him a birthday cake that looked like a raging forest fire—their paid cameras rolling without pause. Our luck came when Senator Stennis stumbled while mounting the stairs to the stage. I did what is now called creative spinning and decided he had been pushed by unprincipled Republican thugs trying to get a few deceitful frames of film. I am sure he only tripped going up the steps, but evidence that he was not physically capable could have been a turning point in the campaign. My comments made newspapers from New York to Jackson. We reprinted these small news accounts by the tens of thousands and distributed them throughout Mississippi. The voters were outraged that their idol, this model of southern chivalry, had been molested. The red-hot film of an old man stumbling—and later sleeping on the stand as Governor William Winter spoke—became useless.

Making television commercials in steamy Mississippi in August was another problem. In Jackson my New York crew and I filmed the senator in early mornings, when his energy level was highest. By 11 A.M. on most days, the crew had retired to air-conditioned motel rooms and swimming pools. Bob Fiore, our cameraman, wore knee pads and shot from low angles to give the diminutive candidate more height, moving constantly to give an illusion of activity on the part of Stennis. Bob truly learned to walk on his knees. The commercials were a series of quick cuts and moving shots that created the feeling of energy and drama.

I kept running into the traditions of the old Senate. When we filmed in Washington, I arranged for several senators to give testimony to Stennis's place and importance in the Senate. I called and scheduled Senators Bentsen, Texas; Johnston, Louisiana; Nunn, Georgia; Long, Louisiana; and DeConcini, Arizona. At our morning meeting as I explained our afternoon shooting schedule, I saw Stennis glower and draw himself erect.

"Sir, who called those senators?"

I was astonished and didn't understand his anger or body language. There had been no problem scheduling the senators. Stennis was loved by all.

"I did, Senator."

"No, no, no, no. You can't do that. You can't call those senators direct. That, sir, is senator-to-senator business. Now you go sit down at that typewriter and make a list of senators you want, and I'll take care of it."

I typed out the list, and he folded it and put it in his coat pocket. That was the last I saw of it, but I spent the afternoon interviewing senators.

I grew to truly love this man and much of what he represented. There were times I felt I was degrading him to bring him into modern politics. He had no understanding of the great demand for money in modern campaigns. We were asking him to raise two million dollars, whereas in the past he had spent only about $5,000 per election. He would just wring his hands, and I would report to Senators Bentsen and Long, who were looking out after his welfare. They helped raise money. Finally, in desperation, I reminded the old senator that he was chairman of Armed Services and had spent billions of dollars with the defense industry. What about LTV? I asked him. What about McDonnell Douglas?

"Would that be proper?" he asked. I'm sure I was glib with my answer in 1982, but that question has bothered me for years since. Is it proper for a public official to take money from companies and institutions over which he or she holds great power? Is it proper for state treasurers to collect campaign money from banks? Is it proper that fundraising must start for the reelection campaign the day after the election? Who gets first call on a public official's time, the person who votes and writes a note or the person who raises $100,000? The answers are obvious and an insult to democracy.

Long before the Senate tied itself in knots over the McCain-Feingold campaign finance reform bill in 2001, Senator Stennis had put his finger on something that none of the reformers in modern politics wanted to touch: It is not only bad form to take money from industries regulated by Congress, it's an inherent conflict of interest. What Congress has done over the years is to practically legalize bribery.

In a way, Senator Stennis's naivete about campaign financing mirrored the old-fashioned attitudes he had held through much of his career about race. When John Stennis started out in politics, Mississippi was a one-party state, as was most of the Deep South. The Mississippi Democratic Party of his youth was all white. Blacks, for obvious reasons, had tended since the time of Lincoln to lean Republican. But across the South, and most especially in Mississippi, blacks were simply discouraged—either by odious legal means such as "poll taxes" or, if that didn't work, by threats of violence— from voting at all. If candidates like Stennis could avoid a Democratic primary, they didn't need to raise money for general elections against Republicans. Their victories were assured.

Historical ironies abound, of course, and not the least in Mississippi. All over the country, blacks left the Republican Party in droves during the Great Depression, settling their hopes on the same man my father put his trust in: Franklin Delano Roosevelt. This occurred despite the fact that most of the legendary segregationists in American politics, such as George Wallace, Orval Faubus, and Strom Thurmond, began their public lives—and, in some cases ended them—in the Democratic Party. Mississippi itself boasted, if that is the word, some of the most virulent racists in American politics, all of them Democrats. Their number included Theodore G. Bilbo, who frequently compared blacks to monkeys, and Ross Barnett, the hapless racist who served as governor when the University of Mississippi was integrated at the point of U.S. Army bayonets.

In 1948, when thirty-seven-year-old Hubert H. Humphrey, then mayor of Minneapolis, electrified the Democratic National Convention with an appeal to the party to "get out of the shadow of states' rights and walk forthrightly into the bright sunshine of human rights," Strom Thurmond led southerners on a walk right out of the convention. John Stennis, who'd replaced Bilbo in the Senate the year before, went with him—along with the entire white establishment of Mississippi. (Louisiana's senator Russell Long refused to participate in the walkout; he stayed and tried to hold the party together so that it would not be split on racial lines.) In 1964 and 1965, Stennis and Mississippi's other senator, fellow Democrat James O. Eastland, were key participants in the filibusters that delayed and threatened passage of the Voting Rights Act and other landmark civil rights legislation pushed by LBJ, Hubert Humphrey, and the national Democrats.

While all this was going on, the modern version of the Republican Party in Mississippi was gaining a foothold, led by a Barry Goldwater conservative named Clark Reed. His appeal was not to disenfranchised blacks, but to conservative *whites* who felt the national Democratic Party had turned too liberal. One of the issues it had gone liberal on, of course, was race. And so, in the 1970s and 1980s, a historical shift occurred. In Mississippi and all across the South, whites began drifting to the Republican Party in national elections, while retaining their fealty to old Democratic Party warhorses like John Stennis in statewide and local contests.

It may be unfair to say that Republicans in Mississippi today are racists, even if they've inherited—or courted—the racist vote and profited from it. However, without the friction between the races, the Republicans would not have come so quickly to prominence. Certainly Senator Trent Lott makes no overt appeals on the race issue; nor did Haley Barbour, the young Reaganite tapped to run against Stennis in 1982. But one thing is sure, and it's something that, when I think about it, allows me to admire John Stennis to this day. In June of that year, 1982, the Voting Rights Act came under consideration in the Senate for its periodic renewal. Of the southerners who fought against the law in 1965, three were still in office. Two of them, Stennis and Russell Long, were clients of mine. The third was Strom Thurmond himself. When it came time to report the bill to the floor, all three voted Aye.

Days later, after our conversation about fundraising, Senator Stennis called me over to his office. He said he had a surprise. He reached into his desk drawer and handed me a check from LTV. I was astonished. It was for $100. But he was proud and I didn't have the heart to explain. His honor would not allow him to beg. Later, other senators did the dirty work for him and raised more than a million dollars for his campaign.

When the 1982 campaign ended, the American Association of Political Consultants awarded me a plaque for the best television of 1982. In tribute, I took the award to Senator Stennis. He hung it on his wall. I understand that when he died in 1996 in a Mississippi nursing home, he still had the plaque that "Mr. Strother and I won together."

"What is it you do, sir?" It is a good question, Senator Stennis.

Well, obviously, one thing I do is help tell old men the truth—or protect them from the truth. That's why the question was so difficult. Our duties can't be easily defined. I help good candidates win elections. In every campaign, what I do is different.

I'm called a media consultant. Like Senator Stennis said, I make pictures and put them on television. I record scripts and put them on radio. Yet I find that in most campaigns, those duties occupy only about 10 percent of my time. I am hired as part of a team whose only purpose is election. Winning. The boundaries between campaign duties and functions become blurred. When one of my staff members asks whether we should become involved in some function outside the understood definition of our duties, I always answer with a question: "Is there anyone else more capable of performing the task?" If they answer no, then I tell them to fill that campaign vacuum. I am a media consultant, but I am in the business of winning. We win by filling vacuums. Senator Stennis's question, "What is it you do, sir?" is akin to a declaration about the emperor's new clothes. Every candidate thinks he knows. Few do. I am a gear that turns a gear that turns a gear that turns a gear that results in a tiny lever being pulled in a voting machine or a hole punched or a box marked and dropped into a box. At times, I am one of the big gears and at times I am one of the small gears. It all depends on the machine.

I learned more from Senator Stennis, however, than he did from me. I watched the obvious respect he was paid by other Senate monuments. He was a history lesson. Modern campaigns prohibit new people like Stennis from being elected. Now it takes millions of dollars and a made-for-television personality and look. Integrity and intellect must take a backseat to the never blinking eye of the camera and the technology of the consultant.

I had one more encounter with the senator just before he retired. His health had deteriorated and he had lost a leg to diabetes. He was wheeled into a room and placed behind a desk while I waited in another room so I could not see him being handled. I had been asked to produce a film for the Stennis Institute of Politics at Mississippi State University. Over the course of three days I did interviews about his life and career in the Senate. I felt as though he was my father, and my questions were gentle softballs. I wanted him to talk about the changes that had taken place in the Senate, but he would not do that because it would break his code of never speaking ill of any other senator or of the institution itself.

"What is the biggest change you have seen since you have been in the Senate?" I asked.

He thought for a moment and almost whispered, "The wonderful progress made by women and minorities." I left it at that and signaled the cameraman to cut. The expression on his face said it all.

If Senator John Stennis taught me about the orderly traditions and gentility of the Senate, Senator Lloyd Bentsen gave me a lesson in cool efficiency and precision. Without being told, I immediately knew that in his campaign I had to perform on a higher plane to simply meet his minimal expectations. Like my father, he had a code of conduct that defined by example the responsibilities of being a professional, a Texan, and a man. He had bombers shot out from under him in WWII; the squadron he commanded as a twenty-three-year-old major flew in the fierce Ploesti oilfield raids that retarded the entire German war effort. Now his world was an orderly one of good wine, good art, and understatement. Mrs. Bentsen was a charming companion who always appeared when she could help.

Bentsen hired me because of a film I had made in 1980 for a Florida state senator, Dempsey Barron, as a tradeoff for his support of my U.S. Senate candidate, Bill Gunter. Barron was a charming and powerful figure in Tallahassee. He wore hand-tooled cowboy boots, western-cut suits, silver belt buckles, and herded legislators like he did his cattle. The film depicted him as a decisive, commanding individualist who was as comfortable on the back of a horse as he was in the leadership of the state senate. Several portrait-quality scenes showed him riding across a ridge on his Florida Panhandle ranch with a giant orange sun behind him.

I showed Bentsen the five-minute film as part of my presentation. "Mr. Strother," he said, "if you can make me look as good as that cowboy, you are hired."

Like Barron, Bentsen was easy to film. Some candidates naturally exude confidence and seem larger than life. Bentsen and Barron were alike in that regard. Contrary to popular belief, we can make cosmetic changes but can't really change the dynamic of personality that the camera catches as quickly as it does eye color. I could glue Senator Stennis's ears back, but I have never been able to make a weak person look strong. The viewer is too expert at watching television.

I knew that, like my campaign for Long, the Bentsen campaign was a career linchpin. Jack Martin, Bentsen's brilliant young campaign manager, set me up in an apartment in a high-rise across from the beautiful granite Capitol Building in Austin as a silent but powerful message that I was expected to spend a lot of time there. I also represented Senator Dennis DeConcini in Arizona, and Austin was a good jumping-off place between Phoenix, Jackson, Mississippi, for Stennis, and Cairo, Illinois, for Paul Simon. The only difficult campaign to attend was Governor Bill O'Neill's in Hartford, but Morgan shared responsibilities with me there. He had unexpectedly taken himself out of the Bentsen campaign with a stunt that I thought would get us fired by the exacting and private Bentsen.

Early in the campaign we had followed Bentsen to a debate with his opponent, Congressman James Collins, and we were scheduled to ride back to Austin with the senator on a private plane. Bentsen didn't take his man seriously and was remote and relaxed in the debate. I had lost touch with Morgan early in the afternoon when he went off to have a drink with a couple of the college-student campaign volunteers. He met us in the general aviation terminal, and we walked together across the tarmac toward the Beech King Air. Morgan, showing no effect of the alcohol on his breath, left my side and fell in stride with Bentsen. In horror I watched as he put his hand on Bentsen's shoulder, said, "Lloyd, let me tell you how you fucked up in that debate," and began to lecture Bentsen. The senator's face turned to stone, but he said nothing. Bentsen didn't curse, Texans don't touch, and never, never would one employed by the campaign call him Lloyd. I sat in the back of the plane with Morgan while he dozed. Bentsen didn't seem to be troubled about the incident and spoke to me several times about the upcoming film shoot. I thought we had weathered the storm of Bill's little caper until the next morning when I was summoned into Jack Martin's office.

"I want Morgan out of here."

"I understand. I'll do the campaign by myself."

"No, let me make it clear. I want him out of Texas. I never want him back in the state and I never want to talk or hear from him again. And most of all, I never want him in the same place as Bentsen. If Bentsen goes to Washington, I want you to send Morgan to Los Angeles."

I took the hint. Morgan began hanging out in Mississippi, Arizona and Connecticut. And he was brilliant in all three. I moved into the Austin apartment with a New Orleanian, Dan McClung, who specialized in organizing voters with phone banks. I had recommended that the campaign hire McClung instead of a Washington insider whose bid for service was far too high. My wife, lonely and almost deserted, drifted between the house we still owned in Baton Rouge and Washington. Being near perfect in campaigns usually means being terribly imperfect in personal relationships.

Dispatching Bill to Connecticut was good business because it gave me an opportunity to shower attention on Governor O'Neill. I felt it was necessary to represent a New England governor or senator so that I would not be labeled as a southern consultant. My ambition was larger than that.

I had been hired for the O'Neill campaign by two friends of the governor, Jim Wade and George Hannah. O'Neill had taken office following the resignation of Ella Grasso in 1980. She resigned when she became aware her cancer was short-term. O'Neill had been a legislator and then chairman of the Democratic Party. When Grasso's own lieutenant governor opposed her in 1978, she reached out to the affable O'Neill as the replacement. O'Neill and I became instant friends. He was an old-school, back-slapping, blue-collar politician who owned an Irish pub that carried his name across the front. He was the bartender you wanted to sit across from and discuss the game of the week. Though Morgan was more frequently in Hartford, I was drawn there through my affection for O'Neill, Wade, and Hannah.

Connecticut was not Louisiana. In Louisiana (and most southern states), the governor is treated like royalty. Squads of state troopers attend him, radioing ahead the movements of his chauffeured limousine. At the mansion scores of people, including convict labor, cook for him, do his laundry, and wait on him hand and foot. A helicopter takes him to LSU football games. People line up to shake his hand. No restaurant reservations are ever required. In Connecticut, the governor is little more than another public employee and must wait in line like his constituents. O'Neill drove his own three-year-old car and lived in a medium-sized house that badly needed painting. (Because of the frugality imposed by Grasso, he was reluctant to spend money even on paint.) Mrs. O'Neill, a charming woman, had a cook and a maid till 5 P.M., but no other servants. The governor was always embarrassed when too much was made of his presence. He and his wife seldom went to anything but public functions and rarely entertained. (I saw this sort of humility in 2001 when I stood in a long line waiting for a table in an Atlanta seafood restaurant with popular Georgia governor Roy Barnes. He refused to go to the head of the line—a lesson never learned in Louisiana.)

In tune with O'Neill's style, I did not script him, but put him in locations with people he liked and shot miles of film that I later edited into thirty-second pieces. My favorite location was O'Neill's Pub, where he bartended and I filmed a group of working people drinking beer and talking about their friend the governor. I would toss a question on the table along with the next round of beer and step back. The resulting spots were believable and compelling.

Our opponent, Republican Lewis Rome, was represented by my friend David Sawyer, who had done work for me in the Hardy campaign. I took quiet satisfaction when the local newspapers said that O'Neill's television campaign was superior. I had overcome my teacher. The television was pure O'Neill and reflected his character and charm. Morgan and I were delighted when O'Neill won by 7 percent.

Being a one-man band in Texas was occasionally demanding. My new roommate, McClung, shared Morgan's fondness for scotch. He never let it interfere with his work, but our apartment became the watering hole for young volunteers. Often I would return late at night and have to step over bodies sleeping peacefully on the carpet to get to my bedroom. A few times I found my bed occupied and retreated to a nearby hotel rather than try to sort people out in the middle of the night.

I kept my plane at the Austin airport and flew weekly to Phoenix for Senator DeConcini. His campaign run by another young man, Ron Ober, was as highly professional as Bentsen's, but its feel and operation were entirely different. Campaigns usually reflect the personalities of the candidates, and Dennis DeConcini was a warm, friendly person who treated as equals and friends everyone from the volunteers to the Navajos, who were part of his voting block. This climate was perfect for Morgan. He became a favorite with the staff and volunteers, who followed him to rib joints and saloons every night for what seemed to be an endless party. Handsome and a brilliant conversationalist, one of the best-read men I have ever met, Morgan developed a cult following of young coeds with literary aspirations and intellectual pretenses who swooned at his utterances as the clock neared its new beginnings every night. But the next morning he was always on time, cleanly shaven, in his perfectly starched shirt, club tie, and Brooks Brothers suit, with a fresh Pall Mall hanging from his lips. With Morgan covering the details in Arizona, I only needed to fly in for television filming and the important meetings with Ober and the senator. This allowed me to devote an enormous amount of time to Senator Bentsen.

Both of these men inspired my best work—Bentsen through fear, respect, and genuine admiration, DeConcini through his friendship and flexibility. Both of them were great delegators and didn't get involved in the tiny details of the campaign. I was soon to learn that this was the mark of a good politician and campaigner. Amateurs are a nightmare and are usually defeated. They take advice from dozens of people and don't trust their own judgment. Usually they involve themselves with rewriting scripts and petty staff disputes. Both Bentsen and DeConcini were pros of the finest kind, but they were poles apart in the way they handled employees.

In Bentsen's campaign I knew I was responsible only to the campaign manager, Martin, and Bentsen. They made quick decisions and left me to my craft. Never did any other staff members stray from their jobs to involve themselves in an area outside their responsibilities. Never did a staff member second-guess my scripts.

DeConcini, true to his personality, worried about the feelings of his staff. After I finished producing his commercials at the Film Center in New York, I would have to alternate the first showings with the staff in Washington and the staff in Arizona. I didn't mind, but it ran up a lot of airplane miles. I would fly to Washington, quickly show the commercials, then fly to Phoenix so that the staff there could see them the same day. All of this expense and effort was aimed solely at ensuring that none of his people felt frozen out.

Bentsen was different. Once, in a relaxed meeting, I asked him how he avoided squabbling between the Washington and Austin staffs. By now I had found that this kind of bickering was common in most campaigns. Bentsen reflected for a few moments. He could not even understand the question. Squabble? Of course not. Both staffs were there to do their jobs and make his life easier, not more difficult. In Austin and Washington they knew that if they caused trouble, they would be looking for a job. Yet this threat was, as far as I know, never spoken.

The harder I tried to live up to Bentsen's standards, the more problems I seemed to have. He asked me once why I brought a film crew in from New York when there was a lot of talent in Texas. He was right, of course, but I was comfortable with my crew and had confidence they would always give me a high-quality product. I was afraid to gamble on new people with Bentsen. The only caveat Jack Martin had was that I had to play down the fact they were from New York. That rule was violated in a very public way.

Jane Crawford, a New York crew member and the wife of my cameraman, Bob Fiore, was advancing our film shoot. This is an important job and requires an organized person who understands production. Jane worked with local staff to find locations that matched my script requirements. Then she went to the location to look and listen. A location in an airport flight path or next to a freeway can't be used because of sound problems. An observant advance person goes to the location at the time of day it is to be used and checks for everything from barking dogs to obtrusive shadows or reflections. If a nearby school dismisses and the children stay an extra hour for noisy play, the time of filming must be adjusted. If we are shooting inside a building, the advance person checks for available power. Thousands of details must be considered, down to things like flickers from fluorescent lights and the usually unnoticed hum of air-conditioners.

Jane had a wonderful visual sense and was an excellent advance person, but her upbringing in France and New York did not prepare her for Texas. She was riding with a couple of the Bentsen college volunteers when she spotted a restaurant sign advertising chicken-fried steak, the national dish of Texas. For the uninformed, I must explain that a chicken-fried steak—in some places called "country-fried steak"—is a beef round steak pounded to less than one-half inch thick, dipped in a mixture of flour and egg, and deep fried to the consistency of soft shoe leather. It is then smothered with a flour gravy resembling and often tasting like library paste. Usually it covers a whole plate and is served with French fries and pinto beans. Like all rednecks, I love it. Jane said, "Look, they made a mistake. Instead of saying fried chicken and steak they said chicken-fried steak." This caused some chuckles from the college-boy escorts, who lived on chicken-fried steak. At their lunch stop they were joined by a reporter from the *Dallas Morning News*. Jane decided to be adventurous and told the waitress, "I'll try that chicken-fried steak. Rare, please." More laughs.

The reporter wrote a tiny story for the style section about the New

Yorker who ordered her chicken-fried steak rare. I got a look from Bentsen over the top of his morning newspaper. He said nothing. He didn't need to. But the next morning after a day of shooting he called me at about daybreak.

"Raymond. Have you seen the morning paper?"

"No, Senator."

"Well, I suggest you do."

I slipped on some pants and a shirt and rushed to the hotel lobby. Staring at me from the rack was a color picture on the front page of the *Dallas Morning News* of Bentsen being worked on by a makeup artist. What made it worse was that the photographer had captured me at a moment when I was making a comment by pointing my finger. It looked like I was lecturing the senator while he was doing unmanly things like having powder applied with a brush. To make it worse, the story was about me. I got the silent treatment for a couple of days and resolved to be error free for the rest of my life. But things happened.

In 1982, as in many elections, Franklin Roosevelt's Social Security program was causing Republican heartburn. Because of customary Republican opposition to things like cost of living increases, as well as their past efforts to tinker with the system, people would rather have Democrats make decisions about their retirement. My father always said the Republicans opposed this insurance policy from the day it was proposed and have spent a lot of valuable time trying to hack away at it. The only time Republicans seem to get religion is a few weeks before election day, when they try to undo the impression they have made over several decades and assure voters they are the great friends of the federal retirement entitlement.

Like all other Democratic consultants in 1982, I had written Social Security scripts for all of my clients. (In fact, I was still writing Social Security scripts for clients in 2000, but the Republicans have become more clever in disguising their disdain for the program and it is harder to use as a club.) The Bentsen script I had written was to be delivered before a group of Hispanics in San Antonio. Martin had approved the piece, but I knew it was uninspired. I had run out of new ways to create terror in the elderly about the potential loss of their monthly check and the dangers imposed by the Republicans.

I arrived in San Antonio with my New York crew the night before filming and checked into the Hyatt on the beautiful river that runs through town. After dinner with McClung in a Mexican restaurant that specialized in margaritas, I went into the hotel bar alone for a final drink before going to bed. Though I have spent a lot of time in bars, through the years I slowly grew to dislike their forced camaraderie. I was on a stool far removed from any drunk expert on anything, distracting myself by doodling on a napkin. It was bothering me that the script on Social Security to be shot the next day was less than mediocre. It didn't make the point strongly enough that my father made again and again: that the old Roosevelt program was the only investment working people had to protect them from an uncertain future. I knew that my father had been forcefully retired by a refinery attempting to reduce its work force through attrition and his small pension from Gulf wasn't enough to sustain life. His largest paycheck while he worked had been $600 a month. His life had been prolonged because of Medicare. Without that assistance he would have chosen an earlier death over an expensive heart operation. Proud men like my father don't accept charity—even from a son. I was filled with rage as I sat at the Hyatt bar. What I was doing against the Republicans wasn't enough. I wanted to batter them and make them beg for mercy for their callous disregard of working people—my father. The slashes of my pen cut the paper and perhaps even left lines in the bar as I drew a picture of an old frame farmhouse with a windmill behind it and a long dirt or gravel drive leading up to a single garage. I added a sun and some birds in the sky and suddenly it spoke to me. I reached a moment of clarity when I was able to forget what the polls said and reach deep inside for an understanding that defied numbers. Quickly I put a huge mailbox in the foreground of my napkin drawing. Within minutes, as though preordained by the God of my fundamentalist youth, two of my University of Texas volunteers walked into the bar looking for a free drink. Day Cable and Mark Miranda were thirsty and agreeable.

I showed them my napkin. "Do you think you can find this place for me?"

"For a couple of Lone Stars, I'll take a shot at it," Cable answered.

"I only have an hour to shoot this commercial because it hasn't been approved and I want to slip it into the schedule. If you can find the place and find me an older woman who can walk up to the mailbox, I'll shoot at high noon when Bentsen's at lunch."

Around midmorning Cable announced he had found the place and had three women for me to consider. At noon he drove about ten miles outside of San Antonio to an exact copy of my napkin drawing. It was spooky. There was a frame house sitting fifty yards off a blacktopped road with a windmill that was searching unsuccessfully for a breeze in the hell-like Texas heat. Waiting in the shade of a scrub tree were three older women. I looked them over and gave the two I rejected a $100 bill each for their trouble.

"But there's no mailbox," I complained to Day.

"We'll get you a mailbox. First we needed to see if you like the house."

Ten minutes later two volunteers showed up with a battered mailbox on a splintered post, a can of spray paint, and a post-hole digger. While one of them painted out the name on the metal box, the other dug a hole for the post.

"Day, this looks a lot like a stolen mailbox."

"Naw, we just borrowed it for an hour. We'll put it back before the people come home from work."

"But their name will be gone. You're painting over their name."

"There is that. I bet they'll wonder what happened, but it'll look nice with its new paint."

Fiore set up his camera and I walked around the parched dry grass with the old woman, describing how she should conduct herself and what I was attempting to do. I didn't have to explain much. She was on Social Security. She understood as only a poor, dependent person could.

With the camera rolling, I had her walk from the house to the mailbox, open it, look inside, and then, finding nothing, gaze down the lonesome road as if hoping to see the mail truck. I shot it twice more with the lens tightening in on her lined face. Perspiration was beading her forehead and she wiped it off with her hand as she looked down the road, a nervous gesture that added texture to the film. Then I had Bob do a close shot of her opening the mailbox and looking inside. The box was an empty cavern. She wiped perspiration from her forehead and turned back toward the house. The last scene was the empty mailbox on the right side of the picture with a stooped and dejected old woman walking back toward the house. It was a picture story. Even without words it broke your heart.

On the back of another cocktail napkin that was stuffed in my pocket were these words:

What if the checks stopped?

What if the Republicans finally won their battle against Social Security?

All that stands in their way is a group of tough Democrats who understand and care.
But the fight will continue next year . . . and the next.
It's another good reason to vote Democratic.

Taking a huge gamble, I didn't shoot the conventional Social Security script that day of Bentsen talking into the camera. I knew I had the perfect answer.

"Are you sure you don't want me to do a Social Security script, Raymond?"

"I'm sure, Senator." My assurance was more bravado than confidence. I would have shot it, but we were on a tight schedule and I had used too much time at the mailbox.

Weary from filming for three days in the broiling Texas sun, I boarded a Delta plane for New York to have my film developed and then edit it in the Film Center on Ninth Avenue. With Sharon Sachs, my editor from the now famous Russell Long film, I went immediately to work. We began cutting and pasting a "slop" print of the frames that would make the commercial. Even this rough, scratched, taped-together version brought tears to my eyes. I had achieved my fondest wish. When we finished putting together the rough, it was time to have a negative cutter do the final assembly in a sterile room with white gloves. That is when my problems began. All the negative cutters in New York were busy with feature films. Hollywood was in town in a big way.

I begged and pleaded with Noel Penratt, the brilliant film matcher who normally did my work, but she told me she had not slept in three days and could not possibly do the job. I doubled her fee. She refused. I tripled her fee and she accepted. The clock was ticking. The clock is always ticking in political campaigns because there is a wall at the end of the cycle that can't be extended for even a minute. Every day that my Social Security ad was not on the air was a day lost on our most important issue. Besides the mailbox commercial, I had seven others that would air in the next weeks. The success of the campaign was in some tins on the end of the editing table.

At about dark I hired a limo and rushed to Noel's studio to pick up the tin with my assembled negative, then rode across town to a studio on 46th Street to have the negative transferred to videotape and to add the superimposed words and the "paid for" line. I watched the white-gloved technician thread the negative onto the sprocket of the transfer machine and adjust the colors by looking at the first frame. On the viewing screen I could see that my old house and windmill looked like a painting by Andrew Wyeth. It was, in every detail, beautiful. Perfectly rural. Lonesome as a divorced man on Christmas day. I relaxed, and the technician turned on the machine. Seconds later the huge machine screeched to a stop with a sound like worn-out brake shoes against metal. "What the hell?" was all he could say.

He carefully opened the projector gate and pulled out the film. There, directly on the negative, was a piece of masking tape that said, "120 frame dissolve." We had put it on the slop print to indicate where the cutter was to build 120 extra frames into the negative for a dissolve—that wistful effect where one picture slowly overwhelms another. Somehow, the cutter had put the tape onto the negative instead of the work print. The technician carefully peeled it away, but beneath it hundreds of tiny patches of adhesive still clung to the delicate negative. The cooperative technician tried to fix it by cleaning each of the damaged frames with a cotton swab and alcohol. It took almost two hours, and still I could see what looked like a sandstorm. "That's the best I can do," he said with a shrug.

He turned the machine back on and it immediately shut down again with the same problem—another piece of masking tape. Every cut I had made from wide shots to close shots was covered with adhesive residue. Again the willing and perplexed technician began cleaning one frame at a time as the clock ticked toward morning and the day I was to show Bentsen my work.

Later I would find out that my exhausted negative cutter had inhaled too much of the glue used to join the pieces and was hallucinating. She confused the work print with the negative and replaced all of the tape from the work print on the negative. The sun had begun to come up over Manhattan when the weary, red-eyed technician said he had done all he could, and transferred my ruined negative to videotape. I sat stunned. I could barely stand to watch as it played the final time on the screen as it was finished. Every edit place looked to me like the same sandstorm as the first.

With only forty-five minutes left to catch my plane, I put the negative and the finished video commercials in a shoulder bag, woke my driver, and rushed to LaGuardia Airport, managing to board my plane as the door closed. The first-class seat had never felt better. I slept until we landed in Atlanta, where I was to take another flight to Austin. My plane had been in a holding pattern waiting to land—as is so often the case in Atlanta—and I had only minutes to make the connection. I rushed between terminals, stopping only to call Jack Martin and tell him I was on my way. Then I hurried down the concourse and narrowly boarded my connecting flight. I sank into slumber even before the plane taxied. Except on airplanes, I had not slept in days. I awoke with a start at about 10,000 feet, realizing I had left the negative and the commercials in the airport phone booth.

Like a terrorist I began pounding on the door to the cockpit with a flight attendant trying to intercede. Finally the Delta copilot came out to try to calm the madman at his door. I backed up a step so as not to not appear threatening and told him the entire story. He could read my desperation and said he would radio the home office and have them search for the bag. A few minutes later he knelt by my seat and said my bag had been located and would be put on the next American Airlines plane to Austin; he even asked me for a delivery address. I told him that the courier who brought the film would get a $500 bonus if he got it to me within fifteen minutes of the plane landing.

Jack Martin was waiting for me in a small auditorium where a television set and a video machine had been installed. In 1982, video machines were still large and uncommon. I told Jack the story and he didn't comment. Texans are trained from birth not to react. Some call it a poker face. Only the weak show emotions. Clint Eastwood made a fortune keeping a stone face. Martin simply looked at me with pity, as though I had announced a terminal disease. An hour later I could hear Senator Bentsen and his wife outside the room, and I still didn't have the tape. As fate happens, though, a campaign fundraiser and friend of Bentsen's, George Bristol, stopped the senator outside the large double doors and talked to him for more than ten minutes. In that ten minutes a wheezing, sweat-soaked courier rushed into the room with my bag and left smiling with five big bills clutched in his hand.

I couldn't bear to watch, so I looked at the ceiling as the flawed tape played. I knew I was doomed when Bentsen asked to see it the third and fourth time. Then there was silence. He walked over to me, shook my hand, and said, "Good work, Raymond." That was the highest praise one could get from Bentsen. He didn't notice the sandstorm at every edit spot. Bentsen didn't make a mistake. It was simply that I had grown supersensitive to production values and now saw flaws that didn't affect the viewer—even one as critical as Bentsen.

The commercial became the smash hit of the campaign year and was used in forty states to help regain the Senate majority for the Democrats. But I still can't look at it, and I wonder what damage was done to my heart during that week of terror.

But my father had guided me. I wrote from my heart. Finally I had honored working people by punching the Republicans in the gut. I had gambled greatly, stood my ground, and never let the bastards see me sweat. With Social Security as the lever, Democrats won back the Senate in 1982, and the Republicans vowed never to let the issue be used against them again. In fact, when George W. Bush ran for president in 2000, he vowed he wanted to save Social Security. The Republican Party came up with expressions like "putting the Social Security funds into a lock-box" so that greedy politicians couldn't get to them. They knew a bad poll issue when they saw one. Republicans are a little slow, but they live and die by polls—as do the Democrats. For example, after President Jimmy Carter started the Department of Education, the Republicans vowed every year to dismantle it. Polls change. Survival instincts remain. Now the Republicans want to protect the Department of Education and even expand it. I find it amusing that both parties hold three-day retreats where they ponder why Americans have lost confidence in their political institutions.

My prediction is that the great opponents of environmental reform, the Republicans, will soon begin introducing legislation that will cast them as tree-hugging spotted-owl savers. At least now both parties believe and agree on one thing—public opinion polls.

But 1982 was a good year for small-town southern boys with stars in their eyes and the vestiges of righteousness still clogging the arteries in their hearts. We helped win some big races. Made some big money. And we would have made my Daddy proud.

Bentsen won 59 percent to 41 percent.

DeConcini won 59 percent to 41 percent.

Stennis won 64 percent to 36 percent.

O'Neill won 53 percent to 47 percent.

Paul Simon won 66 percent to 34 percent.

The Democrats won back the majority in the Senate.

I won by winning the respect of Washington and securing my place in the rough business of political consulting. I stood proudly in the middle of the ring. Washington is a tough city, and suddenly it was mine. Morgan and I, though, were fatigued. The two of us—along with Randy Thompson, who ran errands and did finish work on our spots, and Connie Choat and Mary Sue Chambers, who kept us scheduled and handled our books—had successfully completed five major campaigns and four of less national significance.

Morgan and I celebrated our victories in Washington. On election day, he said he thought the most important thing we could do was to have a martini at a local Georgetown watering hole, Clyde's, and buy hats. We had three martinis each and stumbled down the street to a hat shop. That became a ritual in our firm. In November 2000, after the Zell Miller Senate race was finished, I spent part of election day by myself in an upscale bar in Lenox Square in Atlanta toasting Morgan. All races are important, and I have a policy of not discriminating among my clients. That means I usually watch election results from my home or office in Washington. In 2000, though, I didn't have the energy to get back on a plane, so I stayed in Atlanta. After the polls closed, I would join newly elected Senator Miller and Georgia governor Barnes to watch the totals flicker across the television screen. Meanwhile, as I sat on a bar stool thinking about Morgan and hat day, Steve Davison, our firm's creative director, reached me by cell phone to say he was at Clyde's in Georgetown and would soon buy a hat. That sort of gesture is why Davison and I are so close. Though Morgan has been dead since 1996, I add a hat to my collection every election day. I have slacked off on the martinis. It no longer takes three.

In earning my graduate degree at Louisiana State University in 1965, I wrote a thesis, "The Louisiana Political Candidate and the Advertising Organization," predicting that the campaigns of the future would abandon grassroots organization and embrace media. I reached this conclusion by examining two Louisiana campaigns for governor in 1963, Gillis Long's and John Mc-Keithen's. Though Long lost to McKeithen and former New Orleans mayor Chep Morrison, his was the campaign of the future. He had a team of consultants from the advertising industry, and they carefully plotted a communications course that is similar to what we do today. They polled and targeted specific groups of potential voters and reached out to them with television, radio, and newspaper. McKeithen, on the other hand, relied on the traditional Louisiana campaign of organizing sheriffs, clerks of court, and other minor public officials to reach voters. It was truly the old against the new.

I began my research during the election cycle and had access to both camps through my dual positions with the Associated Press and the Louisiana Press Association. Gillis Long's media team was headed by a New Orleans ad executive, Jim Carvin, and McKeithen's by the man who later become my partner, Gus Weill. It became evident to me that the old-style campaigning required a different kind of voter than the one that emerged in the age of television. As we proved once again in the Jimmie Davis campaign in 1971, voters would no longer travel long or even short distances to stand in the sun and listen to a politician make promises. Instead, they huddled around a television set in an air-conditioned room.

Gillis Long's was the superior campaign, but he lost to McKeithen. Despite the disorganized campaign, McKeithen staked the final weeks of his efforts on thirty-minute television programs he performed live from a studio to a network of stations. It was truly rough television, without any foundation of research, but McKeithen was a compelling figure. He occasionally even ad-libbed. People were drawn to him. Suddenly his endorsements from legislators and minor political figures became moot as his television created interest and conversation in the state. McKeithen had stumbled into a media campaign without knowing it. There are some things that defy scientific examination, and personal magnetism is one of them. McKeithen looked intelligent and powerful, spoke forcefully, and inspired confidence. Those traits can't be taught.

McKeithen ran second to Chep Morrison, the former mayor of New Orleans, in the Democratic primary, then beat Morrison in the runoff. Since Republicans still didn't count in the state, that amounted to election. McKeithen became Louisiana's most successful governor to date and ushered in the modern era of reform and the restructuring of state government. Many of his reforms were undone by Edwin Edwards.

My thesis was published by a small printer in Baton Rouge, Kennedy Press, and sold 100 bound copies at $25 each. The printer and I shared equally in the profits. That paid for the birth of my second child, Kristan. I was still floating loans at a finance company to make regular payments to the obstetrician for my son's birth and generally catch up with life. Despite my education, I still had redneck problems. The 1953 Chevrolet I had driven since high school would sputter and need a brake job just when a baby got an ear infection or the washing machine motor burned up. I was on friendly terms with a finance company that would lend me $50 until payday. But I was filled with glory. I thought I could see the future and intended to become part of it.

But the Collins and Daley campaigns of 1983 were not the future I had confidently staked out. Martha Layne Collins insisted that one could not win in Kentucky without visiting every courthouse. And in Chicago, I found myself a stranger in a strange land. In that singular city, only organization mattered, and my television was simply a curiosity to keep the home troops happy. Richard M. Daley's mayoral race didn't shake my confidence in media, but it did teach me to put it in perspective. Paid television was of secondary importance in that race, and since then I have come to believe that paid television plays only a minor part in two kinds of race: small ones, such as for city council, where personal contact is of utmost importance;

and the largest of them all, presidential campaigns, where the press does a wonderful job of informing the voters without interference from paid ads.

By 1983, after my string of victories led by Bentsen, Stennis, and DeConcini, I was smug. I thought the lessons of my thesis were obvious and no longer deserved argument or even further consideration. Media always trumped organization. Richard Daley in Chicago and Martha Layne Collins in Kentucky disagreed. Daley was right. Organization and personal contact with ward leaders were far more important than paid media. Chicago was a city of political traditions that live even today. Collins, however, was wrong because she was trying to conduct a rural stump campaign in the style of Jimmie Davis in a society that was urban and suburban. Collins won because her campaigning style did not distract from her media campaign, and she was good on television. Both campaigns taught good lessons. I was still learning that there are no absolutes.

Even before my victories in 1982, I was contacted by the Daley campaign for mayor of Chicago and the Collins campaign for governor of Kentucky. Bill Hamilton was the pollster for both campaigns, and he tilted them in my direction. I took a couple of months off in Scotland, Morgan retreated to Baton Rouge, and then we both moved back into the fray. Bill Daley, later a Clinton cabinet member, installed Morgan and me in an apartment on State Street, and we began helping plan a campaign for Bill's brother Richard M. "Rich" Daley. (Bill and Rich, of course, were sons of the legendary former mayor and quintessential political boss Richard J. Daley.) John Marttila of Boston, an organizational specialist who also understood the importance of message, was brought into the team. With Hamilton, Marttila, and the competent Bill Daley, we had a tight message team. But more lessons were to be learned. Suddenly message and television were not enough.

Shortly after we moved into Chicago, the Collins campaign retained us and we began making regular trips to Frankfort, where Mrs. Collins was serving as lieutenant governor. It didn't take long for me to discover that Kentucky was much like Louisiana. Politicians still suffered the delusion they could be elected by putting together county organizations around minor elected officials.

The stage was thus set for two campaigns that believed in organization to move into the message era. Morgan and I were flying high. Soon we were persuaded by starry-eyed campaign organizers to do media for Winn Moses in his bid for reelection as mayor of Fort Wayne, Indiana. They had read that I had been hired by Daley. It was small potatoes politically, but the cash was good, and our apartment on State Street was only a few miles up the road, so we signed on the dotted line and assumed more responsibilities. I had just come off a year of huge profits beyond my fondest expectations and didn't really need the money. Maybe what made me take a relatively small-time mayor's campaign was simply ego or my self-image of the hired gun who comes into town on the train and cleans out a nest of outlaws. I enjoyed being courted and in control. To be successful, consultants must have control. Usually control is a direct result of reputation. Winn Moses was a delightful man to work with, so it became a pleasure rather than a challenge or inconvenience. Besides, Morgan did most of the work in Indiana, while I concentrated in Kentucky. We shared Chicago.

That honor, in 1983, was a dubious one. Chicago was going through upheaval, mainly because Richard J. Daley had died, leaving his city without a boss to run it. Mayor Daley is remembered for a lot of things, not all of them fondly, by Democrats. True, his ability to perform feats such as coaxing impressive voter turnout rates from unlikely places, including cemeteries, is credited in Republican mythology for narrowly stealing the 1960 Illinois electoral votes—and, thus, the presidential election—from Richard Nixon and giving it to John F. Kennedy. (This legend ignores the fact that the Republicans lost Texas that year, too—by 46,000 votes. Were those votes stolen? Hell, I don't know, but let's just say that Lyndon Johnson's political machine, like the man himself, was not subtle and left little to chance.)

But Daley was also the pro–Vietnam War mayor whose out-of-control police department escalated the violence against antiwar protestors—some of them delegates—so appallingly at the 1968 Democratic National Convention that our nominee, Hubert H. Humphrey, never had much of a chance of winning. For Democrats, Mayor Daley personified Carl Sandburg's famous description of Chicago as a city of big shoulders. And for Chicagoans, he was as dependable as the fierce weather in that town.

Funny, then, that it was a snowstorm that did in the Daley machine. Failure to clear the snow from the streets after a 1979 blizzard outraged the populace and relegated Daley's successor, Michael Bilandic, to a single term in office. Bilandic met his political end that same year at the hands of a five-foot-two, 106-pound former substitute schoolteacher named Jane Byrne, whose irascible manner and unpredictable style of governance earned her numerous politically incorrect nicknames, including "Calamity Jane" and "Attila the Hen."

The job for Morgan and me—and we considered it a noble mission—was to resurrect the Daley machine by engineering the victory of his son Richie to victory over Byrne. The obstacle turned out not to be Byrne; it was that Harold Washington, an African American, had decided it was time blacks shared the power in Chicago.

Martha Layne Collins was a beautiful, strong-willed woman who had been elected lieutenant governor in her own right when John Y. Brown and his former Miss America wife, Phyllis George, took over the Governor's Mansion. Martha Layne's husband, Bill, was a tough, charming mountain man and difficult to assign to a second-fiddle role. He actually ran the campaign—with an iron fist—and was responsible for raising money.

Martha Layne held her own opinions strongly, and we had several arguments that made staff members run for cover. One problem was her insistence on courthouse-to-courthouse campaigning. Her campaign bus also stopped at predetermined secondary spots along the route, where she would be met by friends and supporters, usually ten or fifteen at a time. I climbed on the bus for several days, and it didn't take long to understand that we were wasting her valuable time and the campaign's precious resources. It cost the organization an enormous amount of effort to get supporters to her bus stops and completely took her out of campaign play. One afternoon she came to the back of the bus, where I had my head pressed to the glass watching the beautiful Kentucky scenery float by.

She asked, "What do you think now about this tour?"

"Well, if all of those people who come out to meet you are undecided voters, you can get elected doing this if you can just keep it up for forty-eight more years and nobody dies." As this remark indicates, it was not only her fault we had flare-ups. My smart mouth was partially responsible. I was frustrated that my time and hers was being wasted, but I could have been more diplomatic with a very nice woman who was also breaking new ground for herself and others.

A second source of conflict was her relationship with the press. She hated them and granted interviews only when all but forced to do so. This is a trait I have found in several politicians, but seldom to this extreme. Suddenly I had flashbacks to being kicked off the bus by Jimmie Davis because I insisted he needed to talk to the press. That experience taught me to argue with Martha Layne to a point and then step back before I got myself fired.

It has always been my belief that our system of government only works if public officials are accountable to the people for their actions. The press, even with its warts and biases, is the watchdog for the people and holds our officials accountable. If a person runs for public office, part of the price of admission is dealing with the press. There are two choices—deal with the press or find something else to do with your life other than hold public office. Once in Louisiana, when Governor McKeithen was ranting about the press and threatening to kick their offices out of the Capitol Building, I asked him what would happen if the press didn't watch the legislature. He thought for a few moments, smiled, and said, "Well, I guess Senator Dudley J. LeBlanc would steal the Capitol Building and reassemble it in Abbeville as an insurance company." He got his own joke. Despite his anger, he knew the press is as important to democracy as sunshine is to photosynthesis. I am sure that Governor Collins, now that she has been out of office for a number of years and has had time to reflect, would agree.

We were breaking new ground in Kentucky. A woman had never been elected governor, and there was still a deep strain of male chauvinism in the state. Even worse, we found that older women resented Martha Layne because she was stepping out of their traditional role; also, some women disliked her because she was beautiful. To elect her became a chess game of careful moves and constant research. She was cooperative in television production, and working with Bill Hamilton was a great delight. The campaign would rent a hotel suite in Lexington, and she and I would rehearse for ten or twelve hours before the camera was ever turned on the next day. She had to memorize the scripts because I refused to use cue cards or Teleprompters. I have always believed that the sophisticated American television viewers can discern when a candidate is reading, and the candidate's credibility suffers. The expert viewer can see eye movement and is uncomfortable when the person remains frozen in posture. Only professionals like Dan Rather or Diane Sawyer can get away with reading words that are superimposed over the lens of the camera.

After Martha Layne memorized the words, we would work on inflections, tone, and hand gestures. Except for occasional pauses for club sandwiches or coffee, she tackled the task with ferocity, and when we finished she had the confidence to step in front of the camera and deliver a compelling message without reading. She was damned good.

But we had gender problems. My first campaign had been for Mary Evelyn Parker in the early days of political television, and she was not judged by the same performance standards as candidates are today. Also, she was running for treasurer, not governor. Voters have different standards for different offices. It was once possible to elect women to down-ballot races like treasurer, land commissioner, or even lieutenant governor, but not to the U.S. Senate or to governors' chairs. One of Martha Layne's problems was that she had been elected lieutenant governor by one set of standards and was suddenly playing in a new game with new rules. In 1983, I began to learn about gender bias and electing women.

Coal mining is a major industry in Kentucky, and in 1983 many miners were out of jobs. Putting them back to work was a major plank in our campaign platform. I had the staff arrange for us to film in the bottom of a coal mine so that Martha Layne could show some empathy with miners. We arrived at a remote spot in the mountains early in the morning and were put in tiny individual mining cars that required the passenger to lie almost flat to fit through the claustrophobic tunnel. We loaded our camera equipment and lights were loaded on other cars and began a frightening descent into the bowels of the earth.

We finally emerged in a large cavern with six-foot ceilings; most of the crew had to bend slightly to string cables and install equipment. The only trouble was that the cavern was white. The foreman explained that as a mine was dug, it was sprayed with a fire retardant. But I knew I couldn't shoot in a white coal mine. I needed black.

In a few minutes a machine appeared and dug about fifty feet into the side of the mine without spraying the retardant. Now I had a black mine and five coal miners who could talk to the candidate about their problems. I was going to film their conversation and her answers, and assemble a commercial from the best segments.

There was something wrong, though. The miners—one of them a woman—were scruffy, while my candidate, with her perfect blond hair, looked like the prom queen. She seemed to glow against the blackness. I whispered to our makeup artist, Genie Freeman, and she put a smudge of black on Martha Layne's cheek. Now she looked more like the miners and my crew. I shot for two hours and later assembled beautiful commercials for focus-group testing the next week.

We were using focus groups of actual voters to help us through the bias problems involved in electing a woman in 1983. The testing lab was two rooms separated by a one-way mirror so that we could watch the group interact and listen to their conversations through a mike in the ceiling. The participants were selected randomly from lists of people who matched our problem voters. Bill Hamilton was the moderator. We had already learned in other focus groups that Martha Layne's attire was a major concern. We found we could not use pantsuits and had to be careful with hem length, necklines, and jewelry. Hair style and color were also sensitive items. A male candidate can do an entire campaign with one pinstriped suit and a plaid shirt. In the Collins campaign we even had to worry about how much exposure a particular dress could receive before we needed to pull the commercial. Through the focus-group mirror I would hear things like, "If I see that blue dress again, I'll scream." I actually made commercials using the same script but with Martha Layne in different dresses so I could pound in the message without familiarity with her wardrobe getting in the way.

One night we watched as the focus group viewed my latest batch of commercials. The first three went beautifully. The people understood what we were saying and were impressed with the candidate's delivery and competence. And then the coal mine commercial played. I saw a woman nudge another and whisper. Then, across the table, a woman snorted loudly enough to transmit into our room. Something was wrong. Soon the entire room was debating why a beautiful woman would allow herself to be photographed with coal dust on her cheek. It didn't ring true. They had no idea what was said in the spot because the coal dust made it irrelevant. It was fake.

The next day I went back into the lab and found film clips shot from the clean side of Collins's face. There weren't many, but by quickly cutting to coal miners' faces, I was able to salvage $30,000 worth of production. Now the spot worked—and I learned another lesson.

A few months later I put what the campaign had taught me about the problems of electing women into a *Washington Post* feature that ran in newspapers all over the world. It got me in trouble with Bill Clinton's domineering campaign director, Betsy Wright, and caused a huge flap in the feminist community. In Washington there are only selected truths one can tell.

One of the conclusions I reached in the Collins campaign was that women often reach decisions by a different route than men do. In the Bentsen campaign, Jack Martin, Bentsen, and I would go into a room and leave ten minutes later with all decisions made. It's been my experience that women tend to be consensus builders and arrive at many decisions more gradually, through discussion and compromise. The opinions of Bentsen's friends were never considered, but Collins's friends became major problems. After having done many more campaigns for women, I am no longer sure which viewpoint is correct. I saw good decisions made around a table for Mary Landrieu in her 1996 U.S. Senate campaign, and I have seen headstrong male candidates beat themselves by not listening to advice of any kind.

One problem with Martha Layne's friends was that they convinced her she would lose if she used negative ads. She was adamant that we never mention her opponent's name. Another problem with her friends was that they demanded billboards. I was trying to conserve money for television and had bought no outdoor advertising. "But no one has ever been elected governor in Kentucky without billboards," the friends told us. The complaints grew so large in the back room of the headquarters where they sat together addressing invitations and making calls that I caved in. I put one huge billboard across the street from the headquarters, and all complaints stopped. Regarding negative or comparative advertising, however, the friends almost got their way.

Our principal opponent in the Democratic primary election was Harvey Sloan, the popular mayor of Louisville, the state's largest city and home of the Kentucky Derby. Because of his popularity and constant TV exposure in the largest market, he had a base of votes in the northwest part of the state that we had trouble penetrating. At best, we could nibble around the edges of his voter bloc. Our danger was allowing him to expand his base into the Bluegrass, the central part of the state. If that happened, we could not win. If he had an opportunity to define himself on his own terms, we would lose, but I could not persuade Martha Layne that she was giving her opponent a free ride into her Bluegrass base of support. Poll after poll showed us a few points behind Sloan in a winner-take-all primary. With only days to go, and at the insistence of Hamilton, Larry Hays (her campaign manager), me, and even her husband, Bill, she reluctantly gave us permission to attack her opponent and help define him before it was too late. But even then she feared the opinion of her friends.

I had already made the commercials, so they were on the air within twelve hours. Slowly our polls responded. On election night we narrowly eked out a victory. I was standing in the hotel hall outside the victory celebration when Dr. Floyd Poor, a friend of Martha Layne's and a successful fundraiser, attacked me. He grabbed my tie and swung at me with his fist. I ducked, and several people pulled him away as he screamed, "You son of a bitch, we would have won by a lot more if you hadn't gone negative." A few years later he would run for governor and come in third using his own rules.

In 1983 the Republicans were still not a threat in Kentucky, and Martha Layne coasted through the general election against Jim Bunning, a former baseball pitcher and candidate for the Hall of Fame. Hamilton, knowing it was a no-brainer, turned over the cleanup to a young man in his shop, Harrison Hickman, and I was required to do only one film shoot to put the cap on her final victory.

We lost in Chicago. The stars were not in line. Rich Daley was in the wrong place at the wrong time. Jane Byrne had his father's organization, and Harold Washington had the blacks. There was no place for Richard Daley that year. But our Kentucky win was great and continued a tradition in our firm of helping elect women.

Returning to Washington, I had a new goal. I wanted to make a proposition to Colorado senator Gary Hart and continue my father's war against the politicians who were responsible for killing his son.

Two recurring nightmares haunt me. One is about flying a light plane a few inches above the ground at high speeds, around obstacles and over low fences, attempting to find a hole in the trees or buildings wide enough to be able to climb without stalling. My wing tips clip low bushes, and I wait every second to hear the fatal crunch of metal that means the dream and the life are both over. I wake in a sweat with my fists still tightly clenching the control wheel.

In my other bad dream I am sitting in a video studio at 3 A.M. with malfunctioning equipment and a 9 A.M. deadline for a television spot that will change the complexion and direction of a political campaign.

Both nightmares are based on reality. Both are firmly grounded in experiences that have scared my soul. But the video dream is the worse of the two. For politics is a giant ticking clock that can't be slowed or changed. Like Edgar Allan Poe's dreadful, methodical pendulum, hundreds of clocks tick within the campaign machinery. Each tick shortens the campaign and reduces the opportunities for escape or even survival. Looking back with the cushion of years, I see that the brutal aspect of the underfunded Gary Hart campaign was time. Money and time are related.

I wear an ugly watch on my left wrist. It is large and not even slightly stylish. It is stainless steel instead of gold, an Omega instead of a Rolex. It weighs about eleven pounds and is a source of constant derision from my wife, Sandy. She claims that when I wear it with a tux it looks like I am wearing the grille of a 1958 Nash Rambler. Yet I can't bear to be without that watch. It is the stainless steel control tower of my life. Not only does it tell me the hour and the minute, it also divides the world into seconds and tenths of seconds. It allows me to time the service in restaurants and how long "just a minute" really is when I am waiting for my wife. At night it sleeps only inches from my ear so that when I wake I can hear its ticks. I used to sleep with it on but in the morning looked like I had had a romantic relationship with a cat during the night. "And where do you think that scratch came from?" Sandy would often ask, though she knew that my only mistress was the look-alike for the Nash grille. What she really wanted to do was put a damper on the relationship between me and my ugly watch. "Why don't you dive in your watch?" she often asked me when I put on my mask and tanks and leg knife and fins and a black stopwatch that is a Japanese cousin to my splendid Swiss machine. As marvelous as my watch is, it is not waterproof.

My ugly watch is more than a machine. It is a symbol of my profession. It is a talisman. The watch and its ability to divide the world into tenths of seconds helps elect senators and governors. Its command is final. Those authoritarian ticks can interrupt dinner parties, stop major speeches, play havoc with marriage, and change the political and cultural face of a nation. Tick, tick, tick, tick. (I don't really know where "tock" came from because it is not in the vocabulary of any watch I own. I think that "tock" may simply be a German or a Swiss accent.)

If there is anything to Dante's perception of hell, I will be put inside a ring of ticking clocks without hands and assigned a schedule of television commercials to make for satanic figures who can speak only in three-minute sentences and with a lisp. The electorate will be a host of mink-coat-wearing Republican angels who would rather go to hell themselves than vote for one of my long-tailed devil candidates. The poet Virgil will skip through my ring saying, "You have already missed your deadline, and Errol Flynn has been defeated for governor of hell." Tick. Tick. Then Virgil and his tourist will stick fingers into the videotape machines, causing them to erase, and at the same time jam the computer. That's my kind of hell. And I've been there.

Ticking clocks form the boundaries of what the media consulting business is. The first time constraint is the length of the campaign. Whether two years or only two months, it sets the limit and presses the button on the stopwatch. Everything from research to media involves a separate clock. There are clocks running on fundraising and clocks running on payments. Time must be measured between campaign stops and between handshakes. But those time limitations are easy compared with media production, in which an extra tenth of a second can mean failure. As the clock ticks, a $400-per-hour production studio can click into overtime at $600 per hour, and then possibly to $800 as a technician searches for frames or sounds that can be safely removed. As the clock ticks, the budget for production is depleted. As the budget is depleted, the number of messages to the voters is reduced. The result can be defeat. In the Gary Hart campaign, commercials could not be produced until money was collected to pay for them. That compressed the time for production to hours instead of days or weeks. Then, as the clock in the studio ticked and my heart raced, we faced deadlines that, if not met, would have resulted in dead air time and lost primary elections. More on that later. Tick. Tick.

The campaign clocks are usually wound and started about eighteen months to two years before the election. The candidate often squanders early time by consulting with friends rather than professionals, but the clock is forgiving eighteen months before an election. Even then, though, the campaign machine is running, albeit slowly, toward a stone wall called election day. Every week, day, minute, second, wasted can't be recovered. Gone forever.

The slow ticks of the clock are used for buying custom-tailored clothes, training with a speech coach, and issue-development sessions. Women candidates, particularly in the South, learn methods of avoiding the traditional kiss on the cheek, and breath-control techniques to make their voices more authoritative. In this stage of the campaign, there is a lot of laughter. The ticking of the clock is almost inaudible. Even my ugly Nash Rambler stopwatch ticks very quietly.

Then one day a chart divided into blocks with numbers appears on the headquarters wall. This is the first campaign calendar. Some eager staff member counts the time remaining before the election and posts it on the top of the sheet: "187 Days to Election." It is the first dose of reality. People begin to calculate how many thousands of dollars must be raised every day, and even every hour. They begin to write schedule reminders in the squares. The large empty sheet begins to fill. Rallies, polling dates, direct-mail drops, and interviews begin to show up in various colors of ink. Soon the empty boxes for the next thirty days are filled and become a rainbow. But the inexperienced staff members still take lunches and hours off to lie in the sun on a hill behind the headquarters. Beer drinking still starts at 6 P.M. Sundays are still time off. The neophytes have not yet learned to listen to the ticks.

Spring comes and the campaign staff forms a softball team, or they often meet after work at someone's pool. But now it is not as much fun. The Washington consultants hang around and yell about fundraising and telephone calls. Then the Saturday morning softball game is canceled because only three members show up on the field. Tick. Tick. The pool is now empty on weekends. Lunch comes more often in cardboard containers, and a campaign headquarters smell begins to develop of moldy pizza, spilled beer, poster ink, and discarded gym gear. Paper begins to build into "maybe later" stacks. Squares are checked off the calendar on the wall. The count of remaining days changes. Lost days are lamented. They are gone forever. The calculation for money raising per day is revised. Tick. Tick. June turns to July. Adjustments are made and parts of the campaign are discarded for lack of time and money. Rest days for the candidate are forgotten. Tempers begin to flare. The softball tee shirts are now worn only at the office. Swimming pool tans fade.

Finally somebody in authority looks at the squares on the wall that have been squandered and calls a meeting. Someone is fired. New energy and new fear are instilled in the staff. The clock is beginning to test them. The inexperienced begin to fight, and factions develop that must be dealt with in the next organizational meeting. Some are fired for "budgetary reasons." The clock has run out on money to pay those at the bottom of the pyramid.

At this point a "miracle worker" appears. It is often a spouse, brother-in-law, or friend who complained the loudest. Seldom do these miracle workers know how to solve the problems. Never do they know that they do not know how to solve the problems. The clock continues to tick. Valuable time is wasted in reorganization. Staff members begin leaking information to reporters that firmly places the blame on others. Desperation sets in. Candidates begin to listen to friends who assure them that their opponent is getting no votes—regardless of what the polls say. Tick. Tick.

Now the headquarters never closes. There is not enough time left to accomplish the necessary tasks. The campaign plan, already in tatters, is revised. Slogans appear on the walls. Even the janitors and volunteers begin handing the campaign manager suggestions and scripts for television spots. Other consultants, smelling blood, begin offering "to help." Then they plant items in the press about the failure of the present team to do the job. Large contributors call and ask the candidate "just to talk" to a consultant they know who has worked miracles in other troubled campaigns. At this point panic has set in and the candidate has lost confidence. This becomes the test of his or her fiber. Those who fail the test perhaps don't belong in office. A strong candidate listens to advice, and smiles. Nothing changes. A weak, insecure candidate grasps at straws. I have worked for both.

Senator Lloyd Bentsen's campaigns ran by the clock. Deadlines were made, and there was never a need for excuses. Time was spent productively, every hour used effectively. Campaign manager Jack Martin implemented it and Bentsen demanded it.

Time, however, became my enemy in the presidential campaign of Gary Hart. Because of a cash shortage, everything ran at the last minute. Nothing was completed until seconds before time expired. Hearts beat faster. Sleep came harder. The ticking of the clock pounded inside my head as I ran from mission to mission.

I started my Gary Hart clock ticking after the successful 1983 campaign for Martha Layne Collins. I made an appointment with Hart, whom I had never met. He was the enigmatic senator from Colorado who had run the presidential campaign for George McGovern. He had the reputation of being bright, withdrawn, creative, and inscrutable. But most important, he had always been against the stupid war that killed my brother. My father's anger burned in me. I wanted to lash out at someone, somehow. Hart, I thought, would be my vehicle. He wasn't a go-along-to-get-along Democrat. He drew my father's kind of lines in the dust. I read everything I could find about him, yet when I walked into his office, I talked too fast and my anger spilled out.

"I want to help you run for president," I told him. "I will sweep the floors of the campaign headquarters, or I will produce your media. I owe it to my father and my brother."

Hart just looked at this madman and nodded. Then he asked me to take a seat. We talked for an hour. I told him I thought candidates were becoming puppets who said the same things in the same ways. Media producers, I explained, were too important in the process. "Media consultants," I told him, "should be nothing but extensions for the candidates. I will never tell you what to say. But I will help you say it in thirty seconds."

I don't remember the rest of the conversation. I must have crashed out of the office, because when I found myself in the hall, my heart was pounding and my fists were clenched. I had blown it. I cared too much. I had let my personal feelings supercede my detached professionalism. Then I sagged and shuffled across the Capitol grounds to my office, foiled again by my passion. To care too much in politics is a mistake—a vulnerability that allows the spear of disappointment to penetrate more deeply. And the political skies are filled with spears of disillusionment and failed expectations.

In midafternoon, though, I received a call from Billy Shore, an assistant to Hart and the most decent man in American politics. He said Hart wanted to visit again the next day. Hart showed up at my tiny two-room office to look at my televison work. He settled on a couch and put his boots on a table. I slipped a cassette into the video machine and readied the remote control. Hart and I began talking about media and the responsibility of a media consultant to the truth.

He asked how I would present him and his "new ideas." I told him I would simply turn on a camera, focus it between the middle of his hair and the bottom of his chin, and let him talk. He liked that. Hart resented being turned into an actor. He said he was in my office in part because of my reputation: I did not structure candidates.

He stayed two hours. When he left, the remote control on the table was still untouched. He had hired me without ever seeing my work.

Suddenly I had realized one of my dreams. I had a presidential candidate, even though the pundits were already announcing that he didn't have a chance in hell to win.

I knew my life was going to change again, so I searched for new offices and invested much of my 1983 profits in new staff. I moved from the two cramped rooms on New Jersey Avenue to splendid quarters behind the Supreme Court Building on East Capitol—three condos that occupied an entire floor in a restored building. My office had a large working fireplace and high ceilings. Sandy's decorator from New Orleans came to town, and soon I was sitting behind a reproduction antique desk and my long conference table was slabs of mirror. Instead of Connie badgering Mary Sue in a small office adjacent to mine, I had a staff that buzzed around twelve rooms.

Morgan didn't make the move with me. It was the most difficult decision I had ever made, but at my prompting he opened his own consulting business and ran it for a few months out of my facility. Though we remained friends until his death in 1997, lifestyle problems had finally ruptured our business association. As my overhead skyrocketed and more and more people depended on me, I seemed to grow more conservative and more of a bottom-line businessman. The party had ended. Morgan took up the slack by drinking the scotch I didn't drink and keeping the late hours I could no longer tolerate. It became hard to play high-stakes poker with lobbyists, pundits, reporters, and congressmen most of the night and function clearly the next morning. It was satisfying to me, though, that Morgan became very successful and financially secure. He was a genius and had extraordinary stamina. But few human bodies could withstand Vietnam, never sleeping, three packs of Pall Malls a day, and prodigious amounts of Glenmorangie. His wife, Adrienne, told me that as she drove him to the Houston hospital where he would within three days choke to death with throat cancer, he raspily sang a country song in tribute to her about "*a good hearted woman in love with a good-timing man.*"

Without Morgan, I had no strong person with whom I could share responsibilities. Although I had people to run errands and do postproduction work after I had written and created ideas, I was the point person on every campaign. And a presidential campaign was headed my way like a freight train. I had no concept of its velocity or power and kept accepting other jobs that walked through the door. I hired another copywriter and some bookkeepers and brought a man up from Louisiana, Ron Pohl, to manage my personal finances and the daily running of the office. He had served on the symphony board with me in Baton Rouge and had been personnel manager of a large chemical plant on the Mississippi River. It was imperative that I have someone of his impeccable integrity because while I lived on airplanes, tens of millions of our clients' money flowed through our offices.

By late fall of 1983 I had the infrastructure to handle a presidential campaign, if not people at the top to share the responsibility of making decisions and executing the most important tasks. My organization was bottom-heavy. That meant I was forced to rely on Randy Thompson, an inexperienced production assistant who had been hired by Morgan, to take some of the burden. Thus he was forced into high-pressure situations for which he was not professionally ready. In retrospect I should have offered a partnership to an emerging consultant like Joe Slade White in New York or Frank Greer in Washington. But I was conditioned by my father to make trouble a test of character and to stand against the storm without allowing others to see me sweat. However, under those Brooks Brothers shirts, I was sweating.

In 1983, the promise of the Christmas season rang false and empty. My mood was so bleak and my imagination so stinted that when someone sent a huge holiday poinsettia to my office, I figured if I took it home it would compensate Sandy for my black and incommunicative moods. But when I handed her my peace offering, she was mystified. I couldn't figure out why until I looked at the poinsettia. During my six-block walk home in the icy Washington air, the lush plant had wilted and frozen into something brown and unrecognizable. My gift had turned into an insult. It was thrown into the garbage without ceremony.

New Year's Eve came without popping champagne corks or even a traditional kiss. I was asleep by ten o'clock. The plant turned out to be more than just a bad move by an ornery husband. It turned out to be harbinger of the upcoming presidential campaign.

By 1984, I had begun to notice that in Washington the emperor wasn't always wearing clothes, and few of the best-known pundits seemed to care—or notice. That wasn't a surprise, as there are hypocrites and phonies everywhere. But what was most disillusioning was that the press, which I had always venerated, played an integral role in the city's highly stylized theater of the absurd: formulating and disseminating the most unimaginative conventional wisdom—and then cashing in on it. What finally dawned on me is that Washington is a city of follow-the-leader opinions and little creativity. It has a deaf ear to the deep rumblings in the rest of the country until quakes begin to erupt. Major decisions affecting politics and policy are made by untalented, unproven underlings, often without the knowledge of their bosses. Meanwhile, the pundits, the TV talking heads, the so-called "wise" men and women march in lockstep. They even echo each other's clever phrases and hot words of the week: For awhile, *sea change* was all the rage. Then came *paradigm,* whatever that means. When Bill Clinton went around saying we should "grow the economy," so did all Democrats. Later, Republicans who thought they were being clever would belittle any Clinton idea by saying it depended "on what the meaning of 'is' is." (This dig was inspired by Clinton's famous dodge in the Monica Lewinsky scandal.) In recent years, "big-time" became the clever riposte. This was derivative, too. During the 2000 campaign, Dick Cheney had responded "Big-time!" when George W. Bush leaned over and whispered (into an open microphone) that a certain *New York Times* reporter was a "major league asshole." At least Bush was giving his own opinion. That's refreshing. It's bad enough when the Wise Ones ape each other's opinions, but when they use the same Washington-speak, you know you are listening to people who've actually stopped thinking before they talk. Big-time.

Intellectual intimidation makes original thought dangerous. One can be labeled unworthy if one does not see the obvious truths as recited by the same group of insiders. The advent of cable television news shows was supposed to change all that, but to me it's been disappointing that a small band of personalities continues to dominate Washington thought. They are wrong at least as often as they are right—*Brill's Content* charted how frequently the pundits completely miss the boat—perhaps because they are allergic to old-fashioned reporting. Guys like MSNBC's Chris Matthews and John McLaughlin earn fat salaries by contributing nothing to society except their predictable opinions. The wise men and women attend one another's cocktail hours and dinner parties and, through their incestuous interaction, adjust their opinions—or calibrate their opposition to one another—until they fit into the accepted story line of the week. In this all-too-predictable format, politicians, journalists, and the stray academic are all interchangeable, using each other's phrases, playing carefully rehearsed roles as the house "conservative" or designated "liberal," reading talking points prepared for them by some twenty-something on the payroll of the special-interest-controlled Democratic (or Republican) National Committee. This process is not an enlightening examination of the issues, it's not honest political discourse, and it sure as hell isn't journalism.

Yet obviously there's something seductive about appearing on these shows—I've done it myself, though I can't quite explain why. I guess all these people are selling something. Lawyers become talk-television personalities as whores for recognition and thus higher fees. Academics, who want to sell books, use their university credentials like a hooker uses hot pants on a corner. For no money they spend hours in television studios to say a few words that add irrelevant historic footnotes to the wisdom of the minute. Doris Kearns Goodwin (before she was discovered plagiarizing other historians) could find her way around many television studios in the dark. If you watch these shows one concludes there are only half a dozen historians in the United States: Doris Goodwin, Douglas Brinkley, Robert Dallek, David McCullough, Michael Beschloss, and Stephen Ambrose, author of best-sellers on the Lewis and Clark expedition and the D-Day invasion. (Even these historians know how weird this is. Ambrose himself once told a friend of mine, "Michael Beschloss is one of my closest friends. But I see Michael on TV more than I really want to.")

Celebrity becomes more important than substance. Famous reporters, politicians, and even consultants clamor for their face time before the cameras. Bob Woodward, who with Carl Bernstein exposed the Watergate scandal of the Nixon administration, is now a political pundit, though he has a completely tin ear for politics. He rearranges what other celebrity pundits say and regurgitates it. It is maddening for a political professional to watch this great reporter sink into an intellectual dance routine.

The networks like this setup because they want the audience to see familiar faces. So a historian who is an expert on Dwight D. Eisenhower gets asked a question about Jimmy Carter, a man he's never studied and never met. Does he decline to answer? Guess again. The network producers don't care. Maybe they never heard of Ike anyway, but the point is the networks don't care because talk is cheap. Literally. Talk shows are cheap to produce. Problem is, the public is getting exactly what it's paying for.

Back at Christmas of 1983, the Wise Ones were certain that my candidate, Gary Hart, was a joke to everyone except me and a small group of fellow true believers. As a result of their pronouncements, we could not raise money and were largely ignored by the major media outlets. At times when the Wise Ones discussed the upcoming presidential campaign among Senator John Glenn, Vice President Walter Mondale, former Florida governor Reubin Askew, and California senator Alan Cranston, they neglected even to mention Hart. On the very morning of the February 28, 1984, New Hampshire primary, a primary Hart would win, the *New York Times* led their paper with an article by Washington bureau chief—and official Wise Man—Hedrick Smith that began this way:

With Senator John Glenn continuing to fade and no new challenger emerging strongly, Walter F. Mondale now holds the most commanding lead ever recorded this early in a Presidential nomination campaign by a non-incumbent, according to the latest New York Times/CBS News Poll.

The nationwide poll, begun immediately after Mr. Mondale's victory in the Iowa caucuses last Monday, shows the former Vice President as the choice of 57 percent of respondents who said they were likely to vote in a Democratic primary or caucus.

Far back, the Reverend Jesse Jackson was preferred by 8 percent. Glenn, from Ohio, and Hart each drew 7 percent, and former senator George McGovern of South Dakota had 6 percent. Three other candidates trailed badly in the survey, conducted by telephone February 21–25.

The incredibly unprescient article went on in the same vein:

In the Democratic race, Mr. Mondale's surge of strength after the Iowa caucuses last Monday left him with unprecedented popularity for this early stage of a Presidential campaign.

The last time opinion surveys recorded such an early overwhelming lead was in 1972, when President Nixon was preferred among Republican voters over Representative Paul N. McCloskey Jr. of California by 83 percent to 6 percent. But Mr. Nixon then had the advantage of incumbency. In February 1968, running as a former Vice President out of office much as Mr. Mondale is today, Mr. Nixon's margin over Nelson A. Rockefeller, then Governor of New York, was 49 to 22 percent . . .

Meanwhile, ordinary Americans—New Hampshire's voters—were instead listening to speeches most Washington Wise Ones never bothered to go hear. "The Washington insiders and special interests have handpicked their candidate for president," Hart said in town after town. "But I offer our party and our country a choice. This election is about the failure of the past and the promise of the future."

Despite Hart's hopeful words, by December the weather was damp and cold and my spirits were as low as they had been since my escape from Louisiana. I withdrew to a leather chair in front of a fire in my library and reread Emile Zola as a way of avoiding the daily newspapers. My television remained as cold as my spirits. The Wise Ones could intrude on my life only if I punched the button on the remote. At the point in my life when I finally felt I could live up to my father's hopes and make a difference, the Wise Ones proclaimed my enthusiasm unfounded and my passions juvenile.

With the longest recession since the Great Depression over, it was "morning again in America" to the Ronald Reagan campaign. To me, it was more like "mourning in America." Federal deficits were spiraling out of control. A frightful new epidemic, AIDS, had hit the country, but no one would talk about it. Spending for military weapons we would never use was up while spending for the cities was down—but my party, the Democrats, had no plan and, seemingly, no philosophy. I wasn't the only Democrat feeling the gloom: between Christmas and New Year's Eve, four different clients who'd been signed up for statewide races called to explain they had decided not to run. As a result, I had beautiful offices, a big staff, a presidential candidate who was a nonstarter, and not enough business to pay the rent. I withdrew more deeply into my chair and switched my readings to Alphonse Daudet and Voltaire.*

But I never let the bastards see me sweat. My daddy said that real men didn't feel sorry for themselves or even seek the counsel of others. After the dreadful holidays finally wound down, I dragged myself to the office to pick up the pieces and try for economic survival.

First I put out feelers for business. There was still minimal competition in 1984, and I soon replaced the clients I had lost. I ended up with candidates I still call friends, like Rufus Edmisten of North Carolina, Frank McRight of Alabama, Senator Max Baucus of Montana, Lindy Boggs of Louisiana, and one of the most unusual clients of my life—though I am

---

*It is a curious and defining fact of my life that my first books were by French writers. A collection of works by Zola, Daudet, Hugo, and de Maupassant was left in my family's possession when my father's brother, Claud Paul, was lost at sea in 1942. He was the second mate of a crew of forty-two that completely disappeared beneath the clear waters of the Caribbean, victims of a German U-boat. As our family's only college graduate until me, he left behind some track letter sweaters he had won as a miler for Texas A&M and a collection of heavy, bound complete works of writers that he read while at sea. I don't remember him, but a family photo shows me sitting on his knee as a two-year-old. More of a family legend than a reality to me, he became my model for life—track, books, college. Later my brother was given his name, and he also perished in war. The bulky books have traveled through life with me.

reluctant to call him a friend—Governor Bill Clinton of Arkansas. Operating capital was no longer a long-term problem, but my spirits were bankrupt because they were invested in the New Ideas of Gary Hart. The pundits continued to ignore him.

With the clock ticking on the campaign, the Wise Ones became even more certain that Hart would soon withdraw. Later I found out that Hart and his campaign manager, Oliver "Pudge" Henkel, had seriously discussed doing just that because they could gain no traction in the face of traditional Washington wisdom. If the Wise Ones don't think you are a candidate, you aren't. As a holding action, Pudge began to cancel telephone lines and fire employees. James Carville, in the middle of his streak of bad luck that seemed to go on for years, was one of the casualties. Pudge was doing everything he could to stretch campaign dollars and keep our dream alive. We were waiting for magic. Part of the austerity was to move the campaign to a headquarters in ramshackle, slumlike offices above a black movie theater in a dangerous section of Capitol Hill. Often the heat didn't work, and the volunteers and the meager staff huddled in overcoats, typing with cold fingers on borrowed computers. More and more meetings were held in my offices, where the temperature was always seventy and the refrigerator was always loaded with beer and soft drinks and the cabinets stuffed with the chips, crackers, and other junk food preferred by our young staff. Because Hart's staff members were infrequently paid, these snacks became part of their diet.

My frustration grew. We had a wonderful press secretary, Kevin Sweeney, who in later years distinguished himself while working for Bruce Babbitt in the Department of Interior. The overall press operation was run by Kathy Bushkin, who became a senior vice president at America Online and a generous philanthropist. The press seemed to like these two, and they did their jobs, but Hart was ignored while Walter Mondale regularly hosted well-attended "brown bag" lunches where the press gathered. As a ploy, I enticed reporters with my secret weapon, gumbo directly from Louisiana. I called my Baton Rouge friend Wanda Williams, one of the great cooks I have known, and asked her to make me a pot of wild duck gumbo, freeze it, and Delta Dash it to me in Washington. Then I got on the phone and invited some reporters I knew, making sure to tell them what I was serving. The gumbo arrived on Thursday morning and was ready for the press when they arrived at noon. I expected two or three reporters, but at least twenty showed up. The gumbo pot was soon empty. This started a series of gumbo dinners that went on until almost five years later, when Hart withdrew from the 1988 presidential campaign.

Thus a politically disinterested Cajun woman from Baton Rouge helped garner attention for an underreported candidate for president. Maybe it was time for the press to engage Hart anyway, but this gumbo event signaled the beginning of new attention to the campaign. To us it seemed like a small miracle. And more were to come. The most significant might have been when a failed film project helped spark a Hart surge.

In June of 1983, when enthusiasm and hope were still running high, I had shot two days of film as the first steps in an introductory biography of the candidate. In accordance with my agreement with Hart, I trailed him with a camera crew recording his comments and musings with people in Colorado, without scripts. I was following the Russell Long model, allowing the candidate to speak unfettered by me. My plan was to inject form later, after Hart had grown comfortable with the camera and my technique. He was concerned that hype would replace substance, and I was working to allow his beliefs and ideas to come through unscreened. A few months later I had to retreat slightly from this agreed-upon approach, but in Red Rocks Park outside Denver that early June, I was still using it to gain the confidence of the candidate. We planned to go later to his boyhood home in Kansas, and then to New Hampshire and Iowa, where the first two election contests would take place.

But the Wise Ones continued to speak. Money dried up. I had a $50,000 investment in Hart and could not afford to shoot any more film for a campaign that was not going to fly. Production was stopped and the first two days of film went on a shelf in cans where it mocked me when I was in the film room. The Hart biography was never produced, which was one of the largest mistakes of the campaign. Voters never got to know this remarkable man in cowboy boots who cared more about his country than any politician I had ever met. When a candidate isn't properly introduced, he or she becomes known only by what people see in newspapers and on television. I felt strongly that if the voters could see the character and intellect of the man, he would become president. I still hold this belief.

There are certain rules of film that can't be ignored—timeless considerations like how to move from one scene to another. If I had been making commercials instead of a documentary when I shot the film in June, I would have shot differently. I would have alternated close shots with wide shots so the film could be cut together without "jump cuts." A jump cut is what happens when you glue two pieces of film together that are similar. Even the slightest change—the closing of an eye or a tiny movement of an arm— makes the scene seem to jump unnaturally when viewed. To solve this problem we often cut to another scene and then back to a similar picture. That is logical to the eye. Therefore, to go from a picture of a person's face looking off into the distance and then to the same face looking down, you need something logical in between, like a sunset. You can also edit from a close shot to a wide shot or a related picture that makes sense, such as a quick shot of a person in the audience listening. After a shot like that, you can go back to almost any scene without jarring the viewer. I had directed the early Hart film simply to record the context of his unfiltered message. He spoke in long paragraphs that were not television friendly—he always insisted on giving more than a surface answer to a complicated problem. In the long documentary I envisioned, I intended to combine his words with scenes of his life. But we had shot no cutaway scenes.

Underfinanced, underappreciated, and facing a supposedly invincible foe, we fancied ourselves to be like Washington's troops in their Valley Forge winter. The Hart campaign slogged on with volunteers and paid staff using talent, determination, and idealism for fuel instead of money. Nonetheless, the campaign clock was ticking. Hart was still in the race, and it was time to take our small, hungry army into the Iowa and New Hampshire primaries. But we needed paid television. In desperation, Pudge asked if I could possibly piece together commercials from the film I had already shot. He explained we didn't have money to shoot new commercials. The consequence of his call turned me into a celebrity.

I buried myself in our editing room with the reels of film. Again and again I looked at the flickering images of Hart in Red Rocks Park. Paul Maslin, a talented associate of Patrick Caddell, made suggestions about which of Hart's comments worked best according to the polls.

In the film, Hart was dressed in jeans and boots, surrounded by people dressed the same way. Some of his answers to their questions were three minutes long. Pudge wanted thirty-second commercials. During the next three days and nights, I studied the reels for places to cut the film and piece it together. By cutting and splicing to reduce the content to thirty seconds, I would be creating sentences and paragraphs in a context that Hart had not used. In effect, his mouth would be mouthing my words. I was nervous because changing his intentions and saying something counter to his philosophy would violate our agreement and be dishonest for a media consultant.

I called Hart's official pollster, Dotty Lynch, and we talked at length about the Hart message and what parts of it might sell in Iowa and New Hampshire. She told me we should talk about generational change. This made sense because the anointed Democrat, Vice President Walter Mondale, was a fifty-six-year-old Minnesotan whose claim to the nomination rested primarily on a long career in national politics. All campaigns are about change, and candidates who run on experience often find themselves fighting to survive. Later, Mondale would have to fight for his political life. (Similarly, in the 2000 election, Al Gore's experience failed to be persuasive enough as a reason for election.) Our Hart slogan, "A New Generation of Leadership," was already being used to contrast us with Mondale, Glenn, and the rest of the pack.

With resolve to keep the campaign alive, I invested even more money in the Hart film and hired an editor. Together we rearranged the tiny snippets of film into coherent twenty- or twenty-five-second pieces. The result was something that sounded good if one could turn away from the screen. But the images would make the viewer seasick as they jumped from one Hart scene to another.

Television at its best must work on several levels. Not only did I want viewers to hear compelling messages from Hart's mouth, I wanted our commercials to reflect his futuristic goals and thinking. In an era when computers were just becoming a hot item, I wanted to identify him with the younger generation of voters who were college educated and upwardly mobile. That was a lot to do in thirty seconds.

In an exploration trip to New York in search of new video technology, we discovered a solution to editing the rough Hart footage—a company with a computer program that would make the images turn like a book page. Today this can be done on everyone's home computer. In 1984, though, it was revolutionary British technology, and we paid about $1,000 per hour to use it. The solution to my problem with the jumpy images was simply to turn a page for each new scene. If more information was needed to fill in the blanks in what Hart was saying when the scenes changed, I would add a few seconds of an announcer's voice over the turning page.

Also, we established a grid that seemed to fade off into the back of the television set—a geometric image that suggested something more like Star Wars than the old politics of Walter Mondale and John Glenn. The result was futuristic-looking political television that had never been seen before. Hart's commercials looked like his message, and like him. New. Different. Technical. Smart.

For these different commercials to work, however, they had to be approved by the two women who were in charge of Hart's New Hampshire campaign, Jeanne Shaheen and Sue Casey. I had never met either of them.

Seldom do consultants encounter anyone who has the slightest doubt about his or her own ability to judge good from bad television. I suppose everyone feels qualified after a lifetime of watching, but people who know the least about political communication often have the strongest views. I was disheartened to find that my commercials would never make the air unless these two local amateurs approved.*

I flew the tape to New Hampshire in my plane so I could personally show it. There were four commercials on the reel. Shaheen and Casey made no comment during the first running. I could not read their faces. I looked out the window at neighborhood shrubs. I knew my fate lay in their hands. Then Sue asked that the commercials be shown again. After the second showing, Shaheen said, "Brilliant." Casey agreed. I was exhilarated.

A few weeks after these commercials began running, *Newsweek* ran my picture with a story calling me the "father of high-tech political television." The dusty film on the shelf had turned me into a celebrity. Within hours, Dick Morris called and said his client, Bill Clinton of Arkansas, wanted to talk to me about doing his media. Senator Max Baucus of Montana asked me to produce media for his reelection campaign. John Y. Brown, the former governor of Kentucky, hired me for his pending Senate campaign. Again I was falling up. Ego overrode common sense, and I signed on campaign after campaign.

But if I thought my ship had come in, that was nothing compared to the

---

*History has proved both these women to be exceptional politicians and people. When Hart was forced to drop out of the 1988 presidential campaign that was operated out of Denver, Sue stayed in the community to become a political activist and was elected to the Denver City Council. In 1996, Jeanne became governor of New Hampshire. Sue wrote a fine book about the 1984 campaign called *Hart and Soul*.

quasi-religious fervor experienced by a gruff, rumpled, and dynamic Democratic operative named Patrick J. Caddell. Pat had been a boy wonder in our party, a strategist to the 1972 George McGovern campaign when he was only twenty-one, and a pollster and key adviser four years later in Jimmy Carter's winning run. In his zeal to replicate that feat, Caddell had, in 1983, developed an exotic theory, namely that the next winning Democrat would be Senator Smith. This candidate, whom Pat actually snuck into some polling questions, was a youngish, new-generation Democrat who was pragmatic, individualist in a voice that was moderately liberal, and above all fresh and independent. Senator Smith was based loosely on the John F. Kennedy of 1956 and 1960, but like his namesake (Pat's inspiration was the incorruptible Jimmy Stewart in the Frank Capra film *Mr. Smith Goes to Washington*), he was fictitious. That didn't stop Pat. He saw his creation as the natural mantle for forty-year-old Senator Joseph R. Biden Jr. of Delaware. But Joe Biden didn't want to run against Reagan, preferring to wait four years. So Pat tried Senator Smith's message out on a forty-two-year-old House member, Richard A. Gephardt of Missouri. But Gephardt also wanted to wait until 1988 to run for president. And so Pat turned to Gary Hart.

He and Hart met one day in my offices and went to a local tavern, the Jenkins Hill Bar, to discuss Pat's possible involvement in the campaign. I understand that in their meeting, Pat emphasized that the campaign should be expressed in generational terms—as had Dotty Lynch. Pat thought this tactic would lure back into involvement those who had demonstrated with McGovern against the Vietnam War. He assured Hart that this message would give him a second place in Iowa and perhaps even a first place in New Hampshire. Pat, a pollster and strategist, brought a lot of credibility to the campaign. He had been the wonder boy for Jimmy Carter and had a kingmaker reputation. We knew the Wise Ones would like Caddell.*

---

*After 1984, a disillusioned Caddell gave up politics and moved to California, where he became an adviser to movie producers and a writer and consultant for the television show *West Wing*. Some saw elements of Senator Smith in Bill Clinton's "new kind of Democrat" campaign in 1992. Pat himself didn't see Clinton as Senator Smith. In fact, he lent his research—and even some of Senator Smith's phrasemaking—to former California governor Jerry Brown. A salient example is Brown's presidential announcement at Philadelphia's Independence Hall, where he said, "Our cause is clear. We must restore commitment to our nation, vitality to the values of our society, vigor to our economy, real democracy to our government and purpose to our national life." As it happened,

There is never calm around Caddell. He reached out to various people for help. Soon the press aide to Ted Kennedy, Bob Shrum, would hang around the office at night to talk about message and cadge free dinners from me. With his intellect and charm, he was a great diversion. Sidney Blumenthal, who seemed to spend his whole life trying to work his way into the White House, would sneak into my offices after hours to help write or edit Hart speeches. To my knowledge, we never used any of Sidney's speeches—at least I hope we didn't—but in his moonlighting efforts, Blumenthal walked very close to the ethical edge. At the time, he worked for the *New Republic*. He later put in stints at the *Washington Post* and *New Yorker* magazine. In the 1990s, Blumenthal was considered such a fanatical Clinton apologist that when he finally got his wish and went to work in the Clinton White House, the joke among the press corps was whether Clinton owed him back pay.

I never trusted Blumenthal, and I wasn't sure Shrum's good but predictable and flowery Kennedy-style rhetoric fit Hart. But the truth is that their presence on our fledgling team gave Caddell a measure of comfort—and gave me some breathing room.

Night becomes day. Pat did not sleep and communicated whenever a thought hit his active brain. One night about 2 A.M., I woke to my private phone ringing in my library. I stumbled from the bedroom to the receiver, trying not to wake Sandy. Before I could even speak, I could hear Pat screaming at the top of his lungs that all was lost and my stupidity had cost us the election. Holding the receiver a few inches from my ear, I searched my brain to understand what terrible thing I had done. But then I heard a couple of clues that he did not know to whom he was speaking and he wasn't talking about Hart's campaign.

"Pat, Pat," I screamed, "This is Ray Strother." To be heard over Caddell's screams, one must scream louder.

Caddell had first written this speech for "Senator Smith" and had put some of that material in an unpublished novel, which he showed to a California college professor named Samuel Popkin. Pat thought Popkin was a friend. But Popkin had a horse in the 1992 race, as it turned out, and he dug out Caddell's manuscript and handed it to the Clinton campaign. James Carville gave it to the *New York Times;* George Stephanopoulos gave it to the *Washington Post.* When asked by the press, Pat admitted helping Brown with the speech, but he was not enamored of how it came to light. He thought what Popkin did was less than professional and what the Clinton team did was shady.

There was a slight pause. "Oh, I guess I pressed the wrong key on the automatic dialer." Click. Pat was gone. I went back to bed.

My wife asked, "Was that Pat?"

"Yes."

"You should do to him what we did with the children when they were babies—keep him awake all day so he can sleep at night. Pat's schedule is just turned around."

The next morning, however, I didn't call Pat. I let him sleep because the peace was blissful.

Caddell was troublesome, but he was brilliant, and he taught me a great deal about interpreting raw polling data. Unlike most pollsters, Pat could describe the emotion as well as the message of a spot. One of his theories was that a group always identifies with the music of its generation. To talk to any particular group, Pat thought we should identify and recall their music. It was Pat who first saw what I was trying to do with the high-tech images of my first commercials. He, better than most pollsters, understood the importance of layering subtle secondary messages on top of the primary message. Pollsters today, though they have become the key players in most campaigns, don't really understand the marriage of emotional and visual images. They are captives of their own cold numbers. As a result of their lack of understanding, television spots have become a catalog of poll data and not as effective as they should be. Political commercials don't work as well as they once did.

For twenty years a battle has raged within political campaigns between image makers and pollsters. In the middle 1990s I finally ran up the white flag. As pollsters achieved superior credence and power, it became extremely difficult for media consultants to win the inevitable confrontations. The new generation of candidates has been trained to accept numbers; poll results have become religion. As a result, the emotional juice has been squeezed out of television commercials. Perhaps that is why we now run three times as many commercials to make the same point as we did twenty years ago. They just don't work as well, because pollsters have forced them into a mold of sameness.

The worst offense against political commercials, however, is the focus group, where people are hired to sit in a room and watch commercial after commercial and comment. When they are promised money they become professional critics and try to earn it by finding fault. Their usual comments are that there is not enough substance and they don't like negative commercials. Because we all know the answers to their criticism before we sit on the other side of a two-way mirror, I wonder why we bother. It might seem harmless, but in fact these groups are dumbing down political television. Producers can make spots that the groups like by giving them what they expect. Thus, in the competitive climate of consulting, media producers are forced to "middle out" their commercials to avoid problems with clients and the wrath of a pollster. The focus group gives the pollster more power in the campaign—exacerbating what is wrong now. Pollsters collect the data and then interpret it—often far beyond the scope of their research. The result is dull, lifeless television, and the public is turning it off.

Of course I make no argument against good research. It is just pseudo research like focus groups and the power vested in a linear person to interpret communication that angers me. Despite the imbalance that exists now, improved modern polling is the most important development in the evolution of political consulting. To run a campaign without a poll is like flying blindly into the dark night in mountainous terrain without a chart or radio.

In the seventies, pollsters Peter Hart and the late Bill Hamilton opened the curtains for me. With their help I could examine my candidates and campaigns as I had never seen them before. I knew not only the prominent issues but how intensely the voters truly felt about them. But neither Hart nor Hamilton prescribed precise words or images. That was my department. Today many pollsters demand that a litany of poll-driven issues be shoehorned into thirty seconds. In a 2000 campaign I even had a pollster ask for revision of a script because the word *richest* was used instead of *wealthiest*. Pace, rhythm, and continuity have been bled from our commercials.

During the 2000 presidential campaign, I was on a political errand in Seattle when I saw a commercial with a stiff Al Gore lecturing a seated audience about crime. I had to laugh. It was another Gore disaster—obviously a case where statistics had won out over style and reason. A candidate noted for his stiffness should not have been lecturing an audience from a distance. He should have been close enough to touch. I am sure Gore's words matched the polling data, but the image aggravated the problem of style and warmth. The humanity had been squeezed out of a man the public already knew was smart, but who had trouble connecting in a human way with voters. I am sure that was a poll-driven spot, approved by people who looked at numbers instead of images. Gore's campaign continued to out-smart itself as his consultants strutted on the stage of egocentric posturing. They jumped day to day in rhythm to slight fluctuations in poll numbers, helping doom their candidate.*

In desperation toward the end of the campaign, Gore withdrew from his professional advisers and depended on his family and his friend Carter Eskew. That was when the campaign reached its depths. Candidates still matter, and their temperament and judgment often are the difference between winning and losing.

Stan Greenberg, one of America's best political pollsters, was released from the Clinton campaign in 1996, reportedly because Clinton didn't think he was definitive enough. He actually prefaced some of his advice to Clinton with sensible disclaimers such as "The numbers tend to indicate . . ." Dick Morris took over and brought in his pet polling firm, Penn and Schoen. With his own pollsters, Dick was back in control of Clinton, feeding him exactly what he wanted. Morris would write paragraphs and dictate language to test in a poll. The result was only a test of which Morris paragraphs worked better than other Morris paragraphs. But Clinton was always a slave to Dick's exact language and would not allow media people to stray from it by even a word. Clinton wanted absolutes, and Morris gave them to him.

Pat Caddell in 1984 was more passionate than either Peter Hart or Bill Hamilton, but like them, he understood communication in a way that transcended numbers. I got along well with Pat. His controlling personality, though, created distress throughout the campaign. The first victim was the official pollster, Dotty Lynch. Pat, on his own, began taking polls and billing the campaign for them, completely ignoring the data brought in by Dotty. Though she remained the official campaign pollster, she was pushed to the sidelines while Caddell ranted and raved to gain complete control of the message. At times I saw the gentle Pudge Henkel put his head down on his desk in utter defeat after losing yet another argument to Caddell. Once I saw Pat, in clinched-fist fury, chase Dotty around his office until she es-

---

*However, it was not entirely the professionals' fault. Gore, in what his team termed "arrogance," often ignored their advice and freelanced. One example is his aggressive move, during a nationally televised debate, into George W. Bush's space. It appeared to be a hostile act. In rehearsal his handlers had set limits to his movement on the stage. For some reason he ignored those limits.

caped by running down the hall. Instead of Dotty, he slugged a filing cabinet while I watched in stunned silence. But his fury brought a lot of focus to the Hart campaign. I am sure part of it was a put-on—an act that worked for Pat just as it does for James Carville.

Gary Hart placed second to Mondale in Iowa and then won New Hampshire, upsetting the Wise Ones in their cozy little parlors in Georgetown. Did they at least take a deep breath, realizing that everything they'd said about the campaign to that point was utter bullshit? Oh no. Instead, they began jostling each other to take credit for predicting Hart's ascendancy. This was a stretch; remember, Hedrick Smith's confident *New York Times* lead ("With Senator John Glenn continuing to fade and no new challenger emerging . . .") was written on February 27, 1984—the day before the New Hampshire primary.

I had traveled around New Hampshire many times with Hart, watching him standing in the snow almost alone, a solitary, heroic figure fighting the odds, greeting people who did not recognize him. He marched on. Vans and cars slid through icy roads into late night so he could talk to six or seven people. Once Sandy and I spent an afternoon with Hart, Caddell, and Ted Sorenson, the famous Kennedy confidant and speechwriter, bumping along back roads between small villages in a van driven by a volunteer. (Sorenson did contribute to at least one Hart speech and maybe more.) Those few people in New Hampshire were the key to winning national attention. Our television was being broadcast out of Boston, and slowly people began to know who Hart was when he stepped out of the campaign van. Television, however, was simply a part of the successful campaign. Hart's hard work and the brilliance of Casey and Shaheen were truly the difference.

The morning of the New Hampshire primary, I left Denver, where I had been meeting with Colorado's lieutenant governor, Nancy Dick, and arrived in Boston to find the entire Northeast snowed in by a fierce storm. At midnight, in only a thin business suit, I had to run from the rental car office with a cup of hot water to pour on the lock before I could force the key into the car's door. As I drove north that night into New Hampshire in snow-blind peril, I realized I was the lead car going across unplowed bridges. It finally struck me that the headlights behind me were people waiting to see if I made it. Little did they know they were following a redneck who had not even seen snow until he was an adult.

The hotel in Manchester was booked solid—and my reserved room had been released to another stranded traveler. Finally, after I pulled a Caddell and yelled enough, I was allowed to sleep on a mattress on the floor of the unfinished penthouse suite. There were no draperies on the huge glass windows, and the snow was beating against them. But the suite was warm, and I was dead tired. The next thing I remember was the phone on the floor next to my mattress ringing. It was bright outside with the sun shining off the snow. I picked up the phone and walked around nude, talking to Israeli radio about the great Hart victory. I was the only Hart person they could find—the hotel desk clerk knew me from my early morning rampage in the lobby. Suddenly it dawned on me that the people on the sidewalks below were being entertained or appalled by a totally nude man walking around with a telephone in his hand. My head still ached. In two days I had had only four hours sleep, a bumpy airplane ride, and a tedious car trip through the blizzard.

Little did that nude man know that was to be the first night of a sleepless year. After getting dressed, I called around and located the site of the Hart campaign's strategy meeting. It was at the home of a New Hampshire supporter of Gary's. When I finally found the house, I had to park almost a block away. A stranger manning the door told me it was a private meeting and to buzz off. He wouldn't listen to my explanation—that I was the campaign's media consultant. I circled the packed house. The scent of fresh meat had attracted political sharks from as far away as Washington, D.C., and California. Some of the Wise Ones wanted in on the feast as well. At the back door I was rebuffed by another stranger. I was literally locked out of the Hart campaign. As I circled the house like a wolf looking for an opening, I heard knocking on glass and saw Pat motioning to me from a window. He opened the window and I climbed in. That was how I got back into the Hart campaign. From that moment on, there were people trying to close doors between me and Hart. I later found out it wasn't personal. In presidential campaigns, it is common for various people to try to make room for themselves or their agendas in the inner circle by pushing someone out.

Later in the campaign, during the New York primary, a California congressman named Henry Waxman tried to force the campaign to fire me, ostensibly because of my failure to make a commercial Waxman wanted promising that, as president, Hart would not sell certain kinds of American-made fighter jets to any Arab nations. Hart didn't allow me to be fired for the simple reason that I was carrying out his instructions. He felt he had already made enough concessions to Israel by promising to move our embassy to Jerusalem. This episode was one of many examples of the great pressures that are exerted by numerous special interest groups to control the dialogue of a campaign for the most important office in the world.

The Hart victory in New Hampshire affected my life like gasoline poured on an already roaring fire. My seven telephone lines at the office never stopped ringing from daylight until midnight. That became a normal workday. Hart's blazing eyes now stared at me from airport newsstands. The press could not get enough of him. Wanda's gumbo was no longer necessary. The Wise Ones began patting themselves on the back, saying they knew it all along. The campaign began to get calls from consultants who were ready to come in and take over. Driving through the middle of the country one night listening to public radio, I heard a Democratic political consultant from the Midwest say it was a miracle that Hart had won, because his television was so bad. This consultant was trying to get a toehold in the business and was angling for some of the Hart television. To my satisfaction, even today he remains a third-stringer. The consulting business was about to change drastically, however; by 1986 this midwesterner's slash-and-burn ambition would be commonplace.

The "Hart look" began to appear everywhere. While waiting to change planes in St. Louis for a visit with Governor Clinton, I saw one of my commercials on the television over the airport bar. The only difference was that the candidate was someone I had never heard of, running for a minor local office. Otherwise, every scene duplicated my spot for Hart. For the next two years I would hear of consultants making presentations in which they claimed that *they* had created the format Hart used. It was becoming a tough business. However, 1984 was only the preamble for what was to follow in the next decade.

The Hart campaign and my year turned into a carnival thrill ride. We would reach roller-coaster highs and then plummet with breathless speed to the bottom. The Hart bounce out of New Hampshire basically eliminated all of the other candidates except Mondale. We racked up primary after primary as Mondale's expensive, top-heavy campaign fought to regain its balance. Our small campaign operated on adrenaline and hope. Money began to come in, but we could never get ahead of the curve. The gauntlet of Tuesday primary elections demanded that we produce and run television before there was money to pay for it. This usually meant that we produced new television spots on Wednesday or Thursday that would run for only four or five days. But in most cases that was enough. Hart now traveled on a chartered jet with a hundred reporters seated in the coach section behind him. I would board his plane at various locations around America and ride for a few hours to try to get back in sync with rapidly changing demands on my time and Hart's. There was never enough time. Fatigue began to wear on us all, and the result was that we made some mistakes. I was riding planes at least six days a week. I produced Hart television in New York, Nashville, North Carolina, Pennsylvania, New Jersey, and Ohio, staying only hours ahead of the primary election deadlines.

I shot one successful series of ads outside a closed steel plant in Ohio under almost impossible conditions. It was overcast and raining with occasional snowflakes. A group of working people like those I had grown up with huddled against rusty metal in a bleak landscape. Although Hart was not endorsed by the unions, the bosses were having difficulty keeping their individual members in line. Many unionized workers carried a grudge against the Carter administration because of its economic record, an attitude that carried over to Mondale, Jimmy Carter's vice president. Those stamping their feet to keep warm around me didn't care what their union leadership had to say. But my candidate was nowhere to be found. His plane was running late.

I didn't know how long I could hold these men. To keep them busy and to help me stay warm, I began wandering through the group screaming angry and provocative questions at them while my camera and sound man followed close behind. I understood these workers' fears and frustration. I was home again in Port Arthur. Soon they began responding.

First man: A good many of us in this valley gave Reagan a chance because we were disillusioned with Carter and Mondale.

Second man [cupping a cigarette, his hot breath vaporizing in the frigid air]: We're still disillusioned with Mondale. He's still the same Fritz Mondale.

Third man [stamping his feet]: We do need something new.

Another worker [motioning at the still factory behind him]: It's kind of hard to feed your family from a factory like this.

First man [rather angry]: Union leadership may get our union dues, but they don't get our hearts and minds.

Another worker: We lost with Mondale before. He had his chance. He got up to bat. He struck out. Now he wants another turn. He hasn't even been out to the field yet.

A worker in a red jacket [with a sigh]: Union leadership asked us to vote for Carter and Mondale and we did. They are asking us to vote for Mondale again.

Angry worker with cigarette: Mondale and Carter was in, they shut all these steel mills, twelve miles of steel mills from one county to the other county. Hart, I think, shows a quality of leadership I'm looking for.

They were not only saying things that helped define Hart, they were echoing conversations I had with my father just before he died. The old labor warrior thought that the paid leadership had hijacked the unions, leaving working men and women just another level of bosses to deal with. He dreamed of crashing into the union executive offices and splintering their antique desks and then burning their limos so the blue-collar members could again take over.

For an hour, looking over my shoulder for the Secret Service detail that would deliver my candidate, I shot roll after roll of film. The workers had expended their anger and were becoming depleted, cold, and wet. Water dripped from my cap into my eyes. I was about to lose the group when the Secret Service motorcade rolled up. Hart bounded out of the car and called me over. He looked haggard and exhausted. His eyes were black circles.

"What are we doing here? I only have about twenty minutes." Hart was abrupt and appeared angry. But it was only fatigue.

"Hell, Gary, I've shot all the film I need. All you need to do is walk into the middle of the group and talk about the problems of the old economy. I'll take what I can get. If you don't talk, I can still produce commercials. These guys are great."

Hart softened up a little and I directed him into the back of a Chrysler van where our makeup artist was waiting. I told her to try to take some of the black out from under his eyes but not to fool with his windblown hair and to avoid powder that would run in the rain. Then I went over to the workers and told them to give Hart pure hell when he came out.

"Challenge him. What new ideas? How are you different from Mondale?"

I placed Bob and his camera in the middle of the group. The sound man jogged beside Hart to clip a mike on Hart's shirt. The result was film magic. The workers' frustration turned Hart on, and for ten minutes he talked while Bob circled with the camera putting him in every shot. Only ten minutes. One roll of film. Hart hammered out this message:

Ronald Reagan represents the past. I think the last administration and Mr. Mondale represent the past. We've got to have new leadership. We've got to have somebody with a vision for this country's future, who has an idea, not only of how to modernize steel mills so that they are competitive in the world but also to diversify and to bring new industries and put the old industries and the new industries together and offer this country hope.

And then Hart left, with all of the lights blinking on the long black limos hustling him to the next event, for which he was already late.

That night, my still-damp Scottish tweed coat smelling like a sheep from the cold rain, I slept for three hours in a chair in the St. Louis airport so I could catch the first flight into Little Rock for a meeting with the Clintons. After a maddening session with Bill and Hillary in which they dissected every word in the scripts, I flew to Raleigh, North Carolina, for a sitdown with Rufus Edmisten, a great redneck candidate for governor who was a relief and a change in style. From there I flew to my Washington office to edit film, then caught a train that night for New York and another meeting. Life was a blur. I felt like a robot. I seldom saw my wife. There was never an airport where I was not being paged. My vision narrowed, and the world seemed to slip by my eyes like images through a train window.

On some almost-empty midnight plane to Atlanta, I was trying to sleep when a flight attendant with political aspirations took the seat next to me. She had *Newsweek* folded to the page with my picture. She wanted to talk politics and to know about Hart. I tried to oblige her but kept falling asleep during the conversation. Then she was gone. When the plane landed and I stumbled off, she pressed a small note in my hand with her address, telephone number, and a message: "If you can't find a hotel room, my apartment is only five minutes away. Call me and I'll pick you up." I staggered down the jetway, tearing the note into little pieces, littering the floor. I didn't want to mistakenly put it in my pocket and have to explain it to Sandy. I didn't have the energy.

Numerous books, some of them quite good, have been written about the 1984 campaign. Hart's loss still bothers me. Against tremendous odds, we came closer than anyone expected and lost by a whisper at the very end. My friends Jack Germond and Jules Witcover, real newspaper reporters who are truly wise, believe that we missed an opportunity to declare victory after the California primary. Jack once told me that had Hart started acting like the presumptive nominee, he could have been the nominee. That year, California went to a confusing method of selecting delegates by congressional district, which worked to Mondale's advantage and gave him nearly as many delegates as Hart. But Hart won statewide—in a state with a long tradition of winner-take-all primaries. Germond and Witcover thought that Hart should have seized the momentum by simply declaring himself the winner. Had he done this, they believe, enough of the Democratic "superdelegates"—party hacks and elected officials—would have come over to our side.

Two other newsmen I respect, Carl Cannon, then with the *San Jose Mercury News,* and Joel Garreau of the *Washington Post* maintain that Hart couldn't have won the nomination that year—though he should have— because the Democratic Party elders had rigged the nominating process too thoroughly in an effort to benefit the eastern establishment. New York, for instance, had many more delegates to the San Francisco convention than California did—even though California is more populous. Cannon and Garreau added up the vote totals from all the primaries and caucuses and discovered that if delegates were apportioned on the basis of population— the way they are in the Electoral College—Hart would have beat Mondale. Call it the Revenge of the Wise Ones.

The Wise Ones themselves, of course, claimed later that the campaign came down to a single quip of Mondale's: "Where's the beef?" Supposedly this question illustrated that Hart didn't really have all that many new ideas. At the time, Wendy's fast food restaurant was running ads that attacked McDonald's. An actress, Clara Peller, opened the lid of an obvious Golden Arches product and said, "Where's the beef?" The slogan, the actress, and the commercial all clicked. In a national debate staged in Atlanta on Sunday, March 5—two days before Super Tuesday—after Hart outlined his economic plan, Mondale said, "You know, when I hear your ideas I'm reminded of that ad, 'Where's the beef?'" The audience laughed and Hart grimaced—the way anyone would if his intelligence had been belittled by a hamburger slogan.

I always found this a superficial explanation of why Hart lost in 1984, but it certainly is true that campaigns often hinge on little things. My own nomination for why, in the end, the Hart campaign came up just short is a different Mondale one-liner, but one that hit Hart in a more vulnerable place—and which particularly stung Pat, me, and Gary's other campaign aides.

Mondale's tart observation came in the midst of the contentious Illinois primary, an election that may have been the pivotal one in who would win the Democratic nomination. The key, of course, was Chicago. At that point, Mondale was still staggering. Caddell argued with Pudge Henkel that we needed to identify Mondale with the old machine politics of Eddie Vrdolyak, chairman of the Cook County Democratic Party. Pudge was adamant: Gary was refusing to run negative advertising. That didn't dissuade Caddell. He could smell victory, and he didn't want what he called "amateurs" destroying our chances. As a result, the diplomatic Henkel gave us permission to write two scripts, one identifying Vrdolyak and one not mentioning his name. In truth, I don't remember writing the fangless version. Pat and I both swore to Pudge that nothing would run without Gary's approval. I wrote a couple of scripts and took them to Pat's office, where he made minor suggestions for changes. Something bothered me about the whole process, so I was terribly careful. Pat agreed that Gary had to approve the commercials and said that I could send them with Connecticut senator Chris Dodd, who was to meet Hart that night for dinner in Chicago. Dodd would then call me—or Pat—with the answer.

Still nervous, I trusted no one with the scripts other than my wife, and I asked Sandy to hand-deliver them to Senator Dodd, who was leaving Washington that night for Chicago. I gave her instructions not to put them in any aide's hands. She was to wait until Dodd himself could take them. She went to Dodd's office and fought off several aides until Dodd personally took the sealed envelope with Hart's name on the front. Then, as double insurance, I took a cab to the campaign headquarters and put copies of the scripts on the desk in front of Henkel, who was on a conference call. I made the familiar "call me" sign language and went home. Around 11 P.M. I called Caddell and asked if he had heard from Dodd. He said he had not but would keep trying. I called again at 12, 1, and finally 2:30. In the meantime my production assistant had produced my scripts and was standing by in Chicago to deliver them to the stations before the Friday noon cutoff, when the logs are closed. Again, time and finances were our enemy. Mondale had been on the air for several days.

At 5 the next morning I woke myself with a cold shower and took a cab to National Airport, where I was to meet Caddell for a trip to North Carolina (we were working together on the Rufus Edmisten campaign). The clock was running out and I still had not heard from Dodd. I called my assistant in Chicago and held him on the line while I waited for Caddell in hope that he would have a message. The last boarding call had been made when I saw Pat jogging toward me. Every second counted. I yelled down the hall, "Did you hear from Chris?" On some dark nights I still think of Pat's answer: "Release the spots."

"Go," I told my production assistant and was soon asleep on the plane. From a campaign briefing in Raleigh on what our polls were showing, I went to New Orleans to meet with Lindy Boggs, a candidate for reelection to Congress, leaving there in early evening for Arkansas and Bill Clinton. I checked into Little Rock's Excelsior Hotel about midnight and was given an emergency call notice from Pudge Henkel. When I opened the door to my room, the phone was ringing. I picked it up and heard Pudge weeping in anger or frustration.

"Why did you do it?"

"What?"

"You ran the negative spots without Gary's approval."

I was stunned but finally convinced Pudge that there had been some sort of mix-up. I added that the spot was scheduled to run only lightly over the weekend, with heavy play on Monday.

"Pull it. Gary said to get it off the air immediately."

I explained to Pudge that it was midnight and it would be impossible to pull the spot at that hour. The earliest we could pull it without taking extreme measures was Monday. I also pointed out that if we tried to kill the spot sooner, it would create news that would harm the campaign. I finally got him to agree that it would be pulled first thing Monday morning. But fifteen minutes later the phone rang again.

"Gary says to pull the spot now!"

"It's impossible, Pudge. We'd have to get station managers to go in from the suburbs to take a spot out of the automated system on Saturday. It would be a disaster."

Pudge agreed to reason with Hart one more time. I sat in a chair with the phone in my lap and must have gone to sleep without replacing the receiver. A bellman pounding on the door woke me. As I replaced the receiver, the phone began to ring. Pudge's message left no doubt. "Call the station managers at home."

By Saturday night we were headline news on every television station. The Sunday newspapers talked about the Hart error. That night in a national debate Mondale asked Hart, "Senator, if you can't run your own campaign, how can you run this country?" That's the line that I believe cut so deep—much deeper than the quip about beef. The Mondale campaign had been trying to paint Hart as an unsteady leader, and we had played into their hands. We went from winning to losing Illinois and perhaps the campaign.

One of the mysteries of the campaign is how the mistake happened. Another is why Hart was so adamant that the spot be pulled. Later I found out that Senator Dodd had put the scripts in Gary's hands in a restaurant as he said he would. Why hadn't Hart seen them? Perhaps, as with the rest of us, the problem was fatigue. Some thought that Hart had perhaps made some sort of arrangement with Vrdolyak and the television spot negated the deal. It would be easy to blame Caddell for the problem and accuse him of free-lancing. There is no doubt he is the best target. Yet there was great confusion and many people communicating. Time is a killer, and campaigns can't afford to wait around to sort things out. Pat may have been dealing with secondhand information.

The morning after the defeat, Hart summoned us all to his Senate office. I expected to be fired. He surveyed all of the ten or so faces in the room and said quietly, "Some mistakes have been made. Let's put them behind us and fight on." When people asked why I am still so devoted to Hart, I simply shrug my shoulders. They wouldn't understand.

But the fight grew more desperate. The clock was ticking on all of my other campaigns, and with Morgan gone I had almost no help dealing with clients. Hart campaign demands occupied me about ten hours a day. And duties for the other campaigns accelerated as the campaign clock ticked. I wrote scripts on airplanes and dictated them over airport telephones to a staff member. We had few computers and no cell phones in 1984, and my office was phone booths across America. Ron Pohl wrote the checks, dealt with the media buyers, and kept my personal financial life on an even keel. Occasionally he would hand me envelopes stuffed with money so I could eat on the road and pay for cabs. I would run out of clean shirts and buy new ones along the way. Emergencies requiring me to leave hotel rooms early would mean discarding shirts I had sent to the hotel laundry. Most of them I never recovered. I estimate the year cost me about thirty shirts and two suits. I became an expert at sleeping on airplanes and eating in rib restaurants and fern bars with young, eager staff members. I gobbled bottles of Tums.

One late night in the campaign plane, Hart summoned me to sit beside him. The team that traveled with him always left the first-class seat open next to Hart. He needed time to think and read. When he needed one of us, we would be called to sit with him.

"What do you think we should do now?"

"I think we should go on television for thirty minutes to counter the Mondale claim that you are all style and no substance."

Hart was excited by the idea and summoned several other staff members to kneel around him. Conventional wisdom makes it hard to convince candidates to use the thirty-minute format. That night I had to do my best selling job.

I wrote a draft of the Hart's remarks, and then Caddell took over. I had no real complaints about having help with the script because I was having to run double-time twenty hours a day and was still losing ground. Pat was a very good speechwriter, as he would later prove as a writer for the TV show *West Wing*. But even with this task off my shoulders, I still needed to make adjustments. Tough decisions. Questions of survival.

Early in the morning after a short and fitful night, I called John Y. Brown and told him I had to resign his campaign. He was furious with me. I really liked Governor Brown and his wife, former Miss America Phyllis George, but they were difficult to work with. Scriptwriting went on forever and filming was almost impossible as Phyllis, with her broadcasting career, would try to direct. I thought it was a time-consuming, nonproductive campaign and the one that I needed to cut.

I was right because Brown was badly beaten later that year in the primary election. My work would have been an exercise in futility. It was tough, though, to disappoint a client. Through the wear and tear of the campaign I had changed my opinion of Brown, becoming ambivalent toward him, but Phyllis made me laugh. I enjoyed driving up to their Bluegrass mansion through the white fences with racehorse colts running around the beautiful pastures. Phyllis told me they didn't own the horses but let their fields be used by a breeder because it seemed to add so much to the house to have beautiful animals at their fences. On one visit she met me at the door with two bottles of champagne and a huge bag of Cheetos. John Y. was in the living room being measured for suits by a tailor, so we had to go to their bedroom to look at the videotape I had brought. We sat in the middle of a large round bed and played the commercials. Occasionally the phone would ring and Phyllis would say, "I can't talk now, I'm in bed with Ray Strother." She had a great sense of humor. Her husband, however, found nothing funny about my resigning from his campaign. I felt the effects for years whenever I tried to get business in Kentucky. His tentacles reached all across the political spectrum, and he made it difficult for candidates to hire my firm.

Even without the demanding Brown campaign, there was no noticeable change in my schedule or workload. My business had grown up around me. I continued to hire support people to make my life easier, but they could not add hours to my day or advise candidates for me. I realize now that, with my eye totally on Election Day, I was overlooking important details of both my business and my personal life.

One tends to lose a sense of reality. Family, friends, and even health and safety are ignored. In the Rufus Edmisten campaign I watched the campaign manager, Charlie Smith, and three other men take off from a mountain airport in Boone, North Carolina, in a single-engine plane. Moments later we heard they had crashed. All walked away from the wreck but Charlie. He had an important campaign event that cost him his life. Later in that campaign, when the race with Eddie Knox, our Democratic opponent in the primary, grew close, it was once necessary to have overnight processing of our film. The campaign clock was ticking, and our margin was going to be razor thin even if we did everything right. The closest lab was in Atlanta, but the professional pilot refused to "go into that giant airport in bad weather." A person from the processing lab was waiting for us at the airport, so I got into my plane, punched up through the rain and clouds, and landed behind a Boeing 747 at minimum landing conditions and hard rain. After handing off the film, I climbed back into the plane and flew to Washington. Twice while on autopilot I fell asleep for minutes at a time. It is obvious now that I had lost my sense of perspective. Had I died, another happy consultant would have been in my place the next morning and the frantic jazz beat would have continued. In reflection, I was no better. I didn't even have time to go to Charlie Smith's funeral. The next day in North Carolina the beat went on.

I mention life and death because that's what the stakes seem to become in this rarified atmosphere. So my thirty-minute program that Pat was working on became the most important event in my life. We had difficulty getting a television network to take the program, but finally CBS in New York allowed us to spend our $200,000 after the 11 P.M. news. It would play all across America. We knew the audience would be small, but our spot would demonstrate Hart's depth and counter the Mondale hamburger claim. And best of all, it would send another signal to the press that Hart was the candidate of substance.

The thirty-minute program turned into a nightmare. Two natural forces collided, a spring blizzard and Pat Caddell. Pat had control of the only working script of the program, and the last I heard was that he was going to New York to finalize it. We were to film Hart at the Ed Sullivan Theater, and Pat was to meet me there with the revised script. We had already spent hours cutting and pasting to fit the thirty-minute format. Despite Pat's great intellect, he refused to be concise. Ideas poured out of his head in torrents. I was terribly concerned that he would again add material, but he was out of touch and could not be found by a score of people searching for him. Pat was lost in New York with the only copy of our speech. Something began to gnaw at my stomach, and I upped my consumption of Tums. Things were beginning to break badly. CBS wanted the show in time for approval before it went on the air. Backing up the clock, I determined that if we could begin shooting at noon, we could be finished by three. It would be a simple script read from a Teleprompter. But Pat was lost. The script was with Pat. And a major spring storm was about to swamp the East Coast.

I had an 8 A.M. Eastern Airline shuttle ticket in my shoulder bag, but as I lay in bed that night I imagined long delays and flight cancellations. Before daylight I dressed, caught a cab to Union Station, and boarded a train. Three hours later I was walking through a blizzard to the Ed Sullivan Theater. Inside it was not a lot warmer than outside. I was met by a Teleprompter operator, a makeup artist, cameraman, lighting director, set designer, and the various crew members needed to make things work in New York. A long table was set up with coffee, soft drinks, juice, water, donuts, chips, bagels, cream cheese, and various vegetables and dips for the crew.

The Teleprompter operator was poised at his keyboard, his fingers hanging over the keys. He shrugged and wandered off toward the refreshment table when I told him the script would soon come. Then I started watching the door to see when Pat would bound in.

At 2 P.M. I got a call on the pay phone from CBS. "Is the tape finished?" I got the same call every half hour. I never told him I didn't have a candidate or a script. At 3 P.M. I began to wade out into the deep snow to clear my head and work off nervous energy. At four I began trying desperately to find the Secret Service detail. I was told he would be there by five. I calculated. We had to put the speech on tape, edit in titles and paid-for lines, and deliver it to CBS in time for a review. At about 5:30 the doors blew open and an army of Secret Service marched in with Hart, Caddell, and actor Warren Beatty, a friend of Hart's. They, like everyone else on the East Coast, had been delayed by deep snow and blizzard conditions.

Beatty came over and shook my hand. We had met several times. "If there's anything I can do, just let me know. I'll take a seat over against the wall." I popped some more Tums. Not only were we late, but I had one of America's best directors watching me work. I considered his most recent movie, Reds, a work of genius.

CBS called again. "Going great," I told the vice president of sales.

Then Pat handed me the script. It had grown to over an hour in length. Both Hart and Beatty saw my distress.

"We'll just cut it a little," Pat said.

Page by page they read the script aloud with people shouting suggestions and changes. Paragraphs were eliminated. Pages were scratched. As a page was completed I would hand it to the prompter operator who tried to decipher the slashes and added words.

CBS called again. "We're almost finished." It was after six.

Beatty was the calm in the storm. Not only was he literate, he was reasonable and constructive. Finally, at about seven o'clock, he suggested that perhaps we should start on the first four or five pages with Hart on camera while he continued to work with Pat and the group.

CBS called again.

I turned on the lights we had been nervously tinkering with all afternoon and found that Hart's deep-set eyes would require even more adjustments. This was done by adding low eye lights that almost came up from the floor—effective, but also making it more difficult to read the Teleprompter. The set was a simple wingback chair a few feet away from a seamless background that disappeared on camera. Hart was lit to be the only focus. With Randy Thompson, my production assistant, taking notes and doing a remarkably good job of trying to keep times, we began shooting while in a small adjacent room the rest of the group—functional only because of the calm leadership of Beatty—grappled with the script.

Hart began reading. After about a minute he stumbled over a word and asked to start at a previous sentence. "You can edit it to a new sentence, can't you?" Of course I could. Randy made notes. Seldom, though, would we go more than a couple of minutes without an interruption that required us to back up. It was going to turn into an editing nightmare. Every time we started again, we had to go back to the completion of a good sentence and start again. However, the old material remained on the tape for us to edit out in the studio.

Joe Mercurio, the media buyer, because of the panic calls he was getting from CBS came to the studio and manned the pay phone. At breaks I would hear him say, "We are adding the finishing touches." Then, there was no more script. We waited for the prompter operator to put in the last of the material and we were finished. We picked up the tape and rushed down the street to a video production studio where we began trying to put together the hundreds of pieces into one coherent program. We had been joined by the great *New York Times* reporter Dudley Clendinen, who frantically made notes. Our announcer was in the sound booth recording an introduction and the paid-for credits. Beatty was lying on the floor of the editing suite with his eyes closed. People were stepping over him. He didn't notice. He was again the only calm in the storm.

By now the vice president of CBS was in the lobby. He wanted his tape. It was almost 11. The show went on at 11:30. As Hart's last words were spoken and we added the announcer reading the paid-for disclaimer, we didn't even have time to rewind or view the final product for flaws. Mercurio ran from the room with the tape under his arm. Beatty walked over and hugged me. He didn't say a word. Then he left.

Suddenly a room of flashing lights and bedlam became calm. I slumped into a chair. Clendinen offered to buy me a drink in a place where we could watch the program. I think even he was a little dizzy. We waded quietly through the snow to a bar with a television blaring at both ends. When we asked the bartender if we could watch a political program, he looked at us like we were crazy. In desperation I gave him $200 to switch the set at our end of the bar to CBS and raise the sound. There were moans and groans from those at the bar. We had replaced a hockey game. Thompson, Clendinen, Mercurio, and I watched the show come on and progress. It didn't seem to have a flaw. Hart was good, and it hung together despite all the editing. But something was dreadfully wrong. When it was over America's CBS screens went blank. Our program, after editing, was only twenty-two minutes long. After a few minutes the network managed to find filler for the dead air. I drank another scotch and walked out into the snow to find a place to finally sleep.

Dudley's April 1, 1984, story began by saying:

It is 8:40 P.M. Thursday. Joseph Mercurio, who buys television time for Senator Gary Hart's commercials, sits in the reception area of the Reeves Video studio on East 44th Street in Manhattan, looking at the front door, willing it to open.

He has paid $123,720 in campaign money to CBS for 30 minutes of time to broadcast a new commercial and fund-raising appeal for Senator Gary Hart. It is to be aired nationally at 11:30 this night. It is to be delivered to CBS in 50 minutes, and it is not yet made. If the campaign misses the deadline the money could be lost.

8:43 P.M. A Cadillac pulls up through the slush outside. The guard buzzes the door open and four men rush in. The first is Raymond Strother, the Washington communications media consultant who makes the Hart commercials. He wears a slouch hat and a coat against the weather, owlish, horn-rimmed glasses and a strained expression. He is working with five gubernatorial and senatorial races as well as the Hart campaign. He has lost 22 pounds in the last month. He has had no more than four hours of sleep for the last 10 nights. He feels weak in the legs. . . .

I didn't know it then, because I still harbored hopes Hart could be our party's nominee in 1984, but that may have been the high-water mark of our campaign. None of us had any illusions that Ronald Reagan would be an easy mark in November (Reagan carried forty-nine states against Mondale), but we figured that Gary could run a credible race against Reagan—giving the Wise Ones a scare in the process—and then come back in 1988 as the most formidable presidential candidate in either party. It was not destined to happen that way, of course, and like most Democrats I have mixed emotions about what transpired in the next twelve years in presidential politics. My own nagging feelings, however, have less to do with the complicated persona of my client from Arkansas, Bill Clinton, and much more to do with unresolved doubts that I did everything I could have for Gary Hart.

The truth of it is that as Hart got hot, I got hot. The siren song came in stereo: Fame and money are the rewards of a consultant who has the touch, and in 1984 I had it. But what if I had resisted some of those other blandishments, and spent all my time and energy on Hart? Would the campaign have worked more smoothly? Would a better-rested media adviser have served the candidate better? What if Pat and I had been in Chicago with Hart at that dinner with Chris Dodd before the Illinois primary? We could have made the case directly to Gary to run the negative spots, and if that appeal didn't work, we would have known never to put them on the air. Then Mondale wouldn't have been able to make his crack about Hart not even being able to run his own campaign, let alone the country. I, for one, have never believed that Mondale's "Where's the beef?" line would have been enough to beat a visionary like Gary Hart.

No one has ever pointed fingers at me or the other Hart advisers in this way; certainly Hart didn't do it himself. In fact, the veterans of that campaign have remained close. It was a fun ride, yes, but Gary Hart was a candidate and a cause we all believed in.

I still do.

I stumbled through the rest of 1984, a wiser consultant with new scars. I had more victories than losses. It is always painful to lose, but two defeats would bother me for years: Rufus Edmisten in North Carolina and Frank McRight in Alabama. But beyond the leaden feeling in my stomach about their losses, something in me had changed. Something about political consulting was also about to change, and I was to become an observer, trying to reason it all out. I no longer felt heroic when I stepped out of airplanes, applauded by troubled campaigns. I suddenly didn't want the spotlight. I wanted to walk in and out of scenes and leave only shallow footprints. I was Peter Sellers in the movie *Being There.* I just wanted to watch. I finally understood that a boy from Port Arthur could not change the world. My father's dream wasn't real. He believed in heroic figures who stood for right and prevailed with blood on their fists and righteousness in their hearts. The little man could triumph and common sense was the only real sense.

The world was still divided into good guys and bad guys, but they both had strings attached from interests far more powerful than they. I also found that voters would vote for hamburger slogans and were influenced by trivia. The greatest fraud was that working people like my father were talked into doing the bidding of the rich and powerful by being distracted by minor issues. How could an hourly worker vote Republican, I still asked myself.

Seven miles from my mountain home in Montana is a bar called the Wise River Club. The regulars are working people I like and admire. They are always there to help the helpless or someone in trouble. More than once they have pulled me out of deep snow or extended little kindnesses. Their only retirement is the Democratic program of Social Security. Their parents are on the Democratic program of Medicare. Their wonderful, income-producing Big Hole River is clean because of Democratic conservation regulations. Their cattle graze on federal land set aside by Democrats. Those who work in the local mines live longer because of Democratic rules protecting them in the workplace. Yet they will vote Republican because they think the Democrats want to take away their snowmobiles. Snowmobiles!

I only observe. In 1984 I learned not to argue. Forces far greater than the workers at the Wise River Club control their vote and their attitudes. I learned I cannot change the world, but maybe I can understand the forces at work—for instance, the congressman who tried to get me fired because I didn't do his bidding on Arab policy. I don't hold it against the congressman. He is like the workers in the Wise River Club.

So 1984 slumped to a finish. I had been battered and I was tired. Sandy and I went to Paris and checked into a large suite at the Plaza Athénée, where for three days I stayed in bed, waking only for room service. Sandy, always a good wit, said that it was easily the most expensive nap she had ever taken. She would later tire of my distraction as I tried to deal with the reordering of my life's core values. I was in a hotel room in Paris that cost more per night than my father ever made in a month. Some good friends had been defeated. A fellow consultant had died in North Carolina. My last virginities had been taken. In November of 1984 I finally came to the conclusion I wasn't going to change the earth. I wasn't even going to adjust it. I enjoyed the craft of political consulting and felt I was better at it than anyone around. I still wanted to help good candidates who would in turn help working people, but I was beginning to believe that I needed professional detachment if I was to survive in the business. I spent most of 1985 alone in a shepherd's cottage outside of Moffat, Scotland, fishing for small trout. Maybe it was a healing process, maybe it was just escape. But when I returned to the U.S., I was somehow different. It was like when you wake in the morning after a sleepless night, a little disoriented.

Occasionally shadows of 1984 creep into my life. In fact, in 2000, when Warren Beatty dabbled with the idea of running for president, I thought I heard the faint echo of Pat Caddell's Senator Smith in his pronouncements.

Show business personalities go in and out of presidential campaigns. There is some sort of comradeship between actors and politicians. Perhaps they are in the same business . . . pleasing people, winning approval. I saw Beatty at the Democratic Convention in San Francisco in 1984. He embraced me and talked to my son, Dane, who was an intern reporter. I didn't see him again until 1999 when I was a Fellow at the John F. Kennedy Institute of Politics at Harvard. Beatty was scheduled to speak to the Forum. It had been fifteen years and I was confident he would not remember a political consultant from a failed campaign, so I avoided the reception for him. Later, though, after he spoke, I was sitting in the living room of the Kennedy School talking to another Harvard Fellow, Dan Lungren, former attorney general of California, when Catherine McLaughlin, executive director of the Institute of Politics, came to get me. "Warren Beatty wants to see you." I went into another room to the warmest reception and embrace imaginable. We were warriors from a battle long ago.

I'm sorry I ever met Bill Clinton. He was a dreamkiller who ended our relationship by damaging my business and adding my body to those he climbed over to reach the White House.

My feelings for and about Clinton have nothing to do with whether he was a good president. I think he was. I also think he is one of the brightest men to ever hold the office, at least in modern times. His kind of intelligence, however, was what the rest of us always hated in college. There was always a student who could return to the dorm late at night, scan the textbook once, and make an "A" on the exam the next day. This student had the sort of memory that could categorize and recall information. But he could not paint. He could not write fiction. He could not create. He could not even formulate original ideas.

Bill Clinton's was that kind of intellect. He could remember faces, names, and everything he read, but he will never be known for a memorable speech because he, in large part, was a micromanager who had little regard for the intellect of others and wrote his own bland, cautious speeches. He didn't know he could not write. That is something I learned early in our relationship. People always remember his delivery; they seldom remember what he said. Bill Clinton didn't coin Churchillian or even John Kennedy-esque phrases that became part of our common experience. He didn't even say anything as remarkable as Nancy Reagan's "Just Say No." In fact, the only two memorable lines of his presidency ("The era of big government is over" and "I did not have sexual relations with that woman, Miss Lewinsky") were calculated falsehoods.

When I was a Fellow at Harvard, another Fellow, Michael Waldman, former director of the White House speechwriting department, showed me a speech he had written that was edited by Clinton until only a handful of the original words peeked out from under the dark marking pen. Another story, however, gave me a glimpse at Clinton's insecurity about his creative ability, as well as his rather casual habit of duplicity.

Dick Morris said that he once gave Clinton a typed draft of a State of the Union speech. Clinton then copied it by hand onto a yellow legal pad. Each time he filled a page, the president got up and left the room to hand it to a White House secretary—apparently so that she and the rest of the staff would believe he was writing the speech himself.

Morris is a good writer. It would be interesting for historians if Dick would go through all of Clinton's speeches from his entire career in politics and underline his own contributions. It would be even more interesting to see his original speeches before Clinton made them safe.

Producing television for Clinton was a nightmare. He wanted to examine each word, often losing the intended purpose of the commercial. When I tried to shoot the sort of spontaneous television I had used with Hart, putting Clinton in the middle of a group of people and filming his remarks, he first demanded scripts. There is no doubt that he was capable of great magic on television, but he was always afraid of losing control. Morris would write script paragraphs and test them in his polls. If a particular paragraph tested well, Clinton would demand that it be used in the commercial without a change. Our "spontaneous" commercials were simply Clinton repeating lines written by Morris. That meant that the visual and emotional part of the commercial was often sacrificed to stay true to those etched-in-stone paragraphs from Morris. Not good science. Not good television.

Why did he use me? Well, it is a crude term, but Bill Clinton was always known as a "star fucker." That meant that he wanted the flavor of the month. When he was first settled in the White House, his guest list looked like Oscar night in Hollywood. He cultivated friendships with the famous. He was not interested in people like the president of General Motors or some great but obscure writer. He wanted Barbra Streisand across the table. He even gave keys to the White House to Harry Thomason and his wife Linda Bloodworth, the rich producers of low-brow television sitcoms. He fed on celebrity. In 1984, I was a political celebrity, so he hired me.

Dick Morris marched me into the Governor's Mansion in Little Rock. "This is the genius who created Gary Hart," he told Clinton. Dick's endorsement, the Hart success, the picture in *Newsweek,* and my media presence resulted in Clinton hiring me without review of my work. Hart had also hired me without looking at my commercials, but he had done so because we agreed philosophically on politics and communication.

I was smitten with Bill Clinton. There was no doubt that we could make television together. His warmth, intellect, and empathy slammed through the lens. But even on our first film shoot, I began to get hints that he would be a difficult candidate to manage. First, he kept deferring to his wife, another lawyer with the misguided notion that she was a wordsmith. Her specialty was to insist that we beat to death some word or phrase that wasn't even important to the commercial. The Clintons considered anything that digressed from Morris's paragraphs risky. And the governor and his wife were on a long march to the presidency. They would not take risks.

In 1984 Clinton didn't tell me he was running for president. In fact, there was never a mention of it. As we left the mansion after my initial meeting with him, I turned to Morris and said, "Bill Clinton will be president." Morris laughed and then explained detail by detail, in a condescending manner, why that was impossible. Morris reasoned that Clinton was a southern governor from a small state who would have trouble raising money. Also, Morris conjectured, Jimmy Carter had wrecked the chances of any southern governor being elected. I remembered my first meeting with Dick, when he was so astonished a southern boy listened to opera, wore shoes, and knew how to read without moving his lips. So another southern president? Never!

Electing a president is the highest achievement in the business of political consulting. By 1985, I was looking years down the road. I thought I had it all figured out. I was confident that Hart would be elected in 1988 and I was already penciling in Bill Clinton for his turn at bat. But where I saw it as a long process, Clinton and his ambitious assistant Betsy Wright were already positioning themselves for a march to the White House.

The Democratic National Committee asked me to produce a television show that would air as a response to President Reagan's 1985 State of the Union Address. I immediately thought this would be an opportunity to promote Clinton on the national networks. The negotiations with the party were difficult. I demanded to use my own production people, select my own spokesman, and avoid featuring the same tired old faces that represented yesterday. The party agreed. I was going to construct a framework that would allow working men and women to express themselves. To do this I came up with a list of young and different Democrats without a Washington taint to moderate discussion groups. I was still sold on the Hart idea of New Democrats, new faces, and new ideas. I was going to edit the sessions into a coherent message and use Bill Clinton as my moderator to tie the segments together. He was the sort of fresh face our party needed in the Reagan era.

This project turned into a bureaucratic nightmare. I should have seen it coming, but even after the Mondale debacle of 1984, the Washington-based Wise Ones on our side of the aisle didn't want this outsider coming in to represent the Democratic Party. For one thing, many of the institutional Democrats had somehow convinced themselves that 1984 was a fluke—or wasn't all that bad. They wanted to blame Mondale, not themselves. In addition, at any given time, about half of the members of the Senate—and even a few in the House—consider themselves viable prospects for the presidency, and they didn't want any more competition. So the staffs of the various politicians got into the fight. Soon there were demands that Senate Majority Leader Robert Byrd, Speaker of the House Tip O'Neill, and future Speaker Jim Wright be given places in the film. It was beginning to look like a collection of the usual suspects, but I thought that the young, fresh-faced governor from Arkansas could still deliver the message of change and newness that I needed.

I filmed in locations around the country. The night before I was to produce the program, two days before the State of the Union, Governor Clinton flew into Washington. I had written pieces for him to read that would introduce the segments I had filmed of working people. He said he wanted to change a few words and went into a private room while we waited. And waited and waited. Two hours later he brought in a script that was too long and didn't properly introduce the people I had filmed. He had subtly changed the direction and tone of the effort. I was trapped by both the clock and my belief in him. We filmed.

The reviews were mostly bad and, I thought, rightfully so. To me the end result was a hodgepodge of old faces, old ideas, political compromises, and poor production values. I was embarrassed. I had lost control of Clinton, the party, and the production. But Clinton called and said, "I thought it was pretty good." I didn't agree, but was undaunted and still filled with hope. Bill Clinton and Gary Hart were the building blocks for my future.

Looking back on that episode today, I see not just Clinton's relentless ambition, but his uncanny political instincts as well. He saw, as too few

Democrats did, that there was no percentage in continuing to treat Ronald Reagan with disdain. The American people weren't buying it, and in any event, we were never going to have to run against Reagan again. Coincidentally, our rebuttal ran on Reagan's birthday, so Clinton veered from the script to say warmly, "By the way, Mr. President, happy birthday tonight."

It was a perfect touch. Moreover, he sneaked in some of the themes he would use regularly for the next fifteen years, including his ubiquitous "bridge to the twenty-first century," while deftly espousing the "New Democrat" theme I had developed from my time with Gary Hart. Clinton conceded that the party had suffered a "resounding defeat" and "knows it has to change." He added, "Perhaps we have lagged behind in recent years, but we're on the move now."

In sketching out where we Democrats wanted to go, Clinton read from the script: "America needs this revitalized Democratic Party because we will work for a government that will go beyond the prison of past thinking, a government that will work in partnership with the private sector to foster economic growth, a government that will operate its own programs with a commitment to excellence and accountability and independence from narrow interests, a government that will not turn away from problems that no people with a heart can ignore."

Two sentences summed it up: "Our critics have said we want too much government, while they want government off our backs. Well, we want the government off our backs, too, but we need it by our side."

This would be one of the themes Clinton stressed in the 1992 campaign—and again in 1996. Today, a comparison between Gary Hart and Bill Clinton would draw snickers among the white wine set, be they Democrats or Republicans, but personal peccadilloes aside, Clinton is the Democrats' direct ideological descendant of Hart. And that 1985 rebuttal is proof of the link.

Like many other people, I had problems dealing with the women in Clinton's life, but I don't mean girlfriends. I never saw Clinton display any behavior toward women that would embarrass him or his wife. The women I had trouble with were those who ran his life, Hillary and Betsy Wright.

It became obvious early in our relationship that I must include Hillary in every film shoot. I made commercials of her talking about her husband

and included her in most commercials. This gave her an opportunity to get involved in scripts and visuals.

Betsy Wright, a brittle, chain-smoking, angry woman, was a bossy but knowledgeable political professional who would order Clinton around as though he were an employee. Dealing with her was more than just difficult. Our first serious encounter was in 1984. I had written an article for the *Washington Post* about the difficulty of electing Martha Layne Collins in Kentucky because of residual sexist attitudes on the part of many voters. In this article I explained how there were double standards for dress and behavior that made a woman's campaign more difficult. Unfortunately, the *Post* held the story for several months and didn't publish it until the political climate was white-hot for a woman to be part of the Democratic ticket. The headline read: WHY A WOMAN CAN'T BE ELECTED VICE PRESIDENT. I had nothing to do with the headline but was smarting at the implications it would have for me in the feminist community in Washington.* So I accepted invitations from all of the networks to address the issue of sexism, in an effort to explain something deeper than the headline the feminists obviously would hate.

As I have written, 1984 was a year from hell and my schedule changed constantly. I had accepted an invitation from ABC to be interviewed in Washington about the article but had to cancel because Lindy Boggs needed me in New Orleans. The network, desperate to keep the planned segment, made arrangements for me to do the show from a New Orleans station. Then I had to cancel again because Clinton was making demands on my time. The network immediately made arrangements for me to do the show from Little Rock. Before daylight the next morning, I was picked up in a limo and delivered to the station. In the interview I explained the context of my article and denounced sexism. I thought it had gone well until the

---

*"If Ferraro is to play the glorious role her suddenly-immense crowd of admirers envisions for her, she is going to have to perform wonderfully well under enormous pressure during the next few months. Political consultant Raymond Strother argued persuasively in the Outlook section last month that the country isn't ready to put a woman a heartbeat away from the Oval Office, a conclusion he reached after trying to help women get elected governor in two states. To prove Strother wrong, Ferraro is going to have to be much more than a plausible candidate. Like Al Smith and every symbolic 'first,' she'll be judged by a double standard. She is going to have to be terrific."—*Washington Post*, July 22, 1984

limo dropped me off at the Governor's Mansion for my meeting with Clinton.

Before I could even ring the bell, Betsy Wright threw open the door and started screaming insults at me. According to her I had endangered Clinton's political future. Reeling a bit, I replied that if she had read the story beyond the headline, she would have found a constructive piece. I also told her bluntly that nobody was going to dictate my speech or my ability to express myself. And remembering that nowhere in the interview had I even mentioned Bill Clinton, let alone claimed I was speaking for him, I asked her what in the hell my interview had to do with Clinton anyway? Still screaming, Betsy said that, as I spoke, they superimposed the name of the Little Rock television station across the bottom of the screen. That, she shouted, linked Bill Clinton with what she considered my antifeminist views.

This bizarre episode demonstrates how controlling and careful the women in Clinton's life were about his future. They supervised him like a small child who might wander off into the street. And nothing—and no one—would stand in their way.

Between Hillary, Betsy, and Dick, I never felt in charge of the Clinton message and was not included in all phases of the campaign. Perhaps that's as it ought to be. Candidates are the ones who hold office after the campaign; they ought to say what's on *their* minds, not the consultants. The rub with Clinton was that although he said he wanted to do my character-building sort of television, what he truly believed in was negative advertising. I often explain to candidates that winning is different than beating your opponent. If a candidate wins because of force of character and ideas, he or she has a platform from which to govern. Clinton's favorite way of winning was to simply bludgeon his opponent. Often, after I had gone back to Washington, Clinton would call a Little Rock advertising agency man, David Watkins, and the two of them would create the crudest, most negative commercials imaginable attacking the other candidate. I wrote Clinton a memo warning him that his manner of winning was destructive. It was a memo I had to write again in 1990:

(Memo to Bill Clinton)
   . . . Unfortunately you have become a master at defeating your opponents, but you have learned little about winning. You end each cam-

paign with an overdrawn emotional checkbook. The good and noble is sacrificed for short-term victories. And one thing I have learned in the last twenty years is that short-term victories are the junk food of politics. They require little thought and add little nutrition to your political life. One result of your philosophy of elections is you have lost respect for the voters. You only want to feed them enough information to make a quick, voting booth decision. Your favorite television style is a reflection of intellectual arrogance that excludes emotions . . . that excludes people. In polls you test carefully worded paragraphs that work only in a vacuum and then attempt to plug them into the public consciousness. It is plastic and cynical.

Bill, voters are not stupid. They make complicated decisions they can't explain but they always have reasons. Your winning by being the only person left standing on election day because of financial and intellectual fire power leaves the voters feeling cheated and disconnected. . . .

I wrote frequent memos to Clinton with the understanding that he wanted to hear others' opinions, no matter how tough. He told me so himself. But the truth is that any form of criticism was met with instant hostility. I don't understand why I didn't see that early on.

It was during the 1980s that Clinton and Morris developed the technique and philosophy that would help Clinton become president. Later, Morris would call the technique "triangulation," but Clinton's method of beating his opponent in the '80s was to embrace him on most issues and then force voters to make a decision based on one distinction. He would say things like, "My opponent and I agree on education, taxes, and crime, so this election is about who can best hold down utility rates." This usually meant that his opponent had taken contributions from utility companies and Clinton could beat him over the head with being too close to special interests. Still, though, every other year—governors then had to run for office every two years in Arkansas—I was in Arkansas filming beautiful scenes of Clinton with people. I was assigned the "soft" part of the campaign. This was considered the least important. I wrote memo after memo to Clinton encouraging him to create an image for himself that could be sustained, so that every two years he would not have to start all over bludgeoning his opponent while his own popularity hovered around 50 percent.

Somehow, while Betsy screamed at me and Hillary ignored me, I grew close to Clinton—or at least I thought I did. I would fly into Little Rock in my plane for visits. We would go to a Mexican restaurant and eat greasy food. Clinton drank nonalcoholic beer. I don't think I ever saw him take a drink of anything stronger. I always knew I was in the presence of a major contender for president, and my ambitions and dreams began to include Bill Clinton.

In 1987, as we planned the next presidential campaign, I persuaded Gary Hart to meet with Clinton. It seemed logical to me that the great but cool intellect and ideas of Hart could be balanced by the warmth and political skills of Clinton. I envisioned a ticket with the cerebral senator from Colorado at the top and the smooth-talking governor of Arkansas as his candidate for vice president. So Hart and I flew to Little Rock for lunch at the mansion with Clinton. I thought it went well. The two seemed to like each other, and my hope was that, in time, some of Hart's idealism would rub off on Clinton. After lunch we were driven back to the airport. Hart peered out the window at the slums of Little Rock and said nothing until we were almost to the plane. By now I was accustomed to allowing him his reflective quietness, but I wanted to see if my plan had worked. I intruded, "Well, what do you think, Gary?"

"About what?" He was still peering out the window.

"About Clinton."

Hart turned to me. "There's no core. He doesn't believe in anything."

End of conversation. Clinton was never mentioned again as long as I knew Hart.

In May of 1987, Hart was forced out of the 1988 presidential race by a *Miami Herald* story about his brief relationship with a woman named Donna Rice, with whom he had traveled for a few hours to the Caribbean island of Bimini. At this point Clinton and I began talking frequently by phone about a presidential race. Also, while trying not to send out ripples about presidential ambitions at home, he began an extensive speaking schedule in New Hampshire, Iowa, Washington, Texas, and other important election states. He did it under the guise of being chairman of the National Governors Association and being on the Education Commission of the States. In many of our conversations Clinton was euphoric about the reception he was getting around the country. People were beginning to awaken to his talent and appeal. Old pros turned their antennas slightly toward the Arkansas governor.

I had written a 100-page memorandum for the Hart campaign that suggested skipping the Iowa primary and downplaying paid media. It was my contention that the media did an excellent job of covering presidential campaigns' day-to-day activities and issues, and we could devote ourselves to substance or the illusion of substance in long television programs. I gave this memo to Clinton but added the caveat that he should ignore his natural instincts and avoid negative campaigning. Clinton was intrigued with my memo and drawn to the idea of breaking the mold of knee-jerk political thinking.

On June 25, at his request, I flew down to Little Rock and stayed at the mansion. Clinton and I talked far into the night. Hillary was not there. In fact, in 1987 and 1988 I seldom saw her. Clinton seemed eager to run, but at the same time troubled. I could not put my finger on the reasons, but he would swing from boyish enthusiasm to quiet reflection. When I got back into my plane the next day, I was not sure about his intentions. However, at about midnight on June 30, he woke me from a deep sleep by saying, "Let's go!"

It was late to gear up a presidential campaign, but I was excited that we were about to begin the process that would make him a real contender four years later, after America had met this charming young man. I didn't sleep that night with visions of the Oval Office in my head and the realization that my dream had been given another chance.

A group of about eight or nine Clinton friends from around the country met with his staff members in Little Rock and began planning a campaign.* In the meeting Clinton was enthusiastic and continued to throw out lines that should be included in the announcement speech. Dick Morris and I had crafted a speech. Plans were made for a public announcement a few days later. After one long night of planning, we each drifted off to our hotels, except for Carl Wagner, who was staying in the guest house behind the mansion. The next morning we met at the long dinning room table and

---

*Several of these friends became prominent in the Clinton presidency. Samuel R. "Sandy" Berger was deputy White House national security adviser and then national security adviser. Mickey Kantor was Clinton's 1992 campaign manager and became U.S. trade representative. John Holum was director of the U.S. Arms Control and Disarmament Agency. Most of the people at the table that day had followed Clinton from the McGovern campaign for president.

began talking again about logistics. Clinton did not join us until noon. Clinton's meetings tended to be conducted late at night, and he compensated by starting later in the day. We were almost finished with our tuna and chicken salad sandwiches when he sat down at the head of the table. Several people tried to get his attention about details for the announcement, but he seemed distracted. His head was down.

"I'm not running," he said dully.

Most of the people at the table thought he was making a joke. The euphoria of the night before was still rampant. We continued talking among ourselves for a few seconds until it began to sink in that a decision had been made. Clinton was truly not running. Our enthusiasm had been in vain. Our travel expenses and time had been wasted. It wasn't that he feared losing. Clinton was convinced that he could run a credible campaign, and even if he lost, set himself up as the man to beat in 1992. He thought that a governor from a small southern state would have to establish his credentials and take over as the leader of the party to succeed. I never thought in 1988 (or even in 1992) that he was running to win the first time. I am confident that his success in 1992 was an unexpected fluke.

Sitting at the end of the table, Clinton looked like a man who had been punched in the stomach. Finally he began to talk about his responsibilities to his family and other excuses.

I turned to Carl Wagner and asked him what had happened. He replied that the night before, he had left for the guest house as Clinton went upstairs to join Hillary in the bedroom. He said that when Clinton went up the stairs, he was still a candidate. When Clinton came downstairs that morning, he was not. The only person he was with in the meantime was Hillary. For reasons that I did not yet understand, she alone had the power to keep him out of the race. Without her help, he couldn't run. And, obviously, her help in 1992 came on her terms.

Even after Clinton decided not to run for president in 1988, our relationship continued to grow stronger. One day he asked me the names of other pollsters in the country. He thought Dick Morris was disliked by the Washington insiders because he represented both Democrats and Republicans. I was shocked that he was willing to throw over his old and trusted friend, but later I was to meet the same fate myself as the 1992 campaign took shape and Hillary took charge.

One of Clinton's great weaknesses, I thought, was his intellectual disregard for—and complete dislike of—the press. He thought he could outsmart them. While sitting in his favorite Mexican restaurant, he tried some of his cleverness on me.

"Don't you think if a reporter asks me whether I have ever smoked marijuana, the perfect answer would be, 'I've never broken the drug laws of our country'?"

"No," I said, "I would think that you were trying to hide the fact that you had used marijuana in England while you were a student." I also explained that he had managed to fool the Arkansas reporters in large part because they were not as aggressive as the press in Washington, where that sort of answer could be a disaster. My words had no effect. Even as president he would use cute and evasive answers to reporters questions and get body-slammed. "It depends on what your definition of 'is' is" will unfortunately go down in history as one of his most memorable lines. He became known as a liar, and the national press corps became even more vigilant. His and Hillary's bitter hatred of the press corps hampered their effectiveness in the White House. Their intellectual smugness and superiority did not serve them well when under the national spotlight.

In 1990 the wheels came off of my relationship with Clinton. I still don't know why, but he was a troubled and irritated man for months. He couldn't decide whether to run for governor again because it would require a promise that he would not run for president. Arkansas never trusted his ambition. One of his strong women, Betsy Wright, had moved away from his circle. I never knew why. Hillary was frosty, but I seldom saw her, so it didn't matter. I kept a film crew in Little Rock for five days waiting for Clinton to decide whether to run for governor. In the meantime, Hillary had Morris run a poll to see if she could be elected if Bill did not run. She could not. In fact, it was an embarrassment that made her angry. She would have had trouble placing third in a three-person race. Arkansas was not fond of Hillary. When people suggested that she should run for the Senate from Arkansas instead of New York in 2000, I smiled to myself.

Finally, Clinton decided to run for reelection as governor, but everything had changed. He knew he would have to lie about not being a candidate for president. That, however, he assigned to the future. Like Scarlett O'Hara, he would "think about that tomorrow." With Betsy Wright, his pillar of strength, out of the picture, he turned to another severe woman

with brittle opinions, Gloria Cabe. Unfortunately, she was out of her element even in a governor's race. Things seemed to be falling apart, and Clinton was suddenly insecure.

The world brightened for a few days in late February 1990, after Morris
brought in a poll showing that Clinton could be reelected. I was called from
my hotel to the mansion to talk about scripts. There seemed to be some
sort of breakthrough. Clinton and I sat until early morning at a tiny table
talking about the poll and how to bring the numbers to life. Looking back
now, it is obvious that Clinton was already trying out themes for use in his
presidential race. His primary concern was welfare reform. I suggested
finding somebody who had come off welfare and was in the work force.
Clinton liked the idea and assigned his staff to find a person and an industry
that would illustrate his administration's success at getting people off welfare.

The staff found a man who had gone from welfare to working for a firm
that refurbished executive airplanes at the airport. I went there and interviewed him. He was perfect. I then wrote a script to accommodate this man
and his story. Finally, there was a gravity to Clinton's work that hadn't existed before. He encouraged high production values and didn't mention
production budgets. The welfare spot could not have been executed better.
I took the finished scripts and a legal release form to the subject. He read
the script and signed the release and the script. We then began several hours
of shooting before Clinton arrived. All Clinton had to do was stand before
the camera and deliver his lines. The worker would be in the background.

The results were wonderful. It was a compelling story and graphically
beautiful. Clinton complimented it and made no changes. That was unusual. I was feeling good about this campaign—and this candidate. Then
disaster struck. When the spot went on the air, the former welfare recipient
renounced it. He said he didn't know he was going to be on television as
having been on welfare. Apparently, the local Republicans had pressured
him to renounce the spot. Arkansas politics can be like that.

The local newspaper ran the story on page one and Clinton raged. He
was like Gore, not Hart or Bentsen. I explained that the subjects in the commercial had signed releases and scripts, but it seemed not to matter. Somebody had put a pothole on his path to the White House. I was called to
Little Rock and met by Gloria Cabe and Dick Morris. Cabe tried to be commanding and as intimidating as Betsy Wright, but all she had down was the

screaming. The signed releases were in my shoulder bag, and it was Clinton's staff, not me, who had found the worker in the first place, so I was confident that when Clinton calmed down and started being reasonable, even Cabe's hysterics would subside. Clinton, though, was not reasonable. He ranted about his political future going down the drain and how I had deviated several words from the Morris poll language. Morris kept trying to smooth things over, but I could see him beginning to move toward Cabe. I don't blame him. It was a matter of survival for him. I am sure he knew by now that Clinton was looking for other pollsters who were more acceptable in Washington.

Finally, sometime after midnight, after the meeting had gone in waves from pleasant and constructive to hysterics again and again, I'd had enough. I was approaching fifty years of age. I had spent a career taking abuse from desperate candidates, cheap-shot artists, and campaign managers filled with little knowledge but much self-importance. They were all present in the room that early morning hour. I packed my shoulder bag and stood up.

"Governor, I think you are just tired, but I am too old to be treated like a child. I am going to my hotel. Call me in the morning and we will get together and work this out."

I had been asleep about an hour back at my hotel when my bedside phone rang. Late-night calls are terrifying. They usually bring bad news like deaths, accidents, and sick children. But this late call was from a weeping Morris.

"I need your advice." Dick paused to gain control of himself. "Clinton beat me up."

I was still coming out of sleep and loosely translated his meaning. There had been a lot of verbal abuse earlier, and I assumed that was what he meant.

"Well, Dick, he beat me up too, but I got up and left."

"No, he really beat me up—with his fists. I tried to do what you did, but when I tried to leave he knocked me down into a table, and Hillary had to pull him off of me."

This woke me up. I could smell trouble. My leaving had ratcheted into a complex situation that compromised Clinton and his ambitions. There was no doubt in my mind that night as I talked with Morris on the phone that Clinton would not be calling me in the morning for a peace meeting.

I calmly gave Morris what I thought was logical counsel. "My advice is to get out of Little Rock."

Dick paused for a few seconds. "I can't do that. He owes me money."

"Get out of Little Rock, Dick. He owes me money too, but if he had hit me, I would be in jail now." This New Yorker had a different reaction than a redneck would have had. I realized that if Clinton had swung at me, Hillary would have had to pull me off him instead of him off Dick, and I would have been arrested by the troopers outside the door.

Dick went back to see Clinton the next morning to collect his money, but their relationship didn't last much longer. A week later I got a call from a television station about a Clinton spot that I didn't make. Frank Greer, with Dick's help, had replaced me. But it didn't save Dick. Bruce Lindsey, Clinton's confidant, called me and said that Frank was being allowed to produce a spot or two, but they would be back to me as soon as the new spots came off the air. "Greer was an awfully good salesman," Lindsey added. Greer is a good salesman, but he is also a good media producer. I knew I was through with Clinton. I just didn't know how through. It would be years.

In 1995 the White House reached me while I was on the road. I was paged in the Atlanta airport and given a time to call Vice President Gore. I called and was told, "He can't talk now, he's in with the president." I was given a time and an inside number to call when I landed at the next airport. I arrived in Louisville and was met by one of my best redneck friends, now our production manager in the firm, Steve Davison. He had arrived early and had cooled down the car with the air-conditioner. He drove and we talked about woodworking and fishing until the prescribed hour arrived. Steve wheeled into a McDonald's that had a phone outside and went in to get a Big Mac. With trucks careening by, I called the number. Gore answered immediately. He obliquely asked what my answer would be if the president wanted me to be communications director of the White House. He made it clear that it was his own idea to find a political professional who could bridge White House and campaign activities. I asked him if he had talked to either the president or the First Lady about my serving in that position. He said he had not. I suggested he do so.

When I got back to Washington, I called my friend Jack Germond for advice. He said simply, "Don't get involved with those people. You will always regret it." His advice was probably sound, but it wasn't tested: I never

heard from Al Gore again. Had I had the misfortune to get the job, I probably would have had to mortgage my ranch to pay the kind of legal fees run
up by all the other staff members who appeared before grand juries.

What is strange, though, is that I pulled for Clinton during his entire
presidency. I guess my daddy's loyalties died hard. Ten or fifteen times I
went on television talk shows to defend him, even after he'd gotten himself
impeached by his habit of trying to outsmart everybody with clever answers—including, stupidly, a federal grand jury. I refused so often to answer
questions about his beating Dick that I endangered some of my friendships
within the press. Because Clinton had turned away from my firm, my competitors had a newspaper clipping to use against us when they made presentations. Not only had Clinton killed my dream, he damaged my business. I
wish I had never met Bill Clinton. But I am glad he was president.

Louisiana, despite its reputation for tolerating corruption, periodically rises up in protest and elects a fresh face and thus a fresh start. Louisianians grow weary of being laughed at and finding themselves at the bottom of every lifestyle measurement in America. For a brief, golden moment, they experience rekindled hopes that their abundant natural resources can be better managed, their children can get a good education, their roads will be paved with asphalt instead of corruption, their colleges funded. Because, despite the straitjacket their history has strapped on them, despite the dumb-Cajun jokes that Louisiana's politicians bring to Washington, despite the hedonistic reputation for letting good times roll, there are as many sober, thoughtful, and serious-minded people in that state as in any other.

The history may be the hardest to overcome. Huey Long made government the court of last resort. He started a tradition that brought free textbooks, school lunches, old-age assistance, charity hospitals, bridges over the Mississippi River, and paved roads. So what if he was a little corrupt? Before Huey there was only ignorance, marshes, and red dirt. He brought the state into the twentieth century. But Louisianians are still paying cultural, emotional, and economic installments on his legacy. When he was assassinated in 1935, Huey's body was buried in front of the Capitol, where a light shines on his statue—but his legacy lived on.

Ever since, good people have been battling to change the direction of the state. Fixing its problems always seems so simple from the outside. In late 1986, Russell Long, Huey's son and one of the most powerful people in America, contemplated leaving his Senate seat and running for governor the following year. The state was in a recession, and Russell Long thought his contacts could help attract new industry. It was to be his final tribute. Bill Hamilton ran a poll showing Long could be elected, and he called me in and told me to start thinking about a campaign. It looked like I was going back to Louisiana. I was eager to help the state and a man I truly admired. Political consulting was going to be a rescue tool like the "jaws of life" in the hands of a fireman. Trumpets would blare and we would ride into the state flying flags of righteousness and change.

But again, something happened. Sandy and I were hanging out in San Sebastian, Spain, eating tapas, drinking cheap red wine, and sleeping late. The year had been as difficult as most even-number years, and I was in my escape mode. In 1986 I had produced media for Clinton's reelection; the first Senate campaign of John Breaux; Congressman W. J. "Billy" Tauzin of the Third District of Louisiana; Rudy Perpich, governor of Minnesota; Jack Brooks in Texas's Ninth Congressional District; a seatbelt campaign for the American Automobile Dealers Association; the reelection of Florida comptroller Gerald Lewis; and about ten other campaigns. On my breakfast tray with the orange juice, coffee, cheese, sausage, and bread was an *International Herald Tribune* with a tiny story that Senator Russell Long had decided not to run for governor. I was disappointed. It was a pleasure to work for someone I liked and who had enough confidence in the campaign decisions I made to keep the political hacks from getting in the way. In my heart, I realized, I deeply wanted to help forge changes in Louisiana.

So I returned from Europe and went to see Bill Hamilton, wondering if there was any salvation in his Louisiana poll numbers. There were. His poll for the never-launched Long effort confirmed what I felt in my gut and what I had learned during John Breaux's Senate race the year before: People were ready to make changes in Louisiana. It was one of those times when their indignation was boiling up. I knew two potential candidates, both congressmen, who I thought could pull off a message of change. But I wondered if they sensed what I did—and whether they had the inclination—to tap into the latent anger Hamilton found in his surveys.

The two congressmen I had in mind were Wilbert J. Tauzin, who always went by "Billy," and Charles Elson Roemer III, known universally as "Buddy." The boyish nicknames masked each man's deep and abiding ambition—and their formidable intellects. Billy Tauzin came from the bayou area of south Louisiana; Roemer represented a north Louisiana district centered in his hometown of Shreveport.

Roemer, because of ancient Louisiana alliances, kept me at arm's length.

Billy was a client and a friend whose integrity I admired. Naturally, I went to him first. I spent several days preparing a memo and asked him to come to my office. There, I explained my theory that Louisianians were tired of their politicians and the political process the way it was practiced there. We needed to offer them a revolution—a campaign that announced change. To do this, I proposed kicking the shins of the political establishment by conducting a campaign that violated all of Louisiana's preconceived ideas of what to expect in a candidate. One manifestation of this approach would be to reject endorsements from legislators, sheriffs, and other minor elected officials.

Unfortunately, because he would have been a great governor, Billy did not agree. Though terribly bright, he was handcuffed by political tradition and felt that one needed to pander to various constituency groups to get elected. His instincts were to run a purely traditional campaign. In our meeting he even suggested renting a train and making "whistle-stop" campaign speeches in a state where people had not ridden trains—or attended political rallies—for a generation. I knew from my experience with Jimmie Davis that a stump campaign was suicide, whether you rode a train or a bus loaded with musicians. The discussion grew heated, and Billy left the office saying only that he would get back to me. He was a little angry and completely sure I was wrong. I felt the same way. After our meeting, I knew I would not work for Billy in that campaign. I called Buddy Roemer.

I had been told for years that Roemer didn't like me. He had been the pollster when I represented "Lightbulb" Powell, and we had squabbled over technique and strategy. Worse, I had run a winning Democratic primary campaign against him in 1978 for a client named Buddy Leach. Roemer, the golden boy, didn't take defeat well, and he came back in 1980, after I moved to Washington, and soundly defeated Leach. We had never spoken since that time except for polite greetings at a high-stakes poker game I occasionally sat in on with congressmen and reporters. These games, attended by both Republicans and Democrats, are so serious there is little conversation, and almost no drinking. Bad judgment could cost several months' pay.

In any event, in January, Roemer agreed to meet me in his Capitol Hill office in the Cannon Building to discuss the 1987 Louisiana gubernatorial race. He had his feet on the desk and was smoking a cigarette. He didn't rise. His body language was a little bit of an insult, but I ignored that and launched into my theory of how he could be elected governor. My thirty-minute appointment turned into two hours. Now Roemer was leaning forward, feet on the floor, shouting agreement and making adjustments in my proposal. Occasionally I would pace in the office, spewing ideas, and Roemer would join me on his feet. It was obvious that he had independently come to the same conclusions. I was simply confirming something he already believed.

When I stood to leave, he delivered the bad news: "I've already hired Deno Seder to do my media." I knew Deno, a talented producer from Shreveport who had begun to make a national name for himself. His unorthodox approach to television would serve Buddy well in a campaign for change. I was disappointed, but I had other things to keep me busy. We were beginning to plan the new Gary Hart campaign for president. I had just bought forty acres of land on the Big Hole River in Montana and had an architect designing a log home. I really didn't want to get involved in a Louisiana campaign without Tauzin or Roemer and ignored several offers to talk to other candidates.

Two days later everything changed.

Roemer called. "I've fired Deno. Let's go to work."

Four years later, the scorned consultant, Deno Seder, would in another quirky circumstance return to the battle that helped take Roemer out of politics. But for the moment, the future looked bright.

After ignoring each other for a decade, Roemer and I had met like two travelers arriving by chance at a crossroads from different routes and discovering that they have the same destination. We were both looking for redemption. Both of us, though we didn't reach an emotional understanding until months later, were warming up for a fight against the establishment. In a strange way, we were both driven by our fathers. His had been punished because of Louisiana corruption, and I was still trying to live up to the mission mine had imprinted on me to help working people. We were both reaching for the same thing and happened to meet because Russell Long decided not to run, because Billy Tauzin got cautious at the wrong moment in history, because of many other strange turns of fate. Maybe it was kismet. But ours was a dance that would go on for years as our lives kept touching. Those two hours would change my life and my relationship with the Democratic Party—and with political consulting itself. Five years later, again by chance, my alliance with Buddy Roemer would almost put me out of business.

There was always a mystical quality to the Roemer saga. Buddy was one of the most complex men I ever met in politics. Harvard educated and inordinately intense, he combined Bill Clinton's intellect with the raw emotional appeal of television evangelist Jimmy Swaggart. He was a walking bundle of contradictions: A lazy man with a high energy level. A man whose attention span was short, but who always had a novel in his pocket in case he became bored—which he did in the middle of dinner parties or Saints football games. When compared with my other client up the road from Louisiana, Bill Clinton, Roemer won all contests hands down, except fire in the belly and work ethic. Whereas Clinton was not creative, memorable phrases rolled out of Buddy's mouth. Clinton had an ability to connect with people and make them nod in agreement. Roemer could make them clap and stamp their feet.

Audiences were refreshed when he said unpolitical things. "I'm a little, skinny, hardheaded, forty-four-year-old man," Buddy would tell them. "Just a politician. But I like my profession. I'm proud to be part of it."

Both Clinton and Roemer were well equipped, but it was not hard to see that Roemer's skills were superior. He was well liked in Washington and a terror in poker games. He always won. But, in another contradiction, he was such a stickler for personal integrity that he always listed his poker winnings on his financial reports—an almost unheard-of gesture—reports that were duly read by the antigambling fundamentalist voters back home. The biggest contradiction of all was that he was planning to run as an anti-Edwards reformer while his father, a north Louisiana political fixture named Charles Roemer, was in prison taking a fall for Edwards. Buddy thought his father was a decent man overwhelmed by a corrupt system. I agreed then and agree now. His father was another victim of institutional corruption in the state.

At that time, however, most political insiders figured that Charles Roemer's conviction made it impossible for Buddy to win as a reformer without denouncing his dad. One night, Buddy was confronted with the Roemer family paradox in a debate. The press and the political establishment had been wondering how he would handle it. In the end, his answer was so sweet and so powerful that it was nearly anticlimactic. He paused briefly before saying simply, "I love my father."

We never heard another word about Charles Roemer.

*   *   *

Roemer was the most unusual candidate I had ever had. I describe Bill Clinton as the first consultant-dependent president. Buddy Roemer was the first candidate I ever represented who believed only in television. We did not use mail, phones, billboards, radio, or yard signs. Because of his certainty that television was the secret to all elections, he barely campaigned. He would usually consent to attend one event a day. The word *work* became a joke for us. At noon I would eat lunch and discuss baseball with Mark McKinnon, who was handling press, campaign manager Harris Diamond, and Len Sanderson, a longtime friend of Buddy's. In the afternoons Roemer would sit in the back office of the campaign headquarters reading novels.

I didn't care if he didn't shake hands or attend political gatherings. We had already set an agenda that excluded all traditional political events. The real problem was that he refused to raise money. I worried that this was taking our reform message a bridge too far. Unlike, say, Bill Clinton, who would sit for hours at a little corner table in the mansion and make money calls, Roemer would put his feet on the desk, make a couple of calls, and then lose himself in a book. While other candidates were on television and radio and Billy Tauzin was riding his train around the state, Buddy was reading novels.

Even if he had worked harder at fundraising, it was tough to contribute to Buddy. For starters, he refused cash. And he wouldn't accept political action committee money or checks from lobbyists or from most of the other contributors who traditionally buy their way in. A few days before election, when the first scent of victory was faintly in the air, some New York brokerage firm sent a tired Louisiana hack to see Roemer with a $5,000 check. The man went into a back room with Buddy for only a few seconds and then rushed out with Roemer behind him. Buddy was enraged. "Next time anybody lets somebody like that near me, they're fired."

We were doing it right, but we didn't have money to go on television. The debates pitting Billy Tauzin, Governor Edwin Edwards, and Roemer were some of the best political theater I have ever seen. Louisiana had three formidable intellects hammering each other, along with some also-rans who provided contrast. Roemer always won. Winning debates, however, is worth little because the audiences are so small. We still floundered. Roemer plugged along in fifth place in the polls. His speeches—those he consented to give—were great. His debates were slam dunks, and we built a small, solid base of reform voters—all six percentage points of them. Our opponents ignored us and began attacking each other on television. We weren't even part of the struggle. Finally, Roemer transferred funds from his U.S. House political account to the campaign. In so doing, he injected a shot of adrenaline—and urgency. For my part, I shot two days of film of Roemer talking to groups of people. I used the same techniques as in the Hart campaign, but the results weren't the same. Buddy came across, in the parlance of TV, as too "hot." He was intense and constantly in motion. I knew this was a problem, I just didn't know initially how much of one. The reason was that the substance of what he was saying was matchless. It was a message I agreed with, and I knew the people of Louisiana agreed with it. It came from Buddy's heart—his father was recently out of prison—and it touched my heart as deeply as it would have touched my father's.

My footage caught Buddy demanding that Edwin Edwards take responsibility for the graft and corruption that kept money from reaching the classrooms and the highways. With Roemer's brilliant articulation, I knew that almost every frame of the film was usable. I had a wealth of spontaneous Roemer scenes that broke political tradition and bore "white-hot" through the television screen. I was sure it would work. Others on the campaign weren't so sure. Mark McKinnon, who later became a media producer and worked with Stuart Stevens to create media for George W. Bush's 2000 campaign, was in charge of press and also helped Roemer with speeches. His work was wonderful. In one of his news releases, Mark had coined the slogan "A Revolution for Louisiana." I read that expression and the media campaign fell into place . . . or at least I thought it did. I had an artist design an animated signature for Roemer that looked like gang graffiti. It splashed on the TV screen on a brick wall after Roemer attacked Edwards and the political establishment. It was beautiful television. But when we showed the commercials to focus-group audiences, it didn't work. Because I was the one who made it, I was the one who had to understand the reason.

Louisiana wanted change. There was little doubt of that. But people in focus groups found my spots unsettling. When the Roemer language was reduced to a small picture in the living room, it was exotic—but also frightening. The voters wanted change, but they didn't want to burn down the state. Also, they knew all they wanted to know about the corruption of Edwin Edwards, and reminding them fought against our original purpose of making Roemer a different kind of politician. If he attacked Edwards, he was simply doing the same thing the other candidates were doing. In short, I had made him one of "them."

I was sent back to the drawing board while some of the staff grumbled about my failure. For days I sat in the edit suite and reviewed the Roemer film. Finally I understood the problem. Except for the criticism of Edwin Edwards, the message wasn't wrong. The candidate was simply too hot. His message was so compelling and I was so familiar with his speech patterns that I didn't see through my camera lens what the voter saw on the television set.

One summer night while sitting at a typewriter in my library, staring down at the occasional drug addict cruising D Street looking for a car to break into, it came to me. Within five minutes I had written the commercial that would be credited for winning the campaign and earn a place on everybody's list of best political television ads. It wasn't complicated. I simply used Roemer's own words and wove them together. Like with Hart, Bentsen, and many others, the candidate's own words are usually the most persuasive. I captured Roemer's speech patterns, his expressions, his intellect, and his resolve—but in a way that challenged and excited voters rather than threatening them. I was terribly excited and woke him up in Baton Rouge. I read him the spot and described it this way, "Hot message, cool candidate."

Roemer was elated. "That's it. You finally got it. Come to Baton Rouge and let's shoot it."

Most of the press, the voters, and the political operatives don't understand television but are quick to make judgments. Republican consultant Doug Bailey uses a wonderful trick in lectures. He shows a commercial and asks each member of the audience to give it a thumbs up or down. He then asks for a group discussion of what made the commercial bad or good. The arguments are heated. People point to camera angles and message lines. Most feel they have an internal meter, unique to them, that allows them to distinguish good political television. And why not? They watch television from the time they are born. They are professional television viewers. If they work in government, a political party, or have experience in the fringes of campaigns, they have an even more exalted view meter. Their opinions are delivered with studied arrogance. So, in his lectures, Bailey always brings the critics crashing to earth. "You are all wrong," he tells them. "None of you has enough information to judge the ads you have seen."

Television ads are crafted for special audiences and for specific tasks at specific times in specific campaigns. There are times when an entire television commercial is crafted to use one magical scene that says something about the candidate. My most successful commercial for Senator Mary Landrieu in 1996 showed a group of women around Mary. It didn't matter much to me what she said because her face told a story of compassion and understanding. Mary seldom objected to anything I wanted to put on television.

But the consultant's nightmare is a candidate who ignores research and forces the production of television on gut feelings. Usually these candidates are looking for the famous "silver bullet" of which so much is made. Silver bullets are usually found after the election is over when people look for a reason the candidate won. The commercial I wrote that night for Buddy became a silver bullet. I arranged for a cameraman from New Orleans, Kenny Morrison, to rent a mottled gray background of splashes of paint on canvas. We rented a small Baton Rouge studio that was deserted on Saturday. Buddy read the script several times and changed my last line. I don't remember what it was before, but he wrote the line that truly made the spot fly. "I don't like Louisiana politics," he said. "I love Louisiana. I love Louisiana enough to make some people angry." Then he began memorizing the script.

Buddy rehearsed before a mirror for about an hour. I bathed the background with ice-blue light and put him in front of it in a coat and tie sitting on a stool. Because of my disdain for cue cards or Teleprompters, we shot the spot eighteen times with me quietly telling him "Hot message, cool candidate" before each take. Finally, when I thought I had heard what I wanted, I put the headset on and listened to the replay on audio tape of the eighteenth take. It was perfect. History was about to be made.

60-Second TV
Spot Title: Angry
Buddy Roemer
Note: (Hot Message, Cool Candidate)
Some insiders say I'm not a good politician because I say things that
    make some people angry.
(Confession) They're right, I do.
Made some people in Washington angry when I refused to take a

Congressional pay raise, passed by the politicians, for the politicians.

(Wistful) I thought the country needed to tighten its belt.

I made the bureaucrats and deadheads in Baton Rouge angry when I said I would reduce the number of state cars and scrub the budget.

I made the polluters angry when I said those that pollute the air and water should pay to clean it up.

(Angry) Clean it up or get out, I said.

I made the education bureaucrats angry when (Amazement) I said I would brick up the top three floors of the Department of Education, cut the consultants, and pay the teachers.

(Sad and honest but not mean) I notice my opponents don't make many people angry. That doesn't surprise you, does it? Politics as usual.

I don't like Louisiana politics. I love Louisiana.

I love Louisiana enough to make some people angry. (Sadness)

With only one month left before the election, the spot finally made it on the air. Because a sixty-second spot costs the same as two thirty-second spots, we did not have as much spot frequency as the other campaigns. That was another rule Buddy and I had agreed to break. It wasn't going to take a lot of viewings to make this spot work. We believed the substance and nature of the spot would overwhelm people into paying attention without our having to beat it into their heads in conventional advertising technique.

After only a couple of days, we began to get the expected response from the other campaigns and the hacks. A legislator stopped my partner, Jim Duffy, on a New Orleans street and said, "Duffy, what you guys up to? In one television commercial you insulted teachers, state workers, industry, and the legislature. You can't get elected that way." Duffy only smiled because he knew that magic had already begun to happen. And as in most winning campaigns, we got lucky.

A day or two before the "Angry" commercial went on the air, the state's newspapers published a poll showing us still in fifth place. This poll wrote off the Roemer candidacy. Therefore, people didn't see us rising until it was too late. Within two weeks we were in second place. With two weeks remaining, I told Roemer he was going to run first and Edwards would run second. He didn't believe me. Money began pouring into the office from people who had never contributed to political campaigns. We made four more television commercials, though I think we needed only the first one. They were all "hot message, cool candidate."

Of course the "Angry" commercial became a legend, a silver bullet. In short order, five or six different people were taking credit for part or all of it. Some people say that Roemer wrote it. In effect, he did. I used his words, his phrases, his inflections, his poetry. All I did was take all the parts and rearrange them into a script. Several people claimed to have written it themselves. Had we lost, there would not have been that problem; I would have gotten all of the "credit." But that is customary in political consulting. Time after time we make presentations, only to have a prospective client say he has seen one or more of our commercials already. Theft is easier than creativity.

On the morning of the election, I flew into Shreveport with a young assistant from California, Stanley Stalford. There were bad omens in the air. If not omens, there was at least a lot of fog, and the airport had planes in holding patterns waiting for instrument minimums to land. Legally one can fly a runway landing pattern on instruments until a designated "missed approach point" and then climb back up into the muck. There were a couple of Delta planes holding, but I decided to take one "look" at the approach. That meant the tower gave me permission to shoot the approach down to minimums. If when the altimeter said 250 feet I did not see the ground, I would abort the landing and join a holding pattern several miles away. I flew down the electronic glide slope, making adjustments in speed, power, and direction as we slid down the invisible string of radio signals. We were encased in thick fog as the altimeter dropped. I turned to Stanley, a game young man, and asked if he knew how to hum the song from the John Wayne movie *The High and the Mighty*. He didn't, so I did. At 300 feet in dense fog I began my checklist in preparation to climb back out when Stanley yelled into the intercom, "I see the ground." Indeed he did. For one magic moment the fog thinned and there was a wide runway only 250 feet below my wheels. We touched down and had to call to tell the tower we were on the ground because they couldn't see us. We were the only plane to land that day. Magic had begun to happen. On the way to the hotel in a rental car, I taught Stanley the theme from *The High and the Mighty* for future flights.

Of course, Buddy won. We huddled in a Shreveport hotel room until

Edwin Edwards called and said he would quit the race and not run it off. In Louisiana, if no candidate gets 50 percent of the vote, the two top vote-getters must have a runoff election.

"Edwards is too smart to run this off," I told Buddy time after time as our advantage mounted. We were a rocket ship still climbing into orbit, and Edwards would have had no chance. He conceded. Buddy was the next governor.

Before I left in my plane that night, I walked up to Buddy, who was sitting in a La-Z-Boy smoking a cigarette, and shook his hand. He didn't get up. He said simply and coolly, "Thanks for your help." The same thing he told people who served his lunch or opened his car door. I used this sort of candidate dismissal in my novel *Cottonwood,* when the fictional consultant wins a longshot election for a wino just to prove a point, but loses his family and becomes a drunk himself in the process. The fictional candidate on election night first recites a list of mistakes the consultant made and then says, "I just want you to know that if you ever need a recommendation for a campaign, you just have them call me and I'll put in a good word for you." Roemer wasn't even that generous on election night.

I didn't hear from Buddy again until he got ready to run for reelection in 1991. But that's not unusual, either. Actually, it's a healthy relationship for an elected official and a consultant. We should not govern, nor should we turn the elected person's term in office into a seamless campaign. But mine and Buddy's paths had crossed in 1987 in a strange, almost mystical way. The 1991 race would be even stranger.

Mike Murphy, one of America's leading Republican media consultants, lamented in 2000 that he made a mistake when he got too involved in John McCain's campaign for president. "I fell in love with the meat," he explained.

It is generally considered bad form in Washington to lose professional detachment and become a true believer. Only amateurs, some think, become cheerleaders. A cloud of cynicism blankets everything. To stick one's head above the cloud invites shots being fired at one's credibility. In one extreme form of this mindset, some reporters in Washington have lost all respect for elected officials, their staffs, and the machinery of politics. Such cynicism may be healthy for a journalist, but I think it is deadly for a political consultant. The best reporters—like the best consultants—are idealists. But our function is different. In my business, to sacrifice sleep, health, and family to help these candidates, one must at least fool oneself into believing it is about more than dollars. My father never told me to get an education to make money. He wanted me to help working people in a way his picket signs and strike violence could not.

One of the reasons I had to flee Louisiana in 1980 was that I had stopped believing in most of the people I was promoting. I saw nothing wrong with "falling in love with the meat." But in Louisiana much of the meat was tainted.

Losing to me is more than a check on a scorecard in *Campaigns and Elections* magazine. When good people I represent lose, even when it is not the fault of the candidate or the campaign, I go into a deep depression. Some losses hurt more than others. Evelyn Gandy's loss for governor of Mississippi in 1983, Frank McRight's narrow defeat for an Alabama congressional seat in 1984, Dave McCurdy's 1994 loss in his campaign for the U.S. Senate in Oklahoma, Roy Barnes's loss for governor of Georgia in

1990, and Jill Docking's 1996 Senate loss to Sam Brownback in Kansas as a result of anti-Semitic campaigning on Brownback's behalf, still hurt inside almost as much as they did on election night. Jill, one of the most noble candidates I've ever known, was defeated while Mary Landrieu was elected in 1996, as I shuttled back and forth between Kansas and Louisiana.

Sure, you win some and lose some. As the great thoroughbred trainer Bob Baffert said with a shrug after his horse Point Given lost the 2001 Kentucky Derby and came back to win the Preakness two weeks later, "Horses beat horses." I like the track, and I don't whine even if I don't cash a ticket at the window all day long. But politics is more than a sport to me, more than the competition, more than the paycheck. For one thing, it's hard to be philosophical when race-baiting is involved. (And race nearly played a role in Landrieu's election as well. In a runoff against Republican Woody Jenkins, she was labeled the "black candidate" by the phone banks and a whisper campaign.) I also believe that the United States, not to mention the people of Oklahoma and Kansas, were shortchanged when we lost those two particular races to second-raters. In both cases I gave a damn. It would be easy to say I cared too much, but I think that is impossible.

So when I got a call early one Sunday morning in 1988 from a *Miami Herald* reporter asking me to comment on Gary Hart's fling with a Florida beauty, I went into an emotional tailspin. I had invested all of my hopes in Hart. He had all of the right stuff. He was intelligent, tough, and loved his country as much as any patriot I had ever met. His wasn't a campaign pose. Hart would get wet-eyed when he talked about the abuses of the past and the hope of the future. I liked it that he wasn't popular with the ass-kissers in Washington and operated as what some called a "lone wolf." And I didn't care about some sexual lapse. By now I understood the human condition and our frailties of the flesh. I had read about how Franklin D. Roosevelt and Dwight Eisenhower had each had a long-term relationship with a woman not his wife while, literally, saving the world from the depression and fascism. I knew also that Presidents John F. Kennedy and Lyndon Baines Johnson had behaved indiscreetly in the same years when they were helping to secure full rights for African Americans. Far better, I thought, for a man to indulge in sexual indiscretions than to betray his country like Richard Nixon, who apparently had little libido, had done.

At the time I received that call—and, in fact, to this day—I never saw Hart behave in any way that would compromise him, his country, or his marriage. But I didn't doubt the reporter from the *Miami Herald*. I had heard rumors. My dreams and my business had been smashed by what the early rock-and-roll singer Clyde McPhatter, and later Elvis Presley, had lamented: "One night of sin."

Once again I had to rebuild my business out of the ashes. I had turned down work for 1988 because I didn't want to make the mistake I had made in 1984, when I stretched myself too thin and perhaps contributed to Hart's eventual defeat. Until that Sunday morning, everything had been going perfectly. Hart was the assumed leader for the presidency, and the Wise Ones and power brokers were showing up with money and help they had denied in 1984. Our opponent would have been Vice President George Bush, a war hero and decent guy, but no match for Hart's intellect, idealism, vitality, or appeal. I will always believe Hart would have defeated Bush and become the forty-first president of the United States—and a good one, too.

Maybe I was partly responsible for Hart's misfortune. In 1986 I introduced him to an old friend of mine from Louisiana, Bill Broadhurst. He was an Edwin Edwards confidant and had moved into the big arena in Washington, where he bought two historic townhouses three blocks from the Capitol. He promptly—and illegally, under local zoning laws—combined the buildings into one. When I asked how he had gotten permission to join the houses, he rubbed his fingers together in the universal symbol of money. "That's how we do it at home," Bill laughed when I asked. He meant no harm. He was just pure Louisiana.

Bill wanted to become involved at the top in Washington. His good friend Congressman John Breaux would soon become a senator when Russell Long retired, and Bill also had a good relationship with the other Louisiana senator, Bennett Johnston, so he was not without valuable connections. He asked me to make a few introductions and help him become involved in a presidential campaign. I introduced him to Gary Hart, and Broadhurst began raising money for the campaign. He also befriended the candidate.

Bill wanted to participate in my annual duck dinner for the press, which had begun in 1984 with Wanda Williams's gumbo. I accepted. I liked Bill and appreciated what he was doing for Hart, and the duck dinner had grown too large for me to host alone. He had ducks, shrimp, and crawfish driven up from the bayous of Louisiana by a team of slightly drunk but screamingly funny Cajun chefs. The dinners grew from twenty guests to a hundred or more and were held in the illegally combined backyards of his townhouses. The only rule was that no client and no elected official was invited. Because there was no implied obligation, the reporters who attended could relax and enjoy an afternoon of drinking wine and eating gumbo. The reporters were my friends, and I never wanted to compromise them. I enjoy eating, drinking, and card playing with them too much to ever use them in business. And, I admit, America's press has been kind to me through the years.

The relationship between Hart and Broadhurst flourished. I don't think the controlled, rigid Hart had ever met a man with Bill Broadhurst's bayou joie de vivre. He made Hart laugh, and nothing Hart could do would be beyond the Louisiana moral boundaries that Billy considered normal. Not that I blame Bill for Hart's downfall. I don't, any more than I blame myself. I still consider the whole thing just bad luck and maybe even political mischief. Bill called and invited me to fly to Miami and meet him and Hart for a boat trip. Hart was working on a speech and could use the solitude and perhaps my help, and Bill wanted a fishing companion when we reached Bimini, where he had left his fishing boat. Hart didn't fish, hunt, or follow LSU Tiger football—thus he failed in many respects as a Broadhurst playmate. It was logical Bill would call me. We made arrangements to meet in south Florida, but the night before I was to catch a morning plane, I got a call from Annette Strauss, who was running for mayor of Dallas and was our client. She was angry. Her opponent had attacked her on television. She wanted me in Dallas immediately.

I liked Annette and her husband, Ted, but I was in the race at the request of one of the grand old men of the Democratic Party, Bob Strauss, her brother-in-law. Bob, one of the true behind-the-scenes power brokers, commanded my respect and was a hard man to refuse. Annette was weeping on the phone and I could never say no to a weeping woman, so I called Broadhurst and told him I would miss the boat trip. The next day Broadhurst and Hart allowed two women to invite themselves onto a yacht, out for a day of boating, and into a devastating snapshot of Donna Rice sitting on Hart's lap. The photo was one of those playful, casual things that could happen to any man who poses for a picture with a pretty woman, but it brought down the campaign and my dreams. With Hart out of the way, George Bush had clear sailing and only minor annoyances like Michael Dukakis to deal with.

That fateful Sunday morning, I sat on the edge of the bed and looked at the phone after I hung up. Was it possible? For a few minutes I lay back on my pillow to regain control. One must always be in control. After I was sure there was no anger, pity, or quaking in my voice, as soon as I was sure no one could see me sweat, I called a friend in Miami and had him read me the entire story. I wasn't ready to condemn Hart. Yes, it was possible that he had been caught with a woman. In fact, I knew it was probable. A major newspaper would not publish a story like that without assurance they were correct. Hart lived only a few doors from me on Sixth Street, and from my second-story bedroom window I could look down on the sidewalk filled with camera crews walking in the direction of his house. Soon it was a mob. I did the logical thing. I went to a baseball game in Baltimore. I didn't want to face the press when I had no answers. My front doorbell was ringing when I left through the back door, where I was picked up by an employee and some of his friends.

We arrived at the stadium so early we had to wait for the gates to open. We watched the ground crew stripe the field, then sat through batting practice. By the time the first pitch was thrown, people around us were talking about Gary Hart and the "bimbo." I hung out at the mustard table by the hot-dog stand and glanced at the game on the monitor hanging from the ceiling. Occasionally a roar would vibrate the metal under my feet. I didn't drink beer at the park or even take a hit from the scotch flask in my friend's pocket. Under emotional stress I always back away from alcohol. A couple of drinks and you reveal too much, show your hole cards, people can see you sweat. At about the seventh inning I called Bill Clinton and told him he should think about getting a presidential race together. I knew that Hart could not survive.

After the game and a neglected dinner in Baltimore's Little Italy, I sneaked into the back door of my house and sat quietly in the dark in my wife's small study off the kitchen. Occasionally a reporter would ring the doorbell. Early that day I had taken the phone off the hook, and our voice mail was full and thus nonfunctional. Just after dark Sandy showed up with her suitcases and a full quotient of jet lag. She had been on a tulip-viewing trip in Holland with some friends from Baton Rouge.

"What's going on?" She had seen the bands of reporters and cameramen milling in front of the house as the taxi dropped her off. I glumly explained as best I could. After about a minute of silent contemplation Sandy asked,

"Where were you last night?" I almost laughed. It did demonstrate some lack of trust. Fortunately, I didn't need an alibi. I was with a friend at his grandson's birthday party at Chuck E. Cheese. There is nothing more innocent than Chuck E. Cheese, unless you make bets on the scores of some of the games kids play in that amusement park disguised as a restaurant. But Sandy's line was funny and got national publicity after I shared it with friends. I was laughing, but it was the forced and sad laughter of Pagliacci from Leoncavallo's opera of the tragic clown.

Once again my business was in ashes all the way up to my neck, with a million-dollar overhead. The fact that my son had just joined the firm made the catastrophe even more painful. He always wanted to go into political consulting, but I had made him find a newspaper job first to hone his writing skills. He had talked the editor of the Lawrence, Massachusetts, *Eagle-Tribune* into hiring him after being originally turned down because of his southern accent. One of my great sources of pride is that both Dane and my daughter, Kristan, were fine reporters, a profession I feel is noble and akin to the clergy.

Ironically, it was Gary Hart who ended Dane's career at the *Eagle-Tribune.* Dane's beat was New Hampshire politics, and the paper, in an attempt to remain objective, took him off it because of his father's relationship with a man who was going to run in the upcoming Democratic primary. Dane loved reporting, but he left the paper rather than accept reassignment.

So I was not simply dealing with an office filled with people with needs, I was about to endanger the professional progress of my own son. I attacked the telephones with a vengeance looking for business. But while I wasn't watching, things had changed. Hungry young consultants trying to establish themselves had swept through the candidate field, often giving away their services to build a résumé. They were working for no fee, and often no commissions on the media buy. Our firm, at the time, charged a fee of $60,000 for a campaign and 15 percent commission on everything spent on paid media. I tried to contract campaigns that would produce at least $200,000 profit in a cycle. Thus, I could cover overhead with five or six campaigns. In 1988, suddenly, fledgling consultants were signing contracts for almost nothing. It turned out that most of them were overcharging even at that price.

Slowly some of my most respected clients signed me, including Senators Lloyd Bentsen and Dennis DeConcini. These multimillion-dollar campaigns saved me again, but I had to build any profit out of small campaigns that had been missed in the new consultant sweep. So when Al Gore called and offered me a deal to do media for the Super Tuesday primary campaigns in the South, I immediately swallowed my pride and accepted at a price far below my standard.

My Gore connection came through a colorful Democratic player from Maryland, Nathan Landau. Nate and I had been on a boondoggle trip to Taiwan with about six other Democrats. It was part of the little island's propaganda effort to win more Democrats to their cause. Coming back in an almost empty first-class compartment of China Air, Nate and I had spent hours talking about presidential campaigns. He was heavily invested in Gore but insecure about how Gore was conducting his campaign. A few weeks later Nate, one of Gore's largest money people, demanded that I do the media or the campaign would risk losing his support.

My first reaction to the Gore offer was to call Jack Martin and Lloyd Bentsen. They had put good money on the line for my help and deserved veto power on my involvement. Jack, Bentsen's campaign manager and friend, simply shrugged and told me to talk to Bentsen. I explained my dilemma to the senator. He showed a great lack of enthusiasm for Gore but said that it would not distract from his campaign if I did only the Super Tuesday election. Bentsen's election that year was developing slowly because no one had the courage to challenge such a heavyweight. It took the Republican Party months to find a fool willing to throw himself on a campaign funeral pyre. Taking on Bentsen was like challenging Matt Dillon after making a pass at Miss Kitty in her saloon in Dodge. But Bentsen was my friend, and he and Russell Long had invented me as a consultant. If Bentsen had shown any hesitation, I would have refused the Gore campaign.

I had another dilemma. By 1988 I truly understood the emerging brutal business of consultant competition. Like others, I had been slammed and criticized. The second- and third-string consultants were out there trying to muscle their way into the business. Gore, however, was being handled by one of the solid firms, the Campaign Group in Philadelphia. I was about to do to them what the pretenders were trying to do to me.

Gore's problem was not Doc Schweitzer, the lead consultant of the Campaign Group. Gore's problem was Gore. (This turned out to be the case again in 2000, when Gore proved his lack of understanding by assembling a team that did not match his needs or personality.) But I had a money-burning machine that needed fuel. I swallowed my feelings about poaching on a good firm—and maybe even some of my integrity—and took the Gore deal. I flew to Norfolk, Virginia, and met the Gore campaign plane, which I would ride for several days to get a feeling for the candidate. I can't film strangers.

I liked Al Gore and was beguiled by his wife, Tipper. They were decent and good people who would serve their country well. Gore told me I was to be the senior media adviser. He said he had not originally come to my firm because his old friend Carter Eskew had promised to do the campaign. Eskew was a junior partner in Bob Squier's firm. Squier was a pro's pro. Eskew bumped around the political business for a while, fell out with Squier, and moved to New York, where he worked in a firm that represented tobacco companies. In my journal I wrote Al's exact words, "Those fuckers let me down." In 2000, Eskew and Gore teamed up again. In an act that appeared pure revenge, Eskew sacked Squier with great public humiliation, and thus began the march of doom for Gore.

In 1988, however, a relaxed, pre-Clinton Al Gore was a pleasure to ride with. We went to North Carolina "pig pickings" and toured industries. At our first large gathering, I was shocked. The warm and personable Gore turned into a mannequin. His body language came directly from some robotics computer, and his speech was artificial. But when he stepped down from the stage and began putting his arm around shoulders and talking to individuals, another Gore appeared. Though I had only two days before I shot film, I now knew what to do. It was simple. I was going to put Gore with real people for a conversation while my camera looked for targets of opportunity.

Gore's campaign staff was almost incapable of helping me quickly come up with people or locations, and I hesitated even to communicate with them because I didn't want a team of amateurs getting in the way. So I went home to redneck Port Arthur, to a language I understood, where I could quickly find help in my daddy's old union. I had a few beers with a weathered refinery worker, Chip Osborn, and we scouted land around the refinery.

We found a patch of oil-soaked ground that did not belong to the refinery, and Chip rounded up a group of men and women to engage the candidate. I intended to film Gore as I had done Hart outside the steel mills in Ohio. I kept the production crew small. Jim Duffy met Gore in a hotel room in Beaumont and briefed him on how we were going to film. No scripts. No lines. Totally unpredictable. Or it seemed that way. Earlier I had met with the union people and grilled them on what I thought the election was all about. The amazing thing to both Duffy and me was that until that meeting in the hotel room, Gore had no central core message for his campaign. In fact, he was a little desperate for direction. For better or worse, we gave him a "worker's protection" message.

My hunch that there would be chemistry between Gore and the workers proved to be right. He was in touching distance and seemed relaxed. I stood behind him, just off camera, and yelled questions for him to answer until the workers grew more confident and took over. The result wasn't magic, but it was good workable television.

30-Second TV
Client: Al Gore
Spot Title: Working People
Al Gore: The working men and women of this country are ready to do their share . . .
Announcer: Corporate greed is strangling our future. Candidate for President, Al Gore.
Al Gore: . . . but the corporations of this nation have to understand that they are American corporations and they've got to start investing more money here for a change and creating more jobs here for a change. That's the only way we are going to rebuild this nation's economic strength.
Announcer: Al Gore, President.

The commercials were immediately approved by Gore and his wife. However, on a Sunday morning two days before they were to go on the air, I got a scorching call from the candidate and Tipper. The *New York Times* had run a story about the new commercials. The Gores considered this meant a breach of confidence on my part. It was no secret that we were shooting film in Port Arthur. An enterprising reporter had simply dropped by my office on a Saturday morning and asked one of my college interns for a look at the new Gore spots. She had no instructions to the contrary and showed him what he wanted. I would not have allowed the reporter to see the spots before they went on the air, but it still did not seem serious to me. When the reporter called me later that day for my comments about the commercials, I made an executive decision that it was too minor an infraction to worry the candidate about. That turned out to be a miscalculation. I didn't know it then, but I know now that for the micromanaging Al Gore, no detail is too trivial.

The spots were about to go on the air, and I tried to persuade Gore that the newspaper story was a minor matter. He was furious and rude. He needed some lessons from my father about control. When Hart lost the Illinois primary because of the mix-up about a pulled television spot, he had calmly gathered the staff together and told us to fight on. There were no recriminations or loss of control. Hart never let people see him sweat. What a contrast Gore was that day as he screamed about a minor miscue. I guess because of the influence of my father, I take the measure of men by how they handle stress and controversy. Gore failed my father's test, as had Clinton. Proof that the newspaper story was utterly unimportant came a few days later when Gore won his Super Tuesday southern state primaries.

I went back to my work for Bentsen, DeConcini, and others. Gore cooled down and didn't hold a grudge. I guess it is hard to blame somebody for winning. The intern had made a mistake. I had made a mistake. Gore overreacted. Presidential campaigns are always on the edge of hysteria. It was a strange year. Before the 1988 campaign season had even heated up, I had gone through three presidential candidates, Hart, Clinton, and Gore. Soon I would be remotely involved in the bizarre Dukakis campaign through Lloyd Bentsen, who became the Massachusetts governor's candidate for vice president.

I am seldom more at home than when I am in Texas. As spring turned to summer in 1988, I flew my plane to Austin and spent most of my time there helping America's best campaign team work for Lloyd Bentsen. Part of it was my debt to Bentsen and part because I enjoyed the good friends and the beef enchiladas at the Texas Chili Parlor. I had a beautiful suite at the Four Seasons Hotel overlooking the lake, and it was an easy flight to Phoenix for Senator DeConcini. By this time Jim Duffy had matured into a first-rate political consultant, and my son was finding his creative wings in production. An organization that had always revolved only around me began to find other orbits, and my quality of life began to improve.

A Texas law signed by Lyndon Johnson allowed Bentsen to accept nomination for vice president while still running for reelection to the U.S. Senate. (This happened again in 2000 when Senator Joseph Lieberman ran both for vice president with Gore and for reelection in Connecticut, which had a similar law.) Our first task was to produce television that explained how and why Bentsen was running for both offices. After a few days of explanation we settled into a normal campaign. Bentsen called me into his suite at the hotel with Martin. Our opponent was forty-six-year-old Beau Boulter, a Republican congressman from Amarillo who was considered ultraconservative even by Texas standards—and who had raised only $300,000 or so in a place where it takes millions to compete statewide. Bentsen wasn't worried about Boulter, but he understood—and made sure we understood—that in a presidential campaign year almost anything could happen. His charge to me was simple. I was to produce media to run in Boulter's own congressional district, a sprawling expanse that encompassed the Texas Panhandle and High Plains. The idea was to put him on the defensive and force him to stay home and defend his conservative base. I created a series of playful radio ads using an announcer with a deep Texas accent. The series was called "Where's Beau?" The announcer opened the spots by asking people to go out and find Beau Boulter because he had a few questions to ask.

60-Second Radio
Client: Lloyd Bentsen
Title: Where's Beau?
Hey folks, if any of you happen to see Congressman Beau Boulter out there any place, would you ask him to come in and listen to the radio?
Now we tried to find him in Washington, but he hadn't been to work in so long they're not sure they'd know him if he showed up.
Ahhh, we just want to ask him some simple things like why he is opposed to catastrophic health care for the elderly.
You know, till Senator Bentsen passed that bill, one long hospital stay could take away a life's savings and force some independent folks to move in with relatives.
Beau, how would you like to be treated like that?
And Beau, why did you go along with the Republicans' tax plan that eliminated the depletion allowance? Hey, the oil industry's barely hanging on now.
Well, Beau, we've got a list of questions as long as your arm, but we're just a little short on radio time.

But don't you worry. We'll be back.

In the meantime stay by that radio.

Beau Boulter never became a factor. Our problem was Mike Dukakis. He couldn't seem to get anything right. His campaign was slow and committee-oriented—and always behind the power curve. Bentsen, a take-charge man, was frustrated by the lack of political understanding throughout the Dukakis campaign. The Texas organization was weak enough that Jack Martin was able to handle them by keeping them pushed out of the way so they could not cause damage.

Bentsen, true to his Texas upbringing and strength of character, never complained or said anything derogatory to me about the Dukakis campaign until it was almost over. For weeks he had attempted to keep the Boston advertising out of Texas. It had been crafted by a group of East Coast advertising executives and their agency people and was little more than politically amateur. Finally, in desperation, Bentsen ordered me to make two commercials to run for the ticket in Texas. After he saw and liked them, he asked me to rush them to Boston for approval. I did. They languished there. Time after time he called to ask if Boston had okayed the spots. Time after time I had to tell him I had heard nothing.

I have related the episode earlier in this book: how, after hanging on the phone for fifteen minutes, I was finally told by a staff member, "Look, sport, I don't know you, I don't know what you're talking about, and you're wasting my time. So go fuck yourself"; how Gay Erwin, a Bentsen assistant and my friend, saw my rage and placed a call to a secret number on the campaign plane, where I repeated the entire conversation to the senator; and how, after a long pause, he said in his controlled voice, "Raymond, you did all you could do. Just forget it. This campaign is over." But he soldiered on as he had when he had flown bombers over heavily protected Nazi fuel depots. Nobody saw him sweat. Real men don't whine or get hysterical or blame others. Lloyd Bentsen was a Texan.

MARRIAGE ON THE ROCKS, UP WITH A TWIST

Early in 1991 I was sitting in front of a fire at Heroes Ranch in Montana sipping a single-malt scotch and talking to my friend Steve Davison. (My wilderness mountainside retreat on the Big Hole River was built as an escape from reality, and even its name reflects its purpose. Because the ranchers all had names over their gates, I, in jest, did the same thing. I named my place after all the "heroes" who tamed the West: Hopalong Cassidy, the Lone Ranger, Tom Mix, Gene Autry. Every year there is a discussion about whether to include John Wayne, but he is voted down because he was such a staunch Republican.) The conversation, as I recall it now, centered on the selection of new woodworking tools in catalogs spread on the table before us. The phone rang, which is always an intrusion when rednecks are looking at their tools, but this was a particularly unwelcome interruption. My wife was on the line from our home on Capitol Hill. She said that she had about all the fun she could stand and when I returned to Washington, she'd have moved out—and that there would be some empty space in the house.

As usual, she wasn't angry. I thought we were a perfect couple because we smiled a lot and rarely argued. So I'm not sure I took her seriously. But when I got home the next week, I found out before I even made it upstairs that she hadn't been kidding. The living room looked as empty as a dance floor after the dance. I called her name, but the only reply was my lonely footsteps echoing in the suddenly barren home. We had had some discussions about the consequences of my distraction, but I had been distracted and hadn't heard very well. Now she had my attention and a new house across Capitol Hill.

People married thirty years or so have their problems, and Sandy and I had hit bad patches before, but nothing like this. As 1991 dawned, I was off track, wandering in a personal and professional wilderness. A man without a stake in the ground somewhere can wander off course. A man with an inflated ego, a new novel in the bookstores, and an airplane with a range of one thousand miles can really wander. (The novel, *Cottonwood*, was about a political consultant who sacrificed his soul to beat his way into the business.) So with my marriage on the rocks, 1991 became my year as a nomad. My travels drew me back to Louisiana.

I had signed a personable new candidate, Richard Ieyoub, a district attorney from Lake Charles, who aspired to be governor of Louisiana and who figured, not unreasonably, that he ought to get himself elected state attorney general first. I was also producing a film for a group of businessmen about the need for education reform. The upshot was that, despite my herculean efforts to escape the place, I was back where I had started professionally. I rationalized this as a case of why not? I knew the terrain and still had personal relationships with maitre d's in most of the good restaurants in New Orleans. My dear gin-rummy-playing friend of many years, Lou Faxon, also unattached, had a couple of empty bedrooms and kept martinis in the freezer. Lou was a partially retired architect and had a lot of time to devote to gin rummy at lunch in the City Club and to late afternoons in his own kitchen cooking elaborate meals that attracted other lonely people like moths to a flame. I would go to book signings for *Cottonwood* around the country, return to Baton Rouge, put my feet on Lou's coffee table, extend my right hand, and almost by magic find it filled with a frozen martini glass. It wasn't a life I would have chosen. I would rather have been married. But my daddy always taught me to play the hand you are dealt with a straight face and without a whimper.

It had been four years since I had talked to Buddy Roemer, and after lunch one day I walked unannounced into the governor's office. I really didn't know what sort of reception to expect. Roemer was sitting at two acres of polished wood with a pen and a single sheet of paper. He looked up and seemed genuinely glad to see me. He jumped up from his seat and shook my hand firmly, a big smile on his face. He seemed almost too glad to see me. He motioned me to a seat across the desk and there were a few seconds of silence. It was obvious this was a man in some sort of pain.

"Patty has left me," he said. "I'm trying to get her back. Why don't you help me with this note?"

"Hell, Buddy, if I was so good at patching up marriages, I wouldn't be sitting here talking to you. Why don't you just call her on the phone or send flowers or something?"

I couldn't imagine my audacity at giving advice about relationships. The governor pushed the paper aside. Maybe he was glad to be able to talk about something else.

"I'm glad you're here. I think I have big trouble getting reelected."

"Are you saying I'm hired for your reelection campaign? Since I haven't heard from you for four years, I thought you were mad at me because I helped you win."

"Ah, you know how I am. You never got the credit you deserved for my election. I got involved in fights with the idiots in the legislature and my wife and just forgot you. But now I'm ready to go back to work."

And that is how I ended up living on the second floor of the Governor's Mansion. Buddy not only wanted me to work for him, he wanted company listening to his Lyle Lovett records, talking about novels, watching professional football games, and eating breakfast every morning at the mile-long table in the formal dining room. Then we might go days without talking as Buddy holed up in his room and I wandered around New Orleans or secluded myself in the velvet cocoon of privacy in the mansion, with state troopers helping me avoid calls and convicts bringing me drinks. When I wandered through the big kitchen at night looking for a glass of milk, I would find platters of freshly baked cookies to help me sleep. The laundry in the basement kept my shirts clean and starched and my pants pressed. My shoes always had a nice shine. It was the best of all worlds. I got to live like a governor, but I didn't have to be one. On Thursday nights there were poker games on the third floor, though in time I learned to stay out of them. The stakes were too high and the players too good.

When Roemer would meet me at the elevator in the hall between our suites, he would look at the heavens and announce with mock drama, "Doomed. We are doomed, Strother."

I normally responded by asking why he didn't go out and campaign. "Too late for all that," he would answer and wander off toward the strains of Lyle Lovett reverberating in his bedroom down the hall. He was partial to Lyle's melancholy, ironic, introspective songs.

Maybe it was already too late, but I was an optimist and thought we could put Humpty Dumpty back together. Buddy had made a mess of his first four years because of his reclusive behavior, his lack of respect for the legislature, and the conniving Edwin Edwards pulling strings in the background.

Buddy had shaken up the system, and the old hacks didn't like it. When he was first elected, he sold the state airplanes and borrowed $1 billion to keep the state out of bankruptcy. Then he tackled a constant problem in Louisiana, tax reform. He made it a death struggle, and it became a platform for his enemies. David Duke, the former Ku Klux Klan leader and former Nazi bad boy, had been elected to the legislature from a suburban New Orleans community in a backlash against blacks. He joined forces with the Edwards loyalists in the legislature to fight or even dismantle all of the Roemer reforms. They needed Roemer to fail if they were to succeed. That Louisiana was the victim didn't seem to matter to them. It was a counter-Roemer revolution. The forces of evil won and Roemer was badly bruised.

Political problems were not enough for the brilliant but troubled Roemer. After his wife left him, he withdrew. He would spend hours by the pool with instructions not to be interrupted, and nights in his bedroom mourning Patty's departure and listening to country music. Legislators had a better chance of talking to President Bush on the telephone than to Roemer. Occasionally we would pile into the governor's limo and drive to the Superior Grill, a Tex-Mex restaurant, where Buddy would get a corner table and sit with his back to the room so he would not be approached by voters.

At this point in my life, Buddy and I were perfect soulmates, if not the perfect campaign machine. Where we differed, though, was that Buddy would reach out for "New Age" help. Danny Walker, an old friend of Buddy's who was an ordained Baptist preacher, tried to fill Buddy's black emotional hole with quick-fix self-help claptrap. When I moved into the mansion, Buddy gave me *All I Really Need to Know I Learned in Kindergarten*, by Robert Fulghum. To please Buddy, I read enough of it to be embarrassed that I was reading it at all, and threw it into a drawer with my socks.

Reading people like Fulghum in private would not in itself have been harmful to Buddy. But he and Walker managed to turn this New Age hokum into a public relations nightmare—and one that played directly into the hands of his critics, who already were trying to portray him as a flake. In January, before I moved in, Walker had conned Buddy into going public with his New Age drivel. Walker conducted a three-day retreat called "Adventures in Attitude" for Buddy's staff. He had the participants put rubber bands on their wrists and snap them every time they had a negative thought. As they pulled the rubber, they were to think, "Cancel, cancel." One can only imagine the belly laughs in the hangouts of the old-style Louisiana pols when the Roemer staff appeared in the governor's office wearing rubber bands.

I think Buddy knew that Walker's juvenile self-help regimen was over the top, but he tolerated the "Adventures in Attitude" session mainly because Walker had invited Patty. Buddy saw this as a way to connect with her. Patty, a smart woman, departed the clinic shortly after the rubber bands started popping. The embarrassed staff soon discarded the rubber bands as well, but the ridicule never stopped. Edwin Edwards, always ready with a needle, said, "Roemer promised us an ethical, scandal-free government and gave us Danny Walker voodooism."

I needed a little help in life myself, but my spiritual adviser was Lou Faxon, with his tonic of true friendship and his holy water of dry martinis. How Buddy Roemer, one of the brightest men I have ever met, fell for such empty intellectual parlor tricks still fills me with wonder. Walker, truly a nice, gentle man in reality, was not to be underestimated, though. He ended up having a corrosive effect in the campaign by making Buddy insecure about negative advertising and killing my chance to attack David Duke when we could have possibly still pulled the election out of the fire.

Thus the 1991 Louisiana governor's race became the strangest election campaign of my life. Seldom is there a more clear-cut case of good against evil. Roemer was an honest reformer with a fount of ideas that would have benefitted the state and its people. Edwards was a living, breathing textbook example of the corrupt—and peculiarly Louisianian—political rogue who had held the state back for so long. He actually called himself the "solution to the revolution." But Edwards, however charming, wasn't the solution to anything. He was part of the problem. Worse, much worse, was David Duke, who stood for an even darker Louisiana legacy, the evils of racism. Duke was a direct intellectual descendant of Hitler in a region of the country that had never come to honest terms with its own past of apartheid, an illegal caste system kept in place by poll taxes, job discrimination, and racial violence, most notably lynching.

If Buddy was conflicted, I wasn't. To me this was even more a crusade than the first Roemer campaign. I dug in and began producing a thirty-minute documentary on the success and promise of the revolution. Buddy

Roemer was Louisiana's best hope to move into mainstream America. But on March 11, 1991, Buddy Roemer put a political pistol to his head and pulled the trigger. On that day, he abruptly changed parties and became a Republican.

There had been rumors circulating for months that Buddy was flirting with this notion, but he personally assured me before I signed on to the campaign that he was going to stay a Democrat. His explanation for the gossip was that he enjoyed the attention he got when he appeared to lean to the right. The rumors persisted and he continued to deny them—right up until the night before he switched.

I had gone to Washington to visit friends and check on the daily machinations of my office. I had been there about two weeks before I headed west on March 10. I was going to Austin but stopping off in Baton Rouge to pick up a couple of suits and shirts from the Governor's Mansion. I called Lou Faxon and told him to freeze the martini glasses and that I would spend the night in what he now called his "fraternity house." When I landed, a state trooper friend picked me up out on the tarmac by my plane and drove me to the mansion. I asked him to wait out front while I collected my clothes. After another trooper let me in, I was met by Harris Diamond, a New York advertising executive who had been Buddy's campaign manager in 1987. I hadn't seen Diamond in years and it was a shock. He was agitated.

Diamond said, "What are you doing here?" It wasn't a pleasant remark. He said it rudely.

Behind him I could see and hear a crowd of people in the dining room. The doors were closed, but through a crack I spotted Mary Matalin. In future years, she would become James Carville's wife, but in those days she was known in Louisiana simply as a Republican operative with close ties to President Bush.

"You need to go," Diamond said.

"I live here. I'm going upstairs to my room and collect a suit. Where's the governor?"

I didn't like Diamond because I never knew exactly whose side he was on. It is an understatement to say his allegiances shifted according to self-interest. He was a close friend of Dick Morris's and had been put in the first Roemer campaign by Morris. Later, as Diamond assumed more control, he helped lead the successful effort to oust Morris from the team.

"You wait here," Diamond commanded and went back into the dining room. He shut the door behind him. Soon Roemer came out, also closing the door, and led me to a small office on the first floor.

"I want to be honest," he told me. "There are a bunch of Republicans from the White House in there trying to talk me into switching parties."

"Don't do it, Buddy."

"You don't have anything to worry about, but when the president of the United States asks you to listen, you give him respect."

Buddy assured me all was well. The next day, March 11, while I was in Austin, he called a press conference on the front steps of the mansion and announced he was becoming a Republican. That night at a book signing for *Cottonwood* at Scholz's Beer Garden, hosted by Texas political heavyweight George Shipley, I saw my friend Jack Martin. I took him aside and explained the Louisiana situation. He advised me to drop Roemer. He was right, but even then I was conflicted. I thought of Buddy as a friend. On my way back to Washington, I stopped in Baton Rouge and collected all of my suits and shirts from the mansion.

When I saw Buddy in the hall, he looked at the heavens and shouted, "We are doomed, Strother. Now we are really doomed."

He laughed and said, "I want you to stay with me. The Republicans are going to staff the entire campaign, but we all want you to do the media." He saw me hesitate. "There's no hurry. Go back to Washington and think about it. You know, before I switched, I was running against the forces of darkness. I'm still running against the forces of darkness. All that has changed is the word that describes my party. I'm still pro-choice. I'm still pro-environment. Nothing has changed. You think about that."

For almost two months I stewed in Washington. I was bored and didn't want to fall into the single-guy trap of hanging out in bars. The Ieyoub attorney general race didn't take much time, because I was going to use his money in a flurry, late in the campaign. In the meantime he was keeping busy slapping backs and shaking hands. He was a wonderful one-on-one politician who fell into the traditional trap of thinking he could shake hands into office. The prospects of my wife coming home with the furniture looked glum, so I began killing time by hiring a decorator and filling the hollow places in the big house.

Finally, Buddy phoned and forced my hand. He called on my friendship and loyalty.

"Raymond, if I went to prison you'd bring me cigarettes?"

"Sure Buddy."

"And if I got sick, you'd give me blood?"

"Of course."

"If I came to your door hungry, you'd feed me?"

"Yes."

"But if I change parties, you run like a scalded dog? I'm still running against Edwin Edwards and David Duke. I'm still running against corruption and hate. If David Duke gets a toehold in the governor's office here, he will have a platform to spew anti-Semitism and racism all over this land. If Edwin Edwards is elected, this state marches backwards for another four years."

His logic overwhelmed me. I was a sucker for a cause. Maybe at a different time in my life I might have given a different answer. But I was looking for meaning, substance, and direction. I tried to think of what my father would have done. Of course he had never voted for a Republican, but he would never have voted for the Ku Klux Klan or for Edwards. At least that is the reasoning I used. He believed you stood by your friends even when they were in great peril. When a worker weakened and threatened to go through a picket line, we didn't curse him, we took him food from our own depleted larder. When schoolyard bullies attacked weak children, my father shamed me into befriending the victims and even standing back to back with them in a fight. "Men don't run," he said again and again.

Two days later I was back in my mansion room but not terribly proud of myself. The conflict raged within, and I withdrew from my friends except for Faxon and a nonjudgmental, hotshot reporter in Washington, Carl Cannon, who was about to become the White House correspondent for the *Baltimore Sun*. When I first walked into the storefront campaign headquarters in a declining shopping center, I felt like I was walking into enemy territory. I had spent years on the other side of the battlefield from these pros sent in from Washington. Sam Dawson, the imported campaign manager, was sitting behind a desk in a stiffly starched button-down shirt and jeans. He had a cigarette burning in an ashtray before him and one in his mouth. The room was filled with smoke.

"You Strother?"

"Yes."

"Hell, son, pull up a chair and let's talk about how we're gonna kick some ass."

Thus I began working for the Republicans—at least for a few months.

Dawson was a real pro and I soon understood why those guys were so effective on the other side. I was accepted—not as a Democrat, but as a fellow professional. Never was there an ideological discussion. The only goal was winning. There is truly a community of political professionals who share language, lifestyle, and focus. They were discreet about their other clients, but I did occasionally learn something revealing. For example, from some vault deep within the bowels of the Republican Party headquarters they had been furnished a reel of my work. It appears they study the work of the opposition consultants so they can try to predict future behavior. Dawson already had a mental list of my "top hits."

Buddy made me feel better by doing all the things a good Democrat should do. He vetoed a repressive abortion bill and fought record-labeling legislation that he considered a violation of the First Amendment. What he refused to do, however, was take David Duke seriously. Duke was running as a saved Christian and depicting his Nazi and KKK past as "youthful in-discretions." Instead of amplifying his theory that the Holocaust never happened, he talked about cutting back the size of government and getting "people" off welfare.

The polls showed Duke far back, and Roemer thought Louisiana was too good to support hate. I didn't share his high opinion of the voters. I thought there was a secret Duke vote that did not show up in polls. Few people would admit on a telephone to a pollster that they supported this former Nazi and KKK chief. At least that was my cynical theory. My dark fear was that a small majority of white voters could possibly vote for Duke, shutting out Roemer. I knew that Edwin Edwards would inherit the black vote. In truth, over his entire career he had been their friend and had earned it. I also knew he had a small core of white support, chiefly among his fellow Cajuns, that could not be shaken from him. This put him in a position to run ahead of Roemer, who would lose conservative Republican and racist voters to Duke and would lose his traditional Democrats. It was my theory that Roemer had jumped off a cliff when he changed parties. But I still believed in the noble cause and slugged away at what I considered a lack of understanding by the Republicans and Roemer. Slowly Dawson came around to my theory. Duke was a disaster waiting to happen. Buddy, in the meantime, was playing "rope-a-dope" from his mansion bedroom. His behavior was reinforced by polls that showed him leading and David Duke stuck at about 11 percent.

Roemer had been a good governor, but because of the smokescreen in the legislature from Duke and Edwards, as well as his own mercurial behavior, only a few people knew it. He was an unconventional politician and needed an unconventional approach. I suggested we go back to the future and produce a thirty-minute documentary. Though the audiences would not be large, I thought it would serve as a monument to substance that would in some way forgive his political ineptness. My theory was that it would cause ripples among thinking people and promote discussion about something other than the clown act in the center ring. I wanted to heal his battered credibility.

My documentary was in essence kicking sand in the eyes of conventional campaign wisdom. Soon there were people trying to stop production. The documentary was rough cut and needed only a few final edits to be finished. We had invested about $100,000, and I needed another $20,000 to complete it. I showed the rough cut to the campaign, and it began to draw fire. It was good. It was damned good. But it became a cause in the campaign. The candidate's father wanted to cut it into thirty-second commercials. P. J. Mills, Roemer's chief of staff, said his young daughter had a better choice of music. Roemer's bumbling press secretary made a list of edits he wanted, even though his entire experience with television was in tuning the set in his living room. Charlie Roemer, Buddy's dad, was a knee-jerk, old-time politician and made the destruction of the thirty-minute format a mission. There was a feeding frenzy within the campaign that Roemer ignored. He didn't back me. The piece died. The campaign didn't want to think outside the box. Hell, they wanted to nail down the lid.

Soon I was to experience another failure. I made a series of commercials that the campaign liked. Roemer talked about the way things were and how he had helped to bring about change. The ads were good solid work using the best spokesperson I had ever seen, Buddy Roemer—or so I thought. When I focus-group tested the spots, they were reduced to ashes. People were now suspicious of Roemer. They knew he was glib and smart and that he could sell refrigerators to Eskimos. They feared being manipulated and smooth-talked. I had to remake the spots without Roemer. By now, however, word had leaked out about my production of a thirty-minute film, and both Duke and Edwards had gone to work producing their own long pieces.

I went into my battle mode and quit drinking. I even thought a couple of times about jogging but never got around to it. I continued to rant about David Duke. Perhaps because he had helped kill my program, Dawson agreed to a series of focus groups on David Duke. One of the Republicans' strong suits was negative research. They had imported a brilliant researcher, Gary Maloney, and he had given us all of the information on the warped personality of David Duke. We did two focus groups (one at 6 P.M. and another at 8) with middle-class voters in a suburban area across the Mississippi River from New Orleans. In the first group we described David Duke in the abstract without using his name. Duke was a hypothetical candidate.

Question: "What would you think of a candidate who had evaded the draft during the Vietnam War and lied about it later?"

Answer: "I can't imagine a man who refuses to serve his country."

Question: "What would you think of a candidate who had plastic surgery to make himself look better?"

Answer: "I'd wonder about his sexuality."

Question: "What would you think of a candidate who hadn't paid his taxes?"

Answer: "I pay my taxes, I expect a politician to."

Question: "What about a candidate who has never held a job?"

Answer: "How can anybody understand our problems if they've never held a job or sweated for a living?"

And so on.

After the group ended, the moderator, Steve Lombardo, came to the room where Dawson and I were viewing the proceedings through a two-way mirror. There was a certain smugness. The voters in the room hated everything about the unnamed hypothetical candidate. How could Roemer be defeated by him? I was not satisfied. I had too much experience in Louisiana. Even in the card room of the City Club, I had heard a prominent attorney say, "I could never vote for David Duke, but you have to admit he's the only one speaking the truth." In the group we had just tested, there was not a single declared Duke voter. I didn't believe it. I wanted to change the second group. I wanted to give them the same information but I wanted to name Duke.

They all went through the motions of saying they could never vote for

Duke, but when we asked about David Duke avoiding the draft a man said, "Everybody of that generation was trying to evade the draft. I went to Vietnam and I would have evaded going there if I could have."

On Duke's plastic surgery a woman said, "What's wrong with a politician having plastic surgery? Movie stars do it. And politicians, after all, are movie stars."

What about Duke not paying taxes? "Only dumb people pay taxes. Politicians and millionaires don't because they're smart. Duke must be smart."

And then, when the moderator hit them squarely in the face with Duke's Klan background, the general response was, "He was a kid. Kids do crazy things."

I was stunned. So was Dawson, the wise old consultant, who put his head in his hands and muttered, "It's all over boys." I agreed. It was obvious that we were on a countdown to defeat. Duke's voters were hidden. The polls lied. Hate was still with us. Ignorance was still king. Louisiana had not grown. Or so I thought.

In desperation, with fifteen minutes left of the two-hour session, I had a note delivered to the moderator in the other room suggesting he ask what would happen to the economy of Louisiana if Duke were elected. Finally the group grew quiet. One man softly said, "People could lose jobs." The other group members agreed. I put my head in my hands on the counter by the view window as though looking through the large bowl of M&Ms before me. I felt as if I had stepped off a curb in traffic and been narrowly missed by a speeding car. There was a tiny chink in the Duke armor. We had a narrow hope to place second to Edwin Edwards and get into a runoff. But I had to paint David Duke as a threat to the economy.

Time was running short. The next day I went to work on commercials that would create economic doubt. I interviewed young, ordinary people about what would happen to jobs if Duke were elected. As usual, the words of the voters were wise—better than I could have written. Those I interviewed, when confronted with a Duke governorship in more than just the abstract, flinched. It was fun for these voters to kick sand in the face of the establishment and the nation's press. It was somewhat satisfying to finally have a way to secretly express racism. Until their brother-in-law's job was in jeopardy, until LSU couldn't recruit black running backs, until the convention and tourist trade dried up, until reality truly set in. I was going to bring the voters a dose of reality.

Three days after the focus groups, I had a series of six commercials. They weren't art. They weren't even clever. These commercials simply sounded an alarm. But feel-good snake oil killed them, and the remote chances of Roemer to pull the election out of the fire died with them. I screened the ads for Roemer and Danny Walker in the family quarters in the mansion. After they showed a couple of times, Walker stood and shook his head, frowning.

"There's nothing to be gained by being negative," he said. "There's nothing to be gained by winning the wrong way. These can't run."

"Listen to Danny," Roemer quietly told me. "I know you're upset about Duke. So is my daughter Caroline. But we're still ahead in the polls, and I want to win right. Not just win. Win right. Show the commercials again."

I rewound them, and Roemer quietly watched them again. I realized that I considered them a small shrub to grab for as we fell off the cliff. Roemer considered them a threat to the Republican votes he would need in a runoff against Edwards. Suddenly I understood that Walker's pablum was an excuse for Buddy to refuse the commercials for what he considered political reasons.

Roemer shook his head. "A bunch of yuppies on TV talking about losing their jobs won't hurt Duke. The numbers just don't show it."

"You must put them on or we lose," I replied. "I can't point to numbers because we can't poll Duke accurately. We need to go after young, upwardly mobile voters who are going to vote for Duke the same way they tried pot when they were younger."

I explained that his future hung in the balance. But it wasn't just his future that worried me, it was mine—and the state's. Edwin Edwards would be trouble for the state for reasons that were familiar even to schoolchildren. And the threats to the economy expressed in my thirty-second spots were mild compared with the ostracism that Louisiana would face if somehow David Duke made it to the statehouse. For me, there were personal issues as well. I had worked with Republicans for the first time in my life—and put my business at great risk in the process—for a higher cause. Losing to Edwin Edwards and David Duke would not only be a disgrace in Washington, it would leave me defenseless against the jackals who were already circling back home.

Roemer stood and interrupted all of my thoughts.

"We're just not going to run them."

With that, he left the room with Walker. I sank into a plush sofa, where I stayed for another hour conjuring up the evils that awaited me in Washington over the following weeks. My competitors would rejoice. The young bureaucrats in the Democratic Party who were trying to feather their nests would finally have a hammer to beat me off of my perch. And, on top of that, evil would prevail in Louisiana. My father and I had lost another fight. Maybe the commercials would not have worked, but at least they were an effort. I took the videotape out of the machine, went to my room, and called my wife. I needed an ally, a sympathetic listener. I was on an island all alone. I didn't call my son because I didn't want to make him insecure any earlier than necessary. Jim Duffy, soon to be my partner, had already written off Roemer's chances. He knew Louisiana and he understood the subtext of the polls. He always did. Finally I wandered to Lou Faxon's house and had a couple of martinis and slept there that night.

The world continued to cave in on the campaign. A south Louisiana businessman, Jack Kent, owned a company that incinerated hazardous wastes. Roemer's environmental reform efforts were threatening to shut down Kent's business. Kent undoubtedly considered both Duke and Edwards far more likely to allow his pollutants to spew into the air, so he had to get rid of Roemer. He hired Deno Seder, the consultant who had been fired by Roemer to hire me in 1987, to create ads attacking Roemer. He would spend $500,000 in the effort. Deno, a good producer, said he took the Kent job because Roemer had bolted parties. I think he wanted to take revenge for being fired. Maybe it was the money. But whatever the reason, he created a brilliant set of commercials. Kent then took them to P. J. Mills, Roemer's chief of staff, and tried to make a deal.

Roemer responded with anger.

"I didn't become governor to make deals like this with people like Jack Kent. If he's violating the law, we should do everything we can to make him stop."

On October 7, the ads went on the air. I responded with an answer charging that Kent's ad was a political payoff for Edwards, but by this time our finances were depleted and we could not nearly match the frequency of Kent's ads. The funeral drums were beating louder.

Roemer continued to take solace in the polls. He didn't display any fear. The Sunday before the election, we watched professional football in the den with a tall, leggy blonde who was visiting Buddy for the weekend. Edwards, they told me, was frantically on the phone talking to black leaders. The girl giggled and flirted. The Saints scored. Pizza was delivered. We acted like Alfred E. Newman from Mad magazine: "What, me worry?"

Though Duke was creeping up, the polling insisted we were still ten points ahead of him. Five days before the election Edwards led with 31 percent, Roemer was second with 30 percent, and Duke had climbed to 20. The yuppies were playing cute, as I predicted. They were finding excuses to vote for Duke. It was over. Roemer disagreed. Roemer finally woke up to the Duke danger the day before the October 19 primary. He came in on a helicopter from a tour in Jefferson Parish and New Orleans, and he was shaken.

"We're doomed, Strother." He was serious this time—and he was right.

The day of the election, my wife showed up to give me support. As always, Sandy was there when I needed her. Carl Cannon dropped by the mansion, partly as a reporter, but more as a friend to offer moral support as the ship sank. We dropped by the moveable feast that was Lou Faxon's house, had a few drinks, and watched LSU beat Kentucky. That night, instead of going to a victory party that was going to turn into a wake, I took Sandy to a local motel. It was the start of our reconciliation.

Of course Buddy lost. The final tally was Edwards, 33.8; Duke, 31.7; and Roemer, 26.5. A host of minor candidates split the rest of the vote. My wife drove to New Orleans to see her sister, and I went to the mansion to pack my things. Roemer was in the kitchen drinking a beer.

"I still don't think running those commercials would have done it," he said, saluting me with a Budweiser.

I had nothing to say. The mansion's cookies now tasted like concrete. I appeared to be the only one in the room who gave a damn about evil's electoral victory. In the hallway I ran into Roemer's mother, who had been a hardworking soldier in the campaign and had stayed most of the time in the mansion. She hugged me and said, "Raymond, we had everything but a candidate." Her eyes were wet.

I didn't have anything to do. My plane was in the shop for minor repairs until Monday afternoon, so I packed my bags and caught a ride with a state policeman to New Orleans to see the Saints play. I had agreed to have a drink before the game with Carl Cannon at the ancient Napoleon House Bar on Chartres Street in the French Quarter. When I arrived the bar was shuttered, but I went down the street to a side door that led into their patio and was greeted by a bartender getting ready for the day. Because I was an old familiar face, I was allowed to select the opera that would play that morning. I picked something tragic by Wagner to match my mood and waited for Carl. When he knocked, I let him in, and for a few minutes we had the opera and the bar to ourselves.

The game had already started when I made my way to the governor's box in the Superdome. It was empty except for Roemer's daughter, Caroline. She was the only person I knew who cared more about the election than I did. We moved to the walled-off private seats in front of the box and listlessly watched the Saints play the Tampa Bay Buccaneers. I don't remember who won. Caroline left in the third quarter. I heard my name being called over the drone of the crowd and saw my friend Bill Morgan sitting with Billy Broadhurst in the neighboring box. Morgan had produced the television for Edwards, and they were celebrating their victory. They asked me to join them. Of course I had to endure some serious roasting and insults, but I arranged to ride back to Baton Rouge with Morgan after the game.

"What do you think?" he asked me.

"I don't think you have enough white votes to win."

Morgan was a political genius. He knew exactly what I meant. Edwards would sweep the black votes, but he was terribly unpopular among whites. His ceiling was about the same as the vote he had received in the primary election.

"You must make this a referendum on the economy," I told him. "You have to scare the hell out of the lower middle class that Duke's election will be an economic disaster."

I walked Morgan through the research we had done—the research Roemer had ignored. We talked in consultant shorthand, and by the time we arrived at the mansion, Morgan had already decided on his course of action. I got two calls that night. One was from Edwin Edwards, who listened while I talked about the economic message. He wasn't friendly, but he was a cool, thoughtful pro. He ended the conversation by showing me he knew more about the inside of the Roemer campaign than we thought: "When I am elected, you can stay in your bedroom at the end of the hall." Later that night I got a call from the publisher of the *New Orleans Times-Picayune,* Ashton Phelps Jr. He wanted me to explain my theory of making the campaign a fight for the economic survival of the state. At the end of the conversation he said, "I intend to devote the entire resources of this newspaper to the defeat of David Duke." He did. David Duke was no longer a cute abstract way to thumb one's nose at the rest of the nation. His election would cost tourism and jobs. Bumper stickers appeared on cars reading, "Vote for the Crook, It's Important." My message was finally getting out.

In the end, Edwards stomped Duke. There were only 617,000 racists who voted for Duke and more than a million people who swallowed their pride and voted their self-interest for Edwards. The scoreboard on election night showed Edwards with 61 percent and Duke with 39. That 39 percent included a slight majority of all white voters. Duke lost, but in my mind Louisiana had once more disgraced itself.

From the time I left him in the kitchen at the mansion, I never saw Roemer again. I called several times in the following years to inquire about his welfare. He didn't return my calls.

I went back to Washington to try to put my marriage back together. That turned out to be easier than the resurrection of my business.

To slip back into redneck parlance, I got the shit gleefully kicked out of me when I returned to Washington after the Roemer campaign. Young, talent-deprived Democratic Party bureaucrats who were trying to help friends and help themselves decided to blackball me. I was no longer pure. I wasn't a good enough Democrat.

It made me angry to be judged by them. They had never served coffee to cold workers on a picket line. They had never prayed to Harry Truman instead of God to end a strike. They hadn't wept when John Kennedy was shot. Their party loyalty was something they learned in Washington martini bars from other hacks whose idea of strenuous physical labor was to loosen their neckties. I didn't respect them, and it always showed. But I understood. They had a good excuse to kick me. I had never attended their strategy sessions or kissed an acre of ass, and I had always considered them irrelevant and more of a hindrance in a campaign than a help. "Please don't send me help from the party" was something they didn't react to very well. But in the years that I ignored them, they grew more powerful because the party began raising obscene amounts of money for campaigns. If one has the gold in Washington, one can call the shots. These bureaucrats suggested to prospective clients that the party wouldn't enthusiastically support a candidate who hired my firm.

My phone didn't ring much. I knew what the immediate future held, so I fired most of the staff, canceled two-thirds of our leased office space, and went into a defensive posture. I spent more time at Heroes, my place in Montana, building furniture and fly-fishing for trout. I would have been fine with that, but I had two partners I cared about. One, Jim Duffy, was a friend; the other, Dane Strother, my only son. So while I appeared stoic in Montana, I burned inside.

The party bureaucrats kicked me for several months until my

back was against the wall and I was forced to do what I was taught in the Redneck School of Life. I came out of the mountains swinging. I fought back with a club in both hands. The party punks had never been in an East Texas saloon fight where their opponent had a pistol tucked in his belt or under the seat in his pickup. The typical redneck brawler had integrity and would fight by the rules if you did. The problem was figuring out the rules. Enough was enough. I knew these people's rules, but they were about to learn honky-tonk rules.

The chairman of the Democratic Congressional Campaign Committee was Beryl F. Anthony Jr., a party insider who represented Arkansas' Fourth Congressional District—almost the entire southern half of the state. I was never sure he knew about the self-serving games and insider dealing his flunkies were engaged in, but I knew he was their boss and that they were trying to put me and my firm out of business. So if Beryl Anthony was their leader, he had to suffer the consequences, if for no other sin than hiring such a weak and venal bunch. Dane, Jim, and I, the three partners, had about a ten-minute meeting and decided to roll the dice. We were going to gamble the future of our firm on exacting justice. We decided if we were being locked out, we had nothing to lose. We would take on the Democratic establishment. If we won, we would be back in business and a force to reckon with. If we lost, we were prepared to shut the doors and find other occupations. It was the kind of gamble I relished, a crap shoot with all of the chips on the table waiting for the next throw. We decided to beat Beryl Anthony—with a Democrat.

Jim Duffy went to Arkansas and found a candidate, W. J. "Bill" McCuen, the secretary of state (and a man who would later go to prison after being convicted of embezzlement from the state and of not paying taxes on kick-backs from supporters in exchange for jobs). While we were down there—and because we had nothing to lose—we also signed on a young woman, Blanche Lambert, who wanted to challenge her old boss, Congressman Bill Alexander. He represented the First District, which took in most of the poor counties of the Arkansas Delta country. Alexander had first won election in 1968 and had risen through the ranks in the House until he was a member of the Democratic leadership. Blanche was a fresh-faced thirty-one-year-old who had grown up in the Delta and who personified integrity.

Dane spearheaded the campaign for Lambert (who is now Blanche Lambert-Lincoln). Jim took over the quest to beat Anthony—with Bill McCuen as his club. Both incumbents had an image problem because of a recent scandal at the in-house bank the congressmen keep for themselves that allowed them to bank by different rules than the average citizen. John Public was penalized with $25 fines for each bounced check. Congressmen simply bounced checks that were held in the bank until covered by their next check. It was a system all Americans would like to enjoy, but which is prohibited by federal law. Alexander had bounced 487 checks, and Anthony 109.

Blanche Lambert initially balked at running negative advertising. Her reservations might have been persuasive in some places, but the timid press in Alexander's district had covered the check-kiting story so sparsely that paid television ads were the only way we had of informing voters about it. In the end, she agreed, but reluctantly. It was a case where candidate decency almost got in the way.

Duffy's candidate, Bill McCuen, didn't have Blanche's scruples. He was willing to do or say anything to beat Anthony. His problem was a lack of money. Duffy, in a brilliant move, overcame McCuen's local leaders' objections and put all of the campaign money into a short television blitz instead of allowing it to be wasted in door-to-door work and other silly traditional methods. We needed a powerful message and one good television spot. As with Lambert, a creative solution was the key. However, Jim Duffy's political skills were as important as the creativity.

While going over the same research that others had seen, Duffy found that while Anthony had been district attorney, before he was elected to Congress, he had prosecuted a woman for bouncing one $324 check for Christmas. With a calculator, Duffy added up the amount of the congressman's bounced checks. They totaled $57,000. He dropped the information on my desk. "We can defeat him purely on hypocrisy," Duffy told me. He asked me to write a spot. It only took about three minutes.

Jim, better than any other consultant I have ever met, has never forgotten how to think outside the Beltway. He knew that a double standard for congressmen went to the heart of what people resented about Washington. By rearranging a few of his words, we made a television spot that would slap the establishment in the face and serve notice our firm was not to be trifled with. But first we needed a way to make the words come to life. To compound the problem, we didn't have money for costly production.

My vision was a simple spot. I sent Dane out to a toy store to buy a rag doll. On his way back, he broke off a small pine branch from one of the trees on the National Mall. In our storeroom we found some Christmas ornaments. We cleared off a table in my office, made a backdrop out of a sheet of blue paper, and decorated the pine bough into what would look on television like part of a full-fledged Christmas tree. We shot the commercial with a home VHS camera. As the announcer read the spot, the camera moved from Christmas decorations hanging from the pine branch to a sad, lonely rag doll. A tinkling music box from my wife's collection played in the background. At the end of the commercial we had the word Beryl bounce to the bottom of the screen and then pop up. The total cost, even with the announcer we hired and the animation at the end, was about $400, which our firm absorbed. We were out for blood. It wasn't personal. I had only met Anthony a couple of times. He was a nice enough man and probably a good enough congressman. But it was life or death for my firm.

30-Second TV
Title: Bounce Beryl
One Christmas Eve, then prosecuting attorney Beryl Anthony arrested a woman for bouncing one $324 check for Christmas. She spent the holidays in jail. As congressman, Beryl Anthony bounced 109 checks for more than $57,000. He didn't go to jail. In fact he's asking to be reelected. Big money has corrupted Beryl.
Secretary of State Bill McCuen represents change.
It's time to bounce the bouncer. Bounce Beryl.

We beat Congressman Anthony in a Democratic primary. The people around him were furious. They swore vengeance on our firm, and then they committed the most hypocritical act I had ever seen. After trying to put me out of business for helping a friend who had switched parties while he was running against the Ku Klux Klan, they jumped into the campaign to help the Republican candidate. Anthony's brother became the congressman's cover in an effort to elect Republican Jay W. Dickey. Even the Clinton organization swung into action, helping win unprecedented African American votes for Dickey. On the strength of an abnormal black vote for a Republican due to the help from Anthony and Clinton forces, Dickey beat McCuen 52-48. Later, as Clinton's reward, Dickey was one of the few Republicans to vote against impeachment.

Of course I'm still bitter about their hypocrisy. But it feels better at night knowing they paid the price. The young bureaucrats and lobbyists who called the shots tried bravado and committed petty acts like telling clients they would not contribute to them because of us, but their power base was gone. They were pathetic remora fish whose shark had died. Soon most of them were looking for other jobs. I don't think any of them found a political consulting firm, no matter how hard they had tried to ingratiate themselves. Talent still matters.

I called the Speaker of the House, Tom Foley, and made an appointment. He was a nice man, far too busy to see a defrocked Democratic consultant, but he gave me his undivided attention while I explained why we had defeated Anthony. I added that unless the party people changed course, I was going after each of his committee chairmen one at a time. It was a bold and empty threat, and he probably knew it, but he also was shocked at the unprofessional actions of people who answered indirectly to him. He had no idea what was going on in the House side of the party.

"It's over," he said.

Foley was true to his word. We were back in business. Redneck justice had prevailed.

Political consulting is a tough business with the fragility of a spring snowflake. A winning season does not necessarily mean you are covered up with business the next year. Things happen. Contracting nonincumbent clients is almost an art form. Many well-intentioned candidates sign a media consultant and then get cold feet when they find money is not easy to raise or when a better-known rival jumps into the race. The consultants troll through the prospective clients and try to sign them before their competitors do. It is fierce competition, with as many as a hundred consultants trying to break down doors to major campaigns. A firm isn't considered top-tier unless it handles senators or governors. Yet, there are only fifty governors, who come up every four years, and 100 senators, who run every six years, in the whole country. And you can only handle candidates for your party. That means that every election cycle brings a mad scramble to win clients. This sales effort becomes a major part of the business and is life and death to new firms.

In 2001, our firm was contacted by some Florida Democrats promoting Vietnam war hero (and U.S. ambassador to Vietnam) Pete Peterson to run for governor of his state. Jim Duffy went to several meetings with the supporters. One of our aggressive competitors was determined enough that he booked passage to Vietnam to make a direct presentation to Peterson. Despite the Vietnam visit, we were hired, so we stopped prospecting in Florida. Peterson was a big challenge and all we could afford to take on in that state. A few weeks later, after former attorney general Janet Reno announced for governor, Peterson dropped out. It was difficult for him to raise money, and the old war hero had a problem with begging. With him out, our Florida business was finished for the 2002 season and we had a budget hole to fill. That is the nature of political consulting and explains why the better firms sign on too much work.

Because the competition is so tough at the top, it takes just a little bad luck to be shut out. An unknown businessman with a lot of money running for Congress looks like a good prospective client. Later, however, when a popular former governor decides to run, the businessman drops out, leaving the consulting firm with no candidate in the race. To avoid this kind of situation, consultants now sign contracts years before elections.

Nonincumbent candidates present another risk. A firm that signs early nonincumbents could easily lose all of its races in the fall or even be eliminated in the early party primaries and sit out October and November watching the bank account dwindle. The only cushion a firm can have is to concentrate on incumbents and roll the dice with other candidates. Incumbents pay the bills. Incumbents seldom lose. And incumbents seldom require as much skill. On the other hand, long shots that come in can elevate a firm from obscurity to prominence.

Because the stakes are so high, selling becomes a war. Anonymous clippings and letters are sent to campaign managers to poison another firm that looks like a winner. Sometimes disgruntled candidates from past campaigns—even those you helped—come out of the hills at night to shoot the consultants they find lying wounded on the battlefield. When I was close to signing former San Francisco mayor Dianne Feinstein for her first U.S. Senate campaign, a friend in the campaign told me that members of Louisiana senator Bennett Johnston's staff had called Feinstein—and other prospective candidates—to warn them that I "had a dark side and they should be cautious." It killed my chances to represent Feinstein's California campaign. I had done media for a successful campaign for Senator Johnston but was presumptuous enough to argue with him six years later when I thought he should hire me without a presentation. Apparently, he doesn't like being questioned. His revenge struck me as petty, mean, and disproportionate to the offense. But I learned something.

I was once asked to meet with Sue Tupper, the campaign manager for Mike Lowry, a candidate for governor of Washington. When I arrived at Tupper's office, she was sitting behind what looked like a Berlin Wall of videotapes from my competitors—more than a hundred of them. I was three months late getting there, but we won the job and Lowry won the election.

Later, after we had become friends, I asked Sue why she had hired us after seeing all those tapes.

"They all looked the same," she said.

There is a reason for that. For twenty years a battle has raged within political campaigns between image makers and pollsters. As a media producer, I now run up the white flag. Pollsters win. The result of their victory, however, is that political commercials don't work as well as they once did. As Sue Tupper said, they all look the same. The emotional juice has been squeezed out of them. Also, their enhanced influence has been responsible for taking campaign professionals from the political headquarters on Main Street to the halls of power.

Like a fundamentalist preacher with the New Testament, pollsters now enter campaign discussions waving computer presentations of graphs and numbers as magic solutions all but ensuring election. They can cure lumbago, dry up warts, and restore zing to passionless marriages. Young campaign aides and candidates listen to their political gospel with rapt attention and unshakable confidence. After election, the candidates suffer withdrawal without regular fixes of numbers relating to their future. The result is a Clinton style of governance that is dominated by numbers rather than ideals.

It wasn't always that way. In the 1960s and 1970s, a media consultant often had to beg candidates to hire pollsters. The science was suspect. Candidates just didn't believe that reliable information could be obtained when fewer than a thousand of their constituents were interviewed. When pollsters *were* hired, they were considered tail fins on a '57 Cadillac—a nice decoration with questionable function. They measured the political climate for a specific time, then moved out of the way to let the candidate and his or her campaign communicate with the voters.

Not now. Today's creative sessions are dominated by pollsters who substitute linear, survey-tested solutions for the many-sided complexities of public policy and communication. The result is perpetual campaigns and paid commercials crammed with words without any real meaning. Of course all political commercials look the same today. They are simply the regurgitation of numbers dictated by pollsters. All good polls have the same information. Therefore, campaigns dominated by pollsters produce television that has an identical look and feel, employing the same buzzwords and stock phrases. That's why Bill Clinton pledges in his election-year rhetoric that America's education policy must be "guided by our faith that every single child can learn" and George W. Bush asserts that the rationale of his education policy is that "no child be left behind."

Keeping the faith. Helping children. Evocative concepts, but when used by pollsters they are simple buzzwords, empty of meaning.

But voters aren't dumb. The end result of this barrage of bullshit is that we must now run three times as many commercials to make the same point as we did twenty years ago.

I make no argument against research. Improved modern polling is the most important development in the evolution of political consulting. I've been a believer since the 1970s, when Bill Hamilton and Peter Hart opened the curtains and let me examine my candidates and campaigns as I had never seen them. The two men were like steady hands that helped steer the course of our efforts. With them, I knew not only the prominent issues, but how intensely the voters truly felt about them. In a New Orleans mayoral race, Peter Hart told me that all of the other candidates would run on street repair because the polls said that was the most important issue. But our campaign, he said, should concentrate on crime. He explained that even though the voters' first reaction was to say street repair, the intensity level on crime was much higher. He was right. We won a place in the runoff. I became a disciple of polling.

What Hart didn't do, though, was prescribe words or images. That was my challenge. Today many pollsters would be able to tell me that crime was the important issue, but they would also crank out a whole list of poll-driven crime answers that must be crammed into our thirty seconds—and maybe even, like the pollster I mentioned earlier, demand revision of a script because it used the word "richest" instead of "wealthiest." For some reason pollsters have come to believe that individual words are more important than the overall impression.

Dick Morris's work for Bill Clinton is a prime example of this syndrome. Morris dictated language to the letter and claimed to find statistical differences in responses to paragraphs that varied by even a hair from what he wanted. Clinton was the first consultant-dependent president. Numbers were a powerful drug that gave him comfort and erased uncertainty.

Another research force that is crushing the life out of television campaigns is focus groups. There was once a time when I had to explain how a focus group worked—how ten people in a room were allowed to express themselves about politics, their lives, and even commercials, and how this could be importantly revealing. Now even the media use focus groups as a gimmick to explain public opinion after presidential debates and major news events. Thus, they use focus groups to create news. And this is poor science. Because the existence of focus groups has become common knowledge, every American is well aware that when one is paid to participate in a focus group, one is expected to be a critic. Participants bring with them their baggage of conventional wisdom and submit to group dynamics. It is amusing to watch aggressive people try to take command in the early moments and shape other participants' opinions. They just can't help themselves. There are always others who don't want to offend or disagree, and look for middle ground that allows them to get through their hour and a half to the paycheck at the other end. Sitting on the other side of the one-way mirror observing a dozen focus-group members, one can discern with great accuracy most of the attitudes they bring into the room. There's a strange sort of game by which people arrange themselves philosophically. The meek surrender. The educated dominate the uneducated. Males dominate females. African Americans become guarded if whites are in the room. They all want something from the group, and it is usually approval.

The media have taught us that negative commercials are bad, and that all commercials must be examined word by word. This, of course, isn't how voters watch television in their own homes, but focus-group participants know they are being paid to dissect and be cynical. No focus group likes ads in which two candidates contrast their records—but professionals know that these are among the most productive messages we put on the air. All focus groups demand what they call substance, and they will always give high marks to any ad that simply regurgitates a list of poll issue items or is longer than thirty seconds. Yet in real life—when they actually go to the polls—they vote for candidates they like and who they feel understand their problems.

Focus groups do not in any way quantify public attitudes. At their best, they allow the poll numbers to come to life so that we hear real voters put their opinions into real language. Yet I once heard an NBC newsreader tell a network-sponsored focus-group respondent that he "represented ten million people." No wonder participants now feel like God. The same thing is happening in campaigns. A new generation of candidates and aides who grew up in a climate where pollsters dominate message will ignore a poll and panic when five of nine focus-group participants disagree with their campaign message or dislike one of their commercials. Focus groups are the rage, and there are often twenty people in the observation area, scribbling in their notebooks and nibbling the cookies and stale sandwiches provided by the research company. They anxiously await truth to be revealed and often come to their conclusions even before the group has ended—and days ahead of the analysis offered by the researcher who was sitting in the room.

I desperately want to be selected for a focus group. I want to turn the discussion to land mines, cruelty to giraffes in zoos, and the importance of eliminating refined sugar from our diets. I want to have the group agree that commercials should be shown upside-down or only in red. Then I want to go home and wait for the inevitable—a surge in paid ads shot through a red filter and screened upside-down lamenting the fate of diabetic giraffes crippled by land mines.

Once, long ago, I believed that my job was to sit in my ivory tower and help candidates communicate the messages that were in their hearts. Now I must spend about two-thirds of my time on selling, television interviews, image enhancement, and fighting with pollsters who are trying to squeeze every candidate, every ad, and every issue into their cookie cutters.

If political consulting is a tough business with the fragility of a spring snowflake, then consultants must find alternate methods of using their highly developed skills to pay the bills and keep the wheels grinding. In short, consultants must have insurance against cyclical swings in their popularity and the downtime between election cycles. Many have begun to give political advice and run campaigns for major corporations. It's called "public affairs."

This is a business that was created by demand. Corporate executives woke one day and realized that they could no longer ignore politics. Microsoft had their entire business threatened before they woke to the need for help in Washington. They realized they didn't speak the same language as the politicians. On top of that, the firms that had always represented them, big advertising and public-relations agencies, moved too slowly and were out of touch with political thinking.

In our industry, we are expected to analyze a problem and react within hours. If a state legislature is about to pass a bill harmful to our clients, we have to be able to turn on the lights and marshal voters to show concern. In his presidential race, Mike Dukakis found that having conventional advertising people communicating for him was like having a huge anchor hanging from his political ankles. They were slow, indecisive, cute, and ineffective. In their world, messages had always had ten months to work—not ten days. A Volkswagen loaded with bottom-feeding political consultants could have done a better job for Dukakis than his crack team of insurance advertising executives.

Business people are catching on. More and more major corporations hire firms like ours as a safety net. Our StrategyDotGov offices in Washington, Atlanta, and Austin now produce almost as much income as our political consulting firm.

Like party bureaucrats, corporate bureaucrats are often defensive and territorial. One day I spent over two hours on a conference call while a corporate team argued and "dialogued" about how to get an appointment with a governor I knew. Finally, without telling them what I was doing, I put the conference call on hold and phoned the governor directly. I set up the appointment and got his views on the subject. Then I plugged back into the conference call and told them when the meeting was and where the governor stood on their issue. There was silence, and then the head of corporate public relations exploded and told me I had stepped far out of bounds. For about five minutes I was berated and threatened. I had made all of their debates and hand-wringing meaningless. They were furious. Then I got redneck arrogant:

"Fine. I'll call and cancel the appointment, and your committee can do it."

That set off another round of panic. "Don't call. Don't rock the boat." This was the second committee meeting of people eating donuts, drinking coffee, and pontificating. The corporate lobbyists danced around the public relations people, who parried with those in public affairs. I admit it wasn't my job to make the appointment or to persuade the elected official to do anything. I am not a lobbyist. I was on the phone to give advice to the business people. I got in the way of their process. And often, process seems more important in corporation bureaucracy than results. But the money is good and people pay their bills on time. With many of our clients, our advice has made a major difference, sometimes saving or helping them earn tens of millions of dollars. Usually this happens when we are removed from corporate politics and put in touch with people in the corner offices atop the corporate headquarters.

I make no claim that we could produce better advertising for General Motors or Kraft than their advertising agencies. We could not. We don't think the way they do, and we don't have their depth of creative talent. And, of course, we don't have their budgets. But if a crippled nun finds a roach in her cheese or a wheel comes off a Buick killing some schoolchildren and there is rioting in the streets, they better give us a call.

The other way political consultants keep their bank accounts in the positive column is foreign work. We are great exporters of political expertise. James Carville works in Israel. Stan Greenberg is credited with the election of Tony Blair, the liberal prime minister of Britain. From the tip of South

America through the continents of Africa and Asia, American consultants have helped elect people. Joe Napolitan, one of the deans of political consulting and a founder of the American Association of Political Consultants and the International Association of Political Consultants, is perhaps the person in the world most responsible for the growth of the craft overseas. Not only did he participate in some of the most important elections of our time, but he also helped guide foreign consultants into the profession. I think he is the most important person in the history of political consulting. And, after all these years, I am not convinced that he is not still the best consultant in the business.

My firm does not do much foreign work because of kinks in my own personality. Some of the younger members think it sounds glamorous, but foreign candidates usually hire consultants they have read about. Therefore they demand my personal attention. But I don't like long airplane rides and never feel in control when there are conversations around me that I don't understand any of except when my name is mentioned. Besides, I'd rather visit other countries on vacation than on the job. So Strother/Duffy/ Strother seldom bids on foreign work. The exceptions tend to be specific jobs requested as favors by friends. That is how I worked on two elections in the Dominican Republic in the late 1990s.

Bill Hamilton, who did scores of foreign campaigns, was representing a candidate in the Dominican Republic who needed guidance. Jacinto Peynado was running for vice president with Joaquin Balaguer, an ancient, corrupt, and legendary strongman who was born in 1906. Peynado wanted the vice presidential seat to set himself up for the presidency when Balaguer retired or died. Therefore, he wanted a separate campaign that did not tie him too closely with the old leader. He would run it with his own money. He needed advice on how to use television.

Hamilton said the campaign would pay me $25,000 to spend a long weekend with the candidate and his team. The money was an attraction but most important was my obligation to my old friend, Hamilton. Had he asked, I would have helped him for nothing. The next week I flew to Santo Domingo.

Armed guards met me at the airport and put me in a VIP room while they retrieved my bags. I already had a problem: I didn't have any bags other than the carry-on that followed behind me on wheels. I told them this, but my Spanish wasn't good enough to stop the official escort from trying to help. So they left me in the room drinking rum cocktails served by a beautiful young hostess for almost an hour while they looked in vain for bags that didn't exist. Finally the young woman, who spoke perfect Miami English, explained to the policemen that I had not lost a bag, and they drove me to the beautiful Jaragua Hotel and Casino on the beach in Santo Domingo. I was ushered into a large suite and told to wait. A couple of hours later, I was picked up by two men with automatic weapons and driven to Peynado's home, a walled complex within the city.

I immediately liked Peynado. He was warm and humorous and spoke perfect English. From a wealthy family, he had been educated at the Taft School in Watertown, Connecticut, and the Wharton School of Business at the University of Pennsylvania. His wife, Margarita, was attractive and his children personable. After the weekend ended and I was paid, he asked me to become his media adviser for the duration of the campaign. I accepted. I was always treated like a visiting celebrity and shown great Dominican hospitality. I grew to truly like and respect the man, his family, and the people in the country.

I never met President Balaguer, one of the world's strangest leaders. He was blind, had never married, and lived with his sister. Many of the less-educated people in the nation thought the old man had some sort of black magic. Some actually prayed to him as they would one of the saints. When he died in July 2002, his residence was surrounded by people who believed that God would personally come down to take the old man away.

The Dominican Republic is, of course, where Columbus really landed in America, and the castle-fortress built by his brother still overlooks the port as a tourist attraction. For the 500th anniversary of Columbus's arrival, Balaguer spent more than a billion dollars of the country's scarce resources erecting a giant building in the shape of a cross, with no function other than that a light atop it projected another giant cross onto the clouds at night when the weather was right. The building became such a scandal that most world leaders ducked the celebration. When I last saw it, in 1996, it was an unairconditioned museum that smelled of mildew and was falling into disrepair.

From the beginning, the campaign was unusual. The Joaquin Balaguer presidential campaign ignored us. The old mystic did mysterious things like rig the vote computers and ride around for public appearances in a version of the Popemobile developed by the Vatican. Meanwhile, our vice presidential run sailed along in an orgy of colorful activities and rum drinks. I would spend one or two weeks at a time in the country, eating, traveling, and laughing with the candidate, who seemed to have his priorities in order. Peynado weighed about 300 pounds and he had earned every pound of it. His home had full-time cooks, and he frequented restaurants in Santo Domingo that would rival or beat those in most cities. A meal with Peynado was usually with ten or fifteen others who happened to be in the house at the time. Evening meals occurred close to midnight and were capped with rum and Cuban cigars. To attend rallies around the country, Peynado had a jet helicopter and two fixed-wing aircraft. He spent occasional weekends at a beautiful condo he owned in Miami Beach and had a jet to shorten the trip. He allowed me to live in the same style in Santo Domingo.

My routine was to be driven to Peynado's house in the late morning by two armed escorts. Milling around outside his wall were scores of poor people attempting to press scraps of paper into visitors' hands. These notes asked Peynado for everything from medical care to refrigerators and automobile repair. My pockets were often stuffed with them. Inside the wall men sat in lawn chairs holding sawed-off shotguns.

Our route to the compound passed the Presidential Mansion, where two dwarfs were always sweeping the walk. Finally, after seeing the dwarfs about ten times, my curiosity overcame political correctness. Rob Schroth, a fine pollster who was affiliated with Hamilton and was fluent in Spanish, and I decided to ask Peynado their story. Sure, he knew the dwarfs. Peynado knew a lot of dwarfs. In fact, there is a dwarf neighborhood in Santo Domingo. Peynado explained that the little people we saw sweeping were retainers to the president and had worked for him for many years. Dwarfs, he said, were often considered magical, or at least good luck when one gambled, and many rich people employed one.

"Do you have your own dwarf? " I asked in wonder.

"Sure, at my Toyota dealership."

"Would you lend me your dwarf to shoot dice?"

Jacinto laughed. "I think we can work that out."

Schroth and I spent the rest of the morning in meetings and then retired to our hotel for the customary nap. Before we parted, we agreed to meet in the lobby at 8 P.M. and cab to a fine seafood restaurant down the beach. At 8 we by chance met on our floor at the elevators and rode down together.

When the doors slid open, there was a huge man holding a dwarf by the arm.

"Mr. Ray, I brought you the dwarf."

Rob Schroth, a man with a rare sense of humor, fell back into the elevator laughing but recovered quickly to join me in a march into the casino—large escort and dwarf in tow. The dwarf created great excitement. People followed him to the dice table, where the stickmen pulled up a stool for him to stand on. Soon people were reaching from three deep around the table to put their money on the "pass" line. The dwarf was magic. Unfortunately, he was also ill tempered and at the wrong place on the table. Dice move clockwise around the table, and the dwarf's stool was to the immediate right of the person with the dice. That meant about twelve people had to shoot before the dice came under his magic spell. He screamed something in Spanish I didn't understand. That's when I found another problem. The dwarfs in Santo Domingo have a distinct dialect. The dwarf was screaming for brandy. Rob understood and immediately produced a drink. The dwarf slammed down about two ounces of Remy Martin and demanded another and another. Soon he was drunk and wobbling on his stool. The large man held him around the waist so he did not fall.

After what seemed like hours, the dwarf finally got his turn with the dice. He could not hold them in one hand so he cupped both hands, drew his arms behind his head, and sent the cubes bulletlike into the forehead of a woman at the other end of the table. One of the sharp corners cut her and blood was running down around her nose, but she refused to give up her place at the magic table for first aid. She simply held a handkerchief over the cut and stayed alert until the dwarf found his range. He won, and won, and won. Pesos flooded the table. There was hysteria in the casino as people began to force their way to the table. Guards came in to hold them back. Rob's and my pockets were stuffed with pesos. Suddenly, in the middle of the madness, the dwarf put down the dice and climbed off the stool.

I screamed, "Where's the dwarf going? Bring him back."

The large man brought the dwarf back under his arm and placed him back on his stool—where he announced that he would not continue his turn unless I agreed to let him be in a commercial for Peynado. Scores of people were yelling in Spanish, and they looked threatening. They had a big investment, and they knew he was my dwarf.

"Rob, tell him he can make a commercial if he'll keep shooting."

A few rolls later he hit a seven and was through. The other people at the table were yelling they would pass their turns at the dice to get the dwarf back as the shooter, but his keeper said, "Mr. Ray, I'm going to take the dwarf home. He's drunk and will pass out."

Rob and I went to a late local restaurant and unloaded a lot of the pesos we had won at the table and told and retold our own versions of the dwarf escapade. The fun ended the next morning when the phone rang.

"Raymond, this is Peynado. Did you tell this dwarf he could make a commercial for me?"

I hesitated and then followed my rule about bad news. Always tell the truth. "Yes, I'm afraid I did."

"Then come get him out of my house. He's been here since daylight waiting to make his commercial."

I called a man I had been working with on television production, Elias Mundez, and told him to open his studio and meet me in an hour. Then I called for my bodyguards and went to Peynado's home to fetch the dwarf. When I got to the studio, Elias was working on a rum hangover and not happy to see me show up with an ill-tempered dwarf. But he was a professional and soon had a blue curtain and a stool for the dwarf.

"What do you want me to say?"

"Say why you like Peynado."

The dwarf talked for about ten minutes into the camera.

"How was that?"

"Brilliant."

The dwarf was sent home, and I thought the episode was finished—at least until I got another call from Peynado. This time he was laughing.

"Raymond, when are you going to run the dwarf commercial?"

"Never."

"Well, get the dwarf off my back. He calls every hour, and my secretary is about to go crazy."

I went back to Elias and we duplicated the dwarf tape 100 times and had the copies distributed in the dwarf neighborhood. I didn't hear any more from the dwarf, but the people around Peynado never let me forget it. Even at that I didn't learn. I made one more dwarf mistake because of my perverse sense of humor. One late night I was sitting by Peynado's swimming pool smoking a Cuban cigar, drinking scotch, and casually listening to his team talk about a parade for the candidate to be held on Saturday. I wasn't part of their discussion, but they yelled, "Have we forgotten anything?"

Continuing the dwarf joke on me, I responded, "Yes, you need a flatbed truck loaded with dwarfs in costumes."

The next Saturday the first float was twenty dwarfs. The others had thought I was serious. It was a fine float.

I said I don't like foreign consulting, but Peynado and his gang were fun. We won, but I doubt our independent campaign had anything to do with the squeaker victory of Balaguer. Corruption played a larger part. Our own State Department delivered stern warnings to Balaguer. They considered the election to have been run illegally and demanded that a new one be held. Peynado went to Washington and brokered a deal to allow the old man to serve two years instead of four. Then they held a new election in which Peynado was a candidate for president. He lost badly. Peynado was not part of the election fraud, but his link to Balaguer sank his chances. Both the Dominican Republic and Louisiana have fits of reform and the occasional rebirth of hope.

Did sea creatures slowly find their way to the shore, develop lungs, grow legs, and begin waging war on other land creatures? Or did God put us here for some purpose we are still trying to figure out? This timeless argument about the evolution of things still bounces around this country, unchanged since the time of the Scopes Trial, between fundamentalists and those I would tend to call more enlightened. But enlightenment can be a relative thing itself. I read a delightful letter in the Bozeman, Montana, newspaper from a creationist who claimed that God is a trickster who planted things like fossil remains and dinosaur bones to fool intellectuals. According to his theory, these fossils were merely decoration, some sort of sleight of hand from the Master Magician. The age of the earth was no more than ten thousand years, he said. Another letter writer was offended and shot back that the Scriptures are clear: the world is 5,000 years old, and the 10,000-year believer was misguided and near blasphemy.

I don't care much about the argument. Some of my distant redneck cousins looked and acted, in my lifetime, like higher apes. And if God is a prankster, as the man thought, perhaps the joke is on him—maybe He assembled man piece by piece from some primordial ooze on a timetable that we don't understand. As a political consultant, I could make a convincing television ad for either side. I could even feature newspaper headlines across the bottom of the screen from publications that agree with either argument. Because I am a fallen-away Southern Baptist, not to mention a lifelong Democrat, I'd inevitably represent the evolutionist side—just as I have Republican consultant friends who would leap to make the 15 percent commissions on the other side.

But not every question in life can be answered by a thirty-second spot or by a poll—or even by an election. Nor should political consultants be involved in every aspect of democracy. It's a fact of modern politics that the role of consultants is changing. But this is evolution, and I can't yet identify the creature that has crawled out of the sea.

We have become public showmen and entertainers instead of thoughtful back-room advisers. We have let the pollsters out of our labs and they have turned into Frankensteins who are no longer content to tell politicians what the people think. They want to manipulate public opinion to help their candidates—by using their polls and our ads to shape what the politicians say after they are elected. There's always reelection, you know. This helps create the most ominous evolutionary change of all. We have changed from advising people on how to get elected to helping them govern. I think this could be dangerous. First of all, few of us have the training to decide the substantive policy issues of the day, many of which involve national security. Second, we've become conduits to political decision-making that involves the kind of money few people can leave sitting on the table. Seldom does a month go by without some special interest calling me to talk to a senator or House member or governor about pending legislation. In 1985, a man offered me a million dollars to have one word changed in a piece of legislation that had something to do with the definition of ship bottoms. Though tempted to take the dough, my reaction was to write a whistle-blowing piece for *Newsweek* about the dangers of the seamless campaign. I was able to do this because I was a successful man whose two children were already through college. What would a younger man with bills and a mortgage and young kids do? Depends on the consultant, I guess, but I have heard of political consultants who do campaign work only for the access it gives them after election. They cut fees and make sweetheart deals because the big money in Washington isn't made managing campaigns but from manipulating the legislative process.

This is the kind of Washington insider game that Ross Perot tried to rat out by running for president in 1992 and 1996. Perot was a flake and an egomaniac, but his suspicions about the insider nature of politics-as-usual were dead-on. In a presidential campaign, large companies and even foreign countries hire top consultants as a possible way to get in the back door of the White House. After the 2000 presidential campaign, the *New York Times* reported that Enron, the huge energy company that went bust, had tried to get close to insiders in the Gore campaign. Since they already had close ties to George W. Bush, this would have given them friends on the inside no matter which man won. In his first year in office, even as he was riding high in the polls because of his performance after September 11, Bush and his vice president were dogged by a nagging little issue that wouldn't go away: whether oil companies were so chummy with Bush campaign people that their voices were abnormally loud when the administration's much-awaited energy plan—the task force was chaired by Dick Cheney—was formulated. I think there was little doubt of that. And while there are laws governing buying gifts, dinners, and champagne for elected officials, there is no law that prohibits special interests from renting the affections of a political consultant—a person who can get an elected official on the phone in the middle of the night.

The Lloyd Bentsen rule was, "You make the campaign commercials, and I'll draft the legislation." As chairman of the Senate Finance Committee, Bentsen set up walls on his staff—like church and state—between the political hacks and the policy wonks. That's all disappearing now. Karl Rove, Bush's top political operative, entered the White House as Bush's top policy man. Mark McKinnon, a Texas Democrat turned Bush Republican (and a friend of mine whom I respect), explained it this way when asked by a reporter about Rove: "Good policy is good politics." Well, maybe, but the evolved Bentsen rule sounds to my ear like this: "How will this vote on legislation affect my next election?" I once had an elected official angrily scream at me, "If you knew this vote was going to affect my reelection, why didn't you call and warn me?" My reflexive smart-assed answer that I didn't give was, "Hell, Congressman, when you made that vote I was desperately trying to get a nesting rainbow trout to hit a Royal Wolff fly in the Big Hole River." I only realized later how revealing my answer was: The campaign over, I headed for the solitude of Montana. That last of the bison. A modern consultant would head to Washington to start up an office that spent the off-year election cycle hooking and netting corporate clients.

But if the beautiful science of the random sample has made consultants greedy, it has had an even worse effect on the politicians. It's hard to produce a true statesman from an environment so cautious and calculating. "How will this look on TV?" or "How will my opponent use this against me?" becomes the pressing question, instead of "What is best for the country?" Polling is the crystal ball to the future, so the pollster wizard becomes an honored guest in the offices of Congress and statehouses. But the media consultant is right behind him, wearing the same path through plush carpets.

I wrote earlier about the pressure applied on me to make commercials that would have committed Gary Hart to a course of not selling fighter jets to Arab nations. Maybe that would have been a good policy; maybe not. The point is that little in my experience, education, or training prepared me to make that decision, and airing such a commercial would have trapped Hart even after he was in the Oval Office. I would have been shaping foreign policy for a future president. I should not do foreign policy.

In exuberance in 1998, I took several commercials to my candidate for governor of Georgia, Roy Barnes. I had conspired with our pollster, Bill Hamilton, and we knew these issue spots would help. Barnes looked at them and politely said, "We can't run these. I can't pass these issues through the legislature, and I don't want to make campaign promises I can't keep." It was a slap on my wrist, but one that was deserved. It made me love the man. I had briefly forgotten the Bentsen rule until Barnes reined me back in. He went on to win the election his way, with his issues, and passed legislation for all of the seventeen campaign promises he did make—and did so in his first session of the legislature.

In 2001, Zell Miller lived up to the promises he made to the people of Georgia in his campaign to replace deceased Senator Paul Coverdell. Miller said he would vote the interests of Georgia and not blindly follow dogma of either political party. He said it and he meant it. Zell ran as a conservative Democrat and early in the Bush administration agreed with the president on tax cuts and other issues, enraging the liberal wing of the Democratic Party. Though I didn't always politically agree with Zell, I did respect him for honoring his campaign promise. Several party bureaucrats called me and demanded that I talk to my former candidate and sway him away from his path of nonpartisan ideology. I explained that I ran campaigns, not government. Usually there was a click on the other end of the line as an exasperated political hack hung up on me.

Though I consider James Carville a friend, he made me angry when he denounced Zell over this and demanded (very publicly) that his own $1,000-dollar contribution to Miller's campaign be refunded. It seemed a little bit disloyal to the old Marine who was taught you never leave your comrade on the battlefield. Zell noted wryly that he'd paid Carville's firm more than $300,000 in fees when James worked on Zell's gubernatorial campaign some years before. Zell wondered: Was James so disgusted that he was planning to return that money? James may have an inflated sense of himself, but if so, then he's the perfect representation of the modern consultant. He thought it only too natural to employ his standing as a famous Democrat to register disapproval with an independent-minded party member. But who elected him? Zell Miller is the duly elected public official representing the people of Georgia—and he should answer to them and to his conscience. Not to Ray Strother or James Carville or any other consultant. No matter how smart we are or how highly paid we are, we are the kitchen help cleaning up the political dishes. I think James stepped out of line.

After James received his contribution back, my partner Jim Duffy and I each gave Zell a check for $1,000. In the lower left corner I wrote, "Carville Refund." Zell looked at the check, shook my hand so hard it hurt, and thanked me in a way that transcended thanks for a contribution. It was an act of friendship and an expression of philosophy that he obviously felt deeply.

James Carville is a brilliant campaign consultant, one of the best in the country, but he shouldn't be running the Senate or, heaven forbid, the White House. Funny thing is that deep down he knows this. When Bill Clinton was elected president, James knew enough not to take a West Wing job. At that time, he even joked about how out of his element he would be in such a position.

But as political consultants have evolved into superstars, James Carville isn't the only person who forgot lessons he once knew. The same could be said of the entire political class—even the nation. Today in America we can judge perception of success or failure of our public officials by reading newspaper polls. And we do. Such polls have an effect on governing. Sometimes this is good. Bill Clinton weathered impeachment because a solid two-thirds of the electorate said for more than a year not only that they didn't want him removed from office over a sex scandal, but that he was, in fact, doing a good job as president. Thus the Senate's vote acquitting him of perjury charges was a victory for popular democracy. Yet there have been times in our nation's history when America needed courageous leaders who were willing to make unpopular decisions. The future depended on it. Had polling been pervasive, this country would look different than it does today. Thank God the Founding Fathers did not have polling. We might still be singing "God Save the Queen" instead of "The Star-Spangled Banner."

(And if Woodrow Wilson and Franklin Roosevelt hadn't been bold, we might have been singing it in German.) I can imagine a media consultant advising Abraham Lincoln that it would be good politics to punish the South after the war. It polls well, the consultant might have said. After all, Mr. President, it's not too early to begin planning for 1868.

Frank Sinatra has a wonderful ballad about the "September of My Years." It starts this way:

One day you turn around, and it's summer
Next day you turn around, and it's fall
And all the winters and the springs of a lifetime
Whatever happened to them all?

I am at the place in life when I truly understand that sappy song. September is on my horizon. Thirty-three years ago, I burst onto the political scene filled with outrageous indignation. I intended to join in the revolution of working people and give them voice. As a college editor and then young Associated Press reporter, I saw things in a brilliant light. As a young political consultant, I wore a flak jacket of smug righteousness. Democratic political consultants were the generals who could lead the forces of truth and reform to victory. Truly, I thought that. But I fear now that I joined a profession that made it difficult to live up to my father's ideals. I started out badly and slipped.

It is no excuse, but for years my only role models were in Louisiana. I was able to exist most of the time by lying to myself about what I was doing and why. I wasn't living up to my father's ambitions of helping people. Mainly, I was supporting an expensive and pleasurable lifestyle, helping myself by helping politicians who were perpetuating Louisiana's tradition of corruption. It was easy to become one of them. Their steaks were prime, their women loose, and their cars sleek. We lived in a world of privilege more reminiscent of eighteenth-century European royalty than of the citizen government touted in speeches at "Jefferson-Jackson" dinners held by Democratic Party organizations each year. And I was the young prince with hungry eyes and pockets filled with hundred-dollar bills. I entertained the privileged insiders and became a caricature of the behind-the-scenes political operator—the glib, voracious manipulator who preyed on the emotional and intellectual weakness of the voters. In reward, the Louisiana establishment hung my picture on the walls of famous French Quarter restaurants and told each other stories about my exploits. Newspapers featured me in their pages, and I was invited to speak before colleges and civic organizations. All before I was thirty-five. But it wasn't enough. Or was it too much? I had to escape.

In 1980 I broke out in Washington with a new identity and a new life, like a con just out of prison who moves into a neighborhood and joins the local church. Washington was my church and the Democratic Party was my faith. And my first Washington experience with the professionals of my generation who were hacking this business into shape and form did not disappoint me. My primary Democratic media competition came from David Sawyer in New York and Bob Squier in Washington. These men gave a damn about their candidates and their issues. Peter Hart and Bill Hamilton were pollsters with grace and integrity who used their science and judgment in a way that allowed candidates and officeholders to make their own decisions. Republican consultants Doug Bailey, John Deardourff, and Bob Goodman were people you would be proud to call your friend. All of these men in both parties had spent years learning their craft and serving their clients.

Every year they got better and better. And I think I did also. We served an apprenticeship of respect for the system and hard work for some worthy clients.

But as Joseph Heller said in his fine book *Something Happened,* something happened. I'm still trying to understand what. Political consulting changed. Candidates changed. The system changed. For years I blamed it all on the Republicans, but I wish the explanation was that simple—or that exonerating of me and my party. It does seem to me that the so-called Reagan revolution in 1980 swept a lot of zealous, single-issue candidates into national politics—people who never grasped that passions, even those legitimately held, must be tempered with compromise for self-government to work. Reagan himself always understood this, but some of the mean-spirited conservative operatives who came to prominence with him did not. They brought to politics an acrimony and a certain baseness that have seldom been in fashion before.

Consultants must share responsibility for these changes. Republicans and Democrats. We gave the new candidates a new way of doing business. The Republican consultant Lee Atwater became the poster boy of bad campaign ethics. Lee believed in winning at any cost. He was not alone, but as the designated King Kong of dirty politics whom the media lionized, the strutting, guitar-strumming Atwater was responsible for another development that corrodes good campaigning, let alone good government: the consultant as media star.

Showmanship began to matter in consulting as cable television networks bloomed and there was more empty time to fill—and the more outrageous the commentary, the better. Soon young consultants were mimicking Atwater. There was money in it. As the quirky, behind-the-curtain consultant for candidates such as Georgia governor Zell Miller and for Harris Wofford in his upset election to the U.S. Senate from Pennsylvania, James Carville was known only to well-connected Democratic political professionals. His partner Paul Begala was even less known. But as the self-styled "Ragin' Cajun" who for good luck didn't change his underwear and ranted and raved like a lunatic, Carville was a media darling who could command $50,000 per speech and would be hired by aspirin and shoe companies for national television ads. He even acted in a movie. It doesn't take long for the word to get out, and now a whole generation of young consultants imagine themselves as the next James Carvilles—down to trying to emulate his in-your-face style.

Several times I have had to laugh as some young would-be Carville disrupted the rhythms of a campaign to pound tables and pace around the room shouting expletives. At one time we all mimicked Joe Napolitan's or Bill Hamilton's low-key, thoughtful, reasoned approach. But you don't rack up $2 million a year in speaking fees that way. It is not only the fault of consultants that classy behavior turned into cheap showmanship. Consultants simply mirror the times. What candidates and their staff want, they get.

In Hollywood, directors and producers say, "Bring me the next Marilyn or the next Brando." In politics, candidates chant, "Bring me the next Atwater or the next Carville." The result is a generation of consultants who can pick up on the style and are loud and mean, but not necessarily as good or thoughtful as were Atwater and Carville. And, as I wrote earlier in this book, the reason there are so many talentless media consultants is that pollsters have made it unnecessary to be creative or even to think. Because of the authority pollsters now have with candidates, they can dictate that their poll questions be transferred to video. Any high school student with a good computer and mom's video camera can do that. It results in terrible, lifeless, cookie-cutter television commercials that bore the viewers. Politicians are so wed to polling that some of the most intuitive and creative consultants— Dick Morris and Frank Luntz—actually act as pollsters in order to sound more authoritative to their prospective candidates. In truth, the genius of both Morris and Luntz is their ear for language that will move voters, not their polling. But poetry can't be quantified—and thus is suspect in today's risk-free and plastic campaigning. For my money, there is not a single good media consultant who has come out of polling. They stress their linear, numbers-based approach and fail to communicate on a personal or emotional level with the voters.

Pollsters have made it possible for people to come out of the party bureaucracy and set up consultant shops. Young people who are little more than receptionists in other consulting firms hang out a shingle. If they can scream loudly, adopt some quirks, never argue with the pollsters, and kiss enough asses of bureaucrats who will recommend them, they can prosper. They can even hang on while some candidates win. Soon they are being quoted in newspapers and seen pontificating on cable television shows to personalities who know less about campaigns than they do. These clips and television appearances then find their way into presentations to candidates who are impressed to have a "famous" consultant talking to them.

My friend Carl Cannon has a theory that journalism suffered after Watergate by the infusion of a new kind of journalist—those who imagined they could achieve the fame and wealth of Bob Woodward. The news business had never attracted people who thought they could get rich as political writers—or even who fancied that they deserved to make the kind of money paid to those they covered. The desire to be a star instead of an objective observer can have a corrosive effect on journalists. You don't get featured in *Hotline,* the daily Bible in the political community, for a thoughtful, fair analysis that takes thirty paragraphs to explain; you get there for a pithy quip, usually at a politician's expense, that is more in the tradition of Dorothy Parker than of Edward R. Murrow. Moreover, talk shows such as *Crossfire,* with their dueling insults, thrive on conflict, not fairness or insight. On-air deftness in this intellectual sandbox results in the obscene contracts paid to "journalists" such as Chris Matthews who master the new style of discourse. Are these people even journalists? Matthews's claim to fame was as former House Speaker Tip O'Neill's spokesman. Celebrity and show-manship have become more important than journalism, ratings more important than substance. Screams replace reason. The ink-stained wretches such as David Broder, Jack Germond, and Jules Witcover became as endangered as the American bison. Journalistic objectivity risked becoming a quaint and troublesome barrier in the path to fame and fortune.

A similar thing happened to many political consultants who entered the business in the late 1980s. They had dollar signs in their eyes. They were the ambulance chasers of our profession. Several of this class are prominent but under constant fire for misspending their clients' money or abandoning candidates before the election so they can avoid blame for the loss. Yet, because candidates have very little understanding of campaigns and their staffs even less, some of these consultants prosper.

Is there anything to be optimistic about? I hope so. In the September of my years, I don't want to sound bitter. Cannon believes there is a silver lining in the infusion into journalism of the post-Watergate class. One advance is that, under pressure from this generation, wages *have* increased for journalists, so that the very best reporters can now stay in the profession without worrying about supporting their families. Cannon also believes that, by and large, the young reporters arriving in the profession today are smarter, better educated, and better writers than their counterparts a generation ago.

I believe—maybe it is just a hope—that consultants hit bottom a few years ago and are rebounding. Several of our Jesse James characters have been discredited or have gone into other lines of work. An army of talented young consultants with degrees from prestigious colleges and an interest in good government, not just campaigning, is beginning to work its way to prominence through experience in local elections. The American Association of Political Consultants (AAPC), working without any real means of enforcement other than ostracism, is setting a good example for young consultants and reaching out to universities to stem the notions that the end always justifies the means and that political consulting is a quick way to big money, like investment banking.

In the 1980s and 1990s, it seemed that people were going into consulting with a set of ethical and professional standards they had learned from the popular media and from bitter and doctrinaire political science professors. I equate this generation of consultants with the Russian mobsters who emerged after the fall of the Soviet state. All of their lives, Russians had been taught that capitalism was a crime and that free enterprise and competition resulted in a few taking advantage of the many. They were taught that the laws of the jungle governed capitalism. The result is a generation of mobsters trying to live up to the images instilled in them through the Communist system.

I was president of the AAPC from 1998 through 2000, and we began a dialogue on ethics and education that is at least exerting peer pressure on consultants who attend our gatherings and must look other consultants in the eye. There are other positive changes. We have a fine magazine, *Campaigns and Elections,* edited by one of our own, Ron Faucheux, another Louisiana native. The magazine also conducts excellent seminars that teach young people the art and science of our craft. Several universities, among them George Washington University, the University of Florida, and American University, have established schools of campaign management. Louisiana State University has a Ph.D. program in political communications: the first in the country. We are stumbling toward an orderly profession of trained consultants who will replace the showmen and the gunslingers.

I said earlier that consultants share the blame for the decline of campaigns, but they are only one small factor. They could not exist without candidates who place winning above principle. Bill Clinton was the first purely consultant-dependent president. The brilliant, if flawed, Dick Morris directed Clinton's entire career. Clinton's policies were largely dictated by polls. His language and even his choice of vacation locations was poll-tested. Clinton didn't take chances. As a result, his motives were always suspect, and that denied him what he most craved—to be seen as a courageous leader. Clinton was replaced by another consultant-dependent president, George W. Bush. White House reporters assure us that Bush bristles when aides talk to him about polling during discussions of administration policy, but I fear he is only fooling himself. His top campaign consultant, Karl Rove, was brought into the White House itself. At least Atwater and Carville had the sense not to do that. But that is politics today. After Bush will come another and another and another, because the system has changed. Even candidates vying for city council seats or sheriff now hire consultants. "Tell me what issues work best," they plead. That system can't be changed—and, as a consultant myself it would be hypocritical for me to say I *want* it to change. But that is why it matters so much to me who goes into our profession, and why, and how they learn the proper role of a consultant. The upside for our profession of having every candidate for office higher than dogcatcher retaining a consultant is that rookie consultants who are formally trained and begin at the bottom constitute a farm team for our profession. These young men and women will eventually earn their way to the top through tests of fire and real life, instead of as hucksters with some friends in high places. Another change in American consulting may be the emergence of truly independent voters who evolve into a loose party that requires independent consultants.

God, but my father would raise an eyebrow at that one. "What's worse than a damned Republican?" he would ask. And answer: "Some fool who can't even make up his mind." But the world changes, and despite the grousing of all the old men, it usually changes for the better. I don't come by optimism easily. Curmudgeon is a more natural role for me. But as I sit here on my Montana ranch, I realize that it's an adopted role, a thick skin to get me through the losses to the other guy's candidates, the disappointments with my own, and the need to pick myself off the floor when some eastern snob gives me and my redneck firm the brush-off. But my optimism about political consulting has a specific source, not just a general one: I work less these days and only participate when my level of enthusiasm for a particular candidate is white-hot; and a few years from now, I will hang it up and leave my firm to my partners, Jim Duffy and my son. Jim Duffy is an honorable person who has seldom compromised his ideals in politics. And Dane is a better father, husband, and consultant than me, and a more idealistic Democrat. My father would be proud of them. And my daddy gets much blame and credit for the structure I have built around me for a life. It was in my redneck genes to distrust authority, be suspicious of bureaucracy, and not suffer fools gladly. Those character flaws would eliminate me from many professions where teamwork is deemed essential and people are allotted little protected spheres of influence. That's why I naturally gravitated toward political consulting, where one can be the Lone Ranger, ride into town on a white horse, kiss all the pretty girls, kick the ass of the bad men, and ride off into the sunset. But even that is changing.

Because of the influence of money and people who raise it, modern campaigns resemble a corporate board meeting. The fundraiser often sits in on strategy meetings—along with the campaign manager, the press secretary, some hack from the party who has access to Washington money, the direct mail consultant, a couple of pollsters, the candidate, the candidate's spouse, the scheduler, and occasionally relatives who once made used-car commercials. That is a nightmare that squeezes creativity out of the product and leaves the pollster in charge. And pollsters should not create. Where Jack Martin, Lloyd Bentsen, and I would sit down and make creative decisions on scripts or spots I had written, there are now often ten or fifteen people who consider themselves part of the "creative team." It is no wonder that all of America's political commercials look the same and lack appeal.

I guess I rant about the system because I never lived up to my father's ideals of helping working people. It wasn't what we thought. One redneck with bloody fists with his back against the honky-tonk wall can't beat the system. But it has been an interesting life. I don't say glamorous. Interesting. Occasionally I have been disappointed in the quality of the people I have helped elect. In several notable elections, good, decent, caring people were beaten by tin-pot idols. My father thought good always prevailed if one was willing to bloody his knuckles. Later I found that we did not have the patent on what was good or bad, no matter what price we paid. There were shades of gray and differences of opinion. Yet when everything seems bleak and I fall into one of my father's blue moods, I think about the post-election mornings I woke and realized I had not only made a difference but had helped elect people even my father would have been proud of, like the great governor Roy Barnes of Georgia, or a woman like Mary Landrieu, who was opposed by the closed-minded racists and single-issue zealots.

I find I am having more and more problems dealing with the defeat of good people. The money earned in losing races like Jill Docking's in Kansas turns to ashes that I would gladly have exchanged for victory. But I guess I lived up to one of my father's dictums.

One day in our small boat out of sight of land in the Gulf of Mexico when my father was watching the gulls throw themselves out of the sky to capture shrimp that were herded to the surface by hungry speckled sea trout, he broke one of his long, blue silences by lamenting, "Raymond, I hope when you grow up you have things to regret." I wasn't absolutely sure then what he meant, but now I know that in his own way he was telling me to take chances, not to be one of those people who lived and died in that gray area of the politically correct and safe. People who were content to dog-paddle through life only left the world as they had found it. To effect change was to put yourself at risk. He knew that if one lives on the edge, mistakes are possible. He made mistakes. I believe he always regretted the violence at the picket lines in his early life. But there was never doubt in his mind about right and wrong. A man had to stand his ground on the picket line when the Texas Rangers attacked with clubs and horses. You had to set an example for others when your family lived only on vegetables out of the small garden and your strength of purpose.

My father was not a cruel man or a bully. He demanded that I be kind to the daughter of a scab. He was outraged when the innocent were hurt, even when the innocent were caught in the crossfire between powerful forces. Once when I was about nine and had my first Red Ryder BB gun, I shot a bird sitting on a limb. It fluttered dead from the cottonwood tree and landed not far from my father's feet where he sat in a rusted lawn chair drinking coffee my mother had brought out. I was excited at the kill. I had aimed. I had hit. I had killed.

"Did you see that shot?" I asked with great enthusiasm.

"Yes, but why did you kill that bird, Raymond?"

"I don't know."

"What good will come of it?"

I hung my head, sorrow radiating into me from my father's sadness. "I don't know why I shot it."

"It'll never sing again, and I like to sit under the tree and listen to birds."

By now I was silently sobbing, not because of the bird but because of my father's quiet rebuke.

"Never hurt anything that doesn't hurt you. Never shoot anything unless you really need food. Then, when you kill it, you have to eat it."

We cleaned and cooked that scrawny bird. It was stringy and went down hard. I never killed another songbird. In the same old rusty chair about two decades later, my father asked my brother a similar question about why he had volunteered to go to Vietnam to fly helicopters.

"Claud, I wish you wouldn't go. Those people have never done anything to us," our father said. "Killing them won't help this country."

In his seventy-fourth year, when he was dying of cancer and sitting in a La-Z-Boy rocker in the living room, he looked around and said, "I've lived all of my life for that air-conditioner, that TV set, the Buick outside, this old house. It seems like it all came down to only that." There was a pause, and the motor of the window air-conditioner seemed abnormally loud. "I hope you do better." Then he slept.

I hope I did. Damn, I tried.

AAPC. *See* American Association of Political Consultants (AAPC)

Abraham, Wilson, 74

Advertising, 58, 60–5, 274–5, 290. *See also* Television programs/commercials

African Americans, 19–20, 99, 137–8, 159, 164, 235, 261, 266, 272. *See also* Racism and race relations

Alexander, Bill, 264–5

Allen, Woody, 48

Ambrose, Stephen, 174

American Association of Political Consultants (AAPC), 91, 95, 139, 276, 292, 293

Anthony, Beryl F., Jr., 264–7

Arizona, 144–5

Arkansas, 213–4, 217, 264–5

Askew, Reubin, 174

Atlanta, 144, 154, 274

Atwater, Lee, 290, 293

Austin, Tex., 243–5, 252, 274

Babbitt, Bruce, 177

Baffert, Bob, 235

Bailey, Doug, 229, 289

Balaguer, Joaquin, 276, 277, 281

Banks, 64–5

Baptist Church, 18–9, 26–7, 37, 49, 249, 282

Barbour, Haley, 131, 132, 133, 135, 138

Barnes, Roy, 6, 85, 115*n*, 144, 154, 234–5, 285, 295

Barnett, Ross, 138

Barron, Dempsey, 141

Barrow, Michael, 118, 121

Baucus, Max, 5, 176, 181

Beatty, Warren, 200–1, 205

Beckley, John, xiii

Begala, Paul, 290

Being There, 203

Bentsen, Lloyd: endorsement of Strother by, 4; as vice presidential candidate, 8–9, 243; television programs/commercials for, 9–10, 127, 141–2, 146–53, 244–5, 295; political campaigns of, 47, 128, 141–3, 145–54, 157, 163, 169, 239, 240, 244–5; as U.S. senator, 122; and Stennis, 134, 136, 137; and Gore, 240; rule of, on political consulting, 284, 285

Bentsen, Mrs. Lloyd, 141

Berger, Samuel R. "Sandy," 215*n*

Bernstein, Carl, 174

Beschloss, Michael, 174

Beychok, Shelly, 86, 87, 90, 93, 109

Biden, Joseph R., Jr., 182

Bilandic, Michael, 158

Bilbo, Theodore G., 138

Billboards, 163

Bismarck, Otto von, 47

Blacks. *See* African Americans

Blair, Tony, 275

Blaze, 121–2

Bloodworth, Linda, 207

Blumenthal, Sidney, 183

Boggs, Lindy, 176, 195, 211

Boulter, Beau, 244

Boustany family, 61–4

Bread commercials, 61–4

Breaux, John, 108, 223, 236

Bribery, 137, 283

Brinkley, Douglas, 174

Bristol, George, 152

Broadhurst, Bill, 236–7, 261, 266

Broder, David, 292

Brooks, Jack, 223

Brown, Jerry, 182–3n

Brown, John Y., 159, 181, 197–8

Brown, Lillian, 118–9, 124–5

Brownback, Sam, 235

Buchanan, Pat, 46

Bunning, Jim, 164

Burns, Robert, 103

Bush, George, 9, 71, 92, 236, 237, 249, 251

Bush, George W., 153, 173, 186n, 228, 271, 283–4, 293

Bushkin, Kathy, 177

Byrd, Robert, 209

Byrne, Jane, 158–9, 164

Cabe, Gloria, 218–9

Cable, Day, 148–9

Cable television news shows, 173–4, 290, 291–2

Caddell, Patrick J., 179, 182–4, 182–3n, 186–8, 194–7, 199–200, 203, 205

Campaign finance reform, 3, 137. See also Fundraising

Campaign Group, 240–1

Cannon, Carl, 193, 253, 260–1, 291, 292

Capra, Frank, 182

Carter, Jimmy, 3, 120, 153, 174, 182, 190–1, 208

Carville, James, 12, 13, 46, 85–94, 97, 98–9, 177, 183n, 187, 251, 275, 285–6, 290, 293

Carvin, Jim, 155

Casey, Sue, 181, 181n

CBS, 199–202

Chambers, Mary Sue, 154, 170

Cheney, Dick, 173, 284

Chicago, 156–8, 164

Choat, Connie, 154, 170

Church, Frank, 4

Church. See Baptist Church

Churchill, Winston, 206

Civility, decline of, 120

Clayton, Bobby, 27–8, 38

Clendinen, Dudley, 201–2

Clinton, Bill: Strother's work for, 10, 12, 46–7, 107, 118, 177, 181, 189, 192, 195, 206–21, 223, 238, 243; and Carville, 12, 85, 88–9, 92, 93, 286; and sex, 27; presidential campaigns of, 46–7, 107, 182–3n, 186, 210, 216; and celebrities, 47, 207; and Morris, 55, 107, 219–20, 221, 271, 293; and southern voters, 71; and marijuana smoking, 74, 217; gubernatorial campaigns of, 106, 107, 217–8; and pollsters, 106, 107, 216, 219, 270–2, 293; makeup for on-camera appearances by, 119; and decline in civility, 120; and Monica Lewinsky scandal, 173, 206; themes of, 173, 206, 210, 218, 270–1; and Blumenthal, 183; personality of, 203, 208, 226; intelligence of, 206, 226; presidency of, 206, 220–1, 227, 272, 293; speeches of, 206–7; television programs/commercials for, 207, 208–11, 218–19; relationship of, with Hillary, 208, 210–1, 216; and negative campaigning, 212–3, 215; and triangulation technique, 213; and Hart, 214; and presidential campaign of 1988, 214–6, 238; and newspaper reporters, 217; alleged physical attack on Morris by, 219–20, 221; impeachment of, 221, 266, 286; and fundraising, 227

Clinton, Hillary, 12, 192, 208, 210–1, 215, 216, 217, 220

Collins, Bill, 159, 164

Collins, James, 142

Collins, Martha Layne, 156, 157, 159–64, 169, 211

Commercials. See Television programs/commercials

Connecticut, 143–4

Consulting. See Political consulting

Cooper, James Fenimore, xvii

Cooper, Whit, 86

Copelin, Sherman, 99

Corporate advertising, 58, 60–5, 274–5, 290

Cottonwood (Strother), 47, 103, 233, 247, 252

Coverdell, Paul, 115n, 285

Cranston, Alan, 174
Crawford, Jane, 146–7
Cundy, Donald, 103
Cutler, Lloyd N., 88

Daley, Bill, 157
Daley, Richard J., 157, 158
Daley, Richard M. "Rich," 156–8, 164
Dallek, Robert, 174
D'Allesandro, David, 9
Dante, 166
Daudet, Alphonse, 176, 176n
Davis, Anna Carter, 72, 76, 78
Davis, Dick, 85
Davis, Jimmie, 69–84, 134, 155, 157, 159, 224
Davison, Steve, 154, 220, 246
Dawson, Sam, 253–4, 256, 257
Deardourff, John, 289
Debates, 135, 142, 186n, 227
DeConcini, Dennis, 128, 136, 142, 144–5, 153, 157, 239, 243
Denton, Jeremiah, 131
Diamond, Harris, 227, 251–2
Dick, Nancy, 187
Dickey, Jay W., 266
DiRosa, Joe, 87–90, 94–102
Docking, Jill, 235, 295
Dodd, Bill, 57
Dodd, Chris, 194–6, 203
Dole, Bob, 120, 122, 123
Dominican Republic, 276–81
Dos Passos, John, 24, 103
Doucet, Daly Joseph "Cat," 48, 51–4, 58, 83, 132
Drugs, 81–2
D'Spain, Jim, 87, 90
Duffy, Jim, 93, 231, 241–2, 243, 259, 263–5, 268, 286, 294
Dukakis, Michael, 7–9, 12, 59, 71, 237, 243, 245, 274
Duke, David, 249, 250, 253–62
Dupuis, George, 73–4, 80, 81, 83–4
Dwarfs, 278–81

East, Charlie, 94
Eastland, James O., 138
Eastwood, Clint, 152
Edmisten, Rufus, 176, 192, 195, 198, 203
Education, 59, 61, 106–7, 108, 222, 271
Edwards, Edwin, 67, 68–9, 86, 107–8, 114, 156, 226–9, 231, 233, 236, 249, 250, 253–5, 257–62
Eisenhower, Dwight D., 35, 121, 174, 235
Enron, 283–4
Environmental reform, 153, 259
Erwin, Gay, 9, 245
Esarhaddon, xi
Eskew, Carter, 186, 241
Ethics, 137, 290, 292–3
Europe, 103, 157, 204–5, 223
Evolution, 282

Farwell, James, 46
Faubus, Orval, 137–8
Faucheux, Ron, 293
Faulkner, William, 24
Faxon, Lou, 247, 250, 251, 253, 259, 260
Fazier, Chris, 74
Feingold, Russ, 3, 137
Feinstein, Dianne, 269
Ferraro, Geraldine, 211n
Fight for Louisiana, The, 115, 118–27, 150
Film editing, 125–7, 150–1, 179–81
Fiore, Bob, 111, 118, 125, 136, 146, 149
Fitzgerald, F. Scott, 103
Fletcher, Roy, 46, 94
Florida, 268
Flowers Industries, 64
Flynn, Errol, 166
Focus groups, 162, 184–5, 228–9, 255–7, 272–3
Foley, Tom, 267
Fontenot, Mary Alice, 51
Foreign campaigns, 275–81
Foster, Mike, 46
France, 204
Freeman, Genie, 161
French, Patty, 42

Fulghum, Robert, 249
Fulmer, Lemos, 42
Fundamentalists. *See* Religious fundamentalists
Fundraising: and campaign finance reform, 3, 137; for Jimmie Davis campaign, 77–8; for Stennis campaign, 136–7, 139; ethical questions on, 137; and Clinton, 227; and Roemer, 227; Hart, 236; and Boulter, 244; and Pete Peterson, 268; and modern campaigns, 294–5. *See also* Money

Gambling, 74, 83, 90, 98, 100–1, 107, 226
Gandy, Evelyn, 234
Garreau, Joel, 193
Gates, John Warne, 23
Gearan, Mark, 88
Gender bias, 161–3, 211–2, 211n
General Motors, 275
George, Phyllis, 159, 197–8
Gephardt, Richard A., 182
Germond, Jack, 193, 220, 292
Gibbs, Leon, 72
Gingrich, Newt, 120
Glenn, John, 174–5, 180, 181, 187
Goldwater, Barry, 105–6, 138
Goodman, Bob, 289
Goodwin, Doris Kearns, 174
Gore, Al, 10, 47, 180, 185–6, 186n, 218, 220, 221, 240–4, 283
Gore, Tipper, 241, 242
Goudeau, Morgan, III, 53
Grassley, Charles, 3
Grasso, Ella, 143
Greenberg, Stan, 186, 271, 275
Greer, Frank, 171, 220
Guggenheim, Charlie, 98, 99
Guidry, Doc, 72, 76
Gumbo/duck dinners, 177–8, 236–7
Guns, 9, 53–4, 296
Gunter, Bill, 115, 127, 141

Hamilton, Bill, 114–5, 117–9, 123, 157, 160, 162, 163, 185, 186, 222–3, 271, 276, 285, 289, 290

Hannah, George, 143
Harbert, Earl, 16
Hardy, Paul, 103, 107–10, 114
Hart, Gary: presidential campaign of, 10, 47, 165, 167, 174–203, 181n, 207, 210, 215, 225, 243; and Donna Rice scandal, 100, 214, 235–8; television programs/commercials for, 125, 167, 178–81, 189–91, 194–7, 199–202, 241, 243, 285; and Vietnam War, 164; hiring of Strother by, 169–70, 208; Strother's hopes for, 169–70, 208, 209, 235–6; and newspaper reporters, 177–8, 193; and negative campaigning, 194–6, 243; and Clinton, 214; and Broadhurst, 236–7; fundraising for, 236
Hart, Peter, 95, 97, 98, 102, 103, 106, 134–5, 185, 186, 271, 289
Harvard University, 7, 12, 13, 91, 205, 206–7, 226
Hatch, Orrin, 120
Hawkins, Paula, 115, 131
Hays, Larry, 163–4
Heller, Joseph, 289
Hemingway, Ernest, 22, 24, 103
Henkel, Oliver "Pudge," 177, 179, 186, 194–6
Henry, Bubba, 98–9
Hickman, Harrison, 164
High and the Mighty, The, 232
Hispanics, 147–8
Holland, 238
Holum, John, 215–6n
Hoover, Herbert, 17, 18
Hubbard, Don, 99
Hugo, Victor, 176n
Humphrey, Hubert H., 138, 158

Ieyoub, Richard, 247
Indiana, 157–8
International Association of Political Consultants, 276
Isaacson, Walter, 100
Israel, 189, 275

Jackson, Jesse, 175
Jackson, Thomas "Stonewall," 71
Japan, 18–9
Jefferson, Thomas, xiii
Jenkins, Woody, 118, 127, 235
John Birch Society, 41
John F. Kennedy, 1917–1963, 99
Johnson, Lyndon, 19, 105, 121, 138, 158, 235, 243
Johnson, Wayne, 30–1, 32
Johnston, J. Bennett, 118, 136, 236, 269
Jones, Robert, 16
Joplin, Janis, 25
Journalists. *See* Newspaper reporters
Jump cuts, 179

Kantor, Mickey, 215*n*
Kennedy, Edward "Ted," 2, 61, 120, 183
Kennedy, John F., 2, 55, 119, 123, 158, 182, 206, 235, 263
Kennedy, Vicki Reggie, 61
Kent, Jack, 259
Kentucky, 156, 157, 159–64, 198–9
Kieffer, Nat, 99
Kirkpatrick, Kris, 115, 119, 124
Knox, Eddie, 198
Ku Klux Klan, 249, 253, 254, 257, 266

Labor movement. *See* Unions
Lambert, Blanche, 264, 265
Lambert, Louis, 114, 115
Landau, Nathan, 240
Landrieu, Mary, 85, 129, 163, 230, 235, 295
Landrieu, Moon, 99, 129
Langdon, Jim, 24–5
Lapham, Harry, 118, 119, 125
Leach, Buddy, 224
LeBlanc, Dudley J., 160
Lee, Robert E., 71
Lewinsky, Monica, 173, 206
Lewis, Gerald, 223
Lewis, John, 20
Lewis, Sinclair, 24
Libraries, 23–6

Lieberman, Joseph, 243–4
Lincoln, Abraham, 137, 287
Lindsey, Bruce, 220
Lombardo, Steve, 256
Long, Carolyn, 119
Long, Cathy, 90
Long, Earl, 45, 107, 121–2
Long, Gillis, 46, 59, 84, 90, 108, 155–6
Long, Huey, 45, 67, 107, 117–8, 121, 124, 126, 222
Long, Russell, 4, 10, 47, 113, 115, 117–27, 130–1, 136–9, 150, 222–3, 225, 236, 240
Lott, Trent, 138
Louisiana, 45–84, 94–115, 117–27, 129, 143, 155–6, 222–35, 236, 247–62, 288–9
Louisiana State University, 41, 42–3, 94, 103, 126, 143, 155, 237, 257, 260, 293
Louisiana Superdome, 58, 129, 261
Lovett, Lyle, 248
Lowry, Mike, 269–70
LSU, 41, 42–3, 94, 103, 126, 143, 155, 237, 257, 260, 293
Lungren, Dan, 91, 205
Luntz, Frank, 291
Lynch, Dotty, 180, 182, 186–7

Mackie, Rick, 126
Magnuson, Warren G., 4
Maloney, Gary, 256
Martin, Jack, 142, 145, 146, 147, 152, 163, 169, 240, 244, 245, 252, 295
Martinez, Angel, 18–9
Marttila, John, 157
Maslin, Paul, 179
Matalin, Mary, 92, 251
Mathieu, Tommy, 109–14
Matthews, Chris, 59–60, 173, 291–2
Mattingly, Matt, 131
Maupassant, Guy de, 176*n*
Mayronne, Harry, 56
McCain, John, 3, 46, 137, 234
McCarthy, Joseph, 121
McCloskey, Paul N., Jr., 175
McClung, Dan, 143, 144, 148

McCollister, Rolfe, 78
McCuen, W. J. "Bill," 264–5
McCullough, David, 174
McCurdy, Dave, 234
McGovern, George, 4, 169, 175, 182, 216n
McKeithen, John, 55, 57, 58, 60, 129, 155–6, 160
McKernan, Jerry, 86
McKinnon, Mark, 227, 228, 284
McLaughlin, Catherine, 205
McLaughlin, John, 173
McNamara, Robert, 19
McPhatter, Clyde, 236
McRight, Frank, 176, 203, 234
Media consultants. See Political consulting; Television programs/commercials
Mercurio, Joe, 201, 202
Merrill, John, 41
Mexicans, 20, 36–7
Microsoft, 274
Miller, Merle, 121
Miller, Zell, 115, 115n, 127, 154, 285–6, 290
Mills, P. J., 255, 259
Miranda, Mark, 148
Mix, Tom, 246
Mondale, Walter, 174–5, 177, 180, 181, 187, 189–94, 196, 197, 199, 202, 203, 209
Money: importance of, xiv, 3, 5, 85; and power, 5; as motivator for political consulting, 12, 292; hundred-dollar bills as "bookmarks," 66; large sums of cash, 112–3. See also Fundraising
Morgan, Adrienne, 171
Morgan, Bill, 46, 93, 128, 134, 142–5, 154, 157–9, 170–1, 261
Morial, Ernest "Dutch," 97, 98, 99
Morris, Dick, 12, 55, 104–7, 114–15, 181, 186, 207–8, 215, 216, 218–21, 251, 271, 291, 293
Morrison, deLesseps S. "Chep," 155, 156
Morrison, Kenny, 230
Moses, Winn, 157–8
Moynihan, Daniel Patrick, 120, 122
Mr. Smith Goes to Washington, 182, 182–3n, 205

Mundez, Elias, 280
Murkowski, Frank, 3–4
Murphine, Ralph, 95
Murphy, Mike, 234
Murrow, Edward R., 291
Music, 24–5, 70, 72–3, 75–80, 82–3, 105, 124, 126, 184, 208, 232, 236, 239, 248, 249, 255, 261, 288

Name recognition, 96
Napolitan, Joe, 93, 276, 290
Nazis, 19
NBC, 273
Negative campaigning, 163–4, 194–6, 203, 212–3, 215, 250, 265, 272
Nelson, Gaylord, 4
New Age, 249–50
New Hampshire, 187–8
New Orleans, 61–4, 77–8, 87–90, 94–5, 97, 99–100, 108–9, 129, 247, 248, 260–1, 271
New York, 109–13
Newman, Paul, 121–2
Newspaper reporters: and Jimmie Davis campaign, 79–82; and corruption in Louisiana politics, 108; and Martha Layne Collins, 159–60; and McKeithen, 160; as watchdog for the people, 160; and George W. Bush, 173; gumbo/duck dinners for, 177–8, 236–7; and Hart campaign, 177–8, 193; and Clinton, 217; and Gore commercial, 242–3; salaries for, 292
Nickles, Don, 4
Nixon, Richard, 55, 158, 175, 235
North Carolina, 241–2
Northwestern State College (La.), 32–4, 38–41
Nuclear weapons, 105–6
Nunn, Sam, 120, 122, 136

Ober, Ron, 144
O'Neill, Bill, 142, 143–4, 153
O'Neill, Mrs. Bill, 143–4
O'Neill, Thomas J. "Tip," Jr., 59, 209, 292
Osborn, Chip, 241–2

Parker, Dorothy, 291
Parker, Mary Evelyn, 48, 51–7, 58, 129, 132, 161
Peller, Clara, 193
Penn and Schoen, 186
Penratt, Noel, 150
Perlmutter, David D., xi–xv
Perot, Ross, 107, 283
Perpich, Rudy, 223
Peterson, Pete, 268
Peynado, Jacinto, 276–81
Peynado, Margarita, 277
Phelps, Ashton, Jr., 261–2
Phoenix, Ariz., 144–5
Photography, 42–3, 132–3
Pierson, Mary Olive, 86
Plato, 56
Poe, Edgar Allan, 165
Pohl, Ron, 171, 197
Political consulting: summary of Strother's main points on, xiii–xiv; winning record of political consultants, 1–3, 85; fees for, 3, 11, 66, 67, 90–1, 95, 239–40, 276; excitement of, 4–5, 58–9; summary of Strother's career, 4–5, 288–9; hiring process for, 6–12; competition within, 10, 239, 240–1; motivation of consultants, 12, 292; Strother's rules for, 57; off-season work for political consultants, 58, 60–5, 274–81, 290; and cost of political advertising, 67; and depression after losing election, 102; and changes in candidates, 124–5; duties of political consultants, 131–3, 139, 169, 283–7; and time pressures, 165–9; and contracting nonincumbent clients, 268–70; and foreign campaigns, 275–81; Bentsen rule on, 284, 285; Strother's reflections on current status of, 289–96; and bad campaign ethics, 290, 292–3; and showmanship, 290–2; university programs on, 293. *See also* Strother, Raymond D.; Television programs/commercials; and specific consultants and clients

Polling and pollsters, 95–7, 103, 104, 106–7, 106n, 114, 134, 175, 184–6, 216, 219, 270–2, 283–7, 289, 290–1, 293, 295
Poor, Floyd, 164
Popkin, Samuel, 183n
Port Arthur, Tex., 14–39, 44, 49, 241–2
Powell, Tommy "Lightbulb," 67–8, 224
Presley, Elvis, 236
Press corps. *See* Newspaper reporters
Prostitution, 48–53, 83
Public-service tapes, 133

Quayle, Dan, 4

Racism and race relations, 19–20, 36–7, 99–101, 107–9, 137–38, 235, 249, 250, 253, 257, 262
Raines, Howell, 6
Random selection, 97
Rather, Dan, 160
Raven, Eddy, 72, 76, 78, 83
Rayburn, Sam, 121
Reagan, Nancy, 206
Reagan, Ronald, 3, 4, 71, 76, 115, 122, 131, 176, 182, 190, 192, 202–3, 208, 209, 210, 289
Redneck culture, 5–13, 71, 81, 105, 121, 123–4, 146, 187, 208, 220, 263, 264, 267, 282, 294, 295
Reds, 200
Reed, Clark, 138
Reedy, George, 121
Reese, Matt, 94–5, 97, 102–3, 115
Reggie, Edmund, 61, 62, 63, 69
Religious fundamentalists, 18–9, 26–7, 49, 66, 70–1, 78, 282
Reno, Janet, 268
Reporters. *See* Newspaper reporters
Rice, Donna, 100, 214, 235–8
Robertson, Pat, 89
Robertson, Willard, 60
Rockefeller, Nelson A., 175
Roemer, Caroline, 258, 261
Roemer, Charles, 226, 228, 255

Roemer, Charles Elson "Buddy," III, 223–33, 247–62
Roemer, Patty, 247–50
Rome, Lewis, 144
Roosevelt, Franklin D., 14, 15, 17, 137, 147, 148, 235, 287
Rose, Ed, 126
Rove, Karl, 284, 293
Rudman, Warren, 3
Ruskin, John, 124

Sachs, Sharon, 125–7, 150
San Antonio, Tex., 147–9
Sandburg, Carl, 158
Sanderson, Len, 227
Sasso, John, 7, 8
Sawyer, David, 109, 110–3, 118, 144, 289
Sawyer, Diane, 160
Scaife, Richard Mellon, 89
Schroth, Rob, 278–80
Schwartz, Tony, 105, 106
Schweitzer, Doc, 240
Scopes Trial, 282
Scotland, 103, 157, 205
Seder, Deno, 46, 225, 259
Seeger, Pete, 15
Sellers, Peter, 203
Sexism, 161–3, 211–2, 211n
Shaheen, Jeanne, 181, 181n
Shields, Mark, 98
Shipley, George, 252
Shore, Billy, 170
Shrum, Bob, 2, 183
Simon, Paul, 10, 128, 142, 153
Sinatra, Frank, 288
Sloan, Harvey, 163
Smith, Al, 211n
Smith, Charlie, 198, 199
Smith, Hedrick, 174–5, 187
Social Security, 147–50, 153, 204
Sorenson, Ted, 187
Southern accent, 7, 8, 12, 13, 59–60, 239. *See also* Redneck culture
Spain, 223
Speer Family, 72–3, 76, 78

Sports, 19–20, 40–1, 107
Squier, Bob, 93, 114, 116, 241, 289
Stalford, Stanley, 232
Starr, Kenneth W., 86, 88–9, 93
Stein, Gertrude, 103
Stennis, John, xiii, xiv, 10, 120, 121, 122, 130–42, 153, 157
Stephanopoulos, George, 88, 183n
Stevenson, Adlai, 99
Stevenson, Robert Louis, 24
Stewart, Jimmy, 182
Stone, Richard, 115
Strauss, Annette, 237
Strauss, Bob, 237
Strauss, Ted, 237
Streisand, Barbara, 207
Strother, Albert Dolph: and concern for working people, xiv, 17, 20, 49, 98, 108, 148, 153, 191, 203–4, 234, 295; physical appearance of, 14; Ray's relationship with, during Ray's youth, 14–20, 27–30, 32–4, 37, 295–6; and unions, 14–5, 191, 253, 296; personality of, 16–7, 37, 171; and Republicans, 16, 17–8, 147, 253, 294; college education for children of, 17, 32–3, 234; employment and retirement of, 17, 44, 148; on Japanese, 17–9; and Baptist Church, 18–9, 27, 37; and son Claud's death in Vietnam War, 19, 44, 164, 169; and advice on standing and fighting, 27–30, 39, 253, 295, 296; on Texas Rangers, 27, 296; and alcohol drinking, 37; final illness and death of, 43–4, 296; on manhood generally, 171, 176, 243, 247, 253, 295–6; dream of, for better world, 203–4, 295–6
Strother, Clara Sue, 19, 29
Strother, Claud (brother of author), 19, 21, 29, 44, 169, 176n, 296
Strother, Claud Paul (uncle of author), 176n
Strother, Dane, 59–60, 93, 205, 239, 243, 259, 263, 264–6, 294
Strother, Kristan, 156
Strother, Mildred, 18–9, 25, 27, 28–9, 33, 37, 98

Strother, Raymond D.: summary of main
points of, on political consulting, xiii–xiv;
and father's concern for working people,
xiv, 17, 20, 49, 98, 108, 148, 153, 176, 191,
203–4, 234, 288, 295; summary of career
of, 4–5, 288–9; and southern accent, 7,
12, 59–60; childhood and youth of, 14–
39, 54, 295–6; father's relationship with,
during youth, 14–20, 27–30, 32–4, 37,
295–6; Baptist upbringing of, 18–9, 26–7,
49, 282; mother of, 18–9, 25, 27, 28–9, 33,
37, 98; and brother Claud's death in Vietnam War, 19, 21, 44, 164, 169, 176n; in
high school and college athletics, 19–20,
40–1; jobs of, as youth, 20–3, 34–8; reading and library use by, 23–6, 175, 176,
176n, 249; fighting during youth of, 27–
32, 38–9; university education of, 31–4,
38–43, 94, 155; wife of, 32, 41–2, 43, 47,
57, 66, 127–9, 143, 165–6, 172, 184, 192,
193, 194, 238–9, 260; homes of, 42, 57–8,
59, 128, 143, 204, 225, 246, 252, 263; and
photography, 42–3; and father's final illness and death, 43–4, 296; first job as political consultant, 43, 44, 55; novel by, 47,
103, 233, 247, 252; separation between
Sandy and, 47, 246–7; and guns, 53–4,
296; fees for and finances of, 57–8, 66, 67,
98, 156, 239–40, 276; rules of political
consulting developed by, 57; and corporate advertising, 58, 60–5, 274–5; children
of, 59–60, 61, 128, 156, 205, 239, 243,
263, 294; as Fellow at Institute of Politics
at Harvard, 91, 205, 206–7; in Europe,
103, 157, 204–5, 223; split with Weill by,
127–8; Washington, D.C., offices and staff
of, 128–9, 170–1, 196–7, 274, 289; awards
for, 139; nightmares of, 165; watch worn
by, 165–6; and father's advice on manhood generally, 171, 176, 243, 247, 253,
295–6; private airplane for, 198–9, 247,
260; and losses of political campaigns,
203–4, 234–5, 295; reconciliation between Sandy and, 260, 262; blackballing
of, by Democratic Party bureaucrats,

263–7; and foreign campaigns, 275–81;
reflections of, on current status of political consulting, 289–96. See also specific
political candidates
Strother, Sandy: in high school, 32; in Baton
Rouge, 41–2, 43, 128–9, 143; jobs of, in
Baton Rouge, 41, 43; homes of, 42, 57–8,
59, 128, 143, 204, 225, 246, 252, 263; and
Ray's busy schedule, 47, 127–8, 143, 192,
193; separation between Ray and, 47,
246–7; automobile for, 57, 128–9; children of, 59–60, 61, 128, 156, 205, 239,
243, 263, 294; and cash as "bookmarks,"
66; and move to Washington, D.C.,
128–9, 143; and Ray's watch, 165–6; and
Christmas holidays in 1983, 172; and
Caddell, 184; and Hart campaign, 194,
238–9; in Europe, 204, 223, 238; reconciliation between Ray and, 260, 262
Superdome, 58, 129, 261
Swaggart, Jimmy, 27, 78, 226
Sweeney, Kevin, 177

Taiwan, 240
Talmadge, Herman E., 4, 115
Targeting, 102–3
Tauzin, W. J. "Billy," 223–4, 225, 227
Teddlie, Ray, 46, 94
Television debates. See Debates
Television programs/commercials: money
for, xiv; for Bentsen, 9–10, 127, 141–2,
146–53, 244–5, 295; cost of, 16, 78,
112–3, 167, 178, 180, 199, 202, 255;
Strother's early political ads in late 1960s
and early 1970s, 56–7; for Mary Evelyn
Parker, 57; Strother's rule against live
television, 57; bread commercials, 61–3;
for banks, 64–5; light bulb commercial for
Tommy Powell, 68; Schwartz's "Daisy"
spot for Lyndon Johnson, 105–6; and
Sawyer, 110–1; lighting for, 111; preparation for, 111; *Fight for Louisiana* and Russell Long campaign, 115, 118–27, 150;
editing of, 125–7, 150–1, 179–81; for

Hart, 125, 167, 178–81, 189–91, 194–7, 199–202, 241, 243, 285; Strother's leaving film behind, 127, 152; for Stennis, 136, 139; for Barron, 141; advance person for film shoot, 146; for McKeithen, 155–6; candidates' rehearsal for, 160–1; for Martha Layne Collins, 160–2; and negative campaigning, 163–4, 194–6, 203, 212–3, 243, 250, 265, 272; cable television news shows, 173–4, 290, 291–2; historians and other academics on cable television, 173–4; and moving from scene to scene, 178–81; and jump cuts, 179; emotional impact of political commercials, 184; and focus groups, 184–5, 228–9, 255–7, 272–3; and music, 184, 255; for Gore, 185–6, 241–3; for Clinton, 207, 208–11, 218–19; for Democratic National Committee (1985), 208–10; for Roemer, 228–32, 250–1, 255–9; for McCuen, 265–6; for Peynado, 279–80. See also Political consulting

Texas, 141–3, 145–54, 243–5
Texas A&M, 176n
Texas Rangers, 27, 38, 296
Thomason, Harry, 207
Thompson, Randy, 154, 171, 201, 202
Thurmond, Strom, 137–8, 139
Time pressures, 165–9
Treen, David, 114
Triangulation technique, 213
Truman, Harry, 134, 263
Tupper, Sue, 269–70
Twain, Mark, 26, 79

Unions, 14–6, 38, 41, 131, 190–2, 253, 296
Unruh, Jesse, 3

Vietnam War, 19, 21, 44, 105–6, 158, 164, 169, 182, 296
Virgil, 166
Volkswagen, 60–1, 274
Voltaire, 176

Voting Rights Act, 138–9
Vrdolyak, Eddie, 194, 196

Wade, Jim, 143
Wagner, Carl, 215, 216
Waldman, Michael, 206–7
Walker, Danny, 249–50, 258
Walker, Mickey, 32
Wallace, George, 71, 137–8
War Room, The, 93
Washington, George, xiii, 14
Washington, Harold, 159, 164
Washington, D.C., 128–9, 154, 170, 172–4, 274, 289
Watergate scandal, 4, 174, 291
Watkins, David, 212
Waxman, Henry, 188–9
Wayne, John, 232, 246
Webb, Skip, 97
Weill, Gus, 43, 55–8, 60, 61, 65–7, 87, 90, 103, 104, 109, 114, 116, 128, 129, 155
Welch, Robert, 41
Wendy's ad, 193–4
West Wing, 182n, 197
White, Joe Slade, 171
White, Mark, 106–7
Whitewater, 89
Wiggins, R. H., 42, 43, 96–7
Williams, T. Harry, 117
Williams, Wanda, 177, 236
Wilson, Dave, 87
Wilson, Woodrow, 287
Winter, William, 136
Witcover, Jules, 193, 292
Wofford, Harris, 290
Women candidates. See Gender bias; and specific women candidates
Woodward, Bob, 174, 291
World War II, 18–9, 141, 176n
Wright, Betsy, 162, 208, 210, 211–2, 217
Wright, Jim, 120, 209

Yacich, Paul, 56, 57

Zola, Emile, 175, 176n